CRITICAL
AMERICANS

CRITICAL AMERICANS

Victorian Intellectuals
and Transatlantic
Liberal Reform

LESLIE BUTLER

The University of North Carolina Press
Chapel Hill

© 2007 The University of North Carolina Press
All rights reserved
Manufactured in the United States of America

Designed by Heidi Perov
Set in Bodoni Book, Bernhard Modern, and Bodoni Poster Compressed
by Tseng Information Systems, Inc.

The paper in this book meets the guidelines for permanence and durability of the Committee
on Production Guidelines for Book Longevity of the Council on Library Resources.

Library of Congress Cataloging-in-Publication Data
Butler, Leslie, 1969–
Critical Americans : Victorian intellectuals and transatlantic liberal reform / Leslie Butler.
p. cm.
Includes bibliographical references and index.
ISBN 978-0-8078-3084-0 (cloth : alk. paper) — ISBN 978-0-8078-5792-2 (pbk. : alk. paper)
1. Liberalism—United States—History—19th century. 2. Politics and culture—
United States—History—19th century. 3. Democracy—United States—History—
19th century. I. Title.
JC574.2.U6B88 2007
320.510973′09034—dc22   2006034390

cloth   11 10 09 08 07   5 4 3 2 1
paper   11 10 09 08 07   5 4 3 2 1

For Frank and Mary Butler
Parents, teachers, friends

*Things do really gain in greatness by being acted on a great
and cosmopolitan stage, because there is inspiration in the thronged
audience and the nearer match that puts men on their mettle.*
James Russell Lowell, "A Great Public Character," 1867

·   ·   ·

*We have lived through a period of the world's history of
surpassing interest & enormous change. But we have seen only the
beginning of the mightiest revolution in human affairs, and we shall
have to quit the stage in the very middle of a most entertaining scene.
I, however, shall not be sorry to go, though my curiosity as to
what is about to happen may never be satisfied.*
Charles Eliot Norton to Goldwin Smith, August 30, 1905

Contents

Preface

This project began with books. Quite literally. On a trip to New York City early in my graduate career, I browsed through shelves of deaccessioned books outside Columbia University's Butler Library. Dusty volumes in shades of navy, maroon, and dark green stretched on for yards: twenty-five cents a book, five for a dollar. I had only recently decided to study American history and was intrigued by the multiple volumes filled with the writings of people whose names were only faintly recognizable: the life and letters of Charles Eliot Norton, the complete prose writings and poetical works of James Russell Lowell, the orations and addresses of George William Curtis, the essay collections of Thomas Wentworth Higginson. Twenty dollars poorer and the car weighed down by an impressive new library of nineteenth-century Americana, I headed back to New Haven and began reading.

What I read fascinated me, and I decided to work through my fascination in a research paper for David Brion Davis. But when I began reading the secondary scholarship concerning this group of Americans, my fascination turned to consternation. The richness and texture of these nineteenth-century writings seemed flattened out in dull abstractions with such names as "The Genteel Tradition" and "Liberal Reform." The scholarly treatment seemed especially perplexing when I compared these figures with their British counterparts (and, it turned out, correspondents), who had engendered a lively and compelling body of scholarship.

While my interest was engaged from the beginning, my sense of the present-day relevance of these writings soon followed. Indeed, in the many years I have worked on this book, I have been struck by the enduring relevance of the concerns raised by these men. I began this project amid a compelling debate over why Americans hated politics or the media or both and over how to make parties more responsive to citizens than to corporations. If this debate called to mind liberal Victorian ideas about the press, public opinion, and democracy, debates over Oprah Winfrey's Book Club further evoked late-nineteenth-century efforts to sort out the relationships among literature, democracy, and the marketplace. When I began writing a new (and final) version of the manuscript in 2004, we had entered into a very different historical moment. A controversial war (deemed a war of liberation by its proponents and denounced as an unnecessary war of aggression by its critics) brought with it inescapable echoes of the late nineteenth century. The curiously evolving timeliness of nineteenth-century liberal debates, the way their resonance has only amplified from year to year, has confirmed my belief that we still have something to learn from this generation of liberal reformers.

This book may have begun with the deaccessioned books from Butler Library found on that cold January day, but it was shaped, nurtured, and completed only with the help of many individuals and institutions. I thank the following sources for their generous financial assistance at various stages of this project: the Graduate School at Yale University; the John F. Enders Research Fund; the Beinecke Library, Yale University; the Nelson Rockefeller Program on Non-Profit Organizations, Yale University; the Mrs. Giles Whiting Foundation; the Massachusetts Historical Society; the American Antiquarian Society; the Intramural Research Grant Program, Michigan State University; the Faculty Development Research Fund, James Madison College; and the Walter and Constance Burke Award and the Nelson Rockefeller Center for the Social Sciences at Dartmouth College.

The directors, librarians, and staff members at the following institutions facilitated my research enormously: the Beinecke Library and Sterling Library, Yale University; Houghton Library, Widener Library, and University Archives, Harvard University; Massachusetts Historical Society; American Antiquarian Society; Bodleian Library, Oxford University; British Library; Library of Congress, Manuscripts Division; British Library for Political and Economic Science, London School of Economics; University Library, University of Cambridge; Huntington Library; Newberry Library; and New York Public Library, Manuscripts Division. I especially thank the Bodleian Library, British Library for Political and Economic Science, Houghton Library, Harvard University Archives, and Massachusetts Historical Society for permission to quote from their collections.

For more than a decade now, I have benefited from the cultivating and critical efforts of several mentors and advisers, whom I am happy to thank here. Cynthia Russett and Frank Turner offered incisive feedback and encouragement at various stages of the book's evolution. Their broad learning and equally broad range of interests provided a continual stimulus to new thinking. David Brion Davis has influenced this project in so many ways and on so many levels that it is hard to know how to thank him. He was willing to take me on as a novice student in American history, and his enthusiastic response to the first research paper I wrote for him led me to believe that there was something to be said about nineteenth-century liberal reformers. He represents the very best of earnest, engaged scholarship and teaching, and it has been a great privilege to have worked with him.

Daniel Walker Howe offered advice and encouragement during some memorable conversations at Oxford University. He also read and commented on an early version of the manuscript, helping me enormously in my revisions. I was fortunate that the University of North Carolina Press found two readers, David Hall and Wilfred McClay, who offered thoughtful comments on not just one but two versions of this book. Their judicious blend of praise and critique helped improve the final product. Hall's involvement has gone well beyond this official capacity: his article, "The Victorian Connection," influenced my thinking about transatlantic liberals at a very early stage in the project; at a very late stage, he suggested the title "Critical Americans," which gave clarity and shape to the final revisions.

Many people have commented on, argued with, or listened to various portions and drafts of this manuscript. I thank Steven Biel, Tom Brown, James Connolly, Nancy Cott, Amy DeRogatis, Ann Fabian, David Hackett Fischer, Sherman Garnett, Julia Grant, Peter Dobkin Hall, Kristin Hoganson, James Kloppenberg, Paul Kramer, Michael McGerr, John McGreevy, Dorothy Ross, Joan Shelly Rubin, David Sacks, Sam Thomas, Alan Trachtenberg, James Turner, and Dick Zinman. I also thank Duncan Bell of Cambridge University and Peter Cain of Sheffield Hallam University, who generously shared with me their forthcoming work on Victorian foreign and imperial policy.

Colleagues at Reed College, James Madison College of Michigan State University, and Dartmouth College have provided stimulating and collegial atmospheres in which to teach and learn. I especially thank Allison Berg and Colleen Tremonte at James Madison College for their friendship and support. I have also benefited from a cadre of helpful research assistants: Natasha Appenheimer, Kelly Miller, and Ed Timke at James Madison College and Lisa Ding, Nikhil Gore, Davida Kornreich, and Laura Pearlstein at Dartmouth College. Amanda Behm was never a research assistant, but I learned much while supervising her thesis on conservative British responses to the American Civil War.

At Dartmouth, the John Sloan Dickey Center for International Understanding ran a wonderfully invigorating seminar on a late draft of the manuscript. I thank the center; its assistant director, Christianne Hardy Wohlforth; and my colleagues around the college who generously read and commented on the entire manuscript: Amy Allen, Michael Ermarth, Carl Estabrook, Jim Murphy,

Annelise Orleck, Jay Satterfield, Ivy Schweitzer, and Allan Stam. Ted Widmer and Caroline Winterer not only read and commented on the manuscript but braved the perils of a New Hampshire January to come and discuss it in person. I thank them all and know that the book is better for their input. At UNC Press, Chuck Grench, Katy O'Brien, and Paula Wald expertly (and patiently) guided the manuscript through the publication process. As copyeditor, Ellen Goldlust-Gingrich helped sharpen many a dull sentence and tie up many a loose end.

Making literally all the difference in the world, as all working mothers know, have been the many trustworthy hands into which I have confidently placed my children while I teach and write. I feel incredibly lucky to be able to thank the loving and professional teachers and staff at the Dartmouth College Child Care Center, who every day transform what could be a necessary evil into a positive good.

Like the work of many academics, versions of this book were written at different moments and in different places: begun in New Haven (Connecticut); revised in Portland (Oregon and Maine), Cambridge and Worcester (Massachusetts), and East Lansing (Michigan); and finally rewritten entirely in Hanover (New Hampshire). Amid the inevitable disorder of these many moves, my family has provided continuity and stability. Without them, nothing (including my sanity) would have been possible.

My in-laws, Patricia and Wally Bigbee, offered encouragement and support as well as endless home improvements. My sisters, Jamie, Alison, Katie, and Jess, and more recently my brothers-in-law, John, Greg, and Tony, have provided an unflagging network of friendship, love, and good humor. Ali went even further, kindly feigning an interest in the subject (sparked by Matthew Pearl's *The Dante Club*, which lent Victorian men of letters a kind of action-hero appeal) and reading around in the manuscript itself. My parents, to whom this book is dedicated, have contributed endlessly to it. Their emotional and financial generosity seems to know no bounds (and I've surely tested them). Even before they required that my sisters and I write weekly summer book reports when we were young, they instilled in me a love of reading and a passion for learning that have never departed. For that, as for everything else, I thank them.

The last word goes to my boys, all four of them. That William Butler Bonner, Matthew Francis Bonner, and Cameron Robert Bonner have delayed the completion of this project will come as no surprise, especially to those who know that high-spirited trio. Will, Matt, and Cameron have provided hours of (usually welcome) distraction from writing and countless moments of (always welcome) exhilaration as they shared with me their zest for living and their curiosity about the world around them. I was either gestating or nursing one of the boys almost the entire time I was writing and revising this book. I look forward with real pleasure to some uninterrupted playtime.

And then there is Bob. I was lucky enough to have met Bob at the beginning of graduate school and smart enough to have married him at the end of it. He has been bound up with this project and with my development as a historian from the beginning—from that initial book-shopping spree at Butler Library long ago to the final round of revisions. He has spent more hours than he probably cares to recall thinking and talking about nineteenth-century Anglo-American liberals and has read every word of every draft of every version of this book (often more than once). In short, his contributions to this project have been colossal. And while he knows that better than anyone, what he may not know is this: vast as those contributions have been, they are the very least he has given me. The rest is too enormous for words.

CRITICAL
AMERICANS

Introduction

They had come to praise Charles Eliot Norton. Gathered in their elegant new building on Boylston Street on a November day in 1908, the members of the Massachusetts Historical Society remembered the life and work of their recently deceased friend with tributes to his high cultivation and cosmopolitanism. Even within the rarified world of Brahmin Boston, Norton had been the prototype of the Harvard aesthete, sustaining exceptionally extensive ties to the transatlantic world of Victorian letters. Here was one of the leading Victorian art historians, a translator of Dante, a confidante of intellectuals on both sides of the Atlantic, the literary executor or editor of Emerson, Carlyle, Ruskin, and Lowell. Here was a man, his friends recalled, whose lifelong work had been to raise the tone of his country and to help Americans smooth what not a few in the audience considered the nation's rough edges.

Most of these tributes were unremarkable, featuring a group of aging Victorians—many of them thick around the middle, even more thin around the hairline—gathered to eulogize one of their own. Amid the remembrances, the antislavery movement veteran and Civil War colonel Thomas Wentworth Higginson stood to speak. He did so with a full head of hair and with an octogenarian frame that hinted at his lifelong athleticism. Yes, Norton had done much for his country, this commander of black troops acknowledged, "but something needs now to be said in turn for that which this country did, in the meanwhile, for him."

Though his speech meandered somewhat, Higginson offered an incisive appraisal of Norton's life. Higginson appreciated how the United States had anchored the Harvard professor in a place where he might put his learning and cosmopolitanism to practical use. America's role as the world's exemplar of popular government, Higginson explained, had strengthened his friend's sense of civic duty and had offered an aspiration noble enough to give purpose and meaning to Norton's life's work. While Old World friends such as the art critic John Ruskin had pitied Norton his vulgar New World existence, Norton had found in it invigoration and commitment as well as a good deal of frustration at times. "The New World had learned much from him," Higginson explained, but "had taught him much" as well. This dynamic of mutual instruction revealed what Higginson considered the "essential Americanism of Norton's career."[1]

Higginson's comments, which he republished with the subtitle "A Link between the Old and New Worlds," captured the transatlantic dimensions of the liberal reform Norton and Higginson had pursued over the course of some six decades. These two friends and their wider cohort of public-oriented men of letters had followed European—especially British—developments over their entire lives. They had read widely in transatlantic periodicals and had entertained scores of transatlantic guests. They had engaged in regular transatlantic travel. Their sense of who they were as Americans, of what they had to offer America as well as what America offered them, was crucially shaped by this international dynamic. Yet in the end, both men had chosen to cast their lot with their own country, where the promise of liberal democracy and cultural diffusion seemed most likely to be fulfilled.

The eighty-four-year-old Higginson's tribute to his eighty-one-year-old friend testified to their longevity no less than to their cosmopolitan frame of reference. Born in the 1820s, this pair had come of age in the midst of the sectional crisis, settled into positions of national prominence during the Civil War, and, after reform careers that spanned the last third of the nineteenth century, died in the early part of the twentieth century. More remarkable than mere length was the dramatic arc of these years, during which the United States transformed from an insecure, largely agrarian republic dedicated to protecting slavery into a powerful, increasingly urban nation fully integrated into a global system of industrial capitalism. Living through this crucial era, they played a role in shaping many of the features of modern America easily taken for granted today. Emancipation, women's rights, national research universities, a nonpartisan career civil service, a forum for principled dissent: all of these developments to varying degrees bear the imprint of these men.

The spectacle of the old abolitionist colonel standing up to honor the Harvard art historian also conveys the common sense of purpose that united men who had at times seemed ideologically and temperamentally quite far apart. While they began life as distant cousins, Cambridge neighbors, and playmates, Higginson and Norton had launched themselves on far different life trajectories by the early 1850s. Higginson experimented with increasingly radical forms of dissent, culminating in his violent attempts to free fugitive slaves in

Boston and his participation as one of the "Secret Six" in John Brown's raid on Harpers Ferry in 1859. During the same period, Norton moved from a conventional career in a Boston merchant house to life as a man of letters in his father's Cambridge home, Shady Hill. His first book had sought to check the revolutionary excesses of European radicals.[2] But the "radical" Higginson and the "conservative" Norton began to converge around the crisis of slavery and national union in the late 1850s. Though their careers took different forms after the war, Higginson clearly recognized a common patriotism and sense of duty that drove both men to political and cultural reform in the last three decades of the nineteenth century. That call to duty was forged in the early 1860s, amid the war for the Union that left such an indelible mark on their subsequent lives.

In this they were not alone. Norton and Higginson belonged to an array of organized groups such as the Massachusetts Historical Society, but they were also members of another, less formal community, a circle of like-minded friends, correspondents, allies, and partners whose shared literary leanings, political commitments, and historical experiences united them during the middle of the century. Higginson and Norton lived the longest of the members of this core group, though they share the spotlight here with two other central figures: the novelist, reformer, and editor George William Curtis and the poet, editor, and ambassador James Russell Lowell. These four friends offer a window onto a wider world of critical engagement. Their manifold activities, the collective scope of their interests, and their self-consciousness about a public role exemplify the tendencies of a broader cohort that swelled, shrank, and shifted over the years. Throughout the mutations of liberal reform, the ties among these four friends provided the basis for a larger circle that would at varying moments embrace such younger men as Charles Francis Adams Jr., Henry Adams, Charles W. Eliot, Richard Watson Gilder, William Dean Howells, William James, Moorfield Storey, and Mark Twain.

This book examines how Norton, Higginson, Lowell, Curtis, and the larger community of liberal men of letters devoted their post–Civil War careers to the reformation of American democracy, to the elevation and broadening of its cultural life, and to a sharp critique of its late-century imperial adventures. It builds on the three insights buried in Higginson's eulogy of Norton: the transatlantic context of their lives; the long range of their collective biography; and the importance of the Civil War within that biography. Posterity has tended to remember them mostly for their postbellum efforts. They have been frozen in time as aging Mugwumps and adherents to the Genteel Tradition, either (somewhat paradoxically) relentless disparagers of all things American and democratic or so smugly comfortable in the world that they did as little as possible to disrupt it. Putting aside this apparent inconsistency, such a narrow view distorts their lived experience and diminishes our historical understanding. To place discrete events in perspective, factor in the importance of hope and expectation in how historical actors perceive any development, and understand the sweep of historical change within one generation, historians must take the longer view.[3]

Taking this longer view reveals the significance of the Civil War as the defining event of these men's lives. This was the moment when they became "liberal," when, as Union publicists, they fought and won, in Norton's words, a "war for liberal ideas and for the establishment of liberal principles." In their four decades of active public life after this watershed, this generation of liberals returned again and again to the significance of this event. To borrow language (loosely) from the twentieth century, in their relationship to the war they were much more "greatest generation" than "lost generation." Far from an alienating or disillusioning experience that represented, in Louis Menand's words, "not just a failure of democracy, but a failure of culture, a failure of ideas," the Civil War remained for these liberals a moment of heady idealism when American slavery was abolished and American democracy vindicated on a world stage.[4] This national (and international) crisis also constituted the moment when their informal community assumed its definitive form as a transatlantic liberal alliance, as the American liberals came into contact with a group of sympathetic Britons—Leslie Stephen, Goldwin Smith, James Bryce, A. V. Dicey, Frederic Harrison, and John Morley, among others—who identified with the Union cause and connected it to their program of liberal reform.

These transatlantic liberals formed a community only in the loosest of terms, a community rooted in friendship, mutual interests, and a network of print rather than tied to specific institutions or organizations. The British liberals closely resembled the Americans in social background and intellectual bearings. All had been born into comfortable (if not necessarily affluent) middle-class families and (with the exception of Curtis) had attended university at a time when only a tiny percentage of Britons or Americans did so. While the Americans had cemented a number of aesthetic ties in the 1850s, involving friendships with Arthur Hugh Clough, John Ruskin, and Thomas Hughes, among others, the relationships that grew out of the 1860s had a more coherent and more clearly liberal focus.[5]

This transatlantic liberal friendship created a community of men who nevertheless enjoyed significant and meaningful relationships with women as friends, wives, relatives, and even occasional colleagues (as in the case of Lucy Stone and Julia Ward Howe, with whom Higginson worked for decades as a coeditor of the *Woman's Journal*). But while women were central to the lives of these men as individuals, no women entered into the group and shared the same degree of friendship, conversational exchange, political conviction, and vocational purpose that the men enjoyed.[6] As the connections between them endured through the decades, emotionally intense relationships flourished, sustaining the men across the span of an ocean. As Leslie Stephen wrote in an uncharacteristically frank 1873 letter to Norton, "You don't know what your friendship has been and will be to me. I have not, and never had many intimate friends, and . . . even my best friends have generally been in sympathy with me only on one side, and that not the most intimate side." Stephen valued the assurance of "finding thorough sympathy" from Norton.[7]

This transatlantic liberal community was forged by shared ambition and sense of duty no less than by social background and manly understanding. In their younger years, these men had been inspired by Ralph Waldo Emerson and Thomas Carlyle (and Samuel Taylor Coleridge and the German Romantics he helped to popularize). These figures had offered a vision of heroic scholars and men of letters who might play a vital role in society. Reaching adulthood, the younger men looked to these earlier models to help fashion a role that would unite personal and national aspirations. The transatlantic liberals used writing —journalism and scholarship—in an attempt to reform, educate, and elevate their nations. Here nomenclature becomes somewhat vexed. While members of this group often described themselves as "men of letters," they shared the sensibilities of later "public intellectuals" in speaking to a broad audience on matters of common concern. A desire to be what Stefan Collini has called "public moralists" blurred into a vocation that in the twentieth century became associated with the work of "cultural critics." Standing behind all these terms is the fact that these men earned distinction through literary pursuits of one sort or another and then parlayed that distinction into a cultural authority that enabled them to unite criticism of art and literature with a broad commentary on the issues of the day. In this achievement, the ideas and example of John Stuart Mill—the most prominent British friend of the Union during the Civil War— came to surpass even those of Emerson and Carlyle in the postbellum decades.[8]

Located quite comfortably in the mainstream of American and British life, these transatlantic liberals were in many respects insiders. They clustered around institutions such as Harvard and Oxford while founding or editing several of the most important (and most enduring) nineteenth-century periodicals. These associations assured access to public platforms, including high-profile diplomatic positions. Such achievements demonstrate that these men were not alienated intellectuals. But from within this comfortable and even privileged position, they crafted a public role that challenged the status quo through regular criticism. They often assumed an oppositional stance toward society, if only rhetorically, and were marked by a willingness to point out when their countries fell short of their professed ideals. With an equal mixture of high-mindedness and self-importance, the transatlantic liberals took it upon themselves to elevate, nudge, challenge, and inspire their citizenries. They found partial fulfillment of their duty in checking complacency (what Higginson would call "spiritual obesity") and keeping before the public a vision of how individuals and the larger nation might venture beyond the pursuit of material wealth toward higher civic and cultural ideals.[9]

I have chosen to highlight this critical function in the book's title. In what has long remained the standard account of Gilded Age liberal reformers, John Sproat effectively used the group's self-identification as the "best men" ironically, as a means of casting them as smug, snobbish elites. This is certainly not a difficult charge to level. I have drawn chuckles by describing my subjects as the deadest, whitest, and least manly men in American history.[10] But I have attempted something quite different here in taking seriously the thought and work of the members of a group who (while undoubtedly pompous) sought to remind Americans of their ideals and were unsparing when they fell short.

The title *Critical Americans* signals that while the intellectuals, political debates, and public life of Victorian Britain play a pivotal role in the following pages, the focus remains on the liberal American protagonists and on the transatlantic dimensions of the American situation. This book is, to paraphrase Daniel Rodgers, a connected rather than comparative history. The focus of the Victorian Americans' intellectual and moral energies on Great Britain requires more careful consideration than most U.S. historians usually offer.[11] Since national commitments were (and are) elaborated in an international framework, this expanded scope is crucial to understanding what being an American (or a liberal) meant and helps to provide an understanding of why intellectually inclined young men would seek to fashion roles as public critics at midcentury.

•   •   •

The role of these liberal critics was complicated by their commitment to democracy. As Stephen recognized in an 1870 article on the press, critics performed an important service in exposing shoddiness, hypocrisy, and corruption; in so doing, however, critics were often "liable to the blame of being a trifle too good for this world." Pointing out flaws might lead to a cynicism or pessimism that would alienate the same public that these critics hoped to reach. While the critical Americans struggled with this difficulty throughout their lives, their criticism was never an end in itself. Becoming public critics did give them a vocation, but the stakes for which they were playing were ultimately much higher. The goal was a renewal of American democracy. "Cultivation" was the concept they repeatedly invoked as a means to achieving that goal. The idea of cultivating a broad reading public pervaded the liberal Victorians' understanding of culture, politics, and statecraft.

Victorian cultivation might seem to lend itself to twenty-first-century scorn as the exclusive concern of snobbish and posturing elites. But to collapse a set of rich and compelling meanings into a reflection on social refinement or the display of polished manners would impoverish our understanding of a concept that continues to animate American life. Cultivation had its roots not in class-bound terms of etiquette but in liberal Protestantism, especially the Unitarianism that set New England liberal reformers on the path to reform. The concept of "self-culture"—most clearly associated with an 1838 lecture by the Unitarian minister William Ellery Channing—championed self-improvement as the development of those moral, religious, intellectual, social, and imaginative faculties that all humans possessed. To achieve one's potential—to become fully human—entailed a process of cultivation. Studying art and literature, performing one's duties to the larger community, and meaningfully participating in civic life all constituted means to this end. The members of the Victorian liberal cohort strove to cultivate themselves and to encourage the cultivation of others by shaping a public life and creating institutions that fostered such individual development. The term "cultivation" is in this respect preferable to its more commonly used cognate, "culture," because the latter has been so often misunderstood or caricatured by scholars as a marker of class distinction or a tool of social control. Cultivation, when tied to the underlying notion of self-culture, represents a more active process and better calls to mind the etymological links to agriculture. As Matthew Arnold summed up (in an expression that was typical rather than formative), culture in nineteenth-century Anglo-America was "not a having and a resting, but a growing and a becoming." [12]

As Arnold's formulation suggested, Victorian liberals saw cultivation as a continual process, not a simple possession. As such, cultivation was open to all selves, not simply persons fortunate enough to attend college, visit European museums, or practice professions. The concept's inclusiveness was an important part of its appeal, both in Channing's initial address to "laboring men" and in the Victorian liberals' tendency to apply its ideals across lines of race, class, and gender. Curtis thus insisted that women, like men, were not simply parents or spouses but were "human beings, with genius, talents, aspirations, ambition." This "other half" of the human race deserved the same opportunities and freedom as men to achieve that genius and aspiration. The same was true of African Americans, who should receive training in active citizenship and the liberal arts, not just the manual education many late-nineteenth-century observers in the American South urged.[13]

Liberal reformers responded to the challenges of a democratizing, urbanizing, and industrializing society by insisting with ever greater emphasis on the universal availability and importance of the concept of cultivation. Such cultivation, in sum, would help democracy adapt to new challenges. Cultivating the aesthetic sense might carve out a place for excellence amid what Carlyle called the "cheap and nasty" of the mass market. Cultivating the moral sense might hold in check the tendencies toward political corruption. Cultivating reason over passion might help Americans conduct foreign policy on more just grounds than an unthinking display of patriotic pride. The individual process of cultivation thus had national and international consequences. More accurately, the individual and the national worked in reciprocal fashion. The nation could be only as cultivated as the citizens within it, and those citizens could become cultivated only as the nation provided the institutional space and legitimacy for doing so. The role of the public critic lay in encouraging this process and checking those forces that most threatened it.[14]

This transatlantic liberal cohort's near-obsession with cultivation provides an important insight into Victorian liberalism more broadly. Many recent scholars have shown that the supposed orthodoxies of Manchester School political economy were neither as orthodox nor as constricted as frequent caricatures suggest. Even were the caricatures accurate, however, this strand hardly stood for all of nineteenth-century liberalism. The cultural and moral dimensions examined here help move beyond the realm of the "dismal science" and rethink whether nineteenth-century liberals were truly interested only in a "negative" liberty.[15] John Stuart Mill (the "doyen of Victorian intellectual liberalism") adhered to a "positive" liberty of self-development that was inherently moral. After his crucial revision of Benthamite utilitarianism along Coleridgean and Carlylean lines, Mill's liberalism converged with Channing's Unitarian self-culture. This Millian liberalism, especially in its political aspect, decisively framed how the transatlantic liberals defined their underlying presuppositions.[16]

The group of Americans examined in this book defined liberalism in terms that went well beyond market forces. Apart from E. L. Godkin, none in this cohort systematically considered economic policy or even political economic theory. Their early careers established two prevailing concerns that largely neglected the workings of markets and the intricacies of exchange: a focus on imaginative development (through cultural expression and creative endeavors) and an increasing involvement in antislavery reform. As a result of these two early interests, the men who became Victorian liberal critics were not only predisposed toward aesthetics and morals but also sympathetic to the lambasting of political economy by the likes of Carlyle and Ruskin.

I have avoided the tendency to treat "liberalism" as a simple dogma or creed, whether as an expression of economic laws or any tidy ideology in the realm of politics and culture. Reducing a set of principles to a rigid system of belief is a fate visited upon far too many "isms" whose coherence is usually more assumed than investigated. It is useful to point out that as a proper name, "Liberalism" had a specific meaning in Britain that it lacked in the United States—the Liberal Party came into being under Lord Palmerston in the 1840s, thrived through the 1860s, and persisted into the Gladstonian ministries of subsequent decades. American usage of the term signaled this sort of party allegiance only during the Liberal Republican movement of 1872 (which was brief and whose presidential nominee, Horace Greeley, failed to win the support of the core Victorian liberal reformers examined in this volume). At the moment that these liberals most closely identified with their transatlantic counterparts, they called themselves Radical Republicans. They adopted the term "liberal" not to establish a party label but to associate themselves with a sensibility that had a long if variable history in religious, political, and economic thought. In Britain, political liberalism existed before the Liberal Party, and as Jonathan Parry has argued, those who first boasted of their "liberal" administration of government were reforming Tories of the 1820s. American liberals at times echoed the efficiency and effectiveness in administrative matters hailed by this charter group of nineteenth-century liberalizers but did not do so with anything like the same focus. Instead, the Civil War and Reconstruction shaped this American version of liberalism, which emerged during a period of upheaval when keeping progressive change moving and on track seemed far more important than retrenchment or administrative competency.[17]

Liberalism in the context of this political, social, and cultural revolution contained an intrinsically expansive cluster of meanings. Most significant were a faith in popular government, a close identification with progress and justice, and a commitment to orderly change and cosmopolitan open-mindedness. Curtis put his finger on these expansive meanings when he explained to readers of *Harper's Weekly* that the "key-note of English as of American liberalism— the secret of peace and welfare—is Justice." Norton carefully distinguished the liberal ideal from mere liberty or freedom when he contrasted the corrosive effects of "partisan narrowness & sectarian bigotry" with the need for greater "liberality of opinion." In this sense, the term conveyed open-mindedness, tolerance, and a willingness to engage in reasoned debate.[18]

Because this book's protagonists were never systematic theorizers, their understanding of "liberal" can best be understood from such concrete associations, which must be examined within specific political, cultural, and rhetorical contexts. It is useful to think of liberalism, like other political theories, as part of a language, providing—as John Burrow has put it—a vocabulary "we inhabit" rather than a set of doctrines to which we subscribe. In this regard, what "liberalism" meant depended more than anything else on two other factors—what set of "illiberal" forces seemed to threaten American democratic promise and what other positive and progressive allies might be enlisted in the struggle to keep reform on track. It was no coincidence that the Americans began to employ the word "liberalism" more frequently during the Civil War years, when transatlantic allies in the Union cause were of greatest importance and when the Millian dimensions of public commitments were formulated in ways that persisted until century's end. The liberalism that helped to end slavery and save the Union could never be reduced to an economic program (although its proponents had a general commitment to the right of property other than in slaves and to free-market trade across international boundaries). What mattered most was a set of moral and political commitments that would assure the continuation of human progress by overcoming those retrogressive tendencies that elevated force over fairness in the pursuit of selfish interest.[19]

In practice as well as on the level of ideas, these liberals' early opposition to slavery persisted in a real (if often condescending) sympathy for racial minorities and in a deeply held conviction that the "hard racism" of the Victorian period was among the most dangerous forms of moral corruption. They supported political equality and popular government as they understood those terms—again via Mill, whose *Considerations on Representative Government* appeared at the same moment that the sectional crisis exploded into war. A dedication to reason, to the free play of ideas, to the educative import of democratic participation, and to the need for individuals to exercise their imaginations to be fully human became central tenets of liberal faith as a result of this 1860s experience. "Liberal" at times became interchangeable with such equally vague but no less powerful adjectives as "advanced" or "progressive." Two points, very much related, bear particular emphasis here. First, these Victorians' understanding of liberalism blended quite easily with other seemingly incompatible political traditions, chief among them republicanism. Second, Victorian American liberals did not respect dogmatic consistency to forge their vision of the good society. They saw no contradiction in emphasizing both private rights and public duties or in insisting that government be both broadly representative and elevated.[20]

This group embraced not only liberalism but democracy. This topic can be addressed with more brevity, because, while not uncontroversial, it has been more easily understood both at the time and in the work of later historians. At least since Tocqueville, the fortunes of the United States and that of popular government in general became so intertwined in the transatlantic imagination that Walt Whitman could assume that readers would agree when he remarked that "America" and "democracy" were in fact "convertible terms." While democracy existed as a national idea, it was also associated with broader trends that extended beyond the borders of the United States. Victorian democrats believed in the (careful) expansion of suffrage, the need for government to respond to the "public opinion" of the nation at large, and the broad dissemination of works of high imagination without regard to the audience's class, race, or gender. Contemporaries assumed that the pursuit of such democratic goals in the United States had broader implications for the rest of the world and were acutely aware of a common democratic wave. The widening of suffrage in both America and Britain in the 1860s (with the Fifteenth Amendment and the Second Reform Act) formed part of this pattern, as did liberals' push for female suffrage during the same period.[21]

Some readers may be surprised by an insistence on these liberal reformers' attachment to democracy. Much scholarship has followed Sproat, whose work has been the most forceful in understanding the leaders of this movement as actively hostile to popular government and to the spirit of democratic culture. Such was clearly not the case, however, at least in any historically meaningful way. Considering those truly antidemocratic conservatives whom liberal reformers took great efforts to dismiss as illiberal reactionaries provides a better understanding of the reformers' stance. Furthermore, their elaborate if non-systematic thinking about the centrality of discussion to democratic practice and their ideal of active democratic citizenship make them current in democratic theory today.[22] During the last decade of the nineteenth century, a sense of despair over the state of American life became more palpable in both their correspondence and their published writings. Godkin and Norton, in particular, became critical of Americans' embrace of imperialism and violence and of the seeming American complacency in the face of rampant materialism and widespread political corruption. Yet neither of these figures ever relinquished his belief in the superiority and desirability of democratic government over all other forms. Higginson and the other surviving members of the American cohort were even less likely to waver in their democratic convictions.

Except in their crankiest moods, what most concerned these figures was how ordinary democratic practice might best conform to those features of the democratic ideal to which they had clung over a lifetime of endeavor. All of these men confronted what they considered national flaws with a strategy of dissent and reform rather than a willful retreat from public life. This fact itself testified to their notion that matters might right themselves and that the people, working through democratic processes, could achieve something better than what had come to pass. To say that the members of this group were disgusted by the materialism, corruption, and jingoism of their era is hardly a sign of their irrelevance or truculence. The concerns of these Victorians in fact bring them much closer to twentieth- and twenty-first-century critics, who have worried about money's role in politics, about voter ignorance and apathy, and about the effects of unthinking hyperpatriotism on foreign policy. The Victorian liberal reformers, like their successors, both prefaced and acted on criticism with a prevailing sense that the people could and should do better.[23]

• • •

In keeping with the biographical thrust of the book, the chapters follow a generally chronological organization as they move from the critical Americans' young adulthoods in the 1840s and 1850s to the end of their lives in the decades surrounding the turn of the century. Chapter 1 explores, in four biographical sketches, how Higginson, Lowell, Curtis, and Norton struggled to find meaningful vocations during a period of political and intellectual ferment. The conventional alternatives for men of their social background—business, law, the ministry, or politics—seemed inadequate to their Romantically inspired literary ambitions as well as their Unitarian and republican sense of duty. Instead, they experimented with versions of reform and authorship that led down different paths, from Higginson's radical (and physical) activism to Lowell's and Curtis's founding of periodicals to Norton's interest in education and art. Along the way, each of these individuals grappled with the sometimes competing forces of duty and personal aspiration, reform and culture, and nationalism and cosmopolitanism. They also faced the sectional crisis as proud New Englanders. Their convergence as opponents of the slave power would be encapsulated in Curtis's address on "The Duty of American Scholars to Politics and the Times," a call to fuse what Higginson called the "progressive literary class" with a commitment to the antislavery movement.

Chapter 2 examines these men's experiences during the Civil War, a crucial moment in the formation of their ideas and in the establishment of their roles as leading shapers of opinion. The crisis that engulfed the nation after Lincoln's 1860 election forced Union publicists to consider the nature of leadership in a democracy. Lincoln's straightforward appeals to the reasoning capacity of ordinary citizens came to seem the best embodiment of democratic statesmanship. Musings on Lincoln's leadership by Curtis, Norton, and Lowell led in turn to an intensive study of the democratic possibilities of public opinion as well as of the important public function performed by those who helped mold that opinion. The Civil War also became an important moment in liberal understandings of the U.S. role in the larger world. The northern intellectuals agreed with Lincoln that with Union defeat, popular government would perish from the earth; they were joined in this view by a small group of Britons who, alone amid a larger hostile public, supported the Union effort. The most prominent among this group was Mill, whose influence and example would grow throughout the 1860s. Norton, Lowell, Curtis, and Higginson developed a more intimate set of ties with younger British intellectuals, whose friendship and liberal political convictions tempered the Americans' more general Anglophobia.

Union victory, the abolition of slavery, and the vindication of democracy resulted in a period of high exultation. Chapter 3 explores this liberal high tide and in many ways forms the centerpiece of the book. The community of American and British intellectuals, who now considered themselves part of a "great liberal party of the world," looked forward to a postwar period of increased liberal progress in both countries. To encourage this progress, they sought to mitigate hostilities between the two countries and to bring about an Anglo-American rapprochement on liberal terms, which meant, for the Americans, siding explicitly (if at times naively) with the Liberal Party against the Tories. During this high tide, liberals focused on the treatment of former slaves, struggling to articulate a policy of "fair play" for freedmen in the United States and for black Jamaicans in Britain. The American liberals' commitment to black suffrage, achieved with passage of the Fifteenth Amendment, was seen as part of the larger liberal expansion of the vote that included the 1867 Reform Act. The transatlantic liberals were not alone in seeing linkages among Union victory, racial fair play, and suffrage expansion. Carlyle connected these events, from a hostile perspective, in "Shooting Niagara," and his shrill reaction provided the perfect illiberal foil against which liberals elaborated their critical role. Mill, Carlyle's onetime friend and frequent foe, provided the quintessentially liberal model of morally engaged public advocacy.

The transatlantic liberals drew on Millian ideas about the educative nature of democratic citizenship while ushering in expanded electorates and rethinking citizenship during a period of constitutional reform. The superiority of democracy as a form of government, liberals argued, lay in the stimulus it provided to citizens' moral, social, and intellectual faculties. Informed discussion, conducted in print, formed the basis of their normative vision of civic life. Because this vision presupposed a "reading citizenry"—able to engage in a larger democratic discussion—it contained potentially restrictive features. But in the midst of the high tide, the liberals seemed mesmerized by the expansive possibilities of uniting citizens across the country in print-based forums, which, not insignificantly, the liberals thought would be shaped in their critical image. With this vision in mind, the transatlantic liberals laid out a reform agenda to prove that public life could be at once broadly democratic and liberally cultivated. The final three chapters of the book explore the contours and dilemmas of this effort in the discrete but connected realms of culture, politics, and international relations.

After emancipation and national reunion had been achieved, the American liberal critics returned to their earlier cultural pursuits, which chapter 4 examines. Higginson spoke for the others in his 1867 "plea for culture," which considered how aesthetic endeavors might prolong the wartime commitment to moral ideals even as the nation entered a prolonged period of peace and "gilded" prosperity. This plea came at the exact moment that British poet and civil servant Matthew Arnold offered his far more iconic definition of culture ("sweetness and light" and the "best that has been thought and said"), which proved so influential through the twentieth century and made "Arnoldian" a suggestive (if often misunderstood) adjective. The American liberals were contemporaries more than disciples of Arnold, and his presence suggests the subtle realignment of Anglo-American interactions that accompanied cultural endeavors, the most dramatic of which was a partial rehabilitation of Carlyle during the 1870s and 1880s. While the Americans reached out beyond their liberal circle, their dedication to the kind of culture associated with Arnold blended easily with the Millian components of their liberalism, nurturing the same processes of self-development and inner growth. In their work on cultural reform, the liberal critics wrestled with the tensions between nationalism and cosmopolitanism and between democracy and authority, but a more general tension accompanied their efforts to define their critical role. Steering a path between critique and despair as the country seemed to become less cultivated with each passing decade, the liberal critics struggled (with mixed success) to combine their severe cultural criticism with a broad democratic faith.

Chapter 5 focuses on political reform through an examination of transatlantic liberal ideas about public opinion, political participation, and the party system. In a seemingly endless stream of writings (most notably James Bryce's 1889 *American Commonwealth*), the transatlantic liberals considered how the press might foster educative citizenship and political discussion. They modeled their ideas in their "higher journalism," which presented a serious and independent discussion of issues to hundreds of thousands of readers. Placing opinion, and especially critical shapers of it, at the center of political life might help ensure that "government by discussion," democracy's great virtue, would flourish. Liberals worried that postwar party machines had stunted rather than facilitated discussion and argument, so they combined their journalistic efforts with an attack on the automatic, blind partisanship that they believed threatened critical, active citizenship. Combining attacks on the spoils system with independent voting and engaged political commentary, they hoped to reform—though not abolish—the party system. Their political activity opened them to charges of effeminacy, most famously for their bolt of the Republican Party in 1884, which the chapter briefly considers before examining some of the larger transatlantic contours of political reform.

The final chapter treats the liberal critics' opposition to the Philippine-American war as their last collective act and thus the closing epoch in their lives. While the chapter focuses mostly on the 1890s, it takes two crucial detours to consider how liberals framed their ideas about international relations in two earlier episodes. The American liberals chronicled for their readers the dramatic clash between the two British political titans—the Liberal W. E. Gladstone and the Conservative Benjamin Disraeli—as they articulated different visions of Britain's role in the world. Preferring Gladstone's pronounced liberal internationalism to Disraeli's no less pronounced conservative nationalism, Curtis and Godkin then followed the Gladstonian Liberals in their move for Irish Home Rule in the 1880s, a position that paradoxically both fractured and reinforced the transatlantic liberal community. Returning to the 1890s, the chapter concludes by showing how Norton, Higginson, Godkin, and their younger allies dissented from their country's increasing jingoism and aggressiveness, which culminated in the Philippine-American war. Compounding the sense of gloom that surrounded this event was the appearance of a transatlantic rapprochement rooted not in the liberal ideals they had cherished and worked toward for decades but in a presumed Anglo-Saxon destiny to rule weaker peoples. The century closed with the aging liberal critics mounting their last concerted campaign.

The epilogue examines briefly how the generation of Victorian liberals fared at the hands of their immediate twentieth-century successors and questions why we in the twenty-first century remain so captive to the moderns' dismissive view. The book closes by noting that succeeding generations have continued to grapple with the same issues faced by the liberal Victorians. The shortcomings of our own diminished public life might chasten our inclination to dismiss without a full hearing critical voices from an earlier era.

Victorian Duty, American Scholars, and National Crisis

Do you ask me our duty as scholars? . . . Thought, which the scholar represents,
is life and liberty. There is no intellectual or moral life without liberty. Therefore, as a
man must breathe and see before he can study; the American scholar must have liberty, first
of all; and as the American scholar is a man and has a voice in his own government, so his
interest in political affairs must precede all others. He must build his house before he
can live in it. He must be a perpetual inspiration of freedom in politics. He must
recognize that the intelligent exercise of political rights, which is a privilege in a
monarchy, is a duty in a republic. If it clash with his ease, his retirement,
his taste, his study, let it clash, but let him do his duty.
George William Curtis, "The Duty of the American Scholar
to Politics and the Times," 1856

By all accounts, George William Curtis was a rousing public speaker. His success depended on his presentation of high-minded Victorian idioms and ideals to audiences eager for clear perspective. At no time were these skills more in evidence than in his 1856 plea for college students to "introduce thought and the sense of justice into human affairs." In considering "The Duty of the American Scholar to Politics and to the Times," Curtis implored the "scholarly class" in his audience to recognize the responsibilities that had made it the "upper house in the politics of the world." Those who did no more than offer a "vague declamation about freedom in general" and then retreat to their studies helped to sanction the canard "that the scholar is a pusillanimous traitor." Only by making the sort of commitment that the times demanded could scholars show society that the "pale student of books" was something more than a "recluse, a valetudinarian, and unpractical and impractical man."[1]

Curtis's oration was heavily indebted to Ralph Waldo Emerson's "The American Scholar," from which Curtis borrowed much of his language. Addressing the Phi Beta Kappa Society of Harvard nearly twenty years earlier, Emerson had sketched a powerful and imaginative vision of the scholar's role. Emerson's address had, in turn, followed in a line of similar orations, most notably Joseph Stevens Buckminster's 1809 "The Danger and Duties of Men of Letters." But if Curtis resembled these predecessors, he also departed from them by rooting the scholar's duty explicitly in "politics and the times," which in 1856 unmistakably meant in the growing sectional crisis. A note of particular urgency thus crept into the address, as he imagined that even the most bookish student would be overwhelmed by the "air that steals in at his window, darkens his study and suffocates him as he reads." The mounting national crisis had become part of this atmosphere, as an imminent storm seemed to be brewing with violence in Kansas and on the floor of the U.S. Senate, where Charles Sumner had recently been beaten by the South Carolinian Preston Brooks. Only the victory of the new Republican Party, Curtis believed, could calm the crisis or at least bring it to an appropriate climax. Curtis had a clear vision of the scholar's duty, and his speech represented an effort to channel the lofty energies of Emerson's solitary Truth-seeker into more immediately political concerns. Curtis called on the young American scholars in his audience "to determine whether this great experience of human freedom, which has been the scorn of despotism, shall, by its failure, be also our sin and shame." American scholars' duty now explicitly included opposition to slavery.[2]

Curtis's call to duty and action did not meet with immediate success, at least in strictly political terms. Though the Republican candidate John C. Frémont carried most of the North, the Democratic James Buchanan emerged victorious. Curtis would have to wait until 1860 to see a Republican elected to the White House. He placed great confidence in Abraham Lincoln and in a party platform that, with the prompting of Curtis and others, included a direct invocation of the Declaration of Independence. Those who voted Republican along with Curtis exhibited a clarifying sense of duty that, one way or another, he thought, could not fail to set the country on a nobler path.

Curtis's 1856 speech set him on a new personal course at the same time that it roused others to action. With this speech, Curtis first expressed his determination to engage in party politics and to act on his sense that a matured conception of a public duty necessarily went beyond writing the light-hearted travel narratives, novels, and satiric social sketches that had thus far made him famous. Curtis had come to believe that what he called the "scholar's office in the State" necessarily involved more than private learning and reflection and that an essential duty involved taking part in the "elevation and correction of public sentiment." Apart from the explicit connection to the antislavery movement, his conception of scholarly responsibility—which would thereafter define his public utterances—was broadly Emersonian. Many of its key elements—the need to "turn and face" the danger, to be the "world's eye," to "cheer, to raise, and to guide men," and to initiate a "revolution" in the "idea of Culture"— had in fact received classic expression in Emerson's 1837 "American Scholar" address.[3]

Curtis used comfortable certitudes when speaking of the scholar's duty, but his assurance masked his tentative evolution toward this ideal. He had struggled with the problem of vocation in his youth and drifted while searching for an appropriate career. Neither the conception of duty nor the drift were exceptional in the mid–nineteenth century, when many men of his social background and generation wrestled with the problem of finding appropriate and satisfying work. These elite northeasterners had been raised in households of middle-class privilege. If they had lacked affluence, they at least had comfort and access to cultural advantages such as exposure to books and a college education. More often than not they had, in Oliver Wendell Holmes's phrase, "tumbled about in a library" and had learned to value the life of the mind and the soul over that of the mere body. They wanted their vocations to exemplify this upbringing as men of ambition and principle.[4]

Curtis and his liberal circle of friends—Thomas Wentworth Higginson, James Russell Lowell, and Charles Eliot Norton—spoke in a Victorian idiom of character and duty that requires some effort to recover. That effort begins by attending to the subtleties of meaning embedded in their words and the specificity of context encircling their biographies. It begins by recognizing the sense of national crisis with which this generation grew up, a sense that all was not right with the American experiment and that the forces of greed and cowardice had clouded its ideals. The conception of duty they invoked while striving to find a role in American society stemmed from their class and place, but it was born as well of the historical moment during which they came of age. All four searched for meaningful and fulfilling work; all responded in some way to a Romantic emphasis on genius and imagination. All four also recognized, however, that the exalted American scholar had to be brought down to earth and had to play a role in the emerging national crisis.[5]

Manlike Let Him Turn and Face the Danger

Thomas Wentworth Higginson reveled in the significance of the moment. "I have never heard of a time in the history of the world," he told an assembled group of Unitarian ministers in 1853, "when there was such a movement going on in the human race, when questions so important were grasping the public mind." Though still a young man, Higginson could speak from experience about the "reforms, practical, social, spiritual" that he had seen "rising for twenty years." He had been involved in many of these efforts as an advocate of temperance, women's rights, free religion, and, first and foremost, abolition. His reform record bolstered his sweeping claim to the Unitarian ministers that "every public man" was at that moment "taxed to the utmost to do his duty to great thoughts and great labors."[6]

Higginson's sense of duty had deep roots, extending in some respects back to the Puritan New England of the 1630s, when the Reverend Francis Higginson established a family tradition of religious and cultural leadership. While the Higginsons' economic standing was ruined by the loss of their fortune during the War of 1812, their cultural influence was preserved by the role that Higginson's father played as steward of Harvard College. In Cambridge, the young Wentworth grew up, earned an undergraduate degree, and nurtured an ambition to be "guiding, governing, pointing out the true course to those who cannot find it unaided." How this ambition might be satisfied in the context of the 1840s, however, would prove to be a more significant challenge than he might have imagined.[7]

Higginson entered Harvard in 1838, one year after Emerson had delivered his stirring address to the Phi Beta Kappa Society. Not until after Higginson graduated from college, however, did his desire to "guide" and "govern" take a literary turn, leading him to consider adopting the Emersonian role of "Man Thinking" as his life's work. With reform and Transcendentalism in the air, this period of "the newness," Higginson later recalled, saw passing "through the whole community a wave of that desire for a freer and more ideal life." Against this backdrop, the barely twenty-year-old Higginson grappled with the problem of vocation and found himself alienated from the conventional career choices—politics, the ministry, the law—all of which seemed too traditional, uninspired, and incapable of capturing the aspirations and longings of an age that the shrewdest observers on both sides of the Atlantic realized was altogether unprecedented.

Higginson began reading Romantic literature and philosophy, mixing

Goethe and Carlyle with a regular immersion in local Transcendentalists. ("The usual dose of Emerson, and to bed," he typically reported in one of his diary entries.) He read the *Dial* with his future wife, Mary Channing, visited the utopian community at Brook Farm, and met local luminaries at Elizabeth Peabody's foreign bookstore.[8] He found his imagination especially fired by the life and writings of Jean Paul Richter, the "moral poet" who had bravely turned to literature when his religious faith faltered and who endured poverty and solitude to pursue his literary calling. Higginson devoured Eliza Buckminster Lee's biography of Richter and began writing poetry, reportedly by moonlight. Higginson soon vowed that he would become a writer—a noble, suffering one at that. In preparation for his Romantic calling, he took additional classes at Harvard while living in a room adorned simply with a Titian print, a bust of the Greek goddess Hebe, and fresh flowers. He imagined himself a "sort of pariah, an outcast of the world," a solitary seeker after Truth. Dining frugally on bread and milk, he read voraciously, attended lectures and musical perfor-mances, and generally sowed his "intellectual wild oats," as he later recalled. Like Emerson's scholar, this aspiring artist was consciously forgoing the "ease and pleasure of traveling the old road" by choosing "poverty and solitude." Hardly a year into this regimen, however, Higginson abandoned his literary plans and entered Harvard Divinity School in the fall of 1844.[9]

Higginson's belated choice of the ministry over literature constituted less a return to a venerable family tradition than a fresh assessment of the impera-tives of the present day. The decision reveals some of his complicated thinking about duty and provides a glimpse into how he negotiated the competing claims of self and society. Like the Romantic-Transcendentalist writers he read and befriended, Higginson sensed a tension between self-development and pub-lic life. Yet for Higginson, that tension arose not simply from distrust of the world's intrusions on individual self-reliance but also from his fear that indi-viduals focusing on the self might neglect their larger public responsibilities. For all his literary aspirations and lifelong love of books, Higginson harbored a profound ambivalence toward an exclusively interior life. He loved literature, nature, and beauty but sensed "inwardly that something more will be sought of me." Even while boasting of his pariah-like seclusion, he could not help thinking that his solitude had a whiff of self-indulgence and social irrespon-sibility. This belief no doubt represented in part a reaction to his real brush with self-indulgence after college, the dandyish "strutting" about in a "beau-tiful combination of gaiters and high heels" and the bohemian posturing as a starving artist. His family had laughed at both the foppish fashion and the

moonlight-drenched poetry, which may have led him, in his later embarrassment, to associate the two.[10]

Higginson's fear of self-indulgent social irresponsibility constituted more
than a personality trait—it stemmed, as was the case with Curtis and others,
from a sense of a deepening national crisis. In a world so much in need of
action, Higginson wondered how one could justify a strictly contemplative life,
how one could cultivate one's inner freedom when so many others were left un-
free, slaves to masters, to alcohol, or to outworn ideas. His engagement to Mary
Channing and consequent association with her family had brought him into
contact with abolitionists and activists of all types who pressed him on exactly
these matters. A subscription to William Lloyd Garrison's *Liberator* was followed by his reading of Lydia Maria Child's *Appeal on Behalf of That Class of
Americans Called Africans*, a work that deeply moved Higginson. "An aesthetic
life—how beautiful," he confided in his journal, "but the life of a Reformer, a
People's Guide, 'battling for right,'—glorious, but Oh how hard!" Higginson
thought he found an answer to his vocational dilemmas—a way to unite ambition and duty, thought and action—as he listened to the antislavery sermons
of William Henry Channing, James Freeman Clarke, and Theodore Parker, all
of whom signaled the possibilities of a modern ministry.[11] "One might accomplish something and lead a manly life even in the pulpit," he realized, using a
common if uncommonly vague adjective.[12] In seeking a career as a Unitarian
pastor, Higginson inverted Emerson's earlier vocational crisis. Where the Concord sage had rejected the ministry and checked "militant humanitarianism"
to discover his true vocation as Man Thinking, Higginson rejected the interi-
ority of Man Thinking to become Man the Reformer.[13]

Man the Reformer Higginson soon became, embarking in 1847 on a veritable multimedia career in a new position at a Newburyport church. He announced his conception of the ministry in his first public address, significantly
titled "The Clergy and Reform." He imagined here an "eternal antagonism"
between the clergy and what he called the "progressive, thinking, or literary
class," further explaining that both groups vied to provide the "moral and intellectual government of the people." Because ministers inherited an "established
station," they as a class incurred a "tremendous responsibility" to prove their
worth. They had to justify their leadership role in society by actually leading,
by "guiding, reforming, and regenerating the world." Though drawing a minister's regular salary allowed him and Mary to wed in 1847, Higginson remained
leery of the institutional prestige of the clergy, identifying strongly with the
"progressive, thinking, or literary class" throughout his life. His skepticism

stemmed from a concern that institutions, while crucial forces in society, often lost touch with the principles that animated them. Individuals had to ensure that institutions remained instruments for social life rather than becoming their own ends; Higginson strove to do this throughout his career as a reform minister.[14]

Higginson's insistence on individuals' crucial role in safeguarding institutions makes plain that his idea of public duty, while wary of self-indulgence, never countenanced self-effacement. Far from it. In fact, in this "age of introversion," he spent a good deal of time engaging in and reflecting on self-development. Here Higginson drew from the Unitarian conception of self-culture, associated most notably with his wife's late uncle, the Unitarian moralist William Ellery Channing. Channing's self-culture meant the building of one's character through the cultivation of all the faculties, especially one's moral, intellectual, and imaginative powers. Significantly, this tradition did not understand self-cultivation as a process occurring in isolation: "Self-culture is social," Channing had urged. The most important branch of self-culture was the "moral" branch, which Channing associated with disinterested conscience and a sense of duty.[15] Even as it was directed toward the public, Higginson's ministerial work nurtured his individual growth as well as the growth of others. While some might have worried about the compromises that reform organizations necessarily entailed, Higginson did not see it that way: "It is worth being a reformer, for the sake of getting the habit of thinking for one's self."[16]

To Channing's catalog of the varieties of self-culture, Higginson added physical culture, by which he meant the development and training of one's physical body through exercise, for which he retained a passion throughout his life. Higginson's focus on the body was not unknown among abolitionists, but it was far more indebted to the broader Victorian fascination with manliness and athleticism. In the 1840s, this trend was especially associated with the "muscular Christianity" of F. D. Maurice, Charles Kingsley, and Thomas Hughes, all of whom put a more progressive understanding on what in Thomas Carlyle's interpretation would come to seem a worship of force.[17] Higginson shared some of this fascination, recording his strenuous hikes and boasting of the gymnastics he performed, all while glorying in his manly feats and "untamed gypsy nature." His emphasis on physical culture was complicated, however, neither being as dependent on gender norms as was typical of the age nor approaching the sense that animal passions had to be released from civilized restraint. However "manly" athletics may have made him feel, he nevertheless urged physical exercise for women as well as men. His attention to the body followed from his conception of dutiful self-development, achieving one's best self and making use of all one's faculties, developing and training them but also submitting them to reason, conscience, and will. Higginson refused to choose between different aspects of development and urged other individuals, men and women alike, to refuse what he saw as a series of false choices. Why did saints (or poets or painters) have to be weak in body, he wondered? Why did people presume that domestication and civilization entailed a diminution of strength? Why did (middle-class) women have to be invalids? Neglect of bodily health and development was false to God as well as to self and society. All human capacities required development. All individuals had minds, souls, and bodies; elements of domestication and wildness; and male and female tendencies. His refusal to choose between what he considered artificial dichotomies echoed the work of Margaret Fuller, one of Higginson's early role models and one of the several Romantics whose biographies he would later write.[18]

Higginson initially felt validated in his choice of vocation, telling James Russell Lowell that "actual experience has thus far enlarged not diminished my view of what the pulpit may be & do, while it lasts." He had found a way to combine cultivating his self with helping others to initiate a similar process of cultivation. His increasing activism—preaching against northern complicity in slavery, advertising abolitionist meetings, and inviting the fugitive slave William Wells Brown to speak at the church—rankled the conservative parish, however. Having vowed after hearing Frederick Douglass speak in 1848 never again to "let one Sunday pass in the professed preaching of Christianity, and leave the name of SLAVERY unmentioned," he chastised his largely Whig parishioners after Zachary Taylor's 1848 election. "A party professing to be anti-slavery and anti-war," he scolded, "has elected to the Presidency one who never could have been chosen, had he not been both a Slaveholder and a Warrior." Faced with drastically thinning pews, he resigned the following year.[19] But his resignation hardly signaled the end of his ministry or his reform work. He sought other outlets through which to cultivate the community: he offered lecture series, wrote a newspaper column, and founded an evening school for working adults. He also turned to politics, running unsuccessfully as a candidate for the Free Soil Party in 1850 after his friend, the Quaker poet John Greenleaf Whittier, declined the nomination.[20]

Higginson's perception of crisis intensified with the passage of the Fugitive Slave Law in 1850. So, too, did his reform activism. He moved to Worcester to lead the new Free Church there and began working closely with the radical Garrisonians—including Wendell Phillips, Parker Pillsbury, Abby and Stephen

Foster, and Lucy Stone as well as Garrison—and dedicating himself to abolition and women's rights. It had become increasingly clear to him that slavery had enlisted force on its side and that consequently the response must be force. Witnessing the conversion of Massachusetts's citizens into slave catchers, Higginson wondered what stood "between us and a military despotism," resolving that reform had to give way to revolution. Active resistance to the Fugitive Slave Law was fine in theory. But Higginson found a chance to practice what he preached in the case of Anthony Burns, a fugitive slave whose Virginia master recaptured him in the spring of 1854 in one of the most electrifying moments in antebellum New England.[21]

Even the Burns case, which seems to mark Higginson's most lawless behavior, showed evidence of his underlying respect for institutions. Active resistance was necessary to protect the past inheritances, to reanimate them, and to render them capable of meeting contemporary challenges. Higginson did not think the Massachusetts citizens responsible for Burns's return were bad people (he admitted that probably none would personally own slaves), although he insisted that converting normally fair people into slave catchers was the exact "tragedy of our American institutions." He took it upon himself to safeguard institutions and to return them to their original underlying principle. In other words, Higginson's refusal to compromise followed not from self-absorption or self-preservation but from his sense of public duty. His disgust at the corruption of institutions led not to a withdrawal from public life but a more radical intervention in it. His commitment always remained to the spirit rather than the form of any institution. As he had explained when running as a Free Soil candidate, the party "organization will never bind us one instant after it seems to us to be plainly false to its principles." Similarly, after determining that the Unitarians were "aimless, hopeless, powerless, and dead," he moved toward more radical forms of religion that might be imbued once more with principle.[22]

Higginson's move toward force in resisting the Fugitive Slave Law worked in tandem with his focus on physical strength and courage. The fight over slavery made his newfound commitment patently clear, as politics, legislation, and moral suasion seemed to make no headway against the steadily escalating demands of southern slaveholders. It was time for force. "All the intellect, all the genius, all the learning ever expended upon the point of Constitutional interpretation," Higginson wrote in 1857, "are not worth, in the practical solution of the slavery question, a millionth part so much as the poorest shot that ever a fugitive slave fired at his master." One had a duty to commit not just mind

and soul but body, a duty to develop one's physical as well as moral and intellectual courage.[23]

Tensions between self-development and self-absorption remained as Higginson moved toward radical opposition to slavery. He took the occasion of an 1858
article to chastise reformers for failing to back up their convictions with physical courage, explaining that both the presence of moral courage and the absence of physical courage often emerged from the same source: an overregard
for the self at the expense of a true understanding of duty. Reformers often were
motivated by an "intense egotism," an obsession with individual purity, and a
fear that even the "slightest indications of popular approbation" signaled an
impure "compromise." But while the "abstract martyrdom of unpopularity"
appealed to many reformers, "when it comes to the rack and the thumbscrew,
the revolver and the bowie-knife, the same habitual egotism makes them cowards." Reformers had to check their egos, Higginson cautioned, and be certain
that neither their concern with moral purity nor their fear of physical danger
led them to neglect their larger duties. He strove in his reform work to unite
physical and moral bravery, doing so in the same way that he balanced his self-
development with larger social duties.[24]

Having "manlike" turned and faced the danger, Higginson's fascination
with violence found a legal outlet in the 1860s when he enlisted in the Union
Army and led the first regiment of former slaves in a war against their onetime masters. Before that new occasion, Higginson created opportunities to
unite the physical with the mental by venturing to Kansas. There he met John
Brown, whose combination of word and deed set the stage for the next act in
American history by offering up a martyrdom that was as far from abstract as
one could imagine.[25]

The World's Eye . . . the World's Heart

Some American reformers who came of age in the 1840s devoted themselves to
breathing new life into old forms such as the university and the clergy. Others
set themselves the task of creating new networks and structures. Nowhere was
such basic building of institutions more important than in the realm of American letters. As the middle of the nineteenth century approached, the greater
Boston area had already produced a constellation of cultural institutions—
most notably Harvard College and the *North American Review*. But any sort
of establishment, especially one with greater than regional influence, was still

in the process of becoming. Such pursuits attracted the powers of dozens of young literary men and women who participated in what would later be recognized as an American Renaissance. Much remained to be done in bringing culture and reform into a common field, in establishing the role of the secular and quasi-professional man of letters, in fostering critical rigor, and in vindicating American culture from its transatlantic critics.[26]

James Russell Lowell was one of the most determined of his generation to commit himself to literature and to fostering the institutions of humane culture in the United States. His talent for mixing "rhymes" with conviviality emerged during his undergraduate days at Harvard, when he was elected to the Hasty Pudding Club and to the office of class poet before being suspended (or, as Harvard then put it, "rusticated") for his rambunctious "neglect of college duties." Lowell proved a more devoted student outside of class than in, devouring all the British literature he could buy or get through the Harvard library. When Lowell graduated in 1838 and returned to his family's Cambridge home, Elmwood, he experienced his own period of "miserable . . . indecision" as he cast about for a vocation with little more sense of direction than Higginson would a few years later. The son of a gentle and gracious Unitarian minister, Lowell briefly considered and rejected the ministry before similarly considering and rejecting business. Through drawn to the luster of a literary career, he ambivalently entered Harvard's Dane Law School in the fall of 1839. In time he would reject a legal career as well.[27]

Young Lowell had kept his distance from Emersonian radicalism while in college, though the Transcendentalist had delivered both his "American Scholar" address and his "Divinity School Address" while Lowell was a student and conversed with Lowell during the young student's "rustication" in Concord. But after college, Lowell began experimenting with new forms of intellectual, spiritual, and personal radicalism that owed a great deal to the Transcendental example. "I am fast becoming ultra-democratic," he told a former classmate only months after graduation, and he chafed at the restrictions of a conventional society that still looked on literature as an amateurish endeavor best pursued by "practical" men in their spare moments from more important concerns. Romantic influences in the matter of vocation would become as crucial for Lowell as for Higginson and for countless other American writers. Alongside Emerson's American scholar stood Coleridge's clerisy and Carlyle's man of letters, allowing young poets to glimpse a sense of a new role and a new legitimacy for literature. Writing poetry while struggling with the tedium of his nearly nonexistent legal practice, Lowell longed to break free and dedicate himself fully to letters as a vocation his generation increasingly considered in quasi-mystical terms.[28]

Lowell's literary ambitions coincided with his engagement to Maria White in 1840, a development that extended his determination to forge a writing career. Maria, the sister of a Harvard classmate, was as bright as she was beautiful, having already participated in Margaret Fuller's famed "Conversations." She and James fell in love while reading Wordsworth together and quickly became engaged but then prolonged their engagement as Lowell tried to demonstrate to her father's satisfaction that he could provide a reliable income through regular labor. Until that day, she and James lived a charmed life, reigning as the "king and queen" of a group of young, intellectually inclined friends known as the Brothers and Sisters Club. Lowell set about earning a reputation, if still not much of an income, with his first volume of poetry, A Year's Life, in 1841. He followed with extensive contributions to the many periodicals then emerging from the prolonged economic depression that had set back literary publishing a few years earlier. Lowell's periodical writing brought him into contact with most of the major literary figures of the day: Edgar Allan Poe at the Southern Literary Messenger, Cornelius Matthews at Arcturus, Margaret Fuller and Emerson at the Dial, Charles Peterson at Graham's Magazine, and Evert Duyckinck and the other Young Americans at the Democratic Review. With a new volume of poetry selling well in 1844, Lowell thought he had scraped together enough money to allow him to quit the law for good and to marry Maria. The couple moved into a newly built cottage on his father's land, which Lowell happily dubbed Elmwood Junior.[29]

Lowell, like Higginson, responded to the call to duty that was part of the milieu of their Unitarian Cambridge circles, though Lowell had more success in using European and American examples to frame literary pursuits as a response to that call. "While philosophers are wrangling, and politicians playing at snapdragon with the destinies of millions," he declared in 1843, "the poet, in the silent deeps of his soul, listens to those mysterious pulses which, from one central heart, send life and beauty through the finest veins of the universe, and utters truths to be sneered at, perchance, by contemporaries, but which become religion to posterity." He elaborated on the religious nature of literature in his 1855 Lowell Institute Lectures, explaining how the offices of "priest" and "poet" were originally united in one person who performed the "highest function" in the community, serving as the "discoverer and declarer of the perennial beneath the deciduous." Even though the roles had been divided by the modern sensibility of the mid–nineteenth century, the poet retained "something of

a religious character" as the "seer" of eternal truths and the "revealer of Deity."
The "function of the poet" held possibilities of truly cosmic importance.[30]

The poet's duties were social as well as imaginative, however, and from the
beginning Lowell's literary work had a reform dimension. "It seems as if my
heart would break," he confided to a friend in 1846, "in pouring out one glorious song that should be the gospel of Reform, full of consolation and strength
to the oppressed." Like Higginson's, Lowell's upbringing had instilled in him
(and his wife's strong principles had reinforced) the belief that individual self-
development depended on a larger social engagement. His second volume,
Poems, published in 1843, made this point explicitly: we ought not "with leath-
ern hearts, forget / That we owe mankind a debt."[31] Criticism of contemporary
barriers to individual development was thus evident in his work: the campaign
against slavery, the protest against the Mexican War, and even to a lesser extent the rights of women became recognizable foci in his writings through the
1840s.[32]

Lowell's sense of himself as a poet remained strong, and he explained to
the editor of the *National Anti-Slavery Standard* that he would "rather give the
cause one good poem than a thousand indifferent prose articles." At least two
of his poems were "good" enough to achieve iconic status among abolitionists:
"On the Capture of Fugitive Slaves near Washington," which repeated his understanding of the connection between self and society ("and they are slaves
most base, / Whose love of right is for themselves, and not for all their race")
and "The Present Crisis," which the literary critic Marcus Wood has termed
the "single poetic anthem" of abolition.[33] Lowell's most successful book, the
Biglow Papers, echoed these poems in attacking the evils of southern slavery
and, just as importantly, northern timidity. This satire, which was written in
Yankee dialect, humorously but ruthlessly skewered American hypocrisy in
the Mexican War. The commonsense wisdom of the New England farmer Hosea
Biglow exposed the ugly proslavery imperialism that politicians and slaveholders had attempted to cloak in grand pronouncements of American freedom and destiny:

> Thet our nation's bigger 'n theirn an' so
>   its rights air bigger,
> An' thet it's all to make 'em free
>   thet we air pullin' trigger.

The overreaching of slaveholders, the duplicity of politicians, and the craven
reticence of the clergy all came in for rhymed scorn. Surely harder to laugh at,

at least for some of his readers, was Lowell's depiction of racial bigotry as a veritable American pastime ("kickin' colored folks about, you know, 's a kind of national"). The *Biglow Papers* proved immensely popular, both in the United States and Great Britain, and bore more responsibility for Lowell's lasting fame than any other work.[34]

What Lowell termed the "prejudice of color" became a frequent theme in his 1840s prose writings, which were copious enough to fill two later volumes. The main theme of his essays for the *Anti-Slavery Standard* and for other periodicals was the idiocy of racial prejudice, which Lowell lambasted with a liveliness and freshness that has lasted longer than the punch of most of his poetry. Lowell saw racialism as tending to deny both individuality and a common humanity in favor of gross overgeneralizations about specific groups. He was much impressed with the dignified and intelligent Frederick Douglass and plotted with Higginson behind the scenes to have the black abolitionist admitted to the Town and Country Club. Lowell found irony in the fact that racial prejudice had taken such root among supposedly equality-loving American democrats. "As if no arrangement of society could be perfect in which there was not some arbitrary distinction of rank," he mused, "we Democrats, after abolishing all other artificial claims of superiority, cling with the despair of a person just drowning, in the dreadful ocean of equality, to one more absurd and more wicked than all the rest." But while he noted the artificial nature of racial difference ("arbitrary" and "absurd"), he also understood the very real effects such prejudice could have on its victims. He recognized that racism — a force "stronger than a constitution, more terrible than the cannon and the bayonet" — could become a self-fulfilling prophecy. An oppressed and despised group was not just systematically denied all opportunity for advancement and achievement but as a result then became vulnerable to the charge of inferior capacities.[35]

Lowell's aversion to racial bigotry reveals a crucial aspect of his general worldview: a humane universalism that marked both his literary criticism and his reform work. In an age of Romantic nationalism, he continued to champion a kind of liberal internationalism, a stance he subsequently modified amid the nationalizing force of the Civil War but never fully abandoned. He came to see the emphasis on difference between peoples as a great obstacle to progress, recently borne out by the dashed hopes of Italian liberation, which had been "thwarted in a great measure by foolish disputes about races and nationalities."[36] His abolitionist anthem, "The Present Crisis," had placed the slavery struggle in a world historical context, across the "broad earth's breast" and on the "thorny stem of Time." Incantations of universal humanitarianism appear over and over again in his verse: "For mankind are one in spirit"; "In the gain or loss of one race all the rest have equal claim." The struggle against American slavery, in this view, constituted only one part of a much larger struggle on behalf of worldwide freedom. "God works for all. Ye cannot hem the hope of being free / With parallels of latitude, with mountain-range or sea." [37]

Though Lowell had associated himself with the Garrisonian wing of abolition throughout the 1840s, he was never comfortable with this group's extremism and found that its members mixed a "little too much mustard" in their salad for his palate. He became especially disenchanted with the Garrisonians' "disunion and non-voting theories," policies that provoked his final split with them in 1850 and the end of his formal connections with the *Anti-Slavery Standard*.[38] The waning of Lowell's abolitionist zeal has often been explained as a consequence of the death of his wife, Maria, in 1853 and the removal of her important radical influence. There is some truth in this view (first promulgated by Higginson), but Lowell's relatively moderate temperament had long made him an uncomfortable ally of the Garrisonians. In addition, his broad-minded universalism also mitigated his commitment to any specific reform such as abolition. He found the immediate abolitionists of his own state too doctrinaire, too single-minded in their focus. With yet another gastronomical metaphor, he explained to a friend that the Garrisonians "treat ideas as ignorant persons do cherries. They think them unwholesome unless they are swallowed stones and all." [39]

In refusing the "stones and all" approach, Lowell, like Higginson, chafed at false choices and adopted whatever suited him as "true" from a variety of supposedly opposing stances: radicalism and conservatism, past and present, national and universal. Even at the height of his radical enthusiasm in the early 1840s, Lowell had carefully insisted on looking critically at the "radicalism of youth" and the "conservatism of age" and combining elements from each. Radicals who ignored what had come before were deprived of much that was worth saving, while "pseudo-conservatives" denied that Truth did not remain the same but continually evolved. The "Past's blood-rusted key" would not open "the Future's portal," as the "Present Crisis" memorably put it, but this view did not imply a simple rejection of prior history. Instead, Lowell called for a reinvigoration of past ideals: "New occasions teach new duties: Time makes ancient good uncouth / They must upward still, and onward, who would keep abreast of Truth." [40]

Lowell's eventual split from radical abolitionism also resulted from his sense that the campaign against slavery constituted only one part of a larger struggle for freedom. This wider campaign was as important for Lowell's poet as for Curtis's scholar or Higginson's activist minister—in each case, lovers of truth and guardians of the ideal in life sought human progress in the broadest of all possible theaters. "Absolute freedom is what I want," Lowell wrote to a friend in 1845, "for the body first, and then for the mind." In terms that recalled Emerson, Lowell explained that he chose to concentrate on slavery "because it is easier to make men conscious of the wrong of that grosser and more outward oppression, and after seeing that, they will perceive more readily the less palpable chains and gags of tyranny."[41]

Lowell valued his antislavery work but also feared that it might distract him from his true literary calling. He ridiculed himself in *Fable for Critics*, his parody of American literary figures, by characterizing his early poetry as a "whole bale of *isms* tied together with rhyme" and predicted that he would never be a great poet until he learned the "distinction 'twixt singing and preaching." (Later, during the Civil War, he wrote to Norton, "I shall never be a poet till I get out of the pulpit, and New England was all meeting-house when I was growing up.") By 1850, Lowell declared himself "tired of controversy" and desired to replenish his more purely literary powers. "I find that Reform cannot take up the whole of me," he confessed, "and I am quite sure that eyes were given us to look about us with sometimes, and not to be always looking forward."[42]

Looking "about" him, Lowell found that the cause of American letters required his services as much as any other reform. A combination of financial necessity and literary ambition fueled his most productive spurt in 1848, when he published his literary lampoon, *A Fable for Critics*, the anti-expansionist *Biglow Papers*, and his medieval verse, *The Vision of Sir Launfal*. Honoring his duty to literature involved more than following his own muse; he also struggled to elevate the standards for American literature by introducing a new sophistication and establishing new directions. He had made an early effort for American letters with his ambitious though doomed attempt at a high-toned literary magazine. The *Pioneer*, first appearing in January 1843, brashly announced a novel experiment in its prospectus: in contrast to the "enormous quantity of thrice-diluted trash, in the shape of namby-pamby love tales and sketches" that appeared in most magazines, the new monthly would "furnish the intelligent and reflecting portion of the Reading Public with a rational substitute," thus offering "a healthy and manly Periodical Literature, whose perusal will not necessarily involve a loss of time and a deterioration of every moral and intellectual faculty." Lowell's defense of literature as "healthy," "manly," and even "rational" betrayed his anxiety about his position in the literary marketplace and more broadly about the role of cultural pursuits in an American society divided ideologically into male and female spheres. Using a gendered language of legitimation, Lowell sought to elevate the stakes of literature by demonstrating both its seriousness and its importance to national identity. During its three-month life, the magazine set out to deliver on its promise of profundity, publishing stories by Poe and Hawthorne; poems by Longfellow, Whittier, and Elizabeth Barrett Browning; and critical reviews of music, art, and literature.[43]

For Lowell, broader literary cultivation represented a national imperative, since America could never be a truly great nation until it had "learned to love art . . . for its humanising and ennobling energy." He knew as well as anyone that Alexis de Tocqueville, Frances Trollope, and Charles Dickens (among others) had repeatedly disparaged American letters and that there was no little truth to Sydney Smith's snide 1820 question: "Who in the four quarters of the globe reads an American book?" Regular calls for a national literature had been issued since that taunt, but they received a new urgency in the 1840s through the spirited yelps of the New York–based Young Americans. Lowell shared his compatriots' general sensitivity to foreign criticism, defensively insisting that if Americans could "frame a commonwealth in which it shall not be a misfortune to be born . . . we shall be as usefully employed as if we should flower with a Dante." Yet he also feared that the frenzied search for a national culture hindered American literature, crippling writers by making them overly self-conscious and deteriorating "our criticism," which "oscillated between the two extremes of depreciation and overpraise." But Lowell went further and dismissed the whole concept of a national literature as presented by the literary New Englanders or the Young Americans. His attitude stemmed from the same cosmopolitan universalism that fueled his aversion to racialism: genius and art were universal, not national, he claimed, and "literature survives, not because of its nationality, but in spite of it."[44]

While Lowell's nationalism would ebb and flow (flowing most energetically during the Civil War), his sense of American literature was always rooted in this larger cosmopolitan international context. The United States was part of the world and had a role to play within it but also had something to learn from that world. "The newspaper, the railroad, and the steamship are fast obliterating the externals of distinct and hostile nationality," he wrote; "human nature is everywhere the same, and everywhere inextinguishable." Yet any objections to a falsely "national" literature did not prevent him from believing that America would make distinctive contributions to world literature. "That

Art in America will be modified by circumstances, we have no doubt, though it is impossible to predict the precise form of the moulds into which it will run," he observed, adding that "new conditions of life will stimulate thought and give new forms to its expression." All that could honestly be demanded of "our literature" was that it "be national to the extent of being as free from outworn conventionalities, and as thoroughly impregnated with humane and manly sentiment, as is the idea on which our political fabric rests. Let it give a true reflection of our social, political, and household life." [45]

National maturity and a cosmopolitan stance required a judicious response to foreign criticism, which was a sore point for many literary figures. An early review of Dickens's *American Notes* (which had been roundly criticized for its supposed "anti-Americanism") allowed Lowell to tackle this aspect of the larger issue. He reminded readers that Dickens's harshest criticism was reserved for slavery ("surely the darkest blot on our national character") and urged Americans to be thankful for frank and honest criticism that might lift the national "gag order" on the topic. Dickens was a "citizen of the world, and belongs as much to America as to England." Lowell urged Americans to overcome their defensiveness and see their failings for what they were: "If our narrowness and cowardice in this matter are not outgrown, we might as well publish expurgated editions of Shakespeare, and all others who satirize and revolt at tyranny, (as all great minds must,) — nay, of the Declaration of Independence itself." [46]

Lowell made his most enduring contribution to American letters more than a decade after the *Pioneer* failed when he helped to found the *Atlantic Monthly* in 1857. He agreed to edit this new Boston periodical in the wake of personal tragedies (including the deaths of three of his young children and of his beloved wife) and of new professional accomplishments. His well-received 1854 Lowell Institute Lectures had been the basis for his appointment as the Smith Professor of Foreign Languages at Harvard in 1855, replacing his friend and fellow poet, Henry Wadsworth Longfellow. Comfortably remarried to Frances Dunlap and ensconced at Harvard, Lowell's position as founding editor of the *Atlantic* allowed him to bring together much of the literary talent and antislavery sentiment around Boston. Those involved had high hopes for the new monthly: as Lowell wrote to Norton excitedly about the plan, "The magazine is going to be free without being fanatical"; although it would "have opinions of its own & not be afraid to speak them," it would pursue them in a "scholarly & gentlemanlike" way. The first issue got off to a good start, with contributions from Lowell, Longfellow, Whittier, Harriet Beecher Stowe, Emerson, Oliver

Wendell Holmes, John Lothrop Motley, Norton, and Parke Godwin. Lowell's heavy reliance on New England writers did not compromise the magazine's cosmopolitan ambitions but instead implied that these Americans had something to contribute to the larger Atlantic world, as suggested by the magazine's title. A testament to its success was its sale of more than twenty thousand copies in its initial issues and a regular circulation of thirty thousand within two years.[47]

The political and literary elements of Lowell's emerging liberalism, which had been evident by the late 1840s, came together again in the pages of the *Atlantic Monthly*, subtitled "A Magazine of Literature, Art, and Politics." In addition to gathering distinguished literary work, the journal plunged almost immediately into turbulent political waters. This attempt to combine high culture with liberal politics remained a characteristic feature of Lowell's subsequent reform career. The magazine declared itself the "organ of no party or clique" but instead the exponent of "what its conductors believe to be the 'American idea,'" "endeavoring always to keep in view that moral element . . . which alone makes the basis of a true and lasting national prosperity."[48] Translated into practice, this mission statement meant an unswerving commitment to the antislavery movement and a pro-Republican political stance. Lowell was determined that under his editorship at least, the new monthly would not stand aloof from the intensifying crisis engulfing the nation. He had found his sense of political outrage increasing steadily through the 1850s and felt a duty to speak out and to allow Higginson and others a new venue for radical abolitionism. Lowell, like his friends, recognized the crisis that was at hand. Anyone "who had not "passed his Master's degree in Black-guardism" must now join the fight.[49]

To Cheer, to Raise, and to Guide Men by Showing Them Facts amidst Appearances

The tensions between art and reform posed fewer challenges for George William Curtis, who approached these two elements as part of his career's natural progression. Like Higginson and Lowell, Curtis followed a path that would make him a writer, editor, and antislavery activist, though he did so in his own way. One difference was that Curtis never attended Harvard College. Instead, he pursued an unorthodox education supervised in the early 1840s by his older brother and financed by his father, a businessman with interests in Rhode

Island and New York. The Curtis boys spent two years at the Transcendentalist settlement at Brook Farm and two more years in the nearby town of Concord. This extended sojourn brought young George into contact with the leading Transcendentalist intellectuals and the neighboring literati while teaching
him the interactions between living in a reform community and thinking about
ideas with a bohemian intensity. On an 1843 visit to Brook Farm, Higginson
recalled meeting the young Curtis, decked out in a flowing poet's "blouse" and
a small "visorless" cap with a tassel that made his distinctly avant-garde commitments clear to all the world.[50]

Curtis used his Brook Farm days to develop friendships with Hawthorne,
Longfellow, and Thoreau, all of whom made lasting impressions. The most important influence was Emerson, however, whom Curtis would class "with Plato
and Bacon, and the other great teachers." The bohemian Curtis immersed
himself in cultivation in both senses of the word—he tended to his vegetable
crops and harvested hay while developing a lifelong love of literature and music.
The early Transcendental influence was seminal in fostering the mutual sense
of independence and connectedness that Curtis later made the ideal for his generation. As his brother recalled after George's death, the "seed then sown took
such deep root as to flower continuously in our later years, and make us both
the confirmed 'Independents' that we were and are, whilst fully conscious at the
same time of the obligation of living in all possible harmony with our fellows."[51]

George and his brother supplemented their informal American education
with a more haphazard four-year tour of Europe and the Middle East during
which they drew "from every source we could, whatever might contribute to
build up and develop, educate and liberalize, the whole man." This "liberalizing" education included many hours touring museums and attending con-
certs, hikes through the Austrian Tyrol, a journey up the Nile and across the
desert, intensive study of foreign languages and literature, and a year enrolled
at the University of Berlin. In letters home, Curtis waxed romantic over the aesthetic delights he was imbibing. He described floating "about in the starlight-
warm midnight" on the Rhine, singing the "lonely" verses of the German poet
Uhland and strumming a borrowed guitar. How "beautifully" the poetry "har-
monises with that summer passage of my life," he wrote to his mother.[52]

The Curtis brothers' travels were not merely one long bohemian rhapsody.
Curtis witnessed firsthand the 1848 political upheavals in Germany, Italy, and
France and sent home letters on French politics to the *New York Tribune* while
living in Paris during the early days of the Second Republic. While he did not
seem overly struck by the historic events, the experience as a whole sparked the

interest in European affairs he manifested throughout his later life. In matters aesthetic, social, and political, four years of foreign travel gave Curtis a "cosmopolitanism which I could never have learned at home." After returning to New York City, Curtis turned his travels into two successful books—*Nile Notes of a Howadji* and *The Howadji in Syria*—that made him a rising literary star in his mid-twenties. He soon followed with *Lotus-Eating*, a domestic travel book based on letters he had sent to the *New York Tribune* from eastern resorts the previous summer. He had quickly carved out a niche for himself as a popular writer and lecturer.[53]

Even more than Lowell's, Curtis's rise in the world of American letters was connected to the sharp upsurge of newspapers and magazines around midcentury. He had early contributed music and art criticism to Brook Farm's *Harbinger*, the *Dial*, and the *New York Tribune*, but by the 1850s he became more closely linked with three important periodicals: *Harper's Monthly*, where he wrote the "Easy Chair" column for the next four decades; *Putnam's Monthly*, a high-toned but short-lived literary magazine; and *Harper's Weekly*, where he authored the "Lounger" column and served as political editor from the Civil War until his death. Most of his extended writings, such as the social satire *The Potiphar Papers* and his two novels, *Prue and I* and *Trumps*, first appeared in serialized form in one or another of these periodicals, whose circulation generated an eager market for their later appearance in book form. The fame he achieved through these various print organs was both reinforced and intensified in 1853 when he decided to join the lyceum circuit, where most of his early lectures focused on matters of art and literature.[54]

Curtis's involvement in the short-lived *Putnam's Monthly* represented an ambitious attempt to forge a new kind of periodical and in this way resembled Lowell's work for the *Pioneer* a decade earlier. "The first genuinely civilized magazine in America," in the historian Frank Luther Mott's words, *Putnam's* hoped to find a national audience of middle-class readers interested in literature, art, and politics who did not need to be enticed with fashion pages or sentimental drivel. Under the stewardship of Charles F. Briggs, Parke Godwin, and Curtis, the magazine promised to be "genuine in itself and genuinely related to the time," heaping "upon our pages the results of the acutest observations, and the most trenchant thought, illustrated by whatever wealth of erudition, of imagination and of experience, they may chance to possess." In direct contrast with the successful *Harper's Monthly*, *Putnam's* refused to rely on pirated English fiction, instead bringing together an impressive list of contributors that included Emerson, Thoreau, Melville, Lowell, Longfellow, Hawthorne, and

Whittier. Excited at the prospect of a first-class American periodical, Emerson urged Curtis to keep the new journal focused on "literature and humanity" and to avoid as best he could "that moribund respectability to which everything American tends." Curtis did his part by contributing poems, music and theater criticism, reviews of new books, social sketches, and various essays.[55]

Curtis's writing and speaking earned him a degree of success—both critical and commercial—that is difficult to appreciate today. The *London Athenaeum* called him "one of the most picturesque and original of American writers," and other contemporary observers regularly classed him with Longfellow, Emerson, Hawthorne, and Melville. Curtis's works sold well and went into repeated editions throughout the nineteenth century, only to fall from popularity in the first decades of the twentieth century. As Norton, a close friend Curtis first met while in Europe, said, "He has resisted more flattery before thirty years old than comes to most men in a the course of a very long life." With his prose works, Curtis clearly achieved what Lowell, whose poetry was never as popular, disparagingly called a "newspaper reputation."[56]

Curtis's popularity unquestionably stemmed from the decidedly light character of his works, which sought less to reveal eternal truths through elevated verse than to entertain his readers and cultivate a sense of beauty in them. In this his model was not so much the weighty Emerson as the urbane William Makepeace Thackeray, to whom Curtis pointed in 1854 as proof that "artists and authors have always been the good fellows of the world." In offering praise for *Vanity Fair*, whose tone Curtis emulated in his novels, he noted that the "mental organization which predisposes a man to the pursuit of literature and art" was "made up of talent combined with ardent social sympathy, geniality, and passion" that "leads him to taste every cup and try every experience." The "very susceptibility to enjoyment" that marked the literary set assured that its members would "always be pleasure lovers and seekers," he concluded.[57]

This Romantic enthusiasm for life and all the sensations it offered was clear enough in Curtis's first book, which attempted to represent the "essentially *sensuous*, luscious, languid and sense-satisfied spirit of Eastern life." Several chapters of *Nile Notes* vividly described his visit to the harem of the Ghazeeyah, or dancing Egyptian girls, where he found himself entranced by the "curious and wonderful gymnastic," the "voluptuous motion . . . starting through every sense and quivering in every limb" of the beautiful young women. This episode provoked a minor stir in polite New York society and caused some critics, including his father, to question Curtis's judgment and taste in including such risqué passages. In responding to his critics and justifying his literary choices to his disapproving father, Curtis insisted on the integrity of the artist's vision: "Had I written a book to please you," he explained, "I could not have published it, because it would not have pleased myself." The artistic duty to a personal vision outweighed any duty to society's conventions. Though Curtis admitted that he might make some literary decisions differently the next time, he stood behind his choices both morally and aesthetically: "The essential spirit of the book is precisely what I wished."[58]

Curtis's emphasis on artistic freedom, however, never led him toward aesthetic nihilism. A moral didacticism pervaded most of his popular writings and speeches, and a clear sense of duty underlay his choice of profession, even if that sense differed wholly from that pervading the dominant tone of middle-class American life, which remained imbued with an evangelical Whiggishness. The controversy over his depiction of the dancing girls allowed Curtis to explain that he was not so much departing from conventional morals as adhering to what he considered a higher conception of value and worth. He mocked the "affected and self-conscious" morality of the "ladies and gentlemen" who condemned his work, complaining that the same people "would sell any daughter to any man, for a sufficient fortune." Such hypocrisy clearly demonstrated that the "moral sense" of New York was "so vitiated" as to be meaningless. Respectable citizens of a proslavery country clung to an outward form of ethics while neglecting the inner spirit of their meaning. Curtis followed his travel books by skewering this polite, wealthy society in two popular social satires, *The Potiphar Papers* and *Prue and I*, that urged simplicity, honest work, and the virtues of private cultivation as opposed to mere public refinement. He mocked the rich (especially those with new money) for wandering from these simple verities in their shallow extravagance and gaudy displays of wealth. In a facetious chapter on "Our Best Society" (composed of three classes: the rich, the pedigreed, and youths who danced well), he explained, "If gilt were only gold, or sugar-candy common sense, what a fine thing our society would be!"[59]

Like Lowell, Curtis recognized a quasi-religious component to his literary work, though he conceived of his cultural ministrations as more social than spiritual in purpose. He sought to elevate and cultivate the periodical-reading middle class by instilling in it an appreciation for simplicity and beauty in art and literature. He often referred to his weekly and monthly outlets at *Harper's* as his "lay pulpit." In a similar vein, William Dean Howells later praised Curtis's "incomparable homilies," while Norton believed that Curtis's lecture on true versus false notions of success represented the work of a modern missionary. Curtis's mission involved chastising Americans for failing to uphold national and humane ideas, for letting greed get in the way of the good. "Commercial prosperity" constituted not a blessing but a "curse if it be not subservient to moral and intellectual progress," he warned his readers, adding, "our prosperity will conquer us if we do not conquer our prosperity."[60]

While Curtis never abandoned his enthusiasm for culture, his sense of duty became increasingly political as the sectional crisis intensified in the 1850s. He had been raised in an antislavery family and had been exposed regularly to abolitionists and reformers of all stripes during his Brook Farm and Concord years, but these associations did not produce in Curtis a sense of particular conviction until the mid-1850s. Then, the spectacle of Bleeding Kansas, the Sumner-Brooks quarrel, and the Dred Scott decision focused Curtis's attention, as did two important personal influences. As with Lowell and Higginson, Curtis's reform spirit was fanned when in 1856 he married into an abolitionist family. By wedding Anna Shaw, he developed a close relationship with her brother, Robert, the future colonel of the black Fifty-fourth Massachusetts Regiment, and with her parents, Francis and Sarah Shaw, wealthy abolitionists whom Curtis had first met at Brook Farm and who had since become intimately involved in transatlantic antislavery reform. Along with Higginson, Francis Shaw had been a member of the Boston Vigilance Committee that attempted to free Anthony Burns, and the family's attitude toward slavery helped nudge Curtis in the direction of greater activism. Indeed, it was no coincidence that Curtis gave his first antislavery speech on Staten Island, where the Shaws had recently made their stately home. By 1859 Curtis had become a familiar—and fiery—enough antislavery orator that he had to face down a hostile mob in Philadelphia to deliver a speech on "The Present Aspect of the Slavery Question."[61]

Of nearly equal importance was Curtis's relationship with Parke Godwin, a political journalist who had once been an active antislavery Democrat. Soon after joining the Republican Party, Godwin drafted its first platform, basing the party's principles on an article he had written for *Putnam's*. This apparently sudden immersion in exalted affairs of national politics nurtured an awakening for Curtis. As Godwin recalled, the "little world" of *Putnam's* was "profoundly stirred" by the events of the day, and the magazine's editors refused to stay aloof from those events. "For the first time in the history of our higher periodicals," he continued, a magazine's "managers had stepped down from their snowy pedestals to take part in the brabble and scuffle of the streets." Godwin insisted that *Putnam's* take a bold stance on political questions, and from the first issues he contributed biting articles and editorials, which he later collected in a volume of *Political Essays*. If the words of "The Duty of the American Scholar" belonged to Curtis, its spirit owed much to Godwin and the example of *Putnam's*.[62]

Putnam's did not become an official outlet of the Republican Party but made its stance clear in offering advanced antislavery political opinion and a sharp critique of those Democrats seemingly under the sway of the slave power. The magazine's editorial voice—a blend of Godwin and Curtis—acknowledged both the benefits and limits of institutionalized parties in much the same way that Higginson had done when he cast his lot with the Massachusetts Free-Soilers. As early as 1844, when he was living at Concord and immersed in studies of "ideal republics," Curtis sensed that he could never be a "party man," as "no party pursues the public good with single aims." He believed that the true "position of a citizen" was "that of a watcher and aider" who might keep public life on track, and he echoed Higginson in declaring that "men are greater than institutions." Curtis also expressed skepticism about parties' tendency to turn away from principle and to "construct a machinery of management which comes to work by its own force, and without reference to the impulses which originally set it in motion." But his seemingly anti-institutional views received more nuanced elaboration in his (and Godwin's) frequent late-1850s *Putnam's* essays. In these writings, Curtis repudiated the "transcendent philosophy" that said that a citizen "should labor to assert his own individual convictions, regardless of the convictions of his neighbors, and steadily refuse to coalesce with them until they shall have reached his standard of judgment." The dutiful citizen faced the challenge of navigating between the Scylla of party bureaucracy and the Charybdis of extreme individualism.[63]

While Curtis's increasing political engagement departed from his strictly literary work in the early 1850s, he understood this change as a natural evolution in his conception of public duty. "As for politics," he recalled some thirty years later in the midst of another political crisis, "I had to make my choice . . . between a life of literary ease and anti-slavery politics, and I am not sorry that I chose the latter." While he believed that his cultural mission was important, political events soon became all consuming, and as he explained, "I should have despised myself had I declined the service that offered itself to me." A less lofty sense of his literary vocation made Curtis more willing than Lowell to relinquish this initial calling, as did Curtis's comparatively candid evaluation of his artistic talents. "With genius I might have done as Milton did," he commented, "but without it I could do only what I could." What he could do included making frequent antislavery lectures, campaigning tirelessly for

Republican candidates John C. Frémont and Abraham Lincoln, and devoting himself to political reform for the next forty years.[64]

Curtis's first political outlet, *Putnam's Monthly*, failed during the economic depression of 1857, though it was effectively (though not at all consciously) replaced by Lowell's *Atlantic*. Lowell's new magazine, like Curtis's old publication, nurtured native writers and situated American letters in a cosmopolitan frame. Just as important, this new endeavor, which quickly became Higginson's publication of choice, used both literature and political commentary to set northern opinion on firm antislavery, liberal grounds. Curtis did not know of his magazine's impending failure when he rose to deliver his address on "The Duty of the American Scholar to Politics and the Times." But he had clearly readied himself for a new stage in his life, which came as all Emersonian Seekers and Poets were pulled down into history and into "politics and the times." He was looking forward as well as glancing back when he insisted that the American scholar was not just "devoted to the contemplation of truth" but represented "in the State, a public conscience by which public measures may be tested." From his vantage point, the members of the "scholarly class" needed to make good on their responsibility to function as the "upper house in the politics of the world."[65]

This Revolution Is to Be Wrought by the Gradual Domestication of the Ideal of Culture

The international dynamic of American Victorianism was evident enough in reflections made by Higginson, Lowell, and Curtis on what men of letters had to offer a world swept by change. But the transatlantic dimensions of Victorians' sense of duty, vocation, and art rose to their highest level in the case of Charles Eliot Norton, who became the most cosmopolitan member of an unusually worldly cohort. Norton spent a good part of his young adulthood contemplating the same matters of reform, responsibility, and imaginative expression that captivated his peers, but his key contribution came in the vital connections he forged between eminent Britons and Americans of the *Atlantic Monthly* set. A series of travels in Europe during the 1840s and 1850s allowed Norton (who was slightly younger than his closest New England friends) to deepen this group's immersion in high Victorian culture. Whether he was facilitating introductions between artists and writers, shepherding friends' manuscripts through publication, or hosting transatlantic travelers, Norton revealed both a capacious mind and a unique talent for nurturing meaningful relationships. These traits would make him the longest and thickest thread in the dense web of Anglo-American friendships formed in the second half of the nineteenth century. As Frederic Harrison recalled in 1912, Norton had played an indispensable and unparalleled role "as friend, as interpreter of movements and ideas, as host or as guest, as an intellectual link between two continents as well as between two nations, and for two generations a centre of Anglo-American thought."[66]

Norton's easy internationalism resulted from his upbringing at Shady Hill, the elegant Cambridge home of his father, Andrews Norton, and his mother, Catherine, the daughter of the wealthy merchant Samuel Eliot. The elder Norton has been mostly remembered as the so-called Unitarian Pope who served as the Dexter Professor of Sacred Literature at Harvard and sparred with Emerson and Theodore Parker. The family's institutional prestige and financial comfort may have mattered less for the younger Norton than its cosmopolitan sensibilities, however, which were evident in his father's immersion in Victorian Unitarianism and in the work he did for the *Select Journal of Foreign Periodical Literature*, which he had founded in 1833, when Charley was six years old. Americans of the mid-Victorian generation typically made a first visit to Europe in their late teens (though Higginson insisted that such foreign travels were best postponed until a slightly older age). Norton's exposure was of an altogether different order, since he first spent time in England at the ripe age of five months, when he reportedly enjoyed the literary company of Sir Walter Scott, Robert Southey, Felicia Hemans, and William Wordsworth (who supposedly even bounced the young Charley on his knee). The Nortons' sense of living in a cultural world unbound by national borders depended as much on print as on travel. His father's parlor was a clearinghouse for international thought and his writing a prime conduit for American exposure to German learning and to philology, the rigorous study of languages as the key to understanding historical texts that was then ascendant in much of Europe.[67]

Andrews Norton was part of a larger Boston group pursuing scholarship in an international context. George Ticknor, the elder Norton's brother-in-law, was even better known, having established himself as the leading student of Spanish literature in the English-speaking world. The outward look of both men lent a distinctly cosmopolitan spirit to their contributions to learning, which they pursued as self-conscious members of a larger republic of letters. Young radicals, soon to identify themselves as Transcendentalists, drew similar inspiration from German ideas even as they took those ideas in a more disquieting and dangerous direction. Not long after Andrews Norton's experiment with the *Select Journal*, Ralph Waldo Emerson oversaw the Boston publication of Carlyle's seminal *Sartor Resartus*, which became the first book-length publication of this early and remarkably influential Anglicization of German Idealism. Charles was twelve years old in 1839, when his father aggressively defended Unitarian "orthodoxy" from the Germanic heterodoxy of the Transcendentalists with his blistering *Discourse on the Latest Form of Infidelity*. To Andrews Norton, the radical ideas of Emerson, George Ripley, and Theodore Parker represented the wrong kind of international engagement.[68]

Norton's postcollege days featured none of the Sturm und Drang or vocational floundering of his peers—the day after his graduation from Harvard in 1846 was also the day he began work for a merchant countinghouse in Boston. Business was a family tradition (from Catherine Norton's side), and this line of work treated the young Norton well enough, affording him time to continue his self-cultivation and sending him in 1849 on a twenty-month international voyage that he later recognized as an important passage toward worldliness. Traveling to India as a supercargo (a task that afforded Norton long hours to devour books), he returned by way of an extended stay in Europe, where, as the Boston wit Tom Appleton put it, this conscientious and dutiful son found the opportunity to "sow his tame oats." Madras, Bombay, Cairo, Venice, Paris, London, Nuremberg: these travels—and the new social and cultural experiences they afforded—further deprovincialized Norton and immersed him in a set of overlapping business, literary, artistic, and political circles. His path crossed with those of other Americans seeking worldliness: in Paris he made the acquaintance of a young wandering bohemian from New York, the "long-haired and sweet-visaged" George William Curtis. The two men traveled together from the Continent to England, dining, talking, touring cathedrals, and forming the basis of a fast and enduring friendship.[69]

After returning home in 1851, Norton soon felt a restlessness born of the scholarly bent he had inherited from his father's side of the family. He began to scratch this intellectual itch with literary and historical reviews for the *North American Review*, then edited by the moral philosopher and family friend Francis Bowen, and by contributing to Curtis's new *Putnam's Monthly*. When his father died in 1853, Charles took on the responsibility of editing Andrews's works, a venture that marked the young man's first experience as a literary executor. At the same time, Norton finished the course of study he had begun two years earlier with a "view to a short essay on Republicanism in Europe." Intellectually drawn to this subject, Norton also considered his book a "pledge to that small portion of the world, who care anything about it, that I do not pass my time idly, and that I still claim Literature as a love who is not to be supplanted in my affections by any other."[70]

Norton's first book-length production, which appeared anonymously in 1853, showed a serious political interest that coincided with his growing immersion in art and culture. *Considerations on Some Recent Social Theories* focused on Europe rather than America, where debates on the future of slavery intrigued him without drawing much from his pen. In its 158 calm pages, the book tried to dampen the utopian ardor of Europe's leading revolutionaries by pointing out the fallacies in Joseph Mazzini's, Louis Kossuth's, and Louis Blanc's calls for "universal liberty" and in their insistence on the people's absolute right to rule in any and all contexts. A republican form of government was not a universal panacea, Norton maintained, but a set of institutions that made sense only in certain historical conditions. It was foolish and even dangerous, he wrote, to talk about liberty without linking the issue to an understanding of a people's collective virtue and morality. If this virtue and morality were not adequately cultivated (as Norton feared was currently true of much of oppressed Europe), then a republic could become as tyrannical as a monarchy. Far better to improve the people first—gradually, carefully—than to impose a new machinery of government on them unprepared. Such conservative musings drew a cool response within his circle, with Curtis ambivalently reporting that although he had read the little book with the "greatest satisfaction," his "own interests lie so much elsewhere, or I should rather say I contemplate the subject from so different a point, that we should both widely differ & closely agree." Parke Godwin gave the book a decidedly lukewarm review in *Putnam's*, while Lowell wrote a sonnet in the volume's honor. "Where Youth & duty go hand in hand, / I ask not if our theories agree," he rhymed, suggesting that the members of their cohort were shaped less by arriving at a similar perspective than by heeding the call of what they recognized as a common sense of responsibility.[71]

The antiutopian skepticism of Norton's first book was genuine, even if it was less thoroughgoing in its reaction than many historians have claimed. Its chief features included a sense of historical relativism, which later formed an important part of Norton's liberalism. His professed objection to unbridled liberty was also capable of subsequent revision, since the most important element was his notion (hardly original) that true liberty was not simply freedom from external restraint but the freedom to do right by God and by one's community. This positive understanding of liberty made it a moral concept rather than a narrowly political or economic one. This expansive understanding even influenced Norton's discussion of the familiar liberal concept of self-possession, which he used to signal his hope that the poor and oppressed of Europe might be helped to "gain possession of their intellectual and moral natures." Only with this intellectual and moral self-possession—achieved through a process akin to Unitarian cultivation—could social progress advance and clear the way for popular rule. While in some sense only educated, morally responsible beings could by definition be truly free, he was equally adamant that the individual as a socially bound, moral agent could move toward autonomy only in harmony with larger collective goals. Like Higginson and Lowell, Norton placed the individual at the center of his conceptual universe and believed that the health of the republic, the capacity for self-government, hinged on the virtue and cultivation of each distinct citizen. But Norton was more insistent than other liberals that the individual was always rooted in a social context and had certain obligations to the larger community. For him, self-interest made sense only if modified with self-denial; individual rights must always be accompanied by larger communal duties. He believed that the selfishness bred by his country's materialism constituted the gravest of all national flaws.[72]

Few at the time or since have noted the call for reform contained in *Considerations*, which demonstrated how far Norton's antiutopianism lay from a simple defense of the status quo. Indeed, the book went out of its way to agree with much of what reformers and revolutionaries diagnosed, arguing that the "contrasts between wealth and poverty, between luxury and misery" that marked much of the world constituted the "reproach of our civilization, of our humanity." Some conservatives wrongly claimed that such inequality was God's will, but according to Norton, God had provided the means to change things: "Each evil that may be overthrown, every wrong that exists, is a motive for exertion, and a suggestion of duty." Discussing socialism, Norton admitted the appeal of such radical programs for reform as the destruction of all individual property, even if he saw them as wrongheaded. Such proposals were "attractive and plausible" because they represented the "exaggerations of right principles and the extravagancies of good feeling." In place of revolutionary schemes for change, Norton substituted an incremental, gradualist view of progress and reform that placed particular emphasis on the key Unitarian notion of education overseen by those "few who have been blessed with the opportunities, and the rare genius, fitting them to lead."[73]

Norton took his prescriptions seriously enough to translate them into actions. His reform endeavors of the 1850s included organizing and teaching an evening school for workingmen (just as Higginson did in Newburyport) and developing a model lodging scheme for the poor (in consultation with pioneering

British experiments). While never as much of a reform activist as his childhood playmate, Higginson; his New York confidante, Curtis; or even his Cambridge neighbor, Lowell, Norton was still pleased that his more moderate efforts had produced a "general flutter of life rattling among the dry bones" of Old Cambridge. What most distinguished his public voice, however, was the sharpness of his condemnation of national materialism. He regularly lectured members of his social class on their duties to society, blasting the "tasteless display, and lavish, reckless wastefulness" of the rich and lamenting that older ideas of republican simplicity languished in an age of excessive wealth.[74]

Norton's 1853 book marked his passage into the world of Boston letters, leading him within a few years to abandon his business career in favor of scholarly pursuits. The additional time allowed Norton to combine the traditional Unitarian reverence for the word with a growing appreciation for images and architecture. Signs of his interest in the visual arts had appeared earlier: Norton's 1846 graduation address had guided a Harvard audience through the worthies of the Italian Renaissance. The young merchant's aesthetic sensibility was further honed during his 1850 stay in Europe, when he met Robert and Elizabeth Barrett Browning and purchased Vasari's *Lives of the Artists* to mark his twenty-third birthday. On his next extended European tour, taken between 1855 and 1857, Norton immersed himself more fully in artistic circles. He formed lasting ties to leading Pre-Raphaelite painters, purchased paintings (two Tintorettos and another by the High Renaissance Venetian Giorgione), and then returned to review the Manchester Art Gallery for the inaugural issue of Lowell's new *Atlantic Monthly*. Out of this trip resulted Norton's next two books—one on Italian travels and one on Dante's *Vita Nuova*—which did less to identify the need to cultivate virtue (a main theme of *Considerations*) than to offer the spiritual example of art history as a means of doing so. Though Norton was hardly alone in believing that the Pre-Raphaelites should be encouraged in rejoining religious and artistic impulses, he refined his perspective through what was already becoming an unusually rigorous research agenda.[75]

During Norton's middecade return to Europe, he befriended John Ruskin, whose *Modern Painters* and *The Stones of Venice* had set him on a path that quickly led to renown as the leading Victorian authority on art history and criticism. As many scholars have noted, Ruskin in time moved from sharing his collection of Turner watercolors with Norton and guiding his European travels to considering the slightly younger American his "first real tutor" and most valued friend. In any strict sense, the image of Norton as the tutor is misleading, though so too is the opposite tendency to present Norton as simply

Ruskin's American disciple. As James Turner has argued, the differences that typified these two friends' approaches to art, spirituality, and the bane of materialism were as revealing as the similarities. The key to understanding their interaction is to appreciate the stances that both men had developed prior to their acquaintance. Their regular correspondence, which was suspended though not ended by wartime tensions of the 1860s, was clearly important for both men. It helped ratify Norton's instinct that his sense of dutiful, cautious reform might be pursued in tandem with the personal satisfactions he derived from engagement with the visual arts. Through a Ruskinian frame of reference, Norton began to link popular virtue—whose important connections with democracy he had already stressed in *Considerations*—with the world of art that he pursued in works such as *Notes of Study and Travel in Italy*. Norton was making important connections, in dialogue with Ruskin as well as others, and recognizing some of the tensions between the allure that imaginative art held in his life and his duty to lead citizens toward a better collective future. In this way, Norton faced up to some of the same basic questions that Higginson, Lowell, and Curtis had confronted when charting vocational decisions at the onset of adulthood.[76]

Norton refrained from drawing any systematic connections between American cultivation and his developing expertise in the fine arts and in literary scholarship. But several casual suggestions demonstrate his understanding of aesthetic development and reveal how the cultural projects he launched by the mid-1850s distinguished his generation from that of his recently deceased father. In assessing the strengths of Andrews Norton, Charles noted that his father's "imaginative faculties had never received much training" and that he suffered from a "consequent deficiency in the exercise and power of imagination." Andrews Norton "sometimes neglected to take into account the variety in human nature, and to give full weight to the fact of the necessary diversity of men's opinions upon the most important subjects." The members of a new generation would achieve a more humane and tolerant cosmopolitanism less by expanding the geographical scope of their parents' worldliness (which was already quite broad) than by attending to those domains of the imagination whose cultivation might produce fresh results that had been stifled by inherited educational processes. For Americans to delve into the arts would be as much a leap toward the future as their contemporaneous embrace of Darwinian science (a development that drew from Norton a genuinely enthusiastic response). In theory, Norton believed that a trained openness to the inherent "variety in human nature" would result from imaginative engagement. In practice, his case proved that this formula contained an important element of truth.[77]

On the eve of the Civil War, Norton had become increasingly concerned with American materialism, a failing he addressed with the urgency his close friends applied to the problem of slavery. Americans seemed to lack a sense of "balance in our lives, in these days of haste, novelty, and restlessness." He hoped that by placing more value on "pursuits which have no end of immediate publicity or instant return of tangible profit," he and his fellow citizens might place themselves in the "freer, tranquiller, and more spacious world of noble and everlasting thought." Such a project would help Americans achieve a sense of their place in history, which to that point was tragically underdeveloped. Part of his mission in delving into the Middle Ages was to demonstrate how "he who lives only in present things lives but half a life," while "living also in the past" taught us how "to value the present at its worth" and to "hold ourselves ready for its end." His fellow Americans might find some aspects of this inheritance surprising and unexpectedly relevant. In probing the thirteenth century, they might see a time when an unfettered protodemocratic spirit produced the great art of cathedrals and learn how the "gilded age" of the Renaissance that followed ushered in a period of derivative ugliness and spiritual deprivation.[78]

Norton's attempt to braid distinct intellectual strands—to intertwine Unitarian stewardship, his ever keener aesthetic sensibility, and the hope that the nation might be cultivated toward greater virtue—was not without its difficulties. His intention, however, was evident: to combine what Lowell recognized (in an *Atlantic* review of *Notes of Travel and Study in Italy*) as an "appreciation of the beautiful in Art" with an "interest in the moral, political, and physical well-being of man." Whatever contradictions existed in Norton's formulation of the links between art and civic morality, they clearly did not dissuade him from expounding, over the remainder of his long life, an understanding of culture he had begun to work out by the time of the U.S. Civil War. James Turner has recently demonstrated that Norton's primary contribution to American intellectual life was institutional in the broadest sense, and his germinal influence is best established by his role in framing new categories such as the "humanities" and even the notion of "Western civilization" within American letters. When Norton died in 1908, Henry James, one of Norton's younger Anglo-American friends, looked back and noticed the curious endeavors that had issued from a "son of the Puritans" who had become as "intellectually transmuted" and as "liberally emancipated and initiated" as was perhaps possible. James appreciated a central paradox in Norton: the farther he seemed to evolve from his early origins, the more stubbornly he clung to the core assumptions of the New England tradition into which he had been born. Norton's status as America's leading art historian and as a persistent voice of reform suggested to the perceptive James how the old New Englander could "still plead most for substance when proposing to plead for style" and "still try to lose himself in the labyrinth of delight while keeping tight hold of the clue of duty." Displaying the confidence of his public convictions and erudite understanding, Norton managed better than anyone of his generation to consider, again in James's words, how one might "still address himself all consistently to the moral conscience while speaking as by his office for our imagination and our free curiosity."[79]

Intellectual friendships lay at the center of Norton's vocation, and the intensity of his relationships provides a clue to his importance in the political and cultural initiatives he fostered across the Victorian Anglo-American world. Initially more important than Ruskin was Arthur Hugh Clough, who arrived in Cambridge in 1852. One of Dr. Thomas Arnold's star students at the Rugby School, a devotee of Carlyle and Emerson, and a sensitive poet, Clough brought his earnest religious questioning to Shady Hill, where he settled in for several months before returning to London for a position in the Education Office. He found Norton to be the "kindest creature" that "ever befriended an emigrant stranger anywhere," and the two remained close friends for the rest of Clough's unfortunately brief life. Travel in the reverse direction introduced Norton to the novelist Elizabeth Gaskell, first briefly in 1850 and then more meaningfully in 1857. Both a Unitarian and a reformer, Gaskell wrote celebrated "industrial novels" that depicted the social dislocation and class conflict of midcentury England. Norton toured Italy with Gaskell and her daughters, sharing with them his expanding knowledge of Venetian art; after spending a few days with the family in Manchester, he then struck up a friendly correspondence with both Gaskell and her daughter, Meta, that would last five decades, long after Elizabeth Gaskell's death. Norton's eclectic and far-flung relationships—which reached into areas of religion, art, culture, politics, and science—underscored both the breadth of his interests and his openness to different perspectives. These relationships also reinforced his harmonious but not necessarily identical efforts to engage the life of the mind and to attend to civic life.[80]

For all Norton's cosmopolitan ease, the core group of like-minded New Englanders—in particular, the reformist men of letters that he befriended during his extended bachelordom of the 1850s—always meant the most to him. Not until the merchant turned scholar reached his mid-thirties did he assume family responsibilities. When he married Susan Sedgwick in the spring of 1862 and began to have children, he had already begun to place his distinctive stamp on Shady Hill. This new stage came amid other currents that would prompt Norton to spend his single decade of married life advocating the cause of American democracy. As with Curtis, Lowell, and Higginson, the crucible of war nationalized Norton's earlier impulses. No less important, the conflict informed how he and his cohort strove to shape American politics and culture in the generation that followed.[81]

The War for the Union and the Vindication of American Democracy

It cannot be repeated too often that this war was a war of ideas, and
that, until one idea or the other has secured a settled triumph, there can be no real
peace between the parties to the war. . . . Having faith in the American system, knowing
that it is the means by which civil order is best secured and advanced—knowing it
to be based upon moral principles of universal application—we must not shrink
from the conclusions to which our faith and knowledge lead us.
Charles Eliot Norton, "American Political Ideas," 1865

War made a confirmed democrat out of Charles Eliot Norton. After a decade of hand-wringing about the future of republicanism during the 1850s, Norton soon found himself rejoicing over the "triumph of popular government and the essential soundness of the people." He marveled at Americans' willingness to undertake a process of sacrifice that raised the entire country from degradation to unexpected heights of idealism. The constancy of citizens through this crisis convinced Norton that a war to preserve the highest American principles might provide the occasion for reinvigorating the country's basic institutions and ideals. The virtue displayed both on the battlefield and in civilian life led him to expect the completion of the experiment that had begun with the American Revolution.[1]

During the war years, peaks and valleys of excitement and despair, euphoria and frustration interrupted Norton's characteristic evenness of temperament. Yet when later recalling the fight for the Union, he and other thinkers of his generation remembered feeling a palpable sense of exhilaration. Purposeful optimism was evident from the earliest days of the conflict. James Russell Lowell noted in March 1861, "I begin to feel more like my old self than I have these ten years." Over the next five years, he burnished his reputation as a national poet and established his credentials as a leading exponent of advanced opinion. Thomas Wentworth Higginson greeted the attack on Fort Sumter with the conviction that the "world is growing better all the time." Recording his experiences as a leader of black troops marked one of the signal contributions to American war literature and shaped his reputation as a man of letters and a reformer well into the twentieth century. George William Curtis was similarly enthralled by the challenge of the war as well as by the shift he finalized in the early 1860s from a life of letters to a career as a journalist and liberal reformer. "I envy no other age," Curtis enthused in 1862, after a period of military setbacks. Returning even to "Persia and Greece and Carthage and Rome to find its parallels," he had to conclude that the "task before us is greater than any people was called upon to accomplish."[2]

A widely shared conviction that the war for the Union involved a basic vindication of democratic governance underlay these expressions of personal gratification. "Let us come out of this conflict victorious in the field," Higginson wrote at the beginning of the war, and the "case of free government is settled past cavil." After four years, Union success would prove doubters wrong about the instability of democracy. In victory, however, even more was assured than the sustenance of popular government. Slavery came to an end (even if illiberal racial prejudice did not), while the corrupting influence of American materialism was tempered (even if it was not completely removed from national life). With such triumphs came an understandable sense of progress and an eagerness to cement America's place in the vanguard of liberal causes across the world.[3]

Understanding liberal reform requires a careful consideration of what E. L. Godkin later described as the "heroic age of the American Commonwealth." Godkin, who was drawn into the circle of these Victorian intellectuals during the 1860s, shared their appreciation for what was "essentially a popular rising which carried the leaders forward often in spite of themselves." He understood as well as they did the rewards of making public duty a central component of one's life work. Henry Adams, another figure whose wartime experience helped shape liberal reform, boldly predicted in 1863 that "our generation has been stirred up from its lowest layers and there is that in its history that will swamp every member until we are all in our graves." In the years to come, the lessons of the war provided an inevitable point of reference. In this wartime crucible, the various individual men of letters became a self-identified group of liberals, grappling with such lasting preoccupations as the nature of leadership in a republic, the way in which public opinion could be shaped and led, and the manner in which Americans could stand for republican principles not just within the Union but throughout the world.[4]

Understanding That a "Democracy Can Think"

Visitors to Shady Hill, Norton's family home in Cambridge, entered a world of elegance and taste. Italian Old Masters and British landscapes hung beside family portraits, as Charles Eliot Norton worked after his 1862 marriage to transform his parents' house into a home for his wife and a growing family. Lush chairs in the library and shelves of leather-bound books presented an open invitation to the possibilities of culture. A similar air of refinement (though one that was more rustic than luxurious) suffused the new home in the Massachusetts hills that Norton purchased in the summer of 1864, a decision that inspired George William Curtis to purchase a summer retreat in the same neighborhood a few years later. Norton's study at the Locusts (as his Ashfield farmhouse was called) combined the urbane simplicity and cultivated learning for which he had already gained a transatlantic reputation. At the heart of this shrine to intellectual cultivation were twin tributes to democratic leadership, which Norton considered an essential part of the larger liberal endeavor. By keeping a photograph of Abraham Lincoln above his mantel and another of John Brown close by, Norton honored the two men who, in quite different ways, dramatized the links between individual character and moral leadership that democratic republics required.[5]

Norton's tribute to Brown was likely to register more surprise among visitors to Ashfield than the image of Lincoln. Yet the photograph of the martyred abolitionist was not an exercise in sentimental recollection. While Brown's violent raid on the federal arsenal at Harpers Ferry smacked of anarchism and disorder on the surface, underneath lay a notion of individual duty and a reverence for a higher law that Norton and the rest of his generation of liberal thinkers found compelling. Though he had not been directly involved in Brown's foiled attempt to spur a slave insurrection (as his childhood playmate Thomas Wentworth Higginson, one of the "Secret Six," had been), Norton had immediately recognized that the raid might "do something to raise the tone of national character and feeling" and establish a new "standard by which to measure the principles of public men." Norton hoped that Brown might serve as a model for selfless devotion to the "mass of the Northern community" that greatly needed the "lesson of manliness, uprightness, and courage which his life teaches." Early in 1860, Norton urged readers of the *Atlantic Monthly* to take the broadest possible view of Brown's character and to consider his example "not merely as lovers of liberty, not as opponents of slavery, but as men who need more manliness, more uprightness, more courage and simplicity in our common lives." Norton's lumping of attributes might imply a valorization of manly action, but it was less Brown's physical boldness than his moral bravery that impressed Norton.[6]

Norton was hardly alone in grasping the possibilities of Brown's strike against slavery. Like Victor Hugo and Ralph Waldo Emerson (both of whom compared Brown to the crucified Christ), Norton discerned a religious aura around this "martyr for liberty" who seemed to be from a "race of men rare in all times and all lands, rare especially in our days," who "thought themselves commissioned to do the work of the Lord." Norton followed other commentators at the time in comparing the supposed Mayflower descendant to the Covenanters and Regicides of the Puritan revolution, identifying Brown as the latest in a series of devout zealots to bring the furious judgments of the Old Testament into his campaign against contemporary injustice. The legacy of Brown's background in the Adirondacks also played a role, which Norton grasped only when he toured the region in 1860. There, in an area seemingly "uninvaded" by civilization, Brown must have been "influenced & formed by such scenery as lay around him." In such a preserve, it was easy for even the most cultivated Boston Brahmin to see how the "presence of God" might be "more constantly & deeply felt" and the "work of his hand more plain" to men such as Brown who were commissioned to accept a divine mission.[7]

After war began, Norton hoped that other Americans might live up to the standard John Brown had set for them. In two successive 1861 efforts, Norton proclaimed that the suppression of the Confederate rebellion would be a healthy corrective to the "false spirit of security, indifference, and boastfulness" that had made the country simultaneously "rich and weak." The discipline required by a major war effort would make clear the true meaning of personal independence, so often "carried to foolish and injurious excess" in America, by demonstrating that only through submission to a larger cause and obedience to a high and honorable sense of duty might one find the "means to display and to develop the best qualities of individual character." A truly independent individual knew when to submit to rightful restraint as well as when to resist tyrannical power. Americans must recognize that, like Brown, they were fighting a "religious war" that required submission not only to military discipline but also to duty, hardship, and the "divine cause of justice, liberty, and humanity."[8]

To be meaningful and enduring, sacrifice would have to continue. Americans were still too hasty and overconfident in their expectations, assuming that the war would be quick and easy work. In an aptly titled article on "The Advantages of Defeat," written for the *Atlantic* in the aftermath of Bull Run, Norton urged readers distraught by military setbacks that the goal was not "to reestablish the old order, but to set up a new one." Such an ambitious undertaking could only be accomplished through a long and costly process. Facing the future with a "simple and manly religious conviction" would prepare Americans for the new order, since Norton believed that an entire generation would be "compelled to frugality" and forced to exchange its "luxurious expenses upon trifles and superfluities" for the "large and liberal costliness of a noble cause." Only a sense of perspective would show his readers that "if defeat has brought us shame, it has brought us also firmer resolve" and convince them that "no man can be said to know himself, or to have assurance of his force of principle and character, till he has been tested by the fires of trial in the crucible of defeat." As he explained in a private letter written that fall, "A too easy & a too early success would have been fatal to the attainment of that permanent peace which is to be based on the destruction of the power of slavery."[9]

Norton's reliance on the need for prolonged suffering in the progress of a moral cause would have made sense to Thomas Wentworth Higginson, who had embraced a more radical brand of politics in the mid-1850s. Higginson's intimate involvement in the Brown raid resulted from an escalating commitment to violent means against slavery, which began with his defense of fugitive slaves in Boston, continued during his trips to Kansas (where in 1856 he served as a brigadier general of the free state forces), and finally brought him and other members of the Secret Six into the inner circles of Brown's strike against Virginia slaveholders. Higginson's involvement in this conspiracy remained one of the more controversial aspects of his entire life. The aid he provided to Brown did not rest on hopes for superhuman deliverance from an inspired prophet. Even though he found much to admire in "that religious elevation which is itself a kind of refinement" that he saw in Brown, the meaning of Higginson's participation, especially his refusal to flee prosecution after the raid was discovered, most concerned him throughout the pivotal moment.[10]

Joining the ring of Brown's conspirators was the culmination of two important trends in Higginson's development through the 1850s. First, it represented his increasingly aggressive response to the national crisis he saw deepening all around him. In the late 1850s, when the slave power had "now gained entire control over the three branches of our National Government," the time for mere exhortation had long passed. Reform, he had explained shortly after the enactment of the controversial Kansas-Nebraska Act, must give way to revolution. Along with radical Garrisonians, Higginson helped to organize the Disunion Convention at Worcester in 1857, even if he found resistance preferable to withdrawal. When given the alternatives, he embraced insurrection and ultimately war as the best means to regenerate American institutions.[11]

Second, Higginson's support for Brown stemmed from an evolving understanding of the importance of physical exertion to self-development. Articles Higginson had written on exercise and physical courage for the *Atlantic Monthly* in the late 1850s and early 1860s had insisted that reformers and intellectuals need not choose between developing their brains and developing their bodies. Higginson followed up this series of articles (published in 1863 as a book, *Out-Door Papers*) with a new *Atlantic* series on black resistance. In "The Maroons of Jamaica" (February 1860) and the "Maroons of Surinam" (May 1860), he explored the courage and bravery of "this heroic race." He then took up matters closer to home with "Denmark Vesey" (June 1861), "Nat Turner's Rebellion" (August 1861), and "Gabriel's Defeat" (September 1862). In addition to offering heavily researched and dramatically written narratives, these stories of black discontent under slavery showed that violence sometimes constituted the necessary recourse. Lest slaveholders take comfort in the disappointing black response to Brown's strike at Harpers Ferry, Higginson affirmed the slaves' willingness to strike for their freedom and to inflict terror under more propitious circumstances. Collectively, the essays on insurrection represented a natural progression from the previous athletic writings, grafting the theme of black resistance and black courage onto the earlier theme of self-culture. Higginson recognized in these key moments of black revolt a common humanity and, as an important part of that humanity, a familiar manifestation of "manly" courage and strength. "Our race does not take naturally to non-resistance," he explained approvingly, "and has far more spontaneous sympathy with Nat Turner than with Uncle Tom." For Higginson to emphasize black assertiveness was particularly crucial when even such a staunch antislavery ally as George William Curtis could observe that a "less mild and flexible race [would have rebelled] but [the slaves] are so soft and hopeless and submissive a race . . . that it did not happen."[12]

Experimenting with radical means of cultivating Americans' character — whether through extended suffering or the expression of individual bravery —

developed from a growing frustration with the state of public affairs and of official moral leadership. Brown's example gave many New Englanders a useful
contrast to what Norton called the "claims and the pretensions of the mass of
our political leaders," who were widely charged with responsibility for obscur-
ing moral perspective. The passage of the Fugitive Slave Law and the shameful
course of events in Kansas clearly demonstrated the aggressions of an aristocratic slave power. But they also revealed, perhaps more ominously, the bank-
ruptcy of northern leadership. Stephen Douglas, whom Curtis could not ex-
coriate in strong enough terms, embodied this political degradation. The fact
that some Americans regarded the Little Giant as a true statesman revealed
like nothing else the "moral prostitution and political peril of the country" before the war. Through the instrumentality of corrupted parties led by leaders
such as Douglas, citizens had been bound by force of law to betray their most
basic values. The lack of principle among politicians had followed their drift
away from such bedrock commitments, a trend that Curtis tried to reverse by
insisting that the Republican Party place that charter of national idealism, the
Declaration of Independence, in its 1860 platform. The need for such a basic affirmation justified low expectations for leaders, who could set themselves apart
simply by avoiding degrading compromises with wrong.[13]

The poor record of northern politicians suggested that while such foreign
observers as Alexis de Tocqueville and John Stuart Mill had perhaps overly
criticized democratic art, literature, and science, their assaults on the lack of
statesmanship and consistency in politics in popular government had the ring
of truth. Lowell anxiously echoed such negative judgments late in 1860 when
he wondered whether it was the "effect of democracy to make all our public
men cowards." Though pining for some leader like Andrew Jackson who might
"take command and crystallize this chaos into order," Lowell was relatively unusual among his circle in keeping John Brown at arm's length, eliciting a gentle
reprimand from Higginson for not printing "*something* manly" about Brown
in the *Atlantic*.[14] While Lowell believed that Americans would rally around the
"slenderest thread of honest purpose and unselfish courage in any man who is
in the right place," he initially found Abraham Lincoln little more promising
than Brown. Late in 1861, Lowell searched for some saving grace in presidential
mediocrity, suggesting to readers of the *Atlantic* that an "honest Chief Magis-
trate of average capacity" might demonstrate the "strength of democratic institutions" better than the "exceptional" man who saved the country without
the full efforts of the people themselves.[15]

While Lincoln had many critics during his first year in office, Lowell's disaffection resulted from the president's relatively cautious policy toward slavery. In a private letter written to Norton in the fall of 1861, Lowell faulted the president for "carrying on [the] war without hurting the enemy" and, worse, for failing to recognize that the "enemy ought to be hurt." Though seemingly unnerved by Brown's violence, Lowell expressed his hope that the "Puritan spirit" might subject the South to the same violent education that Oliver Cromwell had given to Ireland. Norton had similar concerns, especially when he learned that the Lincoln administration had decided in 1862 to return fugitive slaves. Norton called this measure the administration's "greatest mistake (& a criminal one)." Lincoln had squandered the perfect opportunity to announce a "general decree of emancipation, without any of its dangers" and had "violated every moral conviction & every principle of the North in regard to Slavery . . . & succeeded in forcing us all into a complicity in slave owning." Like Lowell, Norton thought the enemy ought to be hurt and declared himself "eager for a fight, for a battle in which our men shall show that they can use steel as well as lead." [16]

In their embrace of fighting and their concerns regarding Lincoln's timidity, Norton and Lowell seemed to share some of Higginson's attraction to violence. But their attitude throughout the war revealed a great deal of ambivalence about the use of force, a perennial dilemma for liberal thinkers who emphasized reason and consensus as the preferred mode of resolving conflict. So while Norton and Higginson agreed that the "events" surrounding Brown's raid, trial, and death had done more to confirm antislavery opinion than "all the antislavery tracts and novels that ever were written," Norton insisted that one of the "events" in question was the "impression made by Brown's character." In this way, he deemphasized Brown's deeds by focusing instead on the martyr's words as the best clue to his character. While his actions, however justified, had been both lawless and extreme, Brown's utterances and his "bearing," Norton believed, were of a different magnitude, especially those "simple and most affecting letters" he had written from jail. These epistles "add a noble chapter to the volume of the literature of the cell," Norton told Arthur Hugh Clough, the British poet who had briefly lived at Shady Hill in the early 1850s. Lowell expressed a similar preference for the word in a poem on the Italian revolution where he compared the muzzle-loading rifle to the printing press: "minié is good, but, spite of change / Gutenberg's gun has the longest range." [17]

As for the fighting itself, the violence and destruction of war might be regrettable but inevitable. As Curtis put it, combat was "incalculably preferable to tyranny or slavery or injustice of any kind." Most northern intellectuals moved during war to the same reasoning that Higginson had long ago adopted: an institution with the threat of force at its core might require an even greater force to uproot and destroy it. Still, while Norton admired the bravery and solidity of the American soldiers fighting the war, he quickly pointed out that they were "not men bred to the art of war, but men of peace" and that they would remain "men who have no lust of conquest, averse to bloodshed, incapable of wanton cruelty." Curtis similarly reminded his readers in *Harper's New Monthly Magazine* in 1862 that "however inevitable, however consecrated by its purpose" war might be, it remained the "remedy of brute force. It is still barbarous and repugnant to every man who would rather owe the amelioration of the race to moral and intellectual rather than to purely physical forces." Their ambivalence on this issue would never disappear, the shadow to their otherwise brilliant celebration of this moment.[18]

After Lincoln began moving step by step toward a policy of emancipation, Norton's and Lowell's attitude toward the president improved considerably. Such praiseworthy policy developments, while crucial, represented only part of their shifting view of Lincoln, a process revealed through Norton's regular wartime correspondence with Curtis, who spent nearly all of the war in New York. In one of these letters, Norton complained about the feeble and "inefficiently written" messages concerning slavery, noting that the president's "style is worse than ever" and remarking that "though a bad style is not always a mark of bad thought—it is at least a proof that his thought is not as clear is it ought to be." The moral emphasis that Norton placed on Lincoln's use of language both resembled Norton's evaluation of John Brown and provided evidence of his growing appreciation for the simple verities of equality and justice that informed American institutions. While clarity of language and purpose was important for the country as a whole, it was especially important for popular leaders, Norton believed, since an enormous responsibility came with communicating such ideals to the larger public. The martyred Brown had conveyed a basic moral lesson in exactly this way with his simple, direct letters from jail and his sincere, moving speech prior to his execution. Norton slowly began to sense that Lincoln might have the same gift for communication, even though, like Brown, the president had suffered the initial "disadvantages of imperfect culture, of self-education, and of little intercourse with men of high-breeding."[19]

By late 1863, Norton had come to echo Curtis's praise of the president, judging that "he rises with each new effort." Norton increasingly spoke of Lincoln's public writings as nothing less than "successive victories" every bit as important as the military triumphs of the Union armies. The president's statements

should be recognized as the "rarest class of political documents," Norton remarked, praising them as "arguments seriously addressed by one in power to
the conscience and reason of the citizens of the commonwealth." Here was a
leader able to use language to set the moral compass of the nation, to inspire
and lead its citizenry, and to establish the meaning of sacrifice and bloodshed.
Lincoln's skill with language became a matter of international commentary:
one of Norton's British correspondents remarked that the Second Inaugural
Address, delivered in 1865, was the "grandest thing that had been written since
the Bible." [20]

In 1864, the question of presidential leadership became more urgent as Lincoln positioned himself to become the first chief executive since Andrew Jackson to win a second term in office. Facing a challenge from the more radical
wing of the Republican Party, those who had criticized his temporizing became
more aware of his "instinct of a statesman" and his "knowledge of how much
is practicable without recoil," which Curtis had seen early in the war. Norton
credited Lincoln with mastering the "art and the duty of a true statesman in
a republic," a role that required him "not to act on what the people ought to
wish and to think" but "to adopt the best course practicable in accordance with
what they actually do wish and think." Lowell more vividly dramatized Lincoln's skill at "so gently guiding public opinion that he seems to follow it," depicting him steering a shaky raft through the rapids of shifting circumstances,
accomplishing his larger goal of moving down the river but keeping himself
always in the main current of the people's wishes to avoid disaster.[21]

Lowell's elevated estimate of Lincoln, which appeared as his first political
article in the refurbished *North American Review* that he and Norton had begun
to edit in 1864, constituted both an opening salvo in a historic presidential campaign and a distillation of liberal ideas about democratic leadership that would
frame this group's commitments for the rest of the century. The article contained, among other things, an admission that Lowell had only gradually recognized the "good sense, the good-humor, the sagacity, the large-mindedness,
and the unselfish honesty" that characterized the president's conduct of public
affairs. With a rhetorical flight that anticipated his 1865 tribute to Lincoln as
the "first American," Lowell described the Union war leader as a "man whom
America made, as God made Adam, out of the very earth, unancestried, un-
privileged, unknown, to show us how much truth, how much magnanimity, and
how much state-craft await the call of opportunity in simple manhood when it
believes in the justice of God and the worth of man." [22]

If Lowell implied that Lincoln was uniquely suited to the challenges of war, he never suggested that the principles of the president's leadership could not be emulated by less divinely chosen statesmen. In contrast to his recent predecessors, Lincoln had been able to "accommodate the conduct of communities to ethical laws, and to subordinate the conflicting self-interests of the day to higher and more permanent concerns." His patience in so doing, Lowell continued, showed the ideal statesman's necessary prudence in waiting "till the sentiment of the people is so far advanced toward his own point of view, that what he does shall find support in it, instead of merely confusing it with new elements of division." Like Norton, Lowell found the secret of Lincoln's success in the manner of his public communication, since the "certain tone of familiar dignity" showed that he was a "true democrat, who grounded himself on the assumption that a democracy can think." In what was perhaps his noblest service, Lincoln had "put himself on a level with those he addressed, not by going down to them, but only by taking it for granted that they had brains and would come up to a common ground of reason." The president found Lowell's article so astute an estimate of the administration's policy that he wrote to the publishers of the *North American Review* to record his praise.[23]

In taking the measure of the Union's war leader, Lowell, Norton, and Curtis emphasized that Lincoln elevated the conflict into something larger than a campaign for territorial integrity against rebellion. While they shared his faith in institutions, they also appreciated his underlying reverence for the values that infused the structures of governance. Brown's actions might have shown the need, during the extreme circumstances of an earlier time, to put aside the regular channels in the cause of conscience. But even then, Norton had sensed that Brown's "chief fault" was his "impatience with the slowness of Providence." Lincoln had a better sense of the process necessary to produce enduring change, even amid armed conflict. His ability to lead the country through changes in its fundamental laws provided a lasting tribute to a statesmanship that, in contrast to the Victorian vogue for Carlylean "hero worship," depended on the people's good sense and willingness to participate in any broad reform. During the war and well afterward, this group's test of leadership involved the lessons imparted to citizens as much as what policies could be accomplished through the wise use of government.[24]

Norton never wrote an exhaustive account of his understanding of leaders in history, choosing instead simply to hang two portraits in his Ashfield study. He clearly understood how individuals made history, however, as is evident in an 1864 letter to the young Indiana editor Jonathan Baxter Harrison. Though insistent that President Lincoln should not be made into the sole focus of the

Union cause lest his personality eclipse the more important principles that he embodied, Norton was compelled to admit that a "great man is the best gift of God to a nation." A danger even lurked, he continued, "lest in our confidence in the democratic principle, we come to neglect the worth and to think too lightly of the value of a preeminent genius, of a born leader of men." Seemingly with Tocqueville's and Mill's criticisms in mind, Norton insisted on the more general point that "our democracy must be liberal enough to include genius." Then, articulating those themes at the core of his developing liberal politics, he declared, "we shall not be true to our own principle in the final expression of it, if it fail to include not merely the elevation of men, but the highest development of the individual man."[25]

Emancipating the Public Opinion of the North

"Whatever other result this war is destined to produce," Lowell confided to readers of the *Atlantic* during the early summer of 1861, "it has already won for us a blessing worth everything to us as a nation" simply by "emancipating the public opinion of the North." With secession, slaveholders no longer could ban free and full discussion, which Lowell had just a few months earlier called the "very life of free institutions, the fruitful mother of all political and moral enlightenment." In accepting what Higginson called the "ordeal by battle" over the "more serious danger of conquering ourselves by compromise," the North had not abandoned its faith in ideas. It had simply committed itself to backing up ideas with action when further compromise seemed a greater threat to those ideas than a resort to violence did. This was a fairly easy leap to make in the spring of 1861, when most observers assumed that secession was more or less a bluff and that any possible conflict would be a quick and decisive restoration of Union authority.[26]

The connection between military action and the "emancipation" of public opinion would be a constant theme among a group of men who distinguished themselves in the early 1860s as Union publicists. Curtis delved into this issue in the fall of 1862, explaining to readers of *Harper's Monthly* that although war was "of the utmost importance in the economy of civilization and progress," it worked primarily in an indirect way. In the "intellectual sphere," he explained, "light necessarily scatters darkness" and the "actual progress of the race" occurred. As a result, Curtis believed, the "brute forces" of armies clashing in battle were not the main point of war. The conflict's true significance lay simply in securing the "conditions under which a change can be effected in the only possible, that is, the intellectual way."[27]

Faith in the power of free ideas to undermine unthinking force had been a major theme of Republicanism and of American abolitionism, which had repeatedly argued that unfettered public discussion would mean the end of bondage.[28] Yet the steadily growing attention to this theme in the early 1860s also represented a key turning point in these liberals' understanding of their role in American society. Fixating on public opinion helped them to make sense of the terrible carnage of war. Doing so also pushed them beyond their earlier commitment to the cultivation of individuals through art, literature, and reform and into an even wider duty broadly to establish principles, to push elected leaders toward important goals, and to instruct the entire citizenry on the true meaning of rapidly changing events. In this context began the liberals' lasting engagement with the relation between public opinion and sound government, a theme that had already become a hallmark of liberal government throughout the Anglo-American world.[29]

Liberal engagement with public opinion took a variety of distinct forms. For Lowell, it meant a stream of political articles for the *Atlantic Monthly*, as he continued to write even after stepping down as the magazine's editor in 1861. In "E Pluribus Unum" (February 1861) and "The Pickens-and-Stealin's Rebellion" (June 1861), Lowell boldly defined the conflict for a jittery public still finding its resolve. He also rediscovered the possibilities of political poetry, primarily through the resurrection of Hosea Biglow in a second series of eleven *Biglow Papers*, mostly published in the *Atlantic*. The papers especially took off when satirizing Britain for its frosty neutrality in "Mason and Slidell: A Yankee Idyll," and, like the first series, they enjoyed a hearty reception across the ocean.[30]

Lowell also teamed up with Norton to edit the *North American Review*, which had been among their earliest outlets for critical writing. The two refurbished this venerable publication as a powerful organ of advanced Republican commentary. Lowell understood that their mission was to make the *Review* "loyal" and "lively" and, most important, to "give it opinions." Liveliness proved a difficult challenge even amid war. Sprightly monthlies such as the *Atlantic* and *Harper's* (soon to be joined by *Scribner's* after the war) seemed to outpace the old quarterlies, which Lowell had come to consider "those megatheria of letters." But a combination of Lowell's celebrity and Norton's editorial acumen helped to stave off extinction by breathing new life into the hallowed quarterly's old bones.[31]

Curtis attempted to shape public opinion through a different set of educative and moralizing venues. He continued to travel the lecture circuit throughout the war, speaking before dozens of audiences about the larger significance of the American crisis, expounding on the "American Doctrine of Liberty," and chastising Americans for their prewar "Political Infidelity." He also developed a more intensive and more regular contact with the northern public through his work in the periodical press. In 1859, he added a "Lounger" column for *Harper's Weekly* to the regular "Easy Chair" column he wrote for *Harper's New Monthly Magazine*, proudly sensing the opportunity this newest "lay pulpit" brought him to reach well over one hundred thousand readers during the war. He relished his ability to offer readers a "chance at hearing things suggested that otherwise there would be no hint of in the paper." With greatly expanded wartime circulation and his promotion to political editor of the *Weekly* in 1863, Curtis flexed his editorial muscles and turned a periodical that had once spoken for conservative Democrats into one of the strongest supporters of the Lincoln administration. His closest friends sensed that such work would lead him to service as a Republican in Congress.[32]

Norton shared a desire "to do or to give something for a cause which has my heart as this has." He too was aware that this something would involve "guiding & defining the popular opinion" by engaging in print journalism, and he thus acknowledged, in a letter to his friend, Meta Gaskell, that the "state of the country imposes duties on us all which occupy our time & change the common current of our pursuits." Norton's wartime experiences as a publicist deserve close attention, since he faced more squarely than perhaps any other Union journalist the complex, multilayered challenges of appealing to and shaping public opinion.[33]

Norton expanded on his early contributions to the *Atlantic* when in 1863 he became the editor and driving force behind the New England Loyal Publication Society. This organization, which was financed by the merchant John Murray Forbes, strove, in Norton's words, "to cultivate the sentiments of nationality and patriotic loyalty, & to promote the advance of freedom and justice." By placing the wartime struggle in a large perspective and framing the issues at stake in the conflict, Norton and the Loyal Publication Society experimented with new ways to "influence and direct public opinion." The effort began by sending out "slips" from metropolitan periodicals to hundreds of small-town papers across the country, especially in midwestern and border states. Norton soon switched to larger broadsides carrying a number of articles and editorials. He threw himself into the work, bringing all the relevant learning that could be mustered in Shady Hill's library and enlisting the help of his vast network of correspondents and friends. By May 1863, he reported to the British politician John Bright that the society was providing "nearly 1000 newspapers in the Loyal States with three or four slips weekly," each of which included "short passages from Burke, Jefferson and others" (articles propounding "good *democratic* doctrine") and political editorials from other papers, both foreign and domestic.[34]

This wartime project of political education caused Norton's already considerable range of contacts to swell. His circle of New York correspondents expanded well beyond Curtis to include Henry Bellows, Frederic Law Olmsted, and, most importantly, E. L. Godkin. Godkin soon came to exercise an enormous influence on American public life, thanks in no small part to his relationship with Norton. A proponent of British liberalism since his days at Queen's College in Belfast, Godkin had emigrated to the United States in 1856 with a modest reputation as the author of a sympathetic *History of Hungary* and as a special correspondent during the Crimean War for the *London Daily News*. Continuing to write for the *Daily News*, he chronicled his observations of the United States—the 1856 presidential election, the continuing crisis of Bleeding Kansas, and John Brown's raid on Harpers Ferry. Though Godkin was in Paris with his new American wife, Elizabeth Foote, when the Civil War broke out, he sent letters to the *Daily News* strongly identifying himself with the Americans during the Anglo-American crisis surrounding the *Trent* affair. He found himself disgusted at the tone of much of the British press, knowing that it failed to speak for liberals such as himself, and he urged his American friends to capitalize on this important minority opinion. "There is a large party in England," he wrote home to an American friend, "composed of dissenters, democrats, reformers of all shades . . . who strongly sympathize not only with Northern anti-slavery principles but Northern theories of government, whose feelings of nationality the North ought to *ménager*."[35]

Returning to the United States in the fall of 1862, Godkin continued his participation in Anglo-American journalism. Sensing a powerful opportunity, he and Olmsted, who had become quite close, began discussing plans for a newspaper of politics and culture modeled on the British weeklies the *Spectator* and the *Saturday Review*. This "newspaper project" led Godkin, at Olmsted's urging, to visit Norton to discuss its prospects. Their meeting at Shady Hill eventually resulted in the weekly *The Nation*, where as editor Godkin became one of the most important voices in late-nineteenth-century liberal reform. But long before that "paper scheme" seemed possible, Norton, impressed with Godkin's "manliness, his strong good sense, his warm & liberal feelings," and the "delicacy of his mind and the quietness of his manner," enlisted him as a contributor to the *North American Review*. From this meeting also emerged a close friendship that endured until Godkin's death some four decades later.[36]

Norton's work with the Loyal Publication Society prepared him for the even more intensive job as Lowell's coeditor at the *North American Review*. The two men agreed that the quarterly was "nearly extinct" but had an ambitious vision for how they might transform it into a "powerful instrument for affecting public opinion on the great questions now at issue." Reading the times, Norton sensed a new "popular demand . . . for clear, sound thought, for thoroughness of learning, for serious criticism, & above all, for the most liberal & at the same time most searching discussion of the principles of religion, morals, politics, literature & art." This judgment gave him hope that the days of the serious quarterly had indeed not disappeared. It is not difficult, even at a distance of nearly 150 years, to detect the palpable changes wrought by Norton and Lowell's editorial direction on their inaugural issue in January 1864, which attracted the notice of, among others, President Lincoln and John Stuart Mill and went into an unprecedented second edition. Norton and Lowell introduced a new liveliness in the journal's political articles and began to set a new standard for its literary criticism.[37]

Higginson's wartime experiences differed radically from those of Norton, Lowell, and Curtis: Higginson fought in the war as a member of the U.S. Army. While not the youngest of the group, he was by far the most adapted to the rigors of military service, both physically and temperamentally. His disciplined gymnastic regimen undoubtedly helped his body belie its forty years, while his embrace of force made him long for the "tonic of war" from the beginning of hostilities. Even so, he did not volunteer until the fall of 1862, since he first had to juggle his desire to join in the fight and his obligations to his wife, Mary, now a complete invalid. Soon thereafter, he was offered a position as colonel of the First South Carolina Volunteers, a regiment made up of former slaves. Higginson's service in the Sea Islands represented a clear (one might even say perfect) culmination of his earlier concerns: his abolitionism, his athleticism, his leadership aspirations, and his literary career. He relished the opportunity to gain personal distinction as well as to strike so central and symbolic a blow by leading freedmen in battle against their former masters.[38]

Higginson's wartime service, however distinct it would be, also contributed crucially to the opinion-shaping work that engaged other liberal men of letters. Indeed, his literary career continued apace with his military career, the one feeding the other. In addition to his wartime articles on black resistance, Higginson published important articles about his experiences with black soldiers in the pages of the *Atlantic Monthly* in 1864 and 1865. Installments of his journal, sent home to his family, circulated widely throughout the Northeast even before the *Atlantic* articles appeared. Norton was among those who read the diary in manuscript and urged Higginson to publish it. Norton assured Curtis that Higginson's account "inspires the completest confidence in the capacity of the blacks for service in war." These writings were among the most carefully detailed accounts of the recently freed southern blacks. A large part of Higginson's task involved rendering the unknown and exotic familiar to a large audience. He accomplished the challenge by treating the "essentially poetic" "Negro Spirituals" as an art form, not unlike Sir Walter Scott's Scottish ballads, and by humanizing his troops as individuals with individual strengths, weaknesses, virtues, and foibles. Higginson's wartime writings often indulged in the patronizing "romantic racialism" of his day, but they also imagined an alliance that might build a vision for the future, where northern intellect and those presumably willing to be guided would unite to push forward what had begun as the good cause of a completed American freedom.[39]

At the suggestion of Norton and others, Higginson agreed to publish his war diary in the pages of the *Atlantic*. Not until 1870 did he gather these observations of black troops into a book, *Army Life in a Black Regiment*, which was rediscovered in the mid–twentieth century as "one of the few classics of military life in national letters."[40] The delay in bringing out the book (and allowing its future translation into French) resulted from a related project Higginson undertook—gathering biographies of the ninety-five Harvard graduates killed in recent combat. Higginson used the preface to this memorial to set forth a ringing claim "that there is no class of men in this republic from whom the response of patriotism comes more promptly and surely than from its most highly educated class." Any "delusions" still present in Europe about the supposed torpor or alienation of "cultivated Americans" from public life would not hold up to the "solid conviction and the absolute law of conscience" that Higginson chronicled after returning to civilian life in 1864.[41]

As Higginson's comments suggest, the experience of war provided an unparalleled opportunity for scholars to embrace those duties Curtis had urged in 1856. This mobilization of men of letters likewise raised expectations for the near future. Higginson realized as much when he declared that the "best monument that we can build to these our heroes is to show that they have renewed our faith, and made nobler the years that are to come." A new understanding of the power of public opinion and a new set of nationalizing institutions would help in this regard. So too would the example of a set of principled publicists who might establish a model of intelligent and reasoned debate.[42]

A Struggle of the Antidemocrats with the Democrats

Gaining public influence was only the first step in assuring that public opinion would be freed from proslavery inhibitions in 1861 and that it would avoid suffering a new round of degradation. If such promising developments were to outlast the passions of war and not suffer a rapid reversal in peace, however, opinion had to be set on a correct understanding of the enormous stakes involved. With such goals in mind, northern intellectuals presented the war as the trial of American democracy against its enemies; the ultimate vindication of popular government thus took on world historical consequences.

Norton summed up the prevailing outlook among northern Republicans when he termed the Union cause a "struggle of the anti-democrats with the democrats." Such a case was not hard to make, even without invoking the basic matter of slavery. As Lowell put it, the "real point, and the only point, at issue" was the "claim of a minority to a right of rebellion when displeased with the result of an election." If this situation were resolved unfavorably, the world's leading republic would not just be divided in two but would be subjected to a continual process of fragmentation. This possible chain of events clearly remained in the minds of Union supporters, who realized that outside observers still doubted whether a democratic government was capable of suppressing a revolt against its legitimacy. As Lincoln acknowledged in his July 4, 1861, message to Congress, the war "presents to the whole family of man, the question, whether a constitutional republic, or a democracy—a government of the people, by the same people—can, or cannot, maintain its territorial integrity against its own domestic foes."[43]

Lowell acknowledged that political theorists across the world and across time "had always taught us that democracies were incapable of the sentiment of loyalty, of concentrated and prolonged effort, of far-reaching conceptions." Tocqueville had wondered thirty years earlier whether a democracy could sustain any prolonged war effort, civil or otherwise. Democracies, the French observer had written with ominous foreboding for Americans engaged in a long, brutal war, were better "suited to directing a peaceful society, or if necessary, to making some sudden and violent effort rather than to braving over a long period the great storms that beset a nation's political existence." Such philosophical conclusions, Lowell observed, came from those who "knew democracy, not by rubbing shoulders with it . . . but merely from books." A more empirical lesson might be gleaned from the present struggle, in which Americans would prove that a "democratic republican government can maintain itself against domestic insurrection."[44]

The Confederate revolt was not just any domestic insurrection, as Curtis and his circle instructed readers again and again. It was the rebellion of that least democratic portion of the country, the slaveholding South, which resembled a feudal society in its landed aristocracy, its enslaved subject class, and the ties of deference and hierarchy that bound nonslaveholding whites in the middle to the ruling class above. Because of its slave system, the South was "aristocratic in instinct, by necessity, in theory and practice" and thus the heart of national antidemocracy that was working to assure a divided American future. None of the liberal principles associated with the democratic North—freedom of speech, equality, the impartial rule of law—had been allowed to take root, let alone to flourish, where slavery prevailed, Curtis and his colleagues pointed out, extending a key tenet of antislavery and Free Soil ideology. Indeed, *Harper's Weekly* argued that secession represented no more than the "effort of the only aristocratic class in the country to destroy popular institutions, because they had learned by experience that under those institutions the people became too wise to submit to an aristocracy."[45]

Opinion-shaping efforts necessarily intensified during the 1864 presidential election, the existence of which, in a time of civil war, demonstrated the trials that a democratic commitment endured. With Lincoln facing severe challenges from both the Democrats and the radical wing of his Republican Party, his supporters faced the prospect that their dedication to democratic processes— popular elections and freedom of speech—might be the undoing of their democratic struggle. The election, Curtis explained, represented a "strain directly along the fibre," the likes of which "no system in history" had ever encountered. It might have seemed that the stakes of the conflict justified all means of zealous electioneering, but Lowell insisted that the election "must be discussed in the higher atmosphere of principle, by appeals to the reason, and not the passions, of the people."[46]

Norton strongly desired Lincoln's reelection but refused to disseminate Loyal Publication Society broadsides in support of the president personally lest his commitment to popular government seem less strong than his party advocacy. "It is of more importance to promote the spread of sound opinion &

just feeling concerning the principles involved in our great struggle," he told a new acquaintance and correspondent from Indiana. If, by sticking to principle, he could "strengthen the love of liberty" and "promote the spread of true ideas of democracy, & confidence in the democratic principle," then he would "indirectly" weaken the "power of McClellanism, of Vallandighamism, of Fremontism" and strengthen the "position of Mr. Lincoln as our best representative of these ideas." Lowell agreed with Norton and might have been speaking of himself when he remarked of Lincoln that "to be moderate and unimpassioned in revolutionary times . . . may not be a romantic quality, but it is a rare one, and goes with those massive understandings on which a solid structure of achievement may be reared."[47]

The insistence on making reason and principle the basis for their campaigns gave these Unionist intellectuals a basis for judging their opponents. In one of his first pieces for the refurbished *North American Review*, Norton confronted the bigoted and unthinking opposition to Republican administration of the war effort. He bolstered his argument by invoking John Stuart Mill, already recognized as one of the most important British advocates of the Union cause. Groups such as the Democratic Society for the Diffusion of Political Knowledge clung to the types of creeds against which Mill had warned in *On Liberty*, Norton explained, relying on influences that exist "outside the mind, encrusting and petrifying it against all other influences addressed to the higher parts of our nature." Democratic appeals to the racism of the American people were especially unfortunate because they represented the antithesis of principled discussion. The racist strain of Copperhead oratory was fundamentally immoral because it revealed a resistance to reason or argument. Such mindless appeals to the worst in the audience were "doing nothing for the mind or heart, except standing sentinel over them to keep them vacant."[48]

After Lincoln's resounding reelection, Curtis exulted that the Union had demonstrated the "general intelligence of the people" and the "security of perfectly free discussion." By so doing, the electorate had offered the ultimate "vindication of the American system of free popular government." Norton found in the results a "greater triumph than any military victory could be over the principles of the rebellion." By casting ballots, the American people had declared their commitment to saving their country at further sacrifice. Moreover, the Unionist intellectuals, like many Republicans, took the election returns as evidence that public opinion had progressed toward the clear emancipation policy that had been overwhelmingly unpopular at war's beginning.[49]

The final extirpation of slavery was the war's coup de grâce, marking the

Union's significant advance toward establishing democracy in the southern
states and reforming it in the northern states. The move against slavery was
even more valuable for having been accomplished through a democratic process. In teasing out this line of argument, the liberal publicists strove to clarify the workings of the American system for their readers and to vindicate it
from critics who saw in emancipation an arbitrary and unconstitutional departure from American tradition. The war years had revealed the true nature of
the American political system — in particular, its fundamental elasticity and
adaptability. Higginson had grasped this idea during the war's first months,
arguing that constitutional interpretation "will always prove plastic before the
popular will." Just because something appeared "*extra*-constitutional," Lowell
explained somewhat more defensively in January 1864, it was not "necessarily
*un*constitutional." History had proved again and again that "all measures will
be found to have been constitutional at last on which the people are overwhelmingly united." Norton commissioned his new friend Godkin to write an article
exposing the "very vague notions" Americans held about their Constitution
and demonstrating that the document was less important than the "principles
which gave worth to it."[50]

Norton explored this aspect of American political adaptability in a postwar
article on "American Political Ideals" that John Stuart Mill enthusiastically
noted. Norton's argument in this piece rested on the American democratic
system's difference from the European governments. While each Old World
polity was a "historic product" with the "supports of tradition, succession, and
force," the United States was "severed from the past," the "product of the fresh
efforts of men striving to do the best for themselves, unimpeded by tradition-
ary forms and authority." For inherited authority, Americans substituted the
moral sense of the people, embodied in such principles as "liberty, justice, and
equality." While these "moral ideas" had been expressed at the founding of the
nation and never changed, the "application" of them "changes with every new
condition of human life" and "according to the advance of mankind in moral
culture and intelligence." This nuanced understanding of an evolving American political system had two important results for Americans in 1865, Norton
believed. First, it demonstrated that all the faults of the 1850s — the "selfish
materialism, the mass of ignorance, the corruption of politics, the atrocities of
slavery" — were mere "excrescences" on the system, capable of removal. Second, Americans benefited from living under what was "essentially a system of
adaptation." The interplay of moral principle with governmental order made

the "whole political system constantly ductile and pliable," constantly capable of progressive change.[51]

But pliable did not mean capricious, and a deliberate and deliberative process had to be followed. If the Emancipation Proclamation represented the progression that might occur within democratic statesmanship, the more difficult and slower work of a constitutional amendment depended on a broader basis of civic participation. How Americans resolved the "position and treatment of the black race," Norton predicted with ominous prescience, would provide the "touchstone of American principles and the prophecy of national prosperity or decline": "The treatment of blacks in the long run must be based not on the necessities of war, or any emergency of transient circumstances, but should be founded on universal principles of universal application and of eternal force."[52]

Norton was hardly alone in recognizing that the revolutionary changes of war taught Americans the enormous responsibility of the citizenry at large. The rule of the people, through opinion, proved itself capable of "outstripping legislative and executive action." In a country where public opinion seemed to matter as much as it did in the United States, the entire enterprise depended on public discussion being conducted at the highest level possible, whether measured in intellectual or in moral terms. The Democratic opposition had shown the dangers of demagoguery and base appeals to prejudice. Unionist intellectuals sought to demonstrate the possibilities of a higher standard.[53]

The human cost of Union victory was as important as its ultimate success, since bloodshed, not simply policy or the outcome of elections, upended the notion that democracies were incapable of sacrificing for ideals. The hundreds of thousands of Union casualties included martyrs with intimate ties to northeastern intellectual circles. Higginson's decision to enlist was unusual more because of his approaching middle age than because of his scholarly background; hardly any leading member of the *Atlantic* and *North American* circles lacked a close link to the battlefield and the ever-mounting human losses. The Nortons had a scare when Arthur Sedgwick, the brother of Charles's new wife, Susan, was captured and imprisoned, although he ultimately reached home safely. Curtis saw a close friend, the writer Theodore Winthrop, die in one of the war's first battles and then mourned his brother, Joseph Bridgham Curtis, killed at Fredericksburg after demonstrating bravery at Antietam. Lowell watched helplessly as three nephews were killed in combat: William Lowell Putnam, the only remaining son of his sister, Mary, at the Ball's Bluff debacle; James Jackson Lowell, son of his brother, Charles, in the Seven Days' Battles; and then, most painfully, the family darling, Charles Russell Lowell, who had risen to command a cavalry brigade before being killed at Cedar Creek. Charles had recently married Curtis's sister-in-law, Josephine "Effie" Shaw Lowell, and the regal glory of this couple was impressive enough to still draw an awed remembrance from William James decades later. At the time of her husband's death, Effie was expecting their first child.[54]

The most significant New England martyrdom came in 1863 when Robert Gould Shaw was killed during the charge made by his regiment of African American soldiers at Fort Wagner, South Carolina. The young colonel's combination of moral and physical courage, his dedication to the cause of emancipation, and his willingness to die in valiant pursuit of the cause provided well-born Yankees with a potent model of heroic sacrifice. Shaw's death reverberated as a personal tragedy for many in the tight-knit cohort of men of letters. Shaw was not just Curtis's brother-in-law but also the son of Lowell's old and dear friend, Sarah Shaw, who had also been an intimate of Norton's in Italy. Higginson, who followed closely the movements of Shaw's Fifty-fourth Massachusetts Regiment, the first black regiment raised in the North, renamed the camp of the First South Carolina Regiment in honor of his fellow Harvard graduate, effectively forgiving Shaw for his earlier waverings on emancipation. Lowell strove to put his feelings into verse that might acknowledge how this blow was among the most deeply felt of his losses. "I write of one, / While with dim eyes I think of three," the poem explained, as its "funereal tread" moved toward a final note of affirmation. Directly addressing the "Dear Land" with a sense of renewal, Lowell recorded his sentiments in terms both deeply personal and capable of application across the northern populace.

> How nobler shall the sun
> Flame in thy sky, how braver breathe thy air,
> That thou bred'st children who for thee could dare
> And die as thine have done![55]

Conquering the Old World

One of the American Civil War's most lasting legacies involved the wartime response of other countries. Of particular significance was the "bitter, bitter alienation" between America and Great Britain, which Thomas Wentworth Higginson recalled with some emotion a full quarter of a century after the Con-

federacy's defeat. As Higginson pointed out in 1890, Anglo-American relations suffered as much from the tensions of the Civil War as from the American
Revolution and Britain's second armed invasion of the United States between
1812 and 1815. The crisis of the 1860s resulted not from a military clash between these transatlantic rivals, though a wider international war seemed imminent at several moments. Instead, Britain's unexpected sympathy for the
Confederacy provoked many Unionists to accuse the "mother country" of a
nearly unforgivable act of betrayal. "All educated England, after taunting us for
years with tolerating slavery," Higginson recalled, "turned and reproached us
more bitterly for giving our very heart's blood to overthrow it." The prevalent
response by the supposedly most cultivated Britons caused lingering American suspicion. But this context also gave rise to a new and enduring type of
transatlantic alliance—an avowedly liberal one—itself to become a main impetus toward progressive accord in the late Victorian period that followed.[56]

The British government's policies during the Civil War were complicated,
as was the interplay of different elements within British society.[57] Yet while
Americans were concerned with the Palmerston government's adoption of neutrality and with the sources of potential Union support among the working class
and dissenting Protestants, what most concerned New England publicists was
the anti-Union animus that issued from the respectable British press and from
the country's leading universities. The pro-Confederate leanings of the *London Times* reawakened some stubborn postcolonial dynamics, as did the ridicule that magazines such as *Punch* heaped on President Abraham Lincoln. A
sneering report by the *Times* reporter William Howard Russell after the Battle
of Bull Run prompted Curtis to predict, "What bitter enemies of England the
war will leave us!" A year later, he drew attention to a recent display of anti-
American sentiment at Oxford University in his regular column for *Harper's
Weekly*. The lopsided vote among undergraduates there led him to the hyperbolic conclusion that "hatred of the United States" was nothing less than an
"epidemic which rages with frightful violence all over England."[58]

The bad feeling led some to hope that the war would finally liberate Americans from their debilitating dependence on leading European opinion makers
in the same way that the conflict forced northern public opinion to overcome
the domination of slave masters and to escape the sway of a demoralized and
demoralizing Democratic Party beholden to proslavery southerners. Lowell announced at the beginning of hostilities that fighting a war for the Union might
"have the good result of making our independence in matters of thought and
criticism as complete as our political emancipation." Curtis pursued the same

line of argument in asking readers of *Harper's Monthly* to scrutinize what he
called "our national sensitiveness to foreign criticism." He did not always practice what he preached, however, and the steady stream of commentary on British insults he served up to readers itself demonstrated the unseemly "eagerness with which our newspapers copy and we all read whatever is said of us in
Europe." Even with his complicity in this collective brooding over Old World
taunts, Curtis recognized that the "indignation or satisfaction with which we
receive" such foreign commentary were the clearest signs possible of persistent
immaturity and lack of national self-reliance. Only with concerted effort could
"this great struggle, by revealing to us our own manhood, release us nationally
from our childish dependence upon European criticism," Curtis concluded,
adding that such a development might also "emancipate our literature from
foreign subservience."[59]

British sneers were even harder to ignore during war than they had been
during peacetime. Foreign attitudes picked at scabs that had barely begun to
heal over the past two generations. Lowell harbored a bitterness that extended
well past the war years, lashing out at pro-Confederate Britons for neglecting
their far more ignoble attempts to put down domestic revolts against central
authority. Those who suppressed the "Irish Insurrection of 1848, or the Indian
Rebellion ten years later" had little right to criticize a war intended to maintain and preserve the world's leading democracy, he reasoned. Like most of his
associates, he was irked not just by British hypocrisy but also by its seeming
indifference to the battle between slavery and freedom. Resurrecting the character of Hosea Biglow, Lowell dramatized the hurt feelings of Jonathan (representing the United States) about John Bull's failure to express enthusiasm
for the North's struggles:

> We know we've got a cause, John,
> Thet's honest, just, an' true;
> We thought 't would win applause, John,
> Ef nowheres else, from you.[60]

Britain's retreat from its leadership of the global campaign for emancipation made sense to the Unionist intellectuals only in the context of the British
rulers' fundamental aversion to popular government. In pursuing this theme,
the liberals invoked many of the same arguments they used to contrast Lincoln's policies with his enemies in the Confederacy and in the Democratic
Party, who had proved themselves unfit champions of New World democracy.
The British founded their system on inherited rank, so this common argument

went, while the South built its self-perpetuating despotism on the ownership of slaves. British actions, Norton explained, simply reflected the "natural and instinctive hostility of an aristocracy, which feels that the current of civilization . . . is turned against it . . . by the advances of the modern spirit of democracy." On reflection, it was remarkable that the country could even remain neutral in a conflict with such clear implications for British destiny. The American struggle was "really the crisis of England," Curtis insisted, explaining that the war constituted "not merely a struggle between secession and Union, or between slavery and freedom" but the "final decisive contest between free popular government on the one side, and government by an oligarchy or a monarch on the other." If the nature of the struggle was thus clear, no less were the stakes. Curtis warned of the dire consequences that would follow the collapse of the world's leading republic. "In every country in the world the suffrage will be restricted, the privileged class strengthened, popular rights reduced, the burdens of the poor man increased, and his opportunities diminished." Americans "shall have brought self-government and humanity itself into merited contempt" simply by allowing the enemies of popular rights to glory in the Union's humiliation.[61]

These American observations won apparent confirmation in the extensive British commentary on the fate of the American Union. One of the key themes of the conservative response was captured in an 1861 prediction by the Earl of Shrewsbury. "I see in America the trial of Democracy and its failure," he wrote, foreseeing "that the dissolution of the Union is inevitable, and that men now before me will live to see an aristocracy established in America." From the perspective of conservative Tories, this reversion to older models of authority was exactly what the New World needed and what a more naturally authoritarian South might achieve. The *London Times* reported that the "whole affair is looked upon in this country as a breakdown of democracy" and "that is one of the main causes of the absence of sympathy" for the Union. Similar views were debated in established British quarterlies in articles such as "Democracy on Its Trial" and "Democracy Teaching by Example." The Tory penchant for linking the South's struggle with that of the European standing order inadvertently allowed British Liberals such as John Bright to link their country's push for an expanded electorate with the struggle against North American slavery.[62]

Framing the struggle as a global clash between aristocracy and democracy helped to spur international interest and turn attention to how the American war might be understood as a continuation of the assault on slavery begun within the United Kingdom. On a more personal level, the broadening of the discussion also reconfigured earlier transatlantic friendships, as the case of Charles Eliot Norton made clear. Norton's insistent vindication of the Union cause further endeared him to the Gaskell family, whose members received his regular commentary about the New England Loyal Publication Society, the North's growing commitment to black rights, and his admiration for Lincoln's leadership. By the end of the war, Elizabeth Gaskell signaled a new stage in her relationship with Norton by dedicating her last novel, *Sylvia's Lovers*, to him. He reciprocated by naming his first daughter for the novelist shortly after her death in 1865. Norton's antebellum web of British contacts suffered from this loss, which compounded the untimely death two years earlier of another close friend, the poet Arthur Hough Clough, at the age of forty-two.[63]

While Norton's democratic zeal impressed the Gaskells, it had the opposite effect on John Ruskin, whose breach with Norton represented the third and most dramatic blow to his antebellum circle of transatlantic friends. Evidence of a possible rupture began with Ruskin's frosty response to Norton's marriage, which Ruskin feared would undermine the intimate bond that the two men had developed. By 1863, Norton's running political commentary had pushed Ruskin to respond with the same acrid, uncompromising formulations perfected by Thomas Carlyle, whose trenchant and pithy attacks on the Union earned him lasting American enmity. "The miserablist idiocy of the whole," Ruskin wrote to Norton in 1863, "has been your mixing up a fight for dominion — (the most insolent and tyrannical — and the worst conducted, — in all history) — with a *soi disant* fight for liberty." Ruskin believed that the North erred by making the question of slavery into one of right and wrong, since this institution simply constituted an "inherent, natural, and eternal inheritance of a large portion of the human race." Unable to ignore such profound differences about the meaning of the American conflict, he concluded that any further correspondence with Norton would be impossible. Continuing to discuss what Ruskin considered a deeply misconceived and unexpectedly sanguinary Union effort would be "just as if I saw you washing your hands in blood, and whistling."[64]

The scrambling of earlier associations set the basis for a new self-consciously liberal alliance that would last far longer than the 1860s. Some elements of a liberal connection were already in place, and in these instances, the war simply reaffirmed and deepened antebellum ties. Thomas Hughes, the Christian Socialist, popular author (of *Tom Brown's Schooldays*), and editor of the British edition of the *Biglow Papers*, assured Lowell in the summer of 1861 that "all that is soundest & noblest in England is sympathizing with you in your great struggle" and urged him not to "judge by newspapers or magazines" the British temper. While Lowell appreciated this gesture and hailed Hughes's stead-fastness, the American remained convinced that Britons more generally were hostile to the United States and grasped that the country would largely be judged through the press. The relatively small number of Union supporters found outlets in publications like *Macmillan's* (where most of Hughes's Ameri-can writings appeared) and in the *London Daily News* (which featured the letters of E. L. Godkin, among others). Such venues might have provided evidence of important moral support but were ill suited for rectifying the prosouthern tilt of the far more powerful voices of the *Times*, the *Saturday Review*, the estab-lished quarterlies, and Walter Bagehot's *Economist*.[65]

The impetus for new, more potent ties between Union friends on both sides of the ocean was related to the growing appreciation for the impact of public opinion within the North. Curtis and Norton reached out to and celebrated such staunch Union supporters as John Bright and Richard Cobden, the two leading northern sympathizers in Parliament early in the war, and did their best to broadcast the writings of leading French liberals such as Count Agénor de Gasparin and Édouard Laboulaye. The differences in age and in tempera-ment with these older men prevented the development of meaningful personal relationships, however, and most of the wartime collaboration ended in 1865. Far more lasting ties developed with a younger set of associates who shared the Americans' aspirations for combining national leadership with cosmopolitan literary engagement. A network of liberal intellectuals took shape over time and had its most lasting form in Godkin's decision to make a permanent home in the United States and to edit the *Nation* magazine. In the 1860s, Godkin's future importance could hardly be imagined, however, and his efforts were seen as no more or less significant than the writings of such better-known young travelers as Edward Dicey and Henry Yates Thompson. The most valuable sup-port for the cause came from the renowned John Stuart Mill. He was a figure of immense importance to a rising generation of young British thinkers, and his path inspired others to follow their conscience and to take pride in the mi-nority status of Union supporter.[66]

Mill's early and active interest in the American conflict came at a time when much of the British public was deeply skeptical about Lincoln's intentions re-garding emancipation. Mill's analysis of "The Contest in America" declared that even if the Lincoln administration was overly hesitant, an immense moral gulf separated the democratic North from the proslavery South. This article, which first appeared in *Fraser's* early in 1862 and was then reprinted in *Harper's Monthly* and as a separate pamphlet, drew extended commentary from American intellectuals. Mill's "curiously-accurate appreciation of all the delicate distinctions of our system" and "exact agreement with the views of the wisest men among ourselves" thrilled Curtis, as did Mill's attack on British hypocrisy. Among the most satisfying parts of his essay was its assault on the disturbing retreat, evident in some of the "most powerful journals," from Britain's historic antislavery commitment. Mill attributed this retreat to the influence of "West Indian opinions and interests" (referring to the former Caribbean ties of *Times* editor John Delane) and to an "inbred Toryism" that was eternally suspicious of liberty. Mill's private correspondence also echoed American convictions about the world historical significance of the war. On the same day that the Union won the battle of Antietam, Mill assured American historian John Lothrop Motley, "if you come well and honourably thru one of the severest trials which a nation has ever undergone, the whole futurity of mankind will assume a brighter aspect. If not, it will for some time to come be very much darkened." [67]

Mill's bracing analysis of the Civil War helped to bolster the Union cause in Britain by inspiring others to publicize their growing sympathy for the North. Support for Lincoln remained a minority opinion, however, and in mid-1862, *Harper's Weekly* still expressed regret at what it called the "mysterious incapacity of intelligent Englishmen, as a body, to understand the American question." Promising signs of change came in the middle of that year, when the publishing office of the Harper Brothers received a new book by the Irish political economist John Elliot Cairnes, *The Slave Power: Its Character, Career, and Probable Designs*. Curtis seized the book and devoured "most of it in their office that morning," subsequently considering himself the "first trans-Atlantic reader" of the most striking analysis to date of slavery's central place in the American Civil War. Curtis realized the importance of a leading British thinker devoting his systematic efforts to the slavery question, especially since Cairnes combined moral insights with the perspective of political economy to argue against slavery's territorial spread. Cairnes contended that the expansionist nature of bound labor had made Confederate secession all but inevitable. This logic supported his claim that the Union was standing up to the aggressions of southern masters. Curtis immediately passed this new foreign commentary to his mother-in-law, Sarah Shaw, who struck up an active and friendly correspondence with its author. Curtis then began to write directly to Cairnes to express how much the "truly patriotic and intelligent American public" appreciated his firm support.[68]

One aspect of *The Slave Power* troubled Curtis, however, and prevented him from doing even more to assure its American circulation. Cairnes originally believed that the slave power's dominance might be best overturned through disunion and the subsequent isolation of bondage rather than the forcible suppression of rebellion by Union arms. Through his letters, Curtis undertook to disabuse Cairnes of this stance and gradually nudged him toward a more consistent Unionist position. "The only proper parallel," Curtis argued to the Irish professor, "would be that of certain counties of England taking up arms against the imperial Government to avoid a prospective injury to the increase of a wrong which outraged the conscience of mankind." In later writings, Cairnes reversed himself on this key point and argued that emancipation required the forcible return of federal authority over the entire slave South. He remained an active force within British circles for coordinating Union efforts, and his status within the pro-Union intelligentsia came to be only slightly lower than that of Mill, who became Cairnes's regular correspondent during this period. Cairnes's faith in New England antislavery grew as his friendship with the Shaw and Curtis families deepened. By naming his son Robert Gould Shaw Cairnes, he gave a transatlantic dimension to the Brahmin tributes to the martyred son and brother-in-law of his newfound American friends.[69]

By 1863, Lincoln's Emancipation Proclamation gave a clarity of purpose to Union supporters, as did the Gettysburg Address, delivered a few months after important federal military victories in Pennsylvania and at Vicksburg. Pro-Union British liberals were emboldened by these successive advances, and a flow of new recruits to the Union cause helped to replace the initial sense of gloom and isolation with hopeful resolve about how America's future might initiate an age of global progress. Some of the most committed Union supporters traveled to the United States to witness efforts to secure freedom and to vindicate popular government. These enthusiastic visitors included a young Cambridge don, Leslie Stephen, who in 1863 carried letters from Thomas Hughes and from Edward Dicey, Stephen's cousin who had recently returned from the United States. Such connections gained Stephen access to Lowell's Elmwood home in Cambridge, where during a two-night stay he established an immediate rapport with both Lowell and Norton. Lowell and Stephen "got so very thick together" over their mutual interest in politics and literature that Stephen later returned for a full week before he sailed for Britain. The pair quickly discovered their shared love of walking, tobacco, and mild irreverence, and they parted fast friends. Hughes was as delighted as he was unsurprised that Lowell had cottoned to Stephen, his latest "consignment," and affirmed that although Stephen had been "very sound in his views when he went out," he had come "back an enthusiast about New England & abolition."[70]

Stephen's American friends were charmed by his character and impressed with his range of ties to other British reformers, writers, and thinkers. His antislavery inclinations stemmed as much from his family heritage as from his New England trip, however, since his grandfather, James Stephen, had been one of the most important antislavery British administrators prior to the Caribbean Mighty Experiment. Stephen also had sound Cambridge University connections, though these led to the same revolt against spiritual coercion in which Clough had participated at Oxford. Of even greater significance was Stephen's rising presence in the world of British higher journalism. After returning from America, Stephen turned his polemical style toward vindicating the Union and lambasting the *Times*, proving that here was a friend who could score points within those most anti-American of all Victorian intellectual venues. Though still in his twenties during his American visit, Stephen soon established himself as a key member of the late-nineteenth-century clerisy, sealing his future reputation as an "eminent Victorian" by marrying the daughter of William Makepeace Thackeray, spending much of his adult life editing the *Dictionary of National Biography*, and siring several children, including a daughter named Virginia, who grew up to become one of the most celebrated modern writers known by the name she assumed after marrying Leonard Woolf.[71]

A year after Leslie Stephen's visit, Norton hosted an equally intriguing and effective pro-Union advocate when Goldwin Smith made the first of countless Atlantic crossings. Smith was nearly a decade older than Stephen and had already achieved one of Oxbridge's most prestigious posts by holding the Regius Professorship of Modern History at Oxford University. Smith had been a writer for the *Saturday Review* (to which Stephen, following his brother, FitzJames Stephen, also contributed after his return), and had begun a series of essays that would establish his reputation as a critic of empire and a supporter of political devolution. These stances might have led Smith to voice pro-Confederate sympathies, but despite his initial hesitancy and his lack of meaningful ties to the British antislavery movement, he became an enthusiastic supporter of the Union after Lincoln issued his preliminary Emancipation Proclamation late in 1862. Smith's first pro-Union article, published anonymously in response to this measure, produced an immediate sensation. Mill, who made a point of sharing Smith's identity with his correspondents, hailed the column as "one of the most powerful and most thorough pieces of writing in [the Union's] defence that has yet appeared." Smith followed this effort with a string of others, including a thorough refutation of recent British attempts to defend slavery as a biblical institution. *Harper's Weekly* quickly began to include him on its list of the "firm, intelligent, and active . . . body of friends" in Europe. Norton began to notice Smith's work in the *North American Review* and the Loyal Publication Society and then initiated personal communications with him with the help of Leslie Stephen and Elizabeth Gaskell. When Smith finally arrived at the Nortons' Shady Hill, the two men immediately hit it off, finding themselves "talking as men talk when they really have something to say and something to learn from each other."[72]

The interchanges between Goldwin Smith and his American friends were a good deal more serious than the easy bantering back and forth that marked the transatlantic ties of Leslie Stephen and Thomas Hughes. In his first letter to Norton late in 1863, Smith described the war for the Union as not only a "good cause" but the "most momentous perhaps, in the issues it involves, for which the blood of man was ever shed." The demise of slavery represented an important beginning, but there was even more to come, he realized. "In its train" would fall the "reactionary influence of the European governments on your Continent," thus making America "in deed and truth, a new world, the scene of new hopes for man." Norton was eager to take the cue and reply in a similarly exalted vein. In one of several nods to Smith, Norton explained to readers of the *North American Review* that the "suppression of the aristocratic and despotic Rebellion of the slaveholders will in itself be the defeat of our foreign enemies" and that "our triumph will be shared by our foreign friends, who are fighting the battle of liberal principles and equal rights in the Old World." Union victory would be an "argument for free popular government to which there can be no demurrer."[73]

Smith used his public appearances in the United States to present the Civil War as a proxy struggle between inherited privilege and democracy, which he noted echoed the forces of liberation and reaction that had begun with the fight of Royalists and republicans during the Cromwellian period. He explained to a Boston audience that "it is rather against the Liberals of England than against you that the feeling of our aristocracy is directed." This contention did not constitute mere flattery but instead showed a growing awareness of how a program of liberal reform developed by the progressive representatives of intellect might transcend national boundaries. The high point of Smith's visit was the 1864 election, which assured him that even an emergency could not disrupt a popular commitment that voters hold leaders to account. Smith's American experiences profoundly affected his development, shaping what he wrote in the

1860s in *Macmillan's Magazine*. They eventually enticed him to leave the Old World for good in 1867, after which he chose to spend nearly all the rest of his life in either the United States or Canada.[74]

Curtis hosted Smith, Stephen, and other British liberals when they visited New York City but took a less sustained interest in developing intimate friendships with these newcomers, either out of inclination or simply because his duties for *Harper's* monopolized his time. Yet despite his failure to cultivate particular intimacy, Curtis played a crucial role in publicizing eminent British intellectuals' support for the North. Late in 1863, Curtis explained in *Harper's Weekly* that supporters such as Mill, Cairnes, and Smith "clearly comprehend the origin and scope of the war" and "spare no effort to enlighten the public mind around them." While the British public as a whole remained hostile to America, it had become clear that "no country torn by war ever had so firm, intelligent, and active a body of friends in another country as the United States now have in England." The band of steadfast allies constituted a reproach to what Curtis called the "feeble flings of Carlyle, the thundering falsehoods of the *Times*, the shrill chorus of abuse from the lesser press, and the long-continued, contemptuous 'neutrality' of the Government." Friends' advocacy served as an antidote to the "passionate hatred of the Union, and maudlin sympathy with a rebellion to establish slavery," Curtis continued, noting that

> while such friends do such work for our cause we have no right to speak of "England" as hostile. For they speak the thought of the leading minds of England. They forecast its future. And it is for their sake, for their tried and true friendship for us, that every loyal American is bound to do all he can by temperate criticism and forbearance, not indeed sparing the sharpest censure of the venal falsehood of the British press, and the meanness of the British Government, to lessen the chances of war between America and England.[75]

Curtis's attempt to separate an "intelligent" and "friendly" England from the rest of the country formed part of a larger trend. The other Unionist intellectuals thought in similarly dichotomous terms both during and after the war, constructing a distinctly transatlantic and liberal notion of "two Englands" that had little to do with Benjamin Disraeli's earlier contrast between the rich and poor. Lowell urged his fellow Americans to remember, even in the press of war, that "England is not the England only of snobs who dread the democracy they do not comprehend" but also the "England of history, of heroes, statesmen, and poets, whose names are dear, and their influence as salutary to us as to her." This England, Americans were unwilling to give up.[76]

Lowell hinted at how much the United States shared with this England and warned that tensions should not end Americans' openness to foreign criticism. "If the result of the present estrangement between the two countries is to make us insensible to the value of British opinion," he explained, "in matters where it gives us the judgment of an impartial and cultivated outsider, if we are to shut ourselves out from the advantages of English culture, the loss will be ours and not theirs." He may well have had in mind his ability to internalize the critique of Charles Dickens twenty years earlier when most Americans rejected the novelist's scorn as a matter of instinct.[77]

Lowell's private correspondence, however, showed his difficulties in remaining open to foreign taunts. Surviving letters bristle with an unmistakable Anglophobia that he summed up when he wrote to Sarah Shaw in 1861, "I shall never feel toward England again as I have been wont to feel. Suppose she is our mother, can't we hate her?" Even liberal allies such as Goldwin Smith did not change Lowell's mind. Writing to Norton in 1865, Lowell argued that a handful of pro-Union Britons could not remedy the underlying hostility between the two countries. These newest allies were "not England and never will be." At war's end, he was thoroughly convinced "that England is an idea, that America is another, that they are innately hostile, and that they will fight us one of these days." A full year after hostilities ended, Lowell opened a letter to Leslie Stephen by noting an "almost invincible repugnance to writing again to England." In harboring this grudge, Lowell insisted that he was no different from the "great body of my countrymen." This was "a bitterness (half resentment and half regret) which I cannot yet get over." By 1869, he was ready to render this attitude in lasting form and to move on by writing one of his most famous essays, "On a Certain Condescension in Foreigners." The primary impetus for England's "condescension" toward America, he argued in this piece, was the country's fear and loathing of American democracy, which only intensified after Union victory. The United States had proved that a "democracy . . . could fight for an abstraction" and that its citizens "held life and goods cheap compared with that larger life which we call country." Such an experience, he gloated, constituted nothing less than the "nightmare of the Old World taking upon itself flesh and blood, turning out to be substance and not dream."[78]

The gradual passing of Lowell's anger toward Britain was part of a personal rapprochement, aided by increasingly meaningful friendships with Stephen, Hughes, and others across the Atlantic. These British liberals soon helped to set things right by struggling for liberal principles against entrenched forces of reaction. In this fight they expected—and received—support from Americans whose cause they had recently aided. Lowell's change of attitude toward Britain (and, by extension, Europe) helped revive his internationalist principles and in turn established the basis for his postwar career as a leading diplomat. He remained proud, however, that America had "conquered the *Old World*" in 1865, as he put it in a letter to Norton at the time. Such a display of national strength was followed by efforts to refashion former enemies in Americans' image. In the immediate aftermath of war, this mission was most evident in the case of southern Reconstruction. But the same demand that conquest be turned to influence operated in the conviction that American events would help shape European politics. As Lowell put it in 1865, "our example and our ideas" would not simply inspire future generations at home but would also "react more powerfully than ever on the Old World, and the consequence of a rebellion, aimed at the natural equality of all men, will be to hasten incalculably the progress of equalization over the whole earth."[79]

The Liberal High Tide
and Educative Democracy

To me it seems that our two countries, on the whole the two most advanced countries of the world, have just successfully emerged from a crisis essentially similar, though by much the gravest and most trying in the US; which has shaken up and dislocated old prejudices, set the stagnant waters flowing, and the most certain consequence of which is that all the fundamental problems of politics and society, so long smothered by general indolence and apathy, will surge up and demand better solutions than they have ever yet obtained.
John Stuart Mill to Ralph Waldo Emerson, 1867

"It is not simply the triumph of American democracy that we rejoice over," the inaugural issue of the *Nation* proclaimed in the summer of 1865, "but the triumph of democratic principles everywhere." This new weekly journal of liberal opinion announced its arrival by noting that the "effects of the revolution through which we are now passing upon European politics" would likely surpass the global ramifications of the American Revolution itself. Reformers in Great Britain and France had clearly understood that the fate of the Union was linked to the prospects for democracy within their own countries. With the coming of peace, the move for even broader changes would be invigorated. Those who had launched the *Nation* were ready to play their part in bringing about a new order. As 1866 opened, the editors had become even more assured that the "guns that announced the downfall of the Confederacy announced not only that the civil war was over, but that modern society had entered on a new path."[1]

By the fall of 1867, such high hopes seemed to be on their way to fulfillment. John Stuart Mill, who kept up with American affairs through subscriptions to both the *Nation* and the *North American Review*, shared his understanding of this moment in a letter to Ralph Waldo Emerson. For Mill to reach out to Emerson was itself significant, since both thinkers had expressed considerable ambivalence about each other's countries and the consequences of transatlantic exchange. Emerson had called on American scholars to cast off Old World influences and had kept some distance from the "mother country" even in his relatively admiring *English Traits* (1855). Mill's aversion to American conformity and the supremacy of a potentially despotic "public opinion" had developed at least since his reading of Tocqueville. His introduction to Emerson in the 1830s had not helped: the British Utilitarian had found the slightly younger Massachusetts Transcendentalist unimpressive. For much of the 1840s and 1850s, Mill had downplayed the New World's positive example and warned of the harm that "Americanization" might pose to liberal principles and individual freedom. His assessment had changed by 1867, however, primarily because of New England leadership in abolishing slavery and containing the worldwide spirit of reaction.

Mill not only proclaimed to Emerson that the two men's countries had "just successfully emerged from a crisis essentially similar" but went on to speculate about how Anglo-Americans who had weathered the storm should ready themselves to overcome the stagnation that he still regarded as the "primary source of almost all social evils." The new mission, he predicted, "will make a most serious demand upon the energies of all cultivated minds, to obtain for thoughts which are not obvious at first sight, their just share of influence among the crowd of notions plausible but false or only half true."[2]

This global mission to establish new truths and to keep progress on track would be the work of a new generation of "cultivated minds" who heeded the example of Mill, Emerson, and other men of letters committed to the greater good. The challenge of making cultivation itself democratic would be taken up by liberal thinkers in Britain and the United States who worked to spread intelligence and culture more widely than even they might have earlier thought possible. At the same time, this new generation of thinkers worked to institutionalize the means for rendering permanent their endeavors in politics and in culture. This generation took earlier strains of thought and, inspired by a sense of civic commitment, worked toward a transatlantic liberal synthesis of broadly edifying culture. If the first half of the 1860s laid the basis for this alliance, the second half of the decade marked its high tide. Facing up to immediate challenges would involve considerable effort. From these activities would come a new understanding of how cultivation might be achieved within the context of mass democracy. In this, the Emersonian principles of self-development and duty would be mediated by what, for the Americans at least, was a heightened awareness of Millian principles of active citizenship and educative democracy.

The Tide Is Turning in Favor of Liberalism

In 1865, amid the "high patriotic exultation" of Union victory, George William Curtis offered yet one more salute to the North's "foreign friends." The triumph of such allies over the "doubts and hostility and ignorance of the ruling class" in Europe earned both thanks and congratulations from Americans, Curtis insisted. With peace came the time for all who had participated in the good fight to step back and consider what the "events of the last four years" had meant. The war years had shown that "all believers in a true popular government, enlightened and just, whether they advocate its claims by eloquent tongues or vindicate its power by irresistible arms, and in whatever country they live," were members of the "great liberal party of the world." Such a vanguard was destined to achieve even greater successes in time, since in their care the "interests of civil order and peaceful progress" were now entrusted.[3]

Curtis's tribute revealed a subtle but significant clue about how his cohort experienced the transition from the war for the Union into the period of postwar Reconstruction. The kinship that had developed with "foreign friends" of a precarious war effort had become by 1865 a self-conscious alliance that focused a considerable part of its attention beyond American borders. The war had not simply vindicated democracy or assured the permanence of the United States; it had demonstrated that a "great liberal party of the world" could overcome menacing illiberal forces that threatened to block further enlightenment, progress, and fair dealing with the powerless. Relief as much as joy accompanied this outcome, as Goldwin Smith explained when he described to his new friend Charles Eliot Norton the catastrophic results Confederate victory would have brought. "English Liberals have just cause to be thankful for the heroic constancy and still more heroic self-control of the American people," he wrote, explaining that "if you had failed in the war, the boast of the reactionary party here would have been fulfilled, and the Liberals would have been completely defeated." But the Union had not failed. "'Conservative Reaction' [was] at an end," Smith pronounced, and he and other university-based liberal reformers now had a chance to remake Great Britain in their image.[4]

It became an article of faith among liberals during the early years of American Reconstruction that a global wave of liberal progress was cresting and that its first landfall would be Britain. The *Nation* magazine revisited this point again and again, claiming that the "tide is turning in favor of liberalism with resistless force." The liberal spirit that the *Nation* had in mind consisted of a number of distinct elements. As the postwar program materialized, its lead-

ing features included a shared commitment to racial "fair play," suffrage expansion, and religious pluralism. The pursuit of these immediate goals would
lead to a common understanding of how the work of molding public opinion
could be part of a larger system of educative democracy. The liberal high tide
was defined at the time not just by its program or its ideals, however, but also
by the underlying sense of momentum. Who liberals were, whom they fought,
and what brought them together was more important in this period than at any
other time.[5]

Despite the regular predictions of continuing progress, the liberal alliance
of Anglo-American intellectuals faced considerable challenges between 1865
and 1870. The forces of illiberalism remained strong in both the Old and New
Worlds, capable of producing considerable mischief even when they were on
the defensive, as was clearly the case in this crucial half decade of activity.
Compounding this challenge were persistent Anglo-American tensions, which
mocked the achievement in 1866 of the long-awaited transatlantic telegraph.
Neither greater ease of communication nor the increasing volume of transatlantic travel could itself ease the rancor between Britain and the United
States that had emerged during the Civil War. Antagonisms kindled during
war resurfaced in the American Congress, in the British Parliament, and in the
press of both countries. A new set of polarizing issues emerged as Irish American Fenians mounted raids into Canada and the U.S. government demanded
that Great Britain provide compensation for damages to U.S. shipping caused
by the *Alabama*, a Confederate warship that had been constructed in Liverpool.
Understanding that such tensions undermined their collaboration toward progressive goals, liberals worked to alleviate hostilities in the diplomatic arena
as well as in seemingly unrelated areas of politics, culture, and even personal
relationships.[6]

While Anglo-American liberals desired greater international understanding, they also shared the ambition of leading their respective countries through
rapid programs of nationalization. Such aspirations were explained in two informal manifestos set forth by Henry Adams and John Morley, each of whom
combined a sense of generational inheritance with a conviction that national
harmony and power could best be nurtured within a cosmopolitan frame of reference. Adams made his pronouncement in 1863, when he was cultivating his
own set of British associates through the American legation. In a letter to his
brother, then serving in the Union Army, Adams explained that the two might
soon become part of a "national set of young men like ourselves or better." Such
a set was destined to "start new influences not only in politics, but in litera-

ture, in law, in society, and throughout the whole social organism of the country—a national school of our own generation." Four years later, John Morley
testified on the eve of his first trip to the United States that the "extreme advanced party is likely for the future to have on its side the most high cultivated
intellect in the nation." Through force of example these "brains" would combine with democratic "numbers" to effect immediate change and to become
the "influential and governing power thirty years hence."[7]

Liberal men of letters in each country understood their national missions
differently, even if the two groups revealed similar combinations of ambition,
self-importance, and naïveté. While both groups hoped to overcome domestic divisions, the challenge facing Americans at the conclusion of a civil war
was clearly more critical. Easing the bitterness that existed between wartime
enemies in the Union and the former Confederacy was crucial, even if most of
the key American liberals believed that this accommodation must not come at
the expense of vindicating and extending the rights of former slaves. The four
million freedpeople had, after all, stood by the nation in the time of its greatest crisis. A nationalizing influence that consolidated the wartime victory thus
became the preferred program for most of the members of this cohort, who
self-consciously identified with the radical wing of the Republican Party during Reconstruction. But the challenges liberals faced in America were further
aggravated by the absence of a clear intellectual, political, and cultural center comparable to London or Paris (as Henry Adams had lamented in imagining a "national school" of young men). The *Nation*, which joined older venues
such as the *Atlantic* and the *North American Review*, embodied the aspirations
of the American liberals in its name and marked the historical distinctiveness
of this postwar generation. The new weekly combined a roster of New England
and British contributors with those from Philadelphia and New York while
locating itself in Manhattan, which was quickly becoming the undisputed center of American publishing. Organized within the North, the magazine, especially at an early stage, carefully focused on what was then transpiring in the
postemancipation South.[8]

When British liberals spoke of representing or influencing the "whole nation," they also did so as a self-consciously advanced segment of an established
party. Their political base of operations was the Liberal Party, which had been
formed at roughly the same time that the American Republican Party had
come into being. Their challenge involved not regional reconciliation or racial
uplift within the body politic but a program of rectifying troubling social cleav-
ages. Much of the energy of British "advanced liberalism" focused on making

the United Kingdom less segmented along lines of class and religion. Morley, Goldwin Smith, Leslie Stephen, and others wanted to make the ancient universities, Parliament, and the press more inclusive of dissenters and the "respectable" working class than had traditionally been the case. These reformers believed themselves specially suited to speak for the nation largely because, like the Americans, they simply assumed that the nation, if fully enfranchised and enlightened, would agree with them. Their advanced principles were confirmed by their advocacy of the American Union, but they were also invigorated by recent imports from Continental sources (especially the perspectives of Auguste Comte) and by their championing of movements for national liberation (as long as they did not, as in the case of the proslavery Confederacy, compromise deeper liberal principles).[9]

The national mission embraced by these two sets of liberals included an attempt to involve their countries in dialogue with the rest of the world. In this way, the cultivation of personal ties with foreign friends was not just a means to an end but an end in itself. Young British liberals yearned to understand how the United States operated, just as the Americans believed that progress at home would be enhanced by knowledge of British and European developments. These transatlantic ties thus became part of the larger project to rejuvenate and to elevate public life by making it more cosmopolitan. The networks that made such cosmopolitanism possible depended on international travel and correspondence, just as had earlier been the case. In addition to these familiar forms of interaction came a new concern in the late 1860s with joint ventures and initiatives that might overcome some of the traditional barriers between recognizably "American" and "British" manifestations of public opinion.

Relationships forged in wartime provided a sure foundation for the personal web of connections. Norton's steady exchange of letters with Stephen, Godkin, and Smith sustained their relationships, as did the more sporadic correspondence that Smith and Curtis established and continued until Curtis's death. If Lowell was at times a less reliable correspondent, he made up for it as a welcoming host who gave a series of British visitors in 1870 a glimpse of American life that would in time have profound echoes. After offering his hospitality to the young Liberals James Bryce and A. V. Dicey (a cousin of Leslie Stephen), Lowell met in person with his friendly correspondent Thomas Hughes for the first time at Elmwood that fall. Hughes proved to Lowell that he was "as frank and hearty and natural a dear good fellow as could be wished." When it came time for them to part, Lowell commented that it was like "saying goodbye to sunshine." Luckily for both men, Lowell's future diplomatic career allowed him to spend a considerable period of time in Europe in the 1870s and 1880s, when Hughes as well as Stephen, Bryce, and Dicey would reciprocate the hospitality.[10]

If public achievements and concerns first produced many of these friendships, personal achievements and tragedies sustained them. The death of Norton's thirty-four-year-old wife, Susan, in 1872 led him to include Stephen in his innermost circle of confidantes. Norton could discuss the "most important matters of thought" with Stephen during long walks through London. These "important matters" largely revolved around religion, as both men were moving away from their parents' traditional faith. So close had they become that Stephen wondered "why should I, a good Briton, find my most sympathetic friend in a Yankee, and find him only to lose him again so soon." When it was time for Norton to return to the United States, Stephen denounced the "cussedness of the universe in putting you and me on opposite sides of the Atlantic." As a token of their closeness and intellectual sympathy, Stephen dedicated his book, *Essays on Freethinking and Plainspeaking*, to Norton. The two had discussed the volume in drafts; Norton believed it to be the "clearest and most definitive statement yet made of the attitude of the thought of serious men who reject the old religion, and of their view of morality, duty, and life." A few years later, Norton provided guidance and support to a grieving Stephen, whose first wife died in 1875.[11]

Norton's liberal interests and penchant for meaningful friendships helped him to immerse himself in British politics between 1867 and 1872, when he enjoyed an extended residence in Europe. Leaving America only after concluding that Reconstruction was on the right path, Norton spent five years nurturing an intense and lasting distaste for Tory conservatism, which only made his ties with John Stuart Mill (at whose home he dined) more lasting.[12] Shortly before Norton left the United States, Godkin had tried to arrange a visit between Norton and John Morley, who had recently become the editor of the *Fortnightly Review*. Godkin noted that in hosting Morley, Norton would have the satisfaction of "knowing that nearly all the statesmen of the new regime in England have passed through your hands." A change in Morley's schedule meant that the two men did not meet until 1869, but they soon found themselves enjoying long conversations on "religion, Utilitarianism, the modern view of Morals, political opinions in England, and the United States." In "belief and opinion I agree him with him more nearly than with most men," Norton wrote in his journal, noting that Morley was "altogether a worthy disciple of Mill." Norton's ties to Morley resulted directly from a lasting friendship with the radical

Comtist Frederic Harrison, who lived in the same Kent neighborhood where Norton and his family took a house. Harrison later recalled his impression of Norton in this period, remarking on his "perfectly open mind, ready to weigh any new view, political, social, or artistic, and yet not at all ready to pronounce judgment without a probing kind of criticism all his own." For his part, Norton found Harrison "by far the ablest" of those "younger men who have lately been taking a part in public affairs." [13]

Thomas Wentworth Higginson's orientation toward Europe experienced the most dramatic change during the Reconstruction period, when he began his first significant interaction with British figures. Higginson had shown less interest than his fellow New Englanders in developing transatlantic ties during the antebellum years, despite his intimate acquaintance with European literature and ideas. His outlook began to change when he moved in 1864 from Worcester, Massachusetts, to Newport, Rhode Island, a coastal resort that drew what Higginson would later describe as a "constant procession of foreign visitors." Higginson made a distinct impression on such advanced British liberals as Lord and Lady Amberley in 1867. In 1870, Higginson struck up valuable friendships with Dicey, Bryce, and Hughes, which served as important facilitators during Higginson's first two trips to Europe in 1872 and 1877. Higginson's reputation as a colonel and a writer had by this point eclipsed his reputation as an antislavery radical, and he was eager to supplement his visits to reformers and politicians such as the Irish Home-Ruler Justin McCarthy and William Gladstone with literary discussions with the likes of Thomas Carlyle. Higginson even managed to arrange an overnight stay with Charles Darwin, who had already become an intimate of Norton (whose sister-in-law had married Darwin's brother). [14]

As a liberal cohort was knit together through travel, correspondence, evolving friendship, and similar cultural styles, these men sought to give institutional form to Anglo-American cultural exchanges. Thomas Hughes was among the first to suggest moving beyond specific reform ties, which had long existed in antislavery, temperance, and other reform circles. "I look forward with intense longing to a real alliance such as there should be between our countries," he wrote to Lowell in 1865. "We want sadly better knowledge of each other," he admitted, suggesting that the best way to rectify this ignorance was to establish an "Anglo-American Committee" that would "cultivate a more intimate knowledge of your politics & specially of all questions at issue between us." A similar organization in the United States "would be equally useful," he continued, "for your folk in general are quite as ignorant as ours." Among the few activities of Hughes's group was its hosting of Higginson in 1872. The effort never really got off the ground, and Hughes realized that a more effective way for Britain to explain itself to America was for him to write "letters or articles on our goings on & thinkings for one of your papers or periodicals." [15]

Henry Yates Thompson undertook a more elaborate if no more successful effort to formalize the emerging Anglo-American ties within the liberal alliance. The effort began in 1866 when Thompson, a recent graduate of Cambridge and the son of a wealthy Liverpool banker, offered to endow a biennial lectureship at his old university on the "History and Political Institutions of the United States of America." Thompson fit the liberal profile quite well, even if he never gained the stature of some of his contemporaries. He had made the requisite liberal pilgrimage to the United States during the Civil War and had spent a good deal of his time with Norton (preferring the strong "abolitionist" views heard at Shady Hill to the comparatively lukewarm sentiments of his hosts, the Edward Everett family).[16] After returning home, Thompson stood unsuccessfully as a Liberal candidate for Parliament in 1865, when Mill, Hughes, and Henry Fawcett were elected. Impressed both by the American people and by the ignorance of his fellow Britons concerning them and determined to correct this ignorance, he proposed that Harvard University appoint a lecturer to teach at Cambridge. Such a transatlantic lectureship might prod Harvard to reciprocate with a lecturer in "English history and English institutions." Together, these positions would "promote an intelligent appreciation of the character and institutions of each country by the educated men of the other." [17]

Although the Cambridge Senate ultimately rejected Thompson's plan, it generated an extensive debate that dramatized what liberals faced in attempting to displace an older and more entrenched establishment within British intellectual life. From the beginning of this project, Thompson realized the possibility of a political backlash from those who would condemn the exchange as a "sort of democratic propaganda." When public discussion of the proposal took place early in 1866 at meetings and through the interchange of pamphlets, the controversy replicated divisions caused by the Civil War. The combined influence of the Anglican Church, the Tories, and other parts of "respectable society" worked to defeat the proposal, which was backed by a much smaller band of self-proclaimed liberals. Before the college Senate voted on the question in February, one opponent questioned the choice of Harvard as a worthy representative of the United States and countered that the school stood for nothing as much as the tyranny and "zeal for an Anti-South idea" that had led to the outbreak of war. "That College," Edward Dodd declared, "is in Cambridge, which is a suburb of Boston, the chief city of a pragmatical little state, which by its literary influences has done more than perhaps any other State in the Union, to soak a continent with blood."[18]

If the memory of the Civil War loomed over the Cambridge lectureship debate, so too did the prospect of a liberal tide crashing onto British shores. At a moment of admitted political turbulence and amid calls to expand the suffrage, the possibility that Cambridge lecture halls might feature, in the words of one opponent, "eloquent panegyrics on the advantages and superiority of a democratic over all other forms of government" seemed a dangerous proposition. If the program had been proposed as "merely a luxury for matured M.A.s, perhaps no harm might result," but for undergraduates, H. R. Bailey of St. John's College concluded, the risk was too great. The Senate needed to be careful lest approval of the lectureship "be construed into an opinion favourable to the Reform Bill."[19]

Leslie Stephen tried to rally enthusiasm, and he was especially pleased with rumors that the first lecturer might be none other than James Russell Lowell. Lowell scoffed at opponents' fears even though the affair clearly piqued him. He complained to Stephen that although he understood that "England *can't* like America, do what she or we will," he saw "no particular use in her taking every opportunity to *tell* us how disagreeable and vulgar we are." Norton and Curtis refused to leave their exasperation to private reflections and published detailed explanations of the proposal and its outcome as way to bolster the nascent liberal alliance. In an 1865 article for the *Nation*, Norton mocked the "heated vision" of one leading opponent by whimsically imagining a Harvard "lecturer, like the tempter at the ear of Eve, instilling the dangerous words of seductive democracy into the hearts of the rising aristocracy." He chastised the anti-intellectualism implicit in the opposition, arguing that resistance to new or different ideas by their suppression seemed wholly unbecoming a "great and venerable university." Such a spirit, he concluded, was "worthy of the darkest age of intellectual weakness and moral decrepitude." Curtis took a similar approach in *Harper's Monthly*, defending Thompson as a "liberal of the best kind," who, "in common with Mr. Mill, Mr. Bright, Goldwin Smith, Professor Cairnes, and our other truest English friends," simply desired the "educated youth of England" to become more familiar with American principles and institutions.[20]

The most jarring aspect of this tempest for Americans came from one of the lectureship's supporters, the novelist and historian Charles Kingsley, who had supported the Confederacy and would soon lead a campaign to defend from prosecution the disgraced governor of Jamaica, Edward Eyre. Kingsley publicly asserted that the refined community of Harvard gentlemen was feeling "swamped by the lower elements of a vast democracy" and as a result had "withdrawn more and more from public life, in order to preserve its own purity and self-respect." This characterization, coming as it did from a member of a Tory Party he had come to hold in contempt, especially irked Norton, who used his piece in the *Nation* to insist that, far from composing "that wretched class of fainéants and dilettantes, ruined by European associations and traditions, who withdraw themselves from public life," Harvard men formed a body of patriotic and devoted public servants who conceived of their duty in explicitly public terms. Kingsley's assumption that educated men feared democracy and thus were withdrawing "more and more from public life" offended Norton and his liberal friends, especially at the precise moment that they championed democracy and sought to establish their public role as opinion shapers. Far from looking to the Britain of tradition and conservatism for support in some rearguard action, the American liberals saw themselves allied with British Liberals as agents for change and progress. If the only way to achieve closer communion with Britain was to stress conservatism, the end was not worth seeking.[21]

Goldwin Smith might have predicted this outcome at Cambridge, since he had railed against a similarly insular Oxford for nearly a decade. Smith's gathering dissatisfaction with the conditions of intellectual debate at the leading British universities played a key role in his resignation from the Regius Professorship in 1867, a step that allowed him to join the faculty of the upstart Cornell University in Ithaca, New York. This was a major coup for the young college, and it helped to focus public attention on an institution that would become a prime breeding ground for postwar liberal endeavors. Smith's presence helped to bring lectures from Lowell and Curtis, among others, though Smith's restlessness (and perhaps his expressed dislike of Ithaca's waterfalls) convinced him to resign in 1871, never again to hold an academic assignment. By this point, Cornell's early vitality had been overshadowed by the excitement associated with Harvard, which undertook its transformation into a research university with the appointment of Charles W. Eliot in 1869. Eliot's ties with British liberals helped the college assume a greater profile, as did his decision to make his cousin, Charles Eliot Norton, the first American professor of fine arts in 1872. Thereafter Harvard offered its undergraduates a variety of what Oxonians had enjoyed from John Ruskin's lectures as the Slade Professor of Fine Arts beginning in 1869.

Despite these glimmers, universities would be a less important embodiment of the liberal alliances during the high tide than would the steadily evolving world of Anglo-American "higher journalism." Godkin's editorship of the *Nation* assured that Britons and Americans would inhabit the same world of print, and from these heady years henceforth the writings of Godkin, Norton, and other Americans appeared side by side with a regular column on British politics by Stephen and subsequently by Bryce and A. V. Dicey. Cross-fertilization of transatlantic reform could be seen in other venues, whether in Hughes's letters to the *New York Daily Tribune* beginning in 1866, Stephen's and Smith's contributions to the *North American Review*, or the perspective that Norton provided in Morley's *Fortnightly*. As each of these examples suggested, transatlantic liberal reform was a community of words as much as friendship, and in this realm the interpenetration of national cultures reached its highest level of intensity. In print, liberal politics would flourish, just as liberal culture had. In print as well, the conceptual defense of educative democratic citizenship would be both articulated and exemplified.

The Total Overthrow of the Spirit of Caste

By 1863, Charles Eliot Norton had begun to tell American readers that the "great question for this nation to solve" was nothing more nor less than the "old, the tiresome, the heretofore ill-answered question of the position and treatment of the black race." He was speaking for radical Republicans more generally when he suggested the need to overthrow Americans' system of racial caste, and he would continue this plea with even greater insistence during Reconstruction. While Republicans devoted much of their attention to post-emancipation southern society, they were aware that illiberal racism was hardly confined to areas south of the Mason-Dixon Line or even to the United States. Norton believed that failing to address this problem would represent an abdication of national duty. "The lesson of the Rebellion is but half learned," Norton wrote, "unless we resolve that henceforth there shall be no fatal division between our consciences, our principles, our theories, and our treatment of the black race." [22]

Where Norton saw duty and conscience, his friend George William Curtis saw the chance for an inspiring national mission, which he characteristically approached as part of a larger international struggle. Curtis made African American rights an increasingly important topic in *Harper's Weekly* and campaigned for black suffrage during his unsuccessful 1864 bid for Congress. The initial unpopularity of this cause did not deter him; he believed that this "good fight" would be just as successful and ennobling as the early antislavery campaign had been. When the war was barely a year old, Curtis dismissed plans for colonizing former slaves outside the United States, arguing that the "notion of getting rid of the laborers at the South because their skin is black is merely a revival of the old prejudices of race which induced so many European nations for several centuries to enact penal laws against Jews and heretics." Efforts to "unlearn this silly, unchristian nonsense" of white supremacy would allow America to set itself apart from Old World corruptions, he continued, and might even help the country realize its "destiny, in the world's progress." This destiny involved an effort to "show that an educated and humane people can rise superior to prejudices which have proved an insuperable obstacle to the besotted planters of the West India Islands." By war's end, Curtis had come to frame the issue in still grander terms, insisting that the "part assigned to this country in the Good Fight of Man is the total overthrow of the spirit of caste."[23]

Events of the immediate postwar period showed that racial prejudice was not an exclusively American phenomenon, even if white hatred of African Americans had reached new levels of bitterness in the New World. European persecution of despised religious outsiders and the incomplete justice provided to former British slaves after their emancipation revealed to the liberals the seemingly universal tendency of the powerful to brutalize the weak. This larger frame of reference came into focus late in 1865, when Americans and Britons simultaneously experienced how the oppression of "darker races" corrupted their respective countries' highest ideals. The liberal consensus that developed in these years insisted that cultivated advancement should be made available to all humans regardless of their outward physical differences. This insistence built on earlier antislavery commitments, which in turn drew from both Christian and Enlightenment ideals of universal humanity and brotherhood. It also deployed a newer Victorian language of "fair play" and reasoned toleration that persisted as a liberal idea through the end of the century.

The liberal critique of racial caste was based on a preference for universal truth over irrational feelings and a sense that reactionary forces depended on popular prejudices in their attempt to compromise the common good. As Lowell had put it in the 1840s, there was something "ludicrous" in founding a "patent of nobility" on "no better distinction than an accidental difference in the secreting vessels of the skin." Diagnosing the issue in these terms allowed Victorian intellectuals to skirt the question of African American difference, which they tended to minimize more than to reject categorically. According to the liberal consensus that emerged, racism did more than discriminate against individuals: it corrupted those who acted on its assumptions, eroded more general social ties, and blocked the United States from realizing its core commitment to human equality. Gaining freedom from a debilitating prejudice had been a means of affirming personal tolerance since the antebellum period, when the surest sign of racial progressiveness was allegiance to the antislavery cause. More practical occasions to display a principled opposition to caste at times presented themselves to northerners, including Higginson and Lowell's unsuccessful effort to enlist Frederick Douglass in the Town and Country Club.[24]

By the time of the Civil War, the emerging Victorian preoccupation with ethnology made race a topic for intellectual consideration, pushing it beyond questions of reform politics and club memberships. As this new science gained credibility, even Lowell sensed that he was becoming "quite a German in respect of Race," though he was eager to have his belief in "that easy formula" ("tempting as it is easy") challenged by the likes of the British historian T. H. Buckle, who claimed that there was "no such thing as hereditary propensities" and instead emphasized the role of institutions in historical development. Lowell's ambivalence signaled a powerful trend evident at Harvard, where the Swiss-born scientist Louis Agassiz fostered an avowedly racialist biology in the 1850s. Even within the circle of antislavery activists, no taboo existed against embracing the hard racial science then emerging in the mid-Victorian world. Theodore Parker, who was one of Thomas Wentworth Higginson's role models and friends, expressed extreme skepticism about African American capabilities both in his private musings and in his public considerations of race. Such intellectual differences were kept in check by a shared hostility to slavery, and the sectional battle kept New Englanders relatively united through the 1850s and into the American Civil War.[25]

A quite different pattern emerged within the British intelligentsia, where internal debates about the question of black "inferiority" became a critical fault line a full decade prior to the American Civil War. The developing alignments were solidified through a famous interchange between Thomas Carlyle and John Stuart Mill about whether England had mismanaged Caribbean emancipation during the mid-1830s. In 1849, just as much of the British public was coming to doubt the effectiveness of tropical free labor, Carlyle produced a biting polemic that satirically attacked the laziness of "Quashee" (as he called the archetypal Jamaican freedman) while skewering both sentimental philanthropy (a "Universal Abolition of Pain Association") and the "dismal science" of political economy. Mill was prodded to respond, motivated by the attack on economics as well as by Carlyle's sneering attitude toward humanitarianism. Highlighting his sober moralism, Mill accused Carlyle of doing the "Devil's work" by "flinging this missile, loaded with the weight of his reputation, into the abolitionist camp" and thus giving comfort to the recalcitrant American "owners of human flesh." Southern planters took satisfaction in Carlyle's assault on antislavery "cant," as did northern Democrats, who reprinted the essay in various forms over the next fifteen years. This sharp debate about black capacity anticipated the opposing stances Mill and Carlyle would take toward the American Civil War as well as staked out two competing visions about difference and human potential that would continue to clash throughout the century.[26]

Wartime northern attitudes toward black southern slaves were driven more by rapid developments in Union policy than by this international discourse about racialist science. No issue focused northern attention on questions of caste more than the enlistment of African American soldiers in the Union Army. Higginson was most intimately involved in this issue both in his service as a colonel of the first black regiment, the First South Carolina Volunteers, and in the series of letters he wrote vindicating African American heroism. Curtis, Norton, Lowell, and their newfound British allies shared Higginson's early and active support for black soldiers, albeit with less public fanfare. By the fall of 1862, Curtis had come to realize that "all our reverses, our despondence, our despair bring us to the inevitable issue. Shall not the blacks strive for their own freedom?" Within months of this pronouncement, his brother-in-law, Robert Gould Shaw, took command of the Massachusetts Fifty-fourth, the first black unit raised in the North. Norton believed that the existence of this regiment "smashes a good many of the eggs among which we have been picking our way so carefully,—eggs labelled slavery, proviso of the constitution, states rights, domestic institution, nigger equality, &c." Military service promised to be a key stage in African American development since, as Norton explained to the British writer Elizabeth Gaskell, the army would serve "as good a school [as] possible for educating the freed slaves into the independence & self-dependence of free citizens."[27]

Similar enthusiasm for black troops and for the cultivating effect of army life came from the Union's most steadfast British supporters. John Elliot Cairnes and John Stuart Mill put greater emphasis on this development than did most foreign observers, in large part because of their interchange of letters with

Leslie Stephen, with George William Curtis, and with Curtis's mother-in-law. (They and other British liberals also followed Higginson's letters from the field, which the *London Daily News* republished). Cairnes admitted that his hopes for America "tend more and more to concentrate themselves upon this one point—the chance of elevating the negroes through military service"—than any other. He admitted that African Americans' patriotic loyalty to the Union surprised him and suggested that slavery must have "been less atrocious" than he supposed since it had not "crushed all manhood out of its victims." Mill was similarly impressed, marveling at the "admirable . . . tone and feeling" of an African American enlistment committee, which the *London Times* had snidely ridiculed. "Degraded and looked down upon as these people are said to be, their strongest feelings were not as negroes but as citizens and republicans," Mill wrote, adding that these men were stirred by the "idea that they were to fight for liberty, and humanity, and civilization." Mill was disappointed that his view was not more broadly shared by the British public, who should have hailed such "high-minded and heroic feelings" and appreciated them even more coming from a "despised and downtrodden race."[28]

During the early days of Reconstruction, what Curtis termed the "heroism, humanity, and unfailing fidelity" of black soldiers seemed the best proof of African Americans' "temper and capacity as freemen." Pledging the national government to protect equal political rights for blacks was nothing less than "our duty to the freedmen," made possible by their desire to help set the American republican experiment on a new course.[29] Higginson, a natural candidate for linking past military service with the questions of Reconstruction, laid out his views in an influential article for the *Atlantic Monthly*. He insisted that former slaves be granted "justice," which he considered simply the "first demand of every rational being." Having played a part in transforming slaves into soldiers, Higginson urged fellow Unionists to take the next step of assuring that "freedmen" became true "freemen." Northern whites should "avail ourselves of [the freedmen's] new-born self-reliance . . . while its first vigor lasts," he urged, "and guard against sacrificing those generous aspirations which are the basis of all our hope." Since time was of the essence, taking steps to "prepare" the former slaves for freedom mattered less than allowing them to exercise it with as few hindrances as possible.[30]

Higginson chose to title his preferred Reconstruction program in terms of "fair play," using a phrase that was becoming a standard liberal stance regarding vexing social and political controversies. This formula held radical potential by invoking notions of justice rather than of rights, as labor reformers and proponents of female suffrage realized in their attempt to invoke the language on their behalf. Higginson's hostility toward masters' "previous monopoly of the soil" (and his 1867 flirtation with the idea of large-scale southern property confiscation) showed what results might follow after northerners determined that southern whites were unwilling to practice fair play. Justice was clearly absent in their recalcitrant passage of Black Codes and in their quest to subordinate African Americans through extralegal violence and intimidation. The same formulation could also, however, legitimate the status quo, since once it seemed that equal "rules" were determined, free operation would sort winners from losers, as if in an athletic contest. As Higginson noted in this same piece, if "fair play" meant to "remove all the obstructions" in the freedman's path, it then meant "to let him alone." The elasticity of this phrase was as notable as its centrality, and over the ensuing few decades, American liberals acted on Curtis's personal intuition that "if we would morally define or paraphrase America, I think we should say Fair Play."[31]

The notion of fair play was implicitly international in that it was not moored to specific laws or national institutions, as became apparent late in 1865, when *Harper's Weekly* suggested that denying former slaves fair play might result in an American counterpart to the "reported horrors of Jamaica." The magazine was referring to the recent reports of a disturbance in Morant Bay that had prompted Governor Edward Eyre to impose martial law on the island's black population and to initiate one of this period's most heated controversies. In a series of repressive actions that lasted for several days, Eyre authorized the killing of more than four hundred black Jamaicans, the flogging of another six hundred, and the destruction of some thousand houses and farms. Most notorious was the execution, after a hasty court-martial, of the landowning mulatto leader George Gordon, who had been Eyre's main political rival in the colonial assembly. This crisis in Caribbean history had wide ramifications, not least for marking a pivotal moment in the history of British attitudes toward race relations. During the following three years, the debate over Eyre's conduct led to a deepening of the split between British supporters of the former Confederacy and those of the Union. The incident also escalated the sense among American and British liberals that in waging a common struggle against violent racialists, they had identified one of the most dangerous of all Victorian-era illiberalisms.[32]

Norton helped to shape the radical Republican interpretation of the Morant Bay atrocities in his last broadside for the New England Loyal Publication Society, which noted that while the initial violence "tend[s] to show the danger" of withholding political power from the former slaves, the white response proved former planters to be "as incapable of self-control and reasonable conduct as . . . the blacks." Other Republican publicists were quick to invoke Morant Bay as they rallied opposition to Andrew Johnson's planned restoration of white rule across the defeated Confederacy. Lowell set the example of Jamaica beside that of the bloody 1866 New Orleans riot, explaining that both events established the folly of leaving power in the "hands of men who would be more than human if they had not the prejudices and the resentment of caste." His remarks signaled an important shift as northern public attention slowly turned from the question of African Americans' capacities as a race to the political and moral incapacity of those whites whom racial animosity had driven to disorder. Even though imperial officials rather than resident planters bore responsibility for the Morant Bay repression, American liberals emphasized what *Harper's Weekly* called the "haughty injustice of the master class." The magazine took up the comparison shortly before congressional Republicans took control of Reconstruction, explaining that the main "lesson of Jamaica" was the "imperative duty of the United States at present to hold the freedmen firmly by the hand, and not to entrust them to those who hate them more than they love their own interest." [33]

The Jamaican events convinced Americans of the deep flaws in Britain's earlier attempt to ensure racial harmony. Their transatlantic rival's shortcomings hardly represented a new theme for Americans, of course. Lowell had linked British racism to its hostility to American democracy in his 1862 *Biglow Papers*, challenging John Bull to choose between the Confederacy's overt racism and the color-blind aspirations of what Lowell considered more truly American ideals:

> The South sayz, "Poor folks down!" John,
> An' "All men up!" say we, — White, yaller, black, an' brown, John:
> Now which is your idee?

The same year, Curtis expressed his hope that the Union would learn from the mistakes made in Jamaica, where there might be freedom but no "real peace." Amid the extreme violence of the Morant Bay affair, this perception of British racial shortcomings became newly relevant. By 1866, E. L. Godkin lamented "how deep-seated the feeling is down in the breasts of the best members of the Anglo-Saxon race, that crimes committed against an 'inferior race' are somehow less heinous than crimes committed against white men, and that even the

'British Constitution' loses some of its virtue when its protection is thrown over a negro."[34]

Goldwin Smith was more attuned than most to the connections between American Reconstruction and the Morant Bay violence, which he publicly called the "strange and fearful epilogue to the Civil War in America." During the summer of 1865, Smith had informed Norton that he regarded the "negro question" as "such a difficulty as perhaps has seldom occurred in politics before," even if he had "learnt by degrees to have almost unlimited faith in the practical sagacity of your nation" to reach a just and lasting solution to the most intractable issues. Eyre's actions convinced Smith that Britons could not wait for American initiative, however, but had to protect their national honor and translate popular outrage against Eyre into action. Vindicating Britain's reputation for justice and humanity across the color line required the prosecution before a court of law of the responsible Jamaican imperial officials. Smith appreciated the initial wave of popular disgust toward Eyre, noting in a letter to Norton that "we have again felt the inspiring example of your victory and the still more inspiring influence of the humanity with which it has been used." As other British liberals joined his efforts to bring Eyre to justice, Smith became increasingly convinced that the prosecution of Eyre would be nothing less than the "decisive test of our morality."[35]

The desire for fair play in the Eyre case inspired the formation of the Jamaica Committee, which was led and staffed primarily by the liberal intellectuals who had supported the Union as well as its turn toward emancipation. Mill and Thomas Hughes led the effort against Eyre in Parliament, where efforts to quell the controversy failed even after a royal commission gathered information following Eyre's removal from power. Leslie Stephen kept readers of the *Nation* informed about the progress of the Jamaica Committee, while John Bright, John Elliot Cairnes, A. V. Dicey, Goldwin Smith, and John Morley kept the case before the British public through lectures and essays. Leading scientists such as Charles Darwin, Charles Lyell, and Thomas Huxley also lent their efforts to the prosecution of Eyre, as did the Comtist Frederic Harrison. At the same time, John Ruskin, Thomas Carlyle, Charles Kingsley, and other supporters of the Confederacy formed an opposing committee intent on defending Eyre, a step that deepened the division among British men of letters over matters of racial justice. By February 1867, Leslie Stephen noted the controversy's pervasiveness, explaining that it was "scarcely possible to mention Governor Eyre's name at a London dinner-table without producing a storm."[36]

Some Britons feared that the Eyre case would permanently split the country between "negrophilites and anti-negroites," as the *Saturday Review* observed during the fall of 1866. Yet the respective camps' positions were shaped not just by their attitudes toward people of color. As the dispute became increasingly contentious, a broader range of disagreements arose over questions of what constituted true manliness, who was capable of intellectual leadership, and what these topics meant for the larger question of democratic change. Mill drew attention to the way in which the episode transcended matters of race when he recounted his service on the Jamaica Committee in his *Autobiography*. He admitted that "there was much more at stake than only justice to the negroes, imperative as was that consideration." According to Mill, the basic question was "whether the British dependencies, and eventually, perhaps, Great Britain itself, were to be under the government of law or of military license." Eyre's ultimate exoneration after a two-year effort to prosecute him thus had ominous ramifications for the future exercise of unregulated imperial force. The episode provided a number of negative examples that would be recalled in later years. One of the images likely to last came in a dispatch from Stephen in 1866, when he described remarks from an imperial official whose stated idea of "fun" was his work in "hanging negroes." *Nation* readers would have been especially outraged by this lieutenant's provocative taunt that "fair play is my motto and true blue is my colors."[37]

Even in America, coverage of the Jamaica controversy eventually focused less on postemancipation race relations than on the dangerously reactionary position taken by intellectuals such as Carlyle and Ruskin. It was hardly surprising, Curtis wrote, that men who had "sympathized with the bloody attempt of Slavery to overthrow our Government" would "think it perfectly right that unresisting people should be shot down at random by a fierce soldiery, and women be whipped with wires for supposed complicity in a supposed plot." The poet Alfred Tennyson's subsequent involvement was more upsetting, since his defense of Eyre caused the "deepest sorrow to thousands of generous hearts who have believed that his sympathy was sure for the most unfortunate race in history." Godkin thought Carlyle's behavior presented a "serious blow to the average morality"; combined with the "apostasy of Charles Kingsley" (who had already roiled the Americans during the Cambridge lectureship debates), such actions would hinder the "progress of liberal ideas." The larger threat seemed to be the public discrediting of men of letters as a group. As Eyre's champions continued "breathing out a scorn for the 'lower classes,' both black and white," Godkin thought that a reaction against intellect seemed likely, noting, "people say, and with good reason, if this is the kind of politician that cultivation makes, let us pray Heaven against it spreading."[38]

In this context, Carlyle came to eclipse Eyre as the most recognizable symbol of a corrupting and dehumanizing racism. The sage's reputation for illiberalism was sealed late in the summer of 1867 when he published a remarkable essay, "Shooting Niagara: And After?," that made even his 1849 "Negro Question" essay seem even tempered. Carlyle used the occasion to point out that "by far the notablest case of *Swarmery*, in these times" was the "late American War, with Settlement of the Nigger Question for result." His diatribe did more than any other piece of writing to link Union victory and emancipation during the Civil War, color-blind justice in the Eyre case, and what Carlyle considered the current Parliament's "inexpressibly delirious" support of "what it calls the 'Reform Measure.'" The article's main point was a castigation of the current push to expand the suffrage, which brought within the boundaries of metropolitan England the same philanthropic follies that had earlier applied only to more distant locales. Despite reformers' "cant," Carlyle believed that democracy meant simply the "calling in of new supplies of blockheadism, gullibility, bribeability, amenability to beer and balderdash, by way of amending the woes we have had from our previous supplies of that bad article."[39]

Carlyle's assault in "Shooting Niagara" completed his fall from favor among the American liberal intelligentsia. The *Nation* called the piece "pure rigmarole, the nonsense of a foolish and conceited old man, which, if written by a person unknown to fame, no intelligent writer would dream of wading through." When a reader complained about the lack of respect toward a recognized Victorian sage, Godkin shot back, "We believe that [Carlyle] is now using the influence he acquired in his earlier and better days to propagate opinions and justify practice which we consider to be immoral and barbarizing and the triumph of which would, in our opinion, be fatal to everything which makes this world worth living in." What the *Nation* hinted at, Lowell asserted unequivocally in a devastating review essay (provoked undoubtedly as much by Carlyle's hostility to the Union as by his support for Eyre). Carlyle's rantings, Lowell regretted, had ceased to be motivated by any faith in human potential or any hope of redemption. Misanthropy had curdled "warning" into mere "denunciation" and soured "remonstrance" into "scolding." Without humane conviction animating it, Lowell explained, criticism was useless: "Of what avail an apostle who shouts his message down the mouth of the pit to poor lost souls, whom he can positively assure only that it is impossible to get out?"[40]

If Carlyle's misanthropy repelled liberals, so too did his abandonment of

ideas in favor of physical strength. His validation of white supremacy seemed
the logical extension of his increasing worship of force and his tendency toward
an authoritarian hero worship that formed the antithesis of the liberal ideal.
He had become the "apostle of brute force," according to the *Nation*, believing that the "only true civilizers and elevators of mankind are the sword and
the whip." This change was all the more tragic, liberals believed, because Carlyle's early work had offered such powerful support for the spirituality of art
and nobility of duty. ("Let us cover the nakedness of our patriarch, and walk
away with eyes hidden," Curtis lamented.) Lowell acknowledged that although
Carlyle might have begun "by admiring the strength of character and purpose
and the manly self-denial which makes a humble fortune great by steadfast loyalty to duty," he was like a man addicted to "stimulants," who "must increase
his dose from day to day as the senses become dulled." He had now reached
the point where "mere strength has become such washy weakness that there
is no longer any titillation in it; and nothing short of downright violence will
rouse his nerves now to the needed excitement."[41]

Carlyle's illiberal attacks on racial "inferiors" and on democracy were most
pertinent during the 1860s, when they provided liberals a perfect foil for their
critical role and reform agenda. Carlyle's extreme pessimism, his assumption that men were really no more than monkeys, and his overall "disdain for
human nature" demonstrated the dangers of a criticism that aimed simply to
tear down rather than to elevate. Critics by necessity spoke unpopular and unpleasant truths, but constructive critics did so with a belief in the possibility
of reform. The absence of any reformist conviction made Carlyle's rants, in
Curtis's loaded words, "merely an ebullition of impotent cynicism." Further,
the Carlylean worship of force, especially in the aftermath of Americans' enormously costly Civil War, revealed the limits of violence as an agent of progressive change while serving to temper the emphasis that some Darwinians would
place on a "struggle for existence." This negative point of reference would again
become relevant before the end of the century, when a wave of Anglo-American
imperialism in the 1890s dramatized the corrupting effects of domination and
showed its particular dangers when imposed on imagined racial inferiors. Many
scholars have pointed out the pivotal role Carlyle played in initiating a period of
hard racism and brutal imperialism of late Victorian Britain, though American
men of letters made Carlyle a less important target of their anti-imperialism
than might have been expected. In the intervening decades, American liberals
put the worst parts of his career in the context of the best. For them, Carlyle
the brutalizer of "Shooting Niagara" remained a vital warning. But they could

not relinquish Carlyle the inspired prophet of *Sartor Resartus*, whose vindication of cultivated duty and aesthetic truth was simply too precious to reject.[42]

To Exercise Their Minds on the Great
Social and Political Questions

Predictions that Union victory would initiate a global wave of democracy seemed to be borne out in the spring of 1867, when within a matter of weeks American and British lawmakers restructured political power as few could have imagined just years earlier. The Congressional Reconstruction Act, passed in March, extended the vote to southern freedmen, assuring that they would be the first group of New World slaves to help set the political terms of a postemancipation settlement. The 1867 British Reform Act seemed almost as significant, at least to liberal observers. This measure both doubled the size of the electorate and demonstrated that Britain could not be insulated from the worldwide advance of popular government. With such transformations under way, even those who had criticized Thomas Carlyle recognized that these tremendous changes brought corresponding challenges.[43] Most Anglo-American liberals looked on this nearly simultaneous expansion of their electorates with a great deal of pride, even if a tinge of anxiety accompanied their optimism. For progressive men of letters, change itself was worthy of congratulation, since it assured that the world's two leading exemplars of liberal civilization would avoid the dangers of crippling stasis and subsequent declension. Leslie Stephen broadcast a prevailing view in the *Nation*, writing, in terms John Stuart Mill might have used, "We can only hope that the democratic deluge will at least put us in motion in some direction or another. Anything is better than sheer stagnation."[44]

American liberals first began their concerted push to expand suffrage across lines of race during the closing months of the war. Early in 1865, James Russell Lowell issued one of the strongest Republican cases for African American voting rights in the *North American Review*, a forum he knew would reach the cultivated American and foreign readers who seemed strongly in need of convincing. For Lowell, the developing program involved keeping faith with core national beliefs. "Our war has been carried on for the principles of democracy and a cardinal point of those principles is, that the only way in which to fit men for freedom is to make them free, the only way to teach them how to use political power is to give it them." Aware that some people still considered popular government unproven, Lowell argued, "If we are to try the experiment of democracy fairly, it must be tried in its fullest extent, and not half-way." Achieving the "fruit of our victory" over the proslavery aristocracy meant acting on the "everlasting validity of the theory of the Declaration of Independence." Nothing less than "Americanizing" the South would answer present needs, and it should be accomplished by "compelling [the South], if need be, to accept the idea, and with it the safety of democracy."[45]

Over the next year, as Lowell became more committed to equal black citizenship, he hailed the "inevitable advance of democracy" in ever more glowing terms. This "clumsy boy giant of popular government" might be "somewhat rude and raw as yet" and "not too well mannered," but America's democratic mission remained sublimely important: its "office" was "to make the world ready for the true second coming of Christ in the practical supremacy of his doctrine, and its incarnation, after so many centuries of burial, in the daily lives of men. We have been but dimly, if at all, conscious of the greatness of our errand, while we have already accomplished a part of it in bringing together the people of all nations to see each other no longer as aliens or enemies, but as equal partakers of the highest earthly dignity—a common manhood."[46]

The zeal that Lowell expressed for democracy in 1865 was confirmed by each of his closest associates, and together this cohort greeted Radical Reconstruction with as much enthusiasm as they had given to the war for the Union. Higginson echoed Lowell's sense of a sacred moment, exclaiming that "through a Red Sea which no one would have dared to contemplate, we have attained to the Promised Land." Norton was only slightly more subdued in expressing his hopes that a "perfect commonwealth might here become a reality." He was convinced that the "ductile and pliable" nature of the American system made it "able to fit itself to every new exigency" and that the wartime emphasis on reconciling the idea of freedom to reality might lead Americans to bring their government "into truer conformity to its principles." Curtis's postwar euphoria was every bit as palpable and even longer lasting. Into the early 1870s, he continued to celebrate the war's bestowal of a "clearer sense of the relations of morals and politics" and to proclaim that the "country was never more hopeful, never fuller of promise, than now."[47]

Support for postwar radicalism coexisted with a more sober recognition that majority rule did not always produce liberal results. A genuine danger lurked, for example, in allowing former Confederates to cast votes and gain popular majorities in the South, and the commitment to preventing a renewed rebellion led most Republicans to support the broad disfranchisement of those who had taken up arms against the Union. The mass of northern voters also exhibited signs of a potentially dangerous illiberalism, especially among those who were most hostile to the idea of black suffrage. This spirit showed, as Norton put it, the "meanness, the ignorance, the folly & the prejudice" of negrophobic Democrats and suggested to him the "unfitness of the majority to possess the very privilege which they deny to the negro." These "unfit" northern citizens were at fault primarily because of their unwillingness to reason, Norton believed, distinguishing between this irrational desire for the racial status quo and the comparatively superficial role that categories such as race or class (or gender) played in the developing liberal idea of popular government. As Lowell aptly put it, the "gist of the matter is in the dark mind and not in the more or less dusky skin." Specious fears about racial difference obscured the true basis of civic competency, Lowell later suggested, optimistically writing that the country was slowly coming to "set a greater value on the color of ideas than on the shades of complexion."[48]

The liberal trust in a sufficiently intelligent democracy developed from the North's wartime sacrifice and from its confidence that Americans were more broadly instructed than any other people in recorded history. The greatest threat during Reconstruction lay not in the lack of popular virtue or intelligence as much as in the dangerous possibility that the wrong sort of leader might unite the corrupted Copperheads of the North with the former rebels of the defeated Confederacy. Such a menace materialized in Andrew Johnson, whose style of leadership liberals found nearly the exact opposite of Lincoln's wise rule. Johnson's decision to take his case for immediate restoration of southern white political rights to northern voters in 1866 showed how easy staunch Unionism could be combined with populist racism. This combination became particularly insulting to liberals when Johnson paid homage to Lincoln's earlier nemesis, Stephen Douglas, the Illinois senator who had died in 1861. Johnson's tributes to this revered Democratic hero caused Curtis to speak out against a party whose leaders "reduced immorality in politics to a science." The popular flattery these men employed showed how they actually "despised" the people, appealing "only to their basest passions and poorest prejudices" rather than to the "deeper and purer springs of popular action." Using similar terms, Lowell recalled that Douglas had "habitually courted those weaknesses in the people which tend to degrade them into a populace, instead of appealing to the virtues that grow by use, and whose mere acknowledgment in a man in some sort ennobles him." Lincoln's faith that a "democracy can think" had transformed Americans into a thoughtful and reasoning citizenry. Taking sharp issue with Johnson's pose as the people's champion, Lowell concluded that "if such a man were the fairest outcome of Democracy, then is it indeed a wretched failure."[49]

British liberals also mixed explicit and enthusiastic advocacy of Radical Reconstruction with a sense of subdued concern, but they were more likely to dwell on the possibility that the training of former slaves for citizenship remained at an early stage. "Every man here whose judgment is worth a straw is for negro suffrage," Thomas Hughes assured Lowell, quickly adding a general preference for "any educational test you like applicable to the whole people, white & black." In *Macmillan's*, John Elliot Cairnes acknowledged that the "proposition to enfranchise at a stroke a whole race of men, but yesterday enslaved" would shock "even liberal politicians" in Britain, especially since the former slaves had been excluded from "every means of enlightenment." Yet Cairnes supported the radical policy, insisting that the "principle of caste in politics" rested on the weak foundation of scientific racism. He further noted that these theories of permanent black inferiority were undermined by black soldiers' courage and by their recent restraint during political gatherings, of which Cairnes had learned from E. L. Godkin's letters to the *London Daily News*. The antiblack hostility shown by former masters in Jamaica convinced him that only one solution existed: the "freedmen must be made the guardians of their own rights." Some French liberals also joined the postwar discussion. Wartime Union ally Count Gasparin lent his support to black suffrage, adding an important corollary when he argued that "in a country in which all men vote, he who is excluded by his race from voting, is no longer a man; or, if you prefer, he is an inferior man, branded with an indelible mark of incapacity, a pariah."[50]

The most striking aspect of such European sentiment was the comparative absence of the doubts expressed by earlier liberals toward American popular government. Tocqueville, Mill, and many who had followed their lead had produced a steady stream of commentary about the American tendency to entrust voters with power before they had proved themselves capable of virtuous, informed, and engaged citizenship. As late as 1860, Mill warned that emulating the United States would make the "political difficulties of the future" all but insurmountable and that Britons faced an "uphill race against time, for if the American form of democracy overtakes us first, the majority will no more relax their despotism than a single despot would." In this aside, Mill echoed the warnings about the danger to individuality that had been the predominant theme of *On Liberty*. He was already revealing what would cause his shift, however, when he acknowledged that popular government represented the future and that "our only chance was to come forward." Rather than resist progressive change (especially that which was all but preordained), Mill would initiate in *Considerations on Representative Government* a discussion about how safely to enfranchise popular power by constructing the most enlightened system of representative government possible. By war's end, though he still believed in the importance of an educational qualification, even he conceded that "at the present crisis the securing of equal political rights to the negro is paramount to all other considerations respecting the suffrage."[51]

An 1865 interchange between Charles Eliot Norton and E. L. Godkin revealed the tensions between American confidence in democracy as an element of national principle and the more cautious (and typical) European liberalism to which Godkin self-consciously subscribed. While the immediate occasion for their dialogue was Godkin's submission of his third major article for the *North American Review*, he and Norton soon found themselves arguing about Lowell's recent tribute to democracy. Godkin considered Lowell's pieces to be too "French" in logically deducing a "right" to vote rather than following the British Utilitarian tradition in evaluating what might produce the best ultimate results for the entire community. Godkin was wary of what might happen through the "proposed addition to the constituency of a million of liberated slaves at present in the lowest state of ignorance and degradation" and suggested that all freedmen have to pass both an educational or literacy test and a "moral" test to display their competence for voting and their "disposition to earn a livelihood or support a family by honest labor." He defended this position on black suffrage as highly principled. Citizens should not be denied the vote on the basis of skin color, he affirmed, but they also should not be granted it on that basis. Being motivated by a "sense of right" (Godkin here might well have used the equivalent phrase, "fair play") was no basis for granting the freedmen the vote, he continued, grumbling that they should not be "admitted to the franchise simply because they are blacks and have been badly treated" or "*because* this is a democracy and negroes are men." In his view, the freedman must "rebuke the presumption of his unfitness for it" raised by the fact of having suffered prolonged degradation as a slave.[52]

Godkin's hesitancy to embrace black suffrage may have been influenced by his Old World background, but it certainly placed him within the mainstream of northern opinion at the time.[53] Even so, Norton refused to publish the article without substantial revisions that would place it in advance of the prevailing Republican stance on this issue, indulging in what James Turner notes was a rare instance of editorial censorship on Norton's part. Norton wanted to ex-

plain himself, however, and did so by acknowledging that the issue "bristles
with difficulties" and that "objections" existed "to any & every plan concerning
the future status of the negro." Even so, he insisted that the best solution was
"that which is in nearest accordance with our democratic principles, — namely
to make [the freedman] a citizen in order that he may become worthy to be a
citizen." Any criteria for voting must be applied on an impartial basis, he reasoned, which would not single out the former slaves as necessarily less capable
than those exercising the right to vote prior to the war. Apparently impressed
by Norton's resolve (if not convinced by his principles), Godkin agreed to "recast all that I have said about the negroes, and put it in a shape which will not
clash with your own opinions and those of the *Review*." [54]

Godkin's agreement to publicly (if tepidly) affirm black voting rights helped
him to secure the editorship of the *Nation* that summer when Norton nomi-
nated him for the post. The position ultimately assured Godkin a far broader
reputation than almost certainly would otherwise have been the case. The cluster of articles that Godkin wrote for Norton's *North American Review* also constituted the key site where he staked out a difficult but crucial rhetorical position as a friendly critic of popular government, willing to discuss its faults as
well as its benefits with the aim of its ultimate vindication. Until the 1890s,
Godkin supplemented the regular round of commentary on events with more
philosophical reflections on the possibilities and limits of democracy. With considerable consistency, he continued to take it as a self-imposed duty to root
out what in 1865 he called "all the delusions" that were "current at present
amongst democrats and aristocrats here and in Europe, as to the real nature,
requirements, and consequences of a democratic form of government." [55] In
the immediate context of Reconstruction, this effort represented both a contribution to political thought and an attempt to impress on American readers
the responsibilities that came with voting, which Godkin believed were insuffi-
ciently appreciated. The article he revised for Norton showed his debt to Mill's
Considerations on Representative Government, explaining that the "steady cultivation, by every possible agency, of a feeling of responsibility to others than
ourselves for the use made of the franchise" would help American voters to
realize "a general advance towards the conscientious performance of this most
important of all our social duties." [56]

While Godkin applied the sensibilities of European liberalism to the American scene, he also self-consciously contributed to the debate over liberal democracy that was raging within Britain. His Reconstruction-era work as a correspondent for the *London Daily News* helped to sustain an acute awareness of

how the process of "Americanization" was extended during the heated struggle for parliamentary reform. In early 1867, as the move for reform was nearing its climax, Godkin predicted that "we are witnessing the last days even of constitutional monarchies" and that the "next century will probably see the whole Western world ruled by a numerical majority, exercising its power either through the medium of one man or of an elected assembly." He believed that the example of the United States should dispel the anxiety that many observers expressed about such a dramatic development. Far from a tyrannical interference in the affairs and opinions of the majority, Godkin asserted, American democracy had produced a country freer and more tolerant than any other. As "singular as it may seem," the United States was "of all countries in the civilized world, that in which the law meddles the least in a man's disposal of his possessions, in which religious worship is freest from legislative control or interference, and in which a man's religious or other opinions, his manners, his calling or mode of life, expose him to least reproach from his neighbors." Given this proven record of liberal democracy in practice, he charged that opponents of British reform expressed only their rank prejudice in warning of illiberal democracy in theory. Those hoping to direct affairs toward progress needed a new strategy that would trust large groups of properly instructed voters to be motivated by justice, a concern for the common good, and a respect for individual rights. The United States was again instructive since "religious toleration, the improvement in the condition of prisoners, the mitigation of the horrors of war, and a hundred other reforms" undertaken in the New World were "brought about, not by the direct agency of a few reformers, but by the success of reformers in persuading the majority into their way of thinking."[57]

Godkin's tribute to liberal democracy within the United States and to the American people's proven record of enlightened reform anticipated arguments set forth in *Essays on Reform*, which appeared just a few months later. The young university-based British liberals hoped that this volume would consolidate their standing as a distinctly progressive segment of the Victorian intelligentsia. From the outset, the contributors promised to show that the "demand for a more national Parliament is not a mere cry to which it would be folly and weakness to give way, or the expedient of a party anxious to attain power by the aid of popular agitation, but a conviction seriously entertained and capable of being supported by arguments worthy of the attention of those who wish to legislate deliberately and in an impartial spirit for the good of the whole people." Its guiding forces were some of the same pro-Union intellectuals who made up the Jamaica Committee, though in this forum the example of the United States was explicit rather than merely implied. Goldwin Smith, who had already applied his Civil War experience to the British call for reform, argued in "The Experience of the American Commonwealth" that most of the flaws associated with the United States were a result not of democracy but of the corrupting effects of slavery, mass immigration, and the "colonial" back-wardness of a culture whose greater refinement would come only with the pas-sage of time. Somewhat more defensively, Leslie Stephen similarly disputed the links between American flaws (which he acknowledged) and the system of popular government (which he predicted could be implemented with far greater success in a stable and enlightened country such as Britain).[58]

Hovering over these and other liberal defenses of democracy was John Stuart Mill's 1861 *Considerations on Representative Government*, a text that only in-creased in importance after Mill entered Parliament and thus became directly engaged in the debates over reform. Though the essay was burdened by several of Mill's well-known "crotchets" — and is often discussed only in this context — it gave philosophical utterance to the educative dimensions of democratic citi-zenship that would animate the transatlantic liberals' vision of popular govern-ment. Mill claimed that two central criteria came into play when judging the goodness of a form of government: to what extent it promoted the "virtue and intelligence" of the people, and how effectively it managed or administered the people's affairs.[59] Based on the first criterion, Mill certainly found represen-tative government — "that in which the sovereignty . . . is vested in the entire aggregate of the community" — to be the best form of government. But he had some concerns about how well democracy met the second criterion, and this is where the crotchets entered in. Mill contemplated a series of schemes to guar-antee that wise and intelligent people would play a large role in governing and thus ensure competence. These conceits ranged from electoral schemes (such as plural voting and proportional representation) to legislative proposals (sepa-rating deliberative bodies such as Parliament from narrowly technocratic ones like his "Commission of Legislation"). Critics from Mill's day to the present have often found these proposals at best bizarrely complicated and at worst "elitist" and undemocratic. But as they gained almost no traction among the young transatlantic liberals, they are of minimal interest here except perhaps as a reminder of the limits that national differences set on political discourse: while American liberals hardly questioned universal manhood suffrage, Brit-ish liberals hardly contemplated it.[60]

What did capture the young liberals' imagination was Mill's more general view of the educative nature of democratic citizenship. Popular government alone, Mill contended, encouraged the "moral and intellectual training" of the people, and this benefit provided its greatest justification. A good despot might be a competent and effective or even "virtuous and intelligent" ruler, but an enormous cost in squandered human potential resulted. The "thinking and active faculties" of the people would receive no stimulation under such a despot, and their "moral capacities" would be "equally stunted." Democracy appealed to Mill and the younger liberals because it cultivated the citizenry, and this educative dimension provided the primary rationale for broadening the franchise in the 1860s, as Mill urged from his seat in Parliament. As in the United States, where average citizens combined a striking patriotism with cultivated intelligence, enfranchising British "manual laborers" not only would give them a political voice in national affairs but also would assure them a noble "course of national education" through their direct involvement in political discussion, argument, and appeal.[61]

The younger liberals echoed Mill in their defenses of an expanded suffrage. A. V. Dicey insisted in his contribution to *Essays on Reform* that free government "rests ultimately on the conviction that a people gains more by the experience, than it loses by the errors, of liberty." James Bryce, who would shortly travel with Dicey to the United States, agreed that democracy had a "stimulating power such as belongs to no other form of government." While this future author of the *American Commonwealth* devoted much of the space allotted to his essay to correcting misperceptions about past historical democracies, he also hailed popular government for providing citizens a sense of fellowship and common purpose and for elevating the "humbler classes" through the enlargement of their "scope of vision and their sense of responsibility."[62]

The American liberals took note of *Essays on Reform* (quite possibly attaching to it even greater significance than it garnered within Britain). The book's appearance convinced Curtis that the "most intelligent and trained minds in England perceive the drift of the current" toward popular government. Curtis introduced the growing (if still cautious) British embrace of democracy to the mass readerships of *Harper's Weekly* and *Harper's New Monthly Magazine*. These outlets rendered foreign developments with broader brushstrokes than was the case in Godkin's *Nation*, where writers assumed a greater familiarity with the intricacies of British politics. Curtis had noted the first signs of British reform in 1864, when he drew attention to the British statesman William Gladstone's plea that "every man who is not presumably incapacitated by some consideration of personal unfitness or of political danger, is morally entitled to come within the pale of the constitution." Despite Gladstone's overt sympathy for the

Confederacy expressed just one year earlier, when he was chancellor of the exchequer, Curtis was now won over by what he called the "sagacity of a statesman who knows that whoever enlarges liberty, in any direction, is dear to the heart of man." By 1867, Curtis welcomed the "revolution in England" as a counterpart to American emancipation and equal rights, privately greeting the university-based authors of the *Essays on Reform* as the "foundations of a new England."[63]

Suffrage reform was most explicitly transatlantic in the case of women's rights, which John Stuart Mill noted had become the "badge of advanced liberalism" by the summer of 1867. His advanced position had made him the obvious ally when a group of British women's rights activists collected more than fifteen hundred names urging Parliament to extend suffrage to all householders regardless of sex. Mill presented the petition and then moved to strike the word "male" from the proposed reform bill, a motion that gained more votes than most observers had expected (earning a respectable 73 votes to 196 against). This showing inspired Curtis to predict that the enfranchisement of women in both countries was "as visible as when the blossom begins to set." Curtis subsequently had the chance to emulate Mill when serving as a delegate to the New York Constitutional Convention in the summer of 1867. That August he made an impassioned case for female suffrage that extended his antebellum commitments while conveying a newfound urgency that the United States match British progress in bringing fully half of the citizenry to equal political rights. Making the case at the state level was easier than pushing Congress to act, since staunch Republicans such as Curtis feared that conflicts between the rights of women and of African Americans might lead to a bitter schism and thus imperil the entire course of Reconstruction. Republican insistence that female suffrage be advanced only after winning black rights outraged activists such as Susan B. Anthony and Elizabeth Cady Stanton, who later blamed the "long years of apathy" on the failure to "settle the broad question of suffrage on its true basis while the people were still awake to its importance." Those who insisted on the priority of African American rights included Curtis and Higginson, who in 1870 helped to form the American Woman Suffrage Association as a pro-Republican (and more avowedly egalitarian) alternative to Anthony's organization.[64]

Earlier Victorian feminism had emerged in the cosmopolitan network of antislavery reform, and these roots were apparent in Curtis's attacks on the "usurpation of sex," which he (like Mill) considered the "last form of caste that lingers in our society." As Britain and the United States simultaneously undertook to establish a new basis for citizenship, advocates of women's rights recognized an unforeseen opportunity to make real strides toward overturning the all-male electorate, which they believed rested on the same irrational basis as did racial qualifications for voting. These efforts began what would be a fifty-year-long campaign in which female voting rights would be finally won in both Great Britain and the United States amid the crisis of World War I. Acknowledging the distance of that achievement, however, should not distract attention from the role that this stage of woman suffrage played in the history of transatlantic liberalism during a period of great change in the late 1860s. As part of the liberal high tide of democratic reform, the issue reaffirmed the more general theory of educative citizenship that endured even after some liberals' enthusiasm for woman suffrage waned.[65]

Mill's vindication of woman's suffrage rested in part on the educative effect of the ballot, thus giving a new dimension to the liberal advocacy of extending the vote to former male slaves and to British workingmen. While Mill admitted that not all women would participate if enfranchised, he reasoned that those who did "would experience that stimulus to their faculties, and that widening and liberalizing influence on their feelings and sympathies which the suffrage seldom fails to exert over every class that is admitted to a share in it." Mill urged other members of Parliament to support a measure that "holds out an inducement to one-half of the community to exercise their minds on the great social and political questions [and] causes the great influence they already possess to be exerted under the guidance of greater knowledge, and under a sense of responsibility." Though no longer serving in Parliament in 1869, Mill still saw signs of progress when women won the vote in municipal elections during the same year in which he published his influential *Subjection of Women*.[66]

Charles Eliot Norton's version of this rationale for female voting is especially noteworthy, given that he was neither a consistent and committed feminist like Curtis and Higginson nor a decided opponent of female suffrage, as Lowell, Goldwin Smith, and Frederic Harrison became in later years. Occupying his typical middle ground, Norton framed a quintessentially liberal stance in 1867 by insisting that "as in every other question of the extension of the suffrage," the real issue was "whether the education of the class seeking it has fitted the generality of the class for its wise exercise." In terms that recalled his argument for African American voting, Norton argued that performing the rights and duties of citizenship were the best civic education. "The mass of women will be made as fit to vote as the mass of men are," he calmly assured *Nation* readers, as soon as women were entrusted with the right, since exercising it would represent an "educational process." Since women still received less schooling than men, those pushing for woman's equality in the political sphere should work for a corresponding equality in the educational sphere. Rehearsing a familiar link between cultivated intelligence and citizenship, Norton insisted that "if the State does its duty in the matter of education [by making it compulsory], there need be no fear of the consequences of the admission of women to the elective franchise. With education and equality of political right, instead of losing loveliness and womanliness, [women] would . . . become more truly feminine, and be no longer the toy and the plaything, but the equal helpmate of man."[67]

Woman suffrage failed at the same moment that the freedmen and "respectable" British workingmen won the vote not because of the strength of the arguments against it but because of larger political currents. Contrary to the sometimes skewed perception of the American liberals, the principled positions taken during this period of constitutional reform constituted only one part of an uncertain political dynamic that in the case of Britain produced what one recent historian has called the "most unintentional revolution in the history of British politics."[68] In both countries, the adoption of major reforms owed its ultimate success largely to the ill-considered intransigence of key opponents. University liberals mobilized their energy by attacking the Liberal statesman Robert Lowe's renegade "Adullamites," just as Americans found their way forward by campaigning against Andrew Johnson's reactionary program. Johnson's initial position on the ticket with Lincoln meant that Johnson became easier to discredit only after he defected to an alliance with racist Democrats and southern whites.

The major achievements of the liberal high tide thus came through a haphazard and unpredictable process that depended on unforeseen contingencies at nearly every turn. Fundamental constitutional reform was not, however, the only product of the late 1860s worth taking into consideration. From the debates of these years, transatlantic liberals developed a new understanding of democratic politics and a sense of how it would (or should) best work. In concert, they had shown that in addition to pulling down old systems and preserving valued ideas, they could innovate with an eye to how the politics of the future might best operate. Looking out from this moment of reform, nothing seemed more important than implementing a sphere of print-based and colorblind reasoned discussion, a conception that had, during a period of rapid change, become the ideal model of democratic civic participation.

Modern Republicans Must Be Reading Republicans

In his 1867 reflections on female suffrage, Charles Eliot Norton noted that it was a "familiar truism which, however, loses no force through triteness, that education, meaning the cultivation of intelligence and character, is the only safeguard and secure foundation of a democracy in which universal suffrage prevails." If anything, this was not merely a liberal "truism." The notion that self-government depended on a citizenry "enlightened" through constant self-cultivation was more like a bedrock conviction that informed nearly every aspect of the transatlantic liberalism that emerged from the 1860s. This ideal model of popular government had roots in earlier experiences. But after the post–Civil War reforms, a view of educative democratic citizenship assumed new durability. The vision that resulted was coherent enough to inform the liberal reform movements in both culture and politics undertaken by Anglo-American men of letters through the early twentieth century.[69]

Differences of opinion existed about what sort of constitutional order would best produce an ideally educated citizenry. A debate that began in 1865 stretched all the way until 1869, when a clash over the Fifteenth Amendment marked a final stage of basic constitutional reform. At issue was whether educational tests remained a legitimate part of the American order or whether they should be eliminated along with suffrage restrictions based on race. During Congress's 1869 winter session (in the wake of Ulysses S. Grant's election as president), the Senate proposed a broad form of the amendment that would have overturned existing statutes (in Massachusetts and elsewhere) that required voters to demonstrate basic literacy. Curtis expressed a shared liberal ambivalence while discussing the issue in *Harper's Weekly*. He agreed with the aim of preventing future encroachment on black voting rights, though he was unsure whether educational or literacy tests in and of themselves should be banned. Godkin and Norton were more decided opponents of the attempt to bar such tests, and both men perceived the measure as a tacit assault on the basic idea of intelligence in politics. Yet even their reflections were tinged by an underlying note of equanimity. "If it should be carried," Norton wrote to Godkin when it seemed likely that the ban on educational requirements would pass, "we shall have to make universal, compulsory education the first aim in all our political efforts." Such an emphasis came naturally to Norton, who had long embraced education as a means of social uplift. His convictions were extended in the same spirit expressed by Britons such as Robert Lowe, who sup-

posedly greeted the passage of the 1867 Reform Bill he had opposed by declaring, "We must educate our masters."[70]

The debate over the Fifteenth Amendment was curtailed when it became
clear that the restrictive measure would be narrowly tailored to the use of race
as a disqualification. It was not the first time—nor would it be the last—that
Republican men of letters reflected on literacy requirements. Although members of this group insisted on educated politics, they were likely to consider
educational requirements in practice a hindrance rather than a help to achieving an informed electorate. This seemingly paradoxical conclusion stemmed
from their understanding of immediate incentives available to the main actors
in the defeated South. Lowell summed up this case in 1865 when he argued that
bringing the freedman into the body politic would give his former master the
"strongest inducement to educate and enlighten him." In contrast, "as a mere
proletary, his ignorance is a temptation to the stronger race," Lowell believed,
adding, "As a voter, it is a danger to them which it becomes their interest to remove." Shortly after the Morant Bay riot in Jamaica, Norton argued along the
same lines that if the extension of the vote to southern blacks depended on their
ability to pass an educational test, planters would retain power simply by doing
their best to perpetuate popular ignorance. Under such circumstances, Norton concluded, the "late slaves will be practically held as serfs, & will hardly
fare even as well as the blacks in Jamaica." Such earlier perspectives resurfaced during the 1869 debate over the final Reconstruction amendment, when
Curtis noted that "nothing will so surely secure general education as general
suffrage," with no restriction on who could vote.[71]

British liberals were as anxious as their American counterparts about how
an expanded electorate might or might not lead to a politics based on informed
discussion. Such concerns were evident in the disillusionment that several leading university Liberals expressed about the final form of the 1867 Reform Bill.
Disraeli's Conservative Party had implemented the bill after Gladstone's government had failed to carry it. With this shift ended the hopes of those who had
planned first to extend the vote to "intelligent artisans" already "fit" for active
citizenship and then to expand it as educational reforms worked to "lift up"
the remaining segments of the population. The *Nation* noted that Disraeli's
bold decision to push for a still broader "household suffrage" showed that
Tories had "stolen a march" by introducing a "large body of persons whom,
in their present state of intelligence, the Conservatives and the rich will be
able to buy or influence." Goldwin Smith wrote to Norton that Disraeli (whom
Smith would later denounce as the "plagiarist of reform") consciously sought

to "overwhelm the more enlightened artisans by the help of a rabble which they reckon on leading by intimidation and corruption." If the worst aspects of society were thus allowed to govern, Conservatism might have a new lease on life, Smith grumbled, and Britain might suffer from the same "rule of a combined oligarchy and rabble" that Americans faced from the wartime Copperhead movement.[72]

The key postreform objective for liberals in both countries was to assure that, as John Morley formulated the issue, "numbers" would follow "brains" in pursuing government policy according to liberal and enlightened principles. In practice, Americans were more interested in equipping these "numbers" with "brains" and in removing from the political process any impediments to popular reason and the intelligence of individual voters. This goal led Americans to construct a normative vision of the ideal American citizen that was comparable to but by no means interchangeable with the model citizen that Catherine Hall and other historians have traced to the reform debates within Great Britain. Liberal Americans would imagine the normative voter as exercising mental faculties through reading, focusing on a process that transcended the ascriptive categories of race and gender that had marked the political nation's boundaries prior to the Civil War. This idea of a reading citizenry had consequences not just for who might be enfranchised but also for what sort of deliberative structures and what style of leadership would be most useful in cultivating American democracy in the aftermath of the liberal high tide.[73]

Godkin conveyed this normative understanding of civic life by contrasting the United States to ancient Athens (not coincidentally one of John Stuart Mill's favorite points of reference in discussing democratic governance). In an early Reconstruction article for the *North American Review* that examined Mill's *Considerations on Representative Government*, Godkin described the ancient practice of gathering in large public spaces, like the agora, where citizens discussed public questions with one another, exchanging opinions and being exposed to the "most enlightened men" in the community. As a result of this practice, a "Greek or a Roman might have been a very intelligent and well-informed man, without knowing one letter from the other."[74]

A large modern republic such as the United States could no longer gather all its citizens together, but Godkin pointed to the newspaper as a "modern equivalent" of the Greek agora and the "only means by which the citizens of a free state can either interchange their opinions or concert plans of political action." This fundamental difference between ancient and modern republics therefore placed a high premium on the ability to read. On this basis, Godkin proposed an impartial, nonracial literacy test as a precondition for the franchise:

> A people who cannot read in modern times becomes the blind tool of an educated few, as naturally as sheep become the prey of wolves. The ability to read is not only the best attainable indication of general intelligence, but the only proof, constituted as society now is, which a man can offer of his fitness to follow or take part in various political discussions of the day, and to possess himself of the facts and arguments necessary to the formation of anything worthy of the name of a judgment on any public measure or public man.[75]

Godkin's sharp warning revealed that the liberals' print-based conception of politics contained notably restrictive dimensions, which would be echoed in the infamous literacy and educational requirements enacted by several states over the last decades of the nineteenth century. As the historian Alexander Keyssar has shown, such measures became the "most popular method of constricting the electorate" during the Gilded Age. As a result of such later developments, it has been tempting to see original liberal qualms about illiterate democracy as signaling a covert plan for later retreat.[76] From this vantage point, Godkin's Reconstruction-era proposal of a literacy test helped to perpetuate what had been the classical republican fear of voters—the concern that a lack of independence (whether in property or in capacity for thought) made the votes of society's most vulnerable citizens susceptible to demagogic control. Keeping the "wrong" elements out of the system seemed to be the main consequence of this linkage, an interpretation that might appear to compromise the liberals' stated enthusiasm for admitting average citizens into the body politic.

Yet unlike later restrictionists, liberals saw literacy as an indispensable (and fundamentally empowering) path to meaningful political participation rather than as a tool of disempowerment. An illiterate voter labored, Godkin observed, "for all political purposes, under mental incapacity" and stood "towards the rest of the citizens very much in the position in which a deaf mute must have stood in Greece." The educative dimensions of democratic citizenship required access to discussion, argument, and opinion, all of which now occurred in print and without which liberals believed voters were effectively disfranchised (as well as dangerous). "Modern republicans must be reading republicans," Godkin insisted in a private letter to the Reverend Henry Bellows in 1867, even going so far as to assert that an "ignorant citizen" was "but one degree removed from a traitor or alien enemy." While Godkin's revealing rhetorical slip (from "illiterate" to "ignorant") certainly registered his larger ambivalence about universal suffrage, his reaction stemmed as much from past experience as from any future threats, especially what he considered the illiberal political subjection of the undereducated white South. "The rebellion was the fruit of ignorance," the *Nation* declared, reasoning that the leaders of the Confederacy "have been able to do what they have done simply because the vast majority of the Southern whites were unable to read the newspapers." Curtis put it more succinctly: "The schoolmaster might have saved us the war."[77]

In his public writings, Godkin emphasized a more positive conception of a reading citizenry, and he did so not only because this approach was more palatable to his audience. In 1869, for example, he argued that educational tests were more likely to endanger aristocracy than to lead to aristocratic exclusion. As proof of this assertion, Godkin pointed out that southern whites always preferred race or property restrictions to educational tests. "By keeping [the voter] ignorant they keep him poor, degraded, and easily managed, and yet get the use of his vote for themselves, without the trouble of arguing with him or convincing him." With universal education and a literate citizenry capable of independent thought and political discussion, such trickery would no longer be possible. In fact, "universal suffrage without education is notoriously the very best basis in existence for absolute or aristocratic rule, because by making people believe they are sharing in the government . . . it prevents discontent, and makes exactions of all sorts safe." An educational requirement, conversely, would enrage those it excluded, thus providing a powerful stimulus to their self-education. They would then enter the political arena with a sense of injury, a sharpened wit, and most importantly, the "idea firmly implanted in them that knowledge ought to rule—an idea which, once it takes hold of a community, makes caste impossible, and distinctions based on color or creed ridiculous."[78]

In short, print-based discursive politics appealed to liberals more for its genuinely democratizing tendencies than for its potential for exclusions. Attention to the advisability of a reading requirement was often overshadowed by liberal reflection about how the mass circulation of newspapers allowed for national and international deliberation. In the same article that discussed the modern agora of print, Godkin exuberantly described how the "newspaper brings the voter in Kansas into almost as close and intimate communion with the voter in New York, as if they met in the market place." He might well have noted that the same system, as his experience made clear, linked people and events in Jamaica, London, and Albany, New York. Lowell, still more enthralled by this system of rapid communication and the "certain metropolitan temper" it lent Americans, offered a lyrical tribute:

One man sitting at the keyboard of the telegraph in Washington sets the chords vibrating to the same tune from sea to sea, and this simultaneousness, this unanimity, deepens national consciousness and intensifies popular emotion. Every man feels himself a part, sensitive and sympathetic, of this vast organism, a partner in its life or death. . . . It is no trifling manner that thirty millions of men should be thinking the same thought and feeling the same pang at the same moment of time, and that these vast parallels of latitude should become a neighborhood more intimate than many a country village.

Such a network held out tremendous possibilities for the future, Lowell continued, since the "newspaper and the telegraph gather the whole nation into a vast town meeting, where every one hears the affairs of the country discussed, and where the better judgment is pretty sure to make itself valid at last. . . . It is this mental and moral stimulus which gives [Americans] the alertness and vivacity, the wide-awakeness of temperament, characteristic of dwellers in great cities, and which has been remarked on by English tourists as if it were a kind of physiological transformation."[79]

This conceptual restructuring of the polity had implications for the men who would present themselves as critical guides through these national and international communication networks. The experience of popular action during the Civil War had caused some liberal observers to doubt whether elected leaders really still counted as much as had formerly been the case.[80] As the people themselves replaced officeholders as the driving force of policy, the prospects for intellectual leadership increased, although not merely any intellectual representative would do. The clash that continued to play out between Carlyle and Mill in the 1860s provided Americans no less than Britons with an important point of reference in solidifying an emerging understanding of how men of letters might best achieve the liberal cultivation of democracy.

At the heart of liberals' objections to Carlyle lay his injunction that "silence is the eternal duty of man." At a time when liberals were coming to distrust Carlyle's version of the heroic oracle and to associate it with the most noxious forms of modern reaction, Curtis drew attention to this fallacy and used it as a negative example to frame a deeper conception of how discussion, democracy, and liberty were mutually reinforcing. "If England and America are indeed the finest countries in the world, they are so because of speech and not of silence," he wrote. What assured these two countries' greatness was the tendency to "invite every man to say his say; to out with it, and not repress and suppress until the forces which can not always be more and more restrained explode the whole system of things into chaos." The "silent" countries existed among the stultifying tyrannies of Asia and Africa, Curtis claimed, and Bismarck and other European reactionaries were heeding that example while trying to govern without broad deliberation. With the controversy over slavery in mind, Curtis added, "in this country, too, we had a system that imposed silence. Speech was as fatal to it as a spark to gunpowder." He followed this string of examples with a summation: "Speech is the salvation of civilization; and in every country we say better foolish speech than none at all, for the liberty of speech and nothing else secures the peaceful progress of society."[81]

By emphasizing discussion (as mediated through widely disseminated print), American liberals revealed the common ground they shared with Mill's conception of popular government. As recent scholars have pointed out, Mill elaborated his devotion to public discussion both in his theoretical writings (especially his *Considerations on Representative Government*) and in the parliamentary example he set during the mid-1860s. His stint as a member of Parliament centered more on words delivered on the floor and outside on the stump than on the advocacy of a particular set of legislative proposals. His political style of public moralism held wide appeal despite the fact that many of his supporters admitted that he was neither a skilled orator nor an especially effective political strategist. The key to his example lay in the clarity of principles that hearers and readers of speeches could glean through careful consideration. To talk to the country through consistently sound published words, to initiate discussion of difficult topics, in itself constituted reform. Through this means, the true national sovereign, the reading citizenry of each country, journeyed toward a better future.[82]

American liberals articulated in the 1860s a vision that they would work the rest of their lives to achieve. The transatlantic faith in educative democracy all but assured that their primary public influence would come through print. Skilled orators such as Higginson and Curtis might periodically continue to travel the lecture circuit, but the print media would give wide airing to their pleas for national cultivation. What each member of this larger cohort discussed would vary in the decades that followed the liberal high tide. Some attended to what Godkin in 1869 termed the "Prospect of Political Art." Others were more likely to establish themselves in the realms of culture. Together, they undertook a collective project framed for a nation freed and united by the bracing experiences of the 1860s. The challenge that lay ahead was achieving comparable progress after the inspiration of sacrifice had passed, the pace of change had slowed, and Americans had embraced peace among themselves and with the rest of the world.[83]

Liberal Culture in a Gilded Age

*Culture is the training and finishing of the whole man, until he sees physical
demands to be merely secondary, and pursues science and art as objects of intrinsic worth. . . .
When this impulse takes the form of a reactionary distrust of the whole spirit of the age, it is
unhealthy and morbid. In its healthy form, it simply keeps alive the conviction that the
life is more than meat; and so supplies that counterpoise to mere wealth which
Europe vainly seeks to secure by aristocracies of birth.*
Thomas Wentworth Higginson, "A Plea for Culture," 1867

In May 1864, as he was recuperating from a mild grapeshot wound and lingering malaria, Thomas Wentworth Higginson established a new home at Newport, Rhode Island. His relocation from a war zone to a coastal resort signaled
a larger self-transformation, as the onetime abolitionist gave up soldiering and
began to fashion a new career as a man of letters. The apparent passage from
hardship to comfort worried Higginson, who was clearly intent on avoiding
the charge of mere indolence and of retreating into "comfort and good dinners." He retained some of his youthful misgivings about the literary life and
the suggestion of self-indulgence it carried. This unease was most evident in
Higginson's series of halting attempts to justify his new direction as an extension of earlier reform commitments. In 1865, he hinted that by preparing a
new edition of the Greek philosopher Epictetus, he was building on his earlier
abolitionism, since this leading Stoic thinker not only had been a slave but
also had been the favorite reading of Toussaint Louverture, the greatest of all
black revolutionaries. Assembling the two-volume *Harvard Memorial Biographies* likewise made sense, given that this commemorative project paid tribute to the wartime service he and others had given to the Union cause. Yet no
such easy rationale could explain why he threw himself into a novel of manners
set among the Newport fashionable. Vindicating this project, which Higginson
pursued between 1867 and 1869, would require developing a completely new
stance toward the needs of the moment.

In 1867, Higginson wrote two pieces for the *Atlantic Monthly* that explained how even light fiction might help to remedy his country's lingering short-comings. In his "Plea for Culture" and his discussion of "Literature as an Art," Higginson insisted that Americans' collective devotion to art and litera-ture would allow the world's leading democracy to continue its moral develop-ment and assure that it would not be "materialized by peace." Intellectual and imaginative cultivation provided the antidote to a "commonplace and perhaps debasing success" that seemed likely to accompany the overthrow of slavery. The higher realms of human expression had the power to guard against "spiri-tual obesity," to place mere material achievements in proper perspective, and to instill the noble "conviction that the life is more than meat." The pursuit of imaginative art was no escapist indulgence; it was difficult, even "strenuous," but it was well worth the effort both for individuals and for the nation. Recall-ing Charles Eliot Norton's writings from the 1850s, Higginson insisted that culture represented the "climax and flower of all civilizations" and noted that American civilization had failed to achieve this distinction. But Higginson be-lieved that the moral discipline of the war had fitted Americans to this crucial task, if they could only channel their recent moral earnestness and energy into intellectual and imaginative pursuits. "The nation has found its true grandeur by war," Higginson avowed. Only with the pursuit of culture would the coun-try "retain it in peace."[1]

Higginson was not alone in considering the possibilities of culture in the aftermath of war (or in worrying about spiritual flabbiness). Over the final third of the nineteenth century, liberal men of letters attempted as a group to fos-ter cultural distinction. They did so with the same sense of purpose that had informed their advocacy of the Union and of Radical Reconstruction. Nearly every aspect of their Gilded Age project could be seen in the goals set forth in 1867, during the transatlantic high tide of democratic reform. If George Wil-liam Curtis's 1856 "Duty of the American Scholar to Politics and the Times" had called a generation to join the political and moral struggle against slavery, Higginson's plea eleven years later focused attention on the pressing tasks of cultural stewardship. He laid out how Americans might be convinced that art, letters, and pure science were "objects of intrinsic worth"; how the Ameri-can university might be remade; and how writers and critics might cultivate a broad, democratic appreciation of aesthetic matters. Such a program sought both to elevate and to broaden national culture. Noting that these vertical and horizontal extensions were mutually reinforcing, Higginson optimistically pointed out that "great men are rarely isolated mountain-peaks" but are more

often the "summits of ranges." Elevate the whole people, and any individual
genius would rise that much higher. The emphasis on general elevation made
cultivation expansive and active. A defensive retreat into exclusive "dens of culture" was not an option; culture required instead both "strenuous effort" and
democratic commitment.[2]

For the remainder of their lives, men who had found their greatest sense of
purpose during the 1860s unapologetically committed themselves to the extension of American learning and to the encouragement of a popular interest
in imaginative expression. For James Russell Lowell, this meant a return to
poetry and an even greater commitment to literary criticism, the breadth of
which would put Lowell in a class by himself in nineteenth-century American
letters. Even after he left Harvard to become a diplomat in Europe, Lowell
drew on his reputation as a man of letters and leading authority on English literature to lay a new basis for Anglo-American liberalism. At nearly the same
time that Lowell took up these foreign duties, Charles Eliot Norton joined the
Harvard faculty, where for more than twenty years he brought into the lecture
hall the same breadth of vision and underlying moral imagination that he had
displayed in the salons and at the dinner tables of the Anglo-American intelligentsia. George William Curtis intensified his political work, which had become the center of his responsibilities during the war for the Union. But from
1865 until his death in 1892, Curtis retained a connection with literature and
art by writing what amounted to nearly twenty-five hundred short essays on
cultural matters in *Harper's New Monthly Magazine*. As for Higginson, his postbellum production was the most impressive of the group, with scores of magazine contributions, hundreds of editorials, and some twenty volumes of essays.
The second half of his life, which stretched from 1867 until 1910, was as busy
as the first half, when his antislavery and military adventures had earned him
a reputation as a "literary colonel." E. L. Godkin transformed the *Nation* into
a leading journal of criticism that paid nearly as much attention to developments in artistic, literary, and historical matters as to political and economic
matters. The editor's insistence on high (some would say unrelenting) critical standards helped make the magazine an authoritative voice that attracted
a staggering array of talented contributors and reviewers.[3]

The liberal critics' cultural endeavors helped them to garner respect — as
well as sporadic resentment — from those who witnessed the effort to create a
national commitment to liberal culture. While engaged with the specific challenges of the American Gilded Age, the liberals' cosmopolitan stance and many
Anglo-American connections made them aware of comparable developments

in Britain. Such alertness formed a central element in their evolving friendships with Leslie Stephen, Frederic Harrison, John Morley, and James Bryce.
Similar transatlantic ties helped set apart a group that would in time be known
as a "genteel" circle of writers, editors, and university professors. This milieu,
which extended well beyond the friendships of Norton, Lowell, Curtis, and
Higginson, represented a new cultural establishment that was both worldly and
staunchly nationalist. The imprint that the members of this generation left on
national life came as much from their insistent championing of the life of the
mind as from their ongoing willingness to take positions on the political issues
of the day. While components of their Civil War experience—their defense of
national values and of individual development—marked their dedication to the
realm of letters, late-nineteenth-century cultural pursuits signaled as well a return to their earliest commitments: to art, to letters, to national culture, all of
which had been subordinated by the more pressing national crisis. The postbellum years brought the thrill of achieving public influence in the areas they
knew best as well as the challenge of elaborating a critical stance that struck a
balance between drawing attention to present faults and expressing consistent
hopes for a more cultivated future.

Something Better Than Riches . . . Something
Utterly Apart from This World's Wealth

After a few warm notices, Higginson's fellow men of letters largely forgot the
plea for culture he set forth in 1867. This neglect resulted in no small part
from the appearance that year of a considerably more trenchant analysis presented by a British poet and civil servant. Matthew Arnold, whom American liberals had previously known for his searching verse, his friendship with
Arthur Hugh Clough, and his intimate knowledge of British and French educational systems, used the pages of the *Cornhill* to explain how "apostles" of
learning might secure the survival of civilization itself. His polemic spoke to
wider needs and aspirations than the brand of literary nationalism set forth
in the American serials. The urgency with which he presented his case ensured that those involved in the liberal high tide would grant him serious consideration. By collecting his essays into a single volume, *Culture and Anarchy*,
Arnold secured lasting renown. This book in time became "one of the most
frequently cited non-fiction prose works in the English language." By encapsulating an "Arnoldian" program, it framed nearly all subsequent discussions

of high culture and liberal democracy. If *Culture and Anarchy* generated debate within the Victorian intelligentsia, it also informed the "culture wars" of succeeding eras, up to and including the present.[4]

Few American critics of the Gilded Age became disciples of Arnold in any meaningful sense of that term. Far more accurate is to speak of them as contemporaries and occasional collaborators in a project that consumed the energies of many who sprang from similar circumstances. The similarities between Arnold and his American liberal counterparts were particularly pronounced. Born in 1822 (three years after Lowell and five years before Norton), Arnold had spent much of his twenties in a Romantic flush: playing the dandy, like Higginson; traveling on the continent and finding himself bewitched by the French actress Rachel, like Curtis; and publishing volumes of earnest, soulful poetry, like Lowell. Like Norton, Arnold had by 1850 settled into a day job, in his case as a civil servant cum school inspector. He had also carried the burden of a well-known father, Thomas Arnold, the fabled headmaster of Rugby, memorialized in Thomas Hughes's *Tom Brown's Schooldays*. Elected professor of poetry at Oxford in 1857, Arnold quickly emerged over the next decade as a prominent cultural critic whose works gained notice on both sides of the Atlantic.

To speak of the liberal Americans' "Arnoldian" view of culture describes a general orientation that emerged out of such shared experiences. There were no unifying doctrines of cultural stewardship such as those associated with "Darwinian" science or even with "Millian" liberalism. Arnold's work mattered not because it formed a particular orthodoxy but because of his "gift of saying what he has to say in a manner that commands attention," to use Curtis's apt description. Arnold's authoritative voice invited men of letters across the Anglo-American world to respond to his critique and to decide whether he might be embraced as a kindred spirit or targeted as a sparring partner. American writers assumed both of these stances, depending on the topic at hand. Their various responses suggest that Arnold's work played a key role in Gilded Age cultural debates primarily through the terminology he created, which lent itself to being quickly internalized and taken as a point of reference. His memorable celebration of "sweetness and light" became a recurrent phrase, as did his pithy definition of culture as the "best that has been thought and said in the world." Like Carlyle with his ranting "Shooting Niagara" or Whitman in his rhapsodic *Democratic Vistas*, Arnold elevated the stakes of culture by folding literary concerns into broader social anxieties.[5]

Arnold focused his seminal 1867 essays on the cultural crisis as it emerged within British society, delineating his country's three main classes along with their respective failings. While the aristocratic "Barbarians" were too concerned with showy exteriors to be interested in culture and the working class "Populace" was too debased, the greatest danger to culture came from the middle-class "Philistines," whom Arnold held responsible for the narrow-minded provincialism, smug complacency, and shallow indifference to art that characterized modern British public life. He lamented the middle class's enthusiasm for commerce, utilitarianism, and the "machinery" of reform and reserved special criticism for the narrow, coarse, and deadening religious nonconformity that he thought dangerously isolated the dissenting middle class from the mainstream of society. He deprecated the Philistine tendency, which he saw epitomized by the Liberal politician John Bright, to evaluate countries by the length of their railroads, their supply of coal, the extent of their franchise, and their number of church buildings. Along with Arnold's indictment came a call for reform, which involved the cultivation of the Philistines (as well as the Barbarians and the Populace) and an effort to evoke their sympathy, intelligence, appreciation for beauty, and faith in what Arnold called "right reason."[6]

Arnold's critique took on a broader frame of reference by borrowing the German poet Heinrich Heine's identification of "Hebraism" and "Hellenism" as the two great rival forces present in Western culture. These dual inheritances differed in style, tone, and thrust, even if both had "man's perfection or salvation" as their end. Hebraism represented the world of Puritan or Dissenting moralism and was correspondingly strict, hard, and dutiful. Hellenism, conversely, represented the world of beauty; it was playful, flexible, and radiant. Hebraism mainly concerned itself with conduct, with "doing," while Hellenism centered on thought, or "knowing." All societies and all individuals needed a balance between the two stances, but Arnold believed that modern Britain suffered from an overdevelopment of stern Hebraism at the expense of a more joyous and playful Hellenism.[7]

Americans found it relatively easy to domesticate this terminology and adapt it to their circumstances, even if Arnold did not focus on the specifically American problems of modern culture until the 1880s. Some elements were lost in translation, however, as with Arnold's attack on nonconformity, which clearly hit a raw nerve with some heirs of the Puritans. Higginson mounted one of the strongest defenses by reminding Arnold of the Miltonic tradition; Higginson was far less concerned about the matter of nonconformity (a category that had little relevance to the American situation) than about defending the New England tradition that had just proved itself during the Civil War. Other men of letters skirted this relatively minor issue and took up Arnold's critique of the middle class and his use of "Philistine" (a term that had earlier been used by Carlyle and Margaret Fuller as an indictment of conventionality). Associating philistinism with modern acquisitiveness and superficiality shifted attention away from distinctively American failings and implied an international mission to cultivate that emerging middle class in whose hands the future of democracy seemed to rest. Attending to this large reading community helped transform literary commentary into the brand of cultural criticism that Arnold would use to contest the cultural preeminence of Carlyle and Mill.[8]

It would be a mistake to give Arnold too much credit for shaping the Victorian liberal understanding of culture and its role in elevating the ideal over the material. As Raymond Williams and others have shown, the notion of culture had evolved over time, rendering the term a conceptual palimpsest that bore traces of Christian, Renaissance, Enlightenment, and Romantic influences. Growing out of an eighteenth-century concern with manners and refinement, a Romantic emphasis on the power of imagination and the perception of beauty, and a liberal Protestant faith in the perfection of character, culture had by the late nineteenth century taken on new meanings and come to serve new needs in a democratizing, industrializing, and scientific age. A vagueness or at least ambiguity often attended the word's usage, but in the most general terms, "culture" was a timeless record of human achievement in literature and art. This was a realm apart from the quotidian concerns of a market-based society, the contemplation of which would help individuals improve themselves. Higginson emphasized the transcendent character of culture as "something better than riches . . . something utterly apart from this world's wealth." Culture's divorce from the mere getting and spending of money was one of its most appealing features in an age increasingly associated with materialism, when nonutilitarian pursuits faced new challenges. Culture was valuable, Higginson explained in a common formulation, because "it makes no money, but helps to make men."[9]

Religious developments as well as social and political dislocations influenced the Victorian concern with culture. Arnoldian "apostles" framed their mission in religious terms and spoke forthrightly about "sacralizing" culture by establishing imaginative expression as a domain separate from the mundane experiences of a dispirited modern existence. Many observers have seen in the fact that *Culture and Anarchy* followed in the wake of the "Higher Criticism" and of Darwinian science a direct connection between the Arnoldian project and the waning power of traditional faith. At Arnold's death in 1888, the *Nation* exemplified this tendency by discussing the "opportuneness" of his essays, which appeared just as Mill, Darwin, and Huxley had "taken hold of the young

men, and destroyed their interest in theological discussions . . . without furnishing them with anything very solid in the nature of a solution to the moral
problem of the universe." Arnold's outlook gained so much influence because
it "hit on a way of providing something which would take the place of a creed,
and cultivate the faculty of reverence and keep alive the faith in the final triumph of righteousness."[10]

American Arnoldians were indeed motivated by commitments to religious
liberalism, though this connection should not be understood reductively. Becoming an "apostle" of culture followed a more general relocation of spiritual
inspiration and a growing liberal emphasis on the supremacy of the individual
conscience. If the homage given to lasting monuments of artistic expression
constituted a response to social dislocation, so too was it a means of venerating
human genius and the capacity for transcendence and permanence outside the
more traditional assurances of faith. Victorian moralists expressed little more
enthusiasm for rejecting Christianity and making its sacred texts obsolete than
had Thomas Jefferson, who famously expressed his humanistic deism by assembling an expurgated version of the Gospels. Mid-nineteenth-century liberal
seekers were influenced as much by the methodologies of the higher criticism
(and in particular by the questions raised about the status of Scripture as revealed truth) as by their inner convictions. Higginson sounded a common note
of liberal Christianity in 1852 when he declared that the "time has come when
an earnest and fearless inquirer can no more study the Bible and believe in its
verbal inspiration, than he can study astronomy and believe that the sun moves
round the earth."[11]

But culture entailed less a demotion of sacred texts than a revaluation of
them. Higginson emphasized the liberation of Hebrew sacred writings from
their inherited trappings. Enlightened appreciation of sacred writing would
constitute an immense improvement, Higginson pointed out, explaining, "We
study this priceless book from childhood, in a manner so constrained and un-
natural, that one half its beauties are veiled from us and reserved for a generation that shall read it without artificial light." Leslie Stephen agreed, insisting
that the Gospels should not be burdened with being thought "true, in the sense
in which a newspaper report is true." Instead, he pointed out in 1869, they
should be understood to convey an "artistic truth as representing a noble phase
of human nature." We should cherish Scripture "not because it is true, but because it is beautiful." If sacred texts were like literature, literature could also
rise to the level of sacred text. Norton gave literature such status in the 1870s,
as he wrestled with how to provide a moral education for his children absent the

Christianity with which he had been raised. Literary texts provided a partial answer. Although he considered Jesus the "dearest saint of humanity," Norton explained to Ruskin, he "would bind up the Gospels with Marcus Antoninus' Thoughts, and regard one as sacred as the other."[12]

Higginson's, Stephen's, and Norton's remarks on the Bible suggest that many liberal Victorians understood their apparent loss of faith as a step toward spiritual wholeness rather than as a crippling moment of existential crisis and spiritual void. A commitment to Darwinian principles may have been less important in Norton's spiritual odyssey than his wartime musings about American liberty and destiny. By 1865, Norton was privately discussing how the United States was on the cusp of embracing emancipation in all its guises, a development that he believed would have direct implications for his country's spirituality. "The progress of freedom in religion will surely follow freedom in politics," he wrote, adding that Americans were destined to "become the most truly and the most unconventionally religious people that the world has known." Norton's journey toward avowed agnosticism later that decade accelerated in a searching dialogue with like-minded friends such as Stephen. These two friends found strength in one another to move beyond the religious convictions of their fathers, even if both in the end insisted that religious truth could be sought only in the confines of radically individual consciences. Joining Higginson in the founding of the Free Religious Association in 1876, Norton wondered if even this ecumenical, largely humanitarian assemblage presented too much organization for as personal a matter as religion.[13]

Norton and Stephen's embrace of "free thought" represented a sober moment in their lives and did as much to bond their friendship as any other factor. But neither man expressed any particularly searing regrets or ever envied his parents for living at a time when faith was less contested. Victorian agnosticism—the inability to know for certain—was not the same thing as atheism; epistemological humility differed in content and spirit from a hostile skepticism. Even the self-proclaimed agnostics, who had dispensed with traditional religion, did not abandon morality or a belief in a power higher than the self. Stephen's strenuous mountaineering in the "sacred" Alps was a typically Romantic way for him to register the smallness of the individual in the cosmic scope of things. At times, even the less robust Norton was enthralled by the untamed splendor of the American interior, and he considered his efforts on behalf of the environment (in the Adirondacks and Niagara Falls) an essentially spiritual activity—"missionary work," as he called it. If the sublime appeal of this natural spectacle both uplifted and humbled, so too did the literary record of human striving and achievement. Norton's conceptualization of "Western culture" included a religious impulse that allowed him the same sense of scope and scale that his more vigorous friends found in the outdoors.[14]

The most acute reactions to wavering faith came not from freethinkers such as Norton, Stephen, and Higginson but from those who sought to achieve personal satisfaction within inherited systems of faith. Lowell preferred a "judicious shutting of the eyes" when it came to the sort of searching questions that led his closest friends toward agnosticism. It was simply impossible for him to ignore, however, the prevalence of such doubts within his milieu, and he chose to dramatize the quest for religious certainty in his 1870 poem "The Cathedral" (thus combining the same poetic musing with an explicit rejection of agnosticism as a viable personal option that Arnold exemplified).[15]

Goldwin Smith went even further, and the intensity of his religious reckoning was extreme even within this liberal cohort. While Smith markedly changed his stance toward political issues over his lifetime, he was consistent in his instinctive hostility to the British ecclesiastical hierarchy. "Religion can be 'established' only in the hearts and minds of men," Smith regularly explained, even as he came to an array of different views about what his heart and mind found most convincing. Long after he had emigrated, he kept himself abreast of debates roiling the Church of England. In later efforts to probe the boundaries of religious faith, he appeared most frequently before groups of liberal Unitarians, the tradition in which all the liberal New Englanders had been reared. The process of searching seemed as important as the final destination, and he dramatized his quest in such collections as *Guesses at the Riddle of Existence*, *In Quest of Light*, and *No Refuge but in Truth*. In later years, Smith fiercely disputed those who labeled him an agnostic. He apparently found even this label too narrow to capture his belief that admitting doubt need not compromise a longing for certainty and his hope that such certainty might be achieved if enough effort was expended.[16]

Whatever might be said about the complex social and religious origins of the Victorians' sacralization of high culture, the effects of their project and its general tenor can be more easily described. The primary results of the Arnoldian dialogue included a further refinement of the relationship of American men of letters to the British intelligentsia, which experienced its own internal rearrangement in response to the question of high culture. While the Americans continued to draw inspiration from John Stuart Mill's idealized version of educative democracy, they became increasingly uneasy about this tradition's apparent undervaluing of works of the imagination. Even Mill sensed a certain void in the liberal project, using his inaugural 1869 lecture as the rector of St. Andrews University to call for greater attention to art, the imagination, and the "cultivation of the beautiful" in British education. This did not keep Arnold from popularizing his suspicion that Harrison and Mill might be "enemies of culture" lurking within the citadel of advanced political liberalism and that they were encouraging the unchecked growth of Philistine egoism.[17]

Repairing his relationship with Ruskin, Norton was increasingly presented with this case, as his friend never tired of assaulting Mill's "logic-chopping" and the soullessness of modern utilitarianism. Lowell's disaffection with the intellectual leader of British liberalism became overt (if vague) while the American traveled in Europe after the war. In response to the news of Mill's death in 1873, Lowell confided to Leslie Stephen that although he "should find it hard to say why I dislike John Stuart Mill," Lowell's "instinct" told him that Mill had "done lots of harm"—in all likelihood a response to Mill's feminism. Amid this reordering of priorities and perspectives, the orbit of transatlantic friendships and correspondents took on subtly new forms. Americans intensified their friendships with culture-minded liberals such as Leslie Stephen and John Morley in the late 1860s and early 1870s and brought newfound enthusiasm to relationships with artists and critics such as Ruskin, the Rossettis, Edward Burne-Jones, Edmund Gosse, William Morris, and Arnold. This last group of figures represented no particular political creed, even if their stance toward Millian liberalism varied from aloofness to outright hostility.[18]

The most dramatic consequence of this realignment of transatlantic ties was the effort to rehabilitate Thomas Carlyle's reputation. Coming to terms with his appalling conduct during the Civil War and the Governor Eyre proceedings required these men to hearken back to their youth, when Carlyle had established himself as a cultural seer and a vindicator of the imagination.[19] Norton, who had already proved himself capable of drawing intellectual sustenance from a diverse array of sources, strove to nurture the common ground that existed by paying a series of regular visits to the old Scotsman during the spring of 1869. Norton accompanied Carlyle on walks around London and recorded their lengthy "conversations" (as often as not monologues by Carlyle). Norton took delight in the old man's "humour" and "playfulness" and sensed that he only half believed his most extreme comments. "After making allowance for the extravagance, the willfulness, and the recklessness of Carlyle," Norton concluded, "there remains a vast balance of what is strong, masculine, and tender in his nature. . . . [H]is individuality is precious in these days of conformity and conventionalism, even in its excesses."[20]

Carlyle's political and social views—especially his attacks on democracy and on the capacities of former slaves and the Irish—continued to distance him from the liberals even as they drew attention to his cultural contributions during the last decades of his life. To reach out to him, transatlantic liberals emphasized his youthful passion; his role in providing a strong, sometimes lonely, voice for cultivation and imagination; and the signs that some of that older spark still lingered in his old age. Stephen confessed himself "almost equally repelled and attracted" by the sage. Acknowledging that "politically and philosophically Carlyle talks a good deal of arrant and rather pestilent nonsense," Stephen could not help but admire his simplicity and integrity as a literary master. His lingering fondness led him gently to object to Lowell's hostile review of *Frederick* when it was reprinted in *My Study Windows* in 1871. Stephen doubted whether Lowell "or any other Yankee can find it in your hearts to be quite just to Carlyle."[21] But no less a Yankee than Higginson would be captivated by Carlyle in London in 1872 and again in 1878. Higginson was so predisposed to think ill of the Scotsman that he initially refused a letter of introduction; however, Higginson came away impressed with Carlyle's warmth and humanity, embodied in his earthy laugh. Carlyle reciprocated the mellowing of American attitudes with a gesture of reconciliation: a gift of all his Cromwell and Frederick research materials to Harvard, which Emerson found both "lovely and redeeming." Norton played the central role in this bequest, thus laying the basis for his later role as Carlyle's literary executor.[22]

When Carlyle died in 1881, the American liberals had gained sufficient distance from the polarization of the 1860s to acknowledge the depth of his influence on their youthful search to combine culture and duty. Curtis explained to his "Easy Chair" readers that the members of an entire generation had received their intellectual orientation by responding to the quite different leadership provided by Carlyle and Mill, that generation's two most important intellectual models. Carlyle was to be remembered for "arousing the young mind of England and America to a high moral earnestness of purpose" and for having blown a "trumpet of moral awakening," while Mill had been responsible for the "direction of that mind into practical channels towards results" and was to be praised for his "elucidation of the true process of reasoning as applied to the management of public affairs." Curtis wanted his readers to understand that these two forces worked together dialectically, a process that the events of the 1860s had possibly obscured. "Neither could have spared the other," he summed up. "One quickened the soil, the other sowed the seed."[23]

An amalgam of Millian liberalism and the veneration of culture associated with Carlyle and Arnold formed the distinctive character of late American Victorianism. The leading men of letters during the Gilded Age would have found it hard to deny this dual inheritance, given the centrality of Carlyle and of Emerson in the antebellum years and the liberals' gravitation toward Mill beginning in the 1860s. The worldview worked out a relation not just to Britain but to all of Europe. Carlyle had helped raise awareness of German Romanticism, while Mill and Arnold worked in a tradition that was equally concerned with continental thought, especially that of France.[24]

What connected the two components of liberal cultivation was an emphasis on the internal development of individuals seeking to achieve what Arnold termed their "best selves." Liberal reformers agreed that modern circumstances demanded that those living the life of the mind should lead by setting an example of sustained inquiry and inner growth. This emphasis owed as much to Romantic theories of cultivation (especially those associated with Coleridge and with German advocates of *Bildung*) as with Arnold. *Culture and Anarchy* represented a step toward making culture a monolithic entity by attempting to enshrine the "best that has been thought and said in the world." The earlier emphasis on process remained in evidence, however, as even Arnold urged readers to remember that culture was "not a having and a resting, but a growing and a becoming."[25]

For all the new terminology provided by Arnold, the liberal Americans were loathe to move very far from understanding culture as first and foremost a process that would ultimately be vindicated by its capacity to change individual lives. Engaging the faculty of the imagination may have harmonized with European trends, but it had also been central to the brand of Unitarian self-culture associated with William Ellery Channing, who had counseled the "unfolding and perfecting of [one's] nature" by a variety of means. Perhaps because of this inheritance, the Gilded Age Americans found lasting meaning in those metaphors of husbandry that hearkened back to the etymological roots of cultivation. "Culture is as much needed for human beings as for the products of the earth," Norton explained in 1888. By keeping in mind the similarities between the harvesting of food and the raising of inner character, critical Americans conveyed that the slightly ethereal scope of Arnold would assume a more earthly—or earthy—character, as Higginson revealed in a striking analogy. "The object of high culture is not to exhibit high culture, but its results," he wrote. "You do not put guano on your garden that your garden may blossom guano." What provided the fertilization in this slightly mysterious process was less important than the completed selves that would flower as a result.[26]

The larger point made in this understanding was that culture was liberalizing through its means rather than through its ends. The study of literature, painting, sculpture, and other artistic forms worked primarily within the context of individuals, awakening the moral sense, developing the imaginative powers, training the perception of beauty, and providing a model of excellence worth striving toward. Norton emphasized the importance of historical texts when he insisted that "our present thought is made stronger & wiser by knowing what the best men have thought & felt in times past." Lowell recurred to the centrality of the Greeks in what he considered the aptly termed "liberal education" of the time. Devoting attention to these distant works was valuable, he explained, because it "emancipates the mind from every narrow provinciality whether of egotism or tradition" and thus became the "apprenticeship that every one must serve before becoming a free brother of the guild which passes the torch of life from age to age." If such comments drew attention to the works of the ancients, cultural work from other periods was also capable of drawing out individuals' most important human qualities.[27]

Insisting on the inward process of growth and development was crucial in an age of mechanical reproduction, Gilded Age fortunes, and increased European travel. New technologies and expanded wealth made culture more widely available but also threatened to shift the focus away from the inner process of culture onto its outer trappings. Arnold had warned of this danger, counseling readers that true culture did not constitute an "engine of social and class distinction, separating its holder, like a badge or title, from other people who have not got it." Though his personal interests tended far more toward politics than culture, E. L. Godkin felt compelled in 1874 (amid the tawdry spectacle of the Beecher-Tilton scandal) to reiterate Arnold's point. In a commentary on "Chromo-Civilization," Godkin objected to the superficial conceptions of culture that understood it as a "smattering of all sorts of knowledge" or as something that could simply be "acquired by desultory reading[,] . . . or traveling in Europe" or owning reproductions of art.[28]

To modern ears, Godkin's distaste for what he called "pseudo-culture," which "a large body of slenderly-equipped persons" mistook for the genuine, smacks of elitist condescension. A closer reading, however, reveals that Godkin's disgust, like Arnold's, stemmed not from the wider availability of culture but from the tendency to convert culture from a means of self-improvement into a means of self-congratulation. Culture, in this incorrect (and even dangerous) view, had misled people into believing "that they have reached, in the matter of social, mental, and moral culture, all that is attainable or desirable by anybody" and elevated them "in their own minds to a plane on which they see nothing higher, greater, or better than themselves." Such an attitude could not have more clearly contradicted what Godkin and his Arnoldian allies saw as the true meaning of culture—that is, the antithesis of complacency. Far from being easy and comfortable, culture was the "result of a process of discipline, both mental and moral" and thus depended on the "protracted exercise of the faculties for given ends." Culture not only was dissociated from wealth (and thus did not simply attach to one who had traveled in Europe or owned nice things) but also had no automatic connection to formal education. "A man who has got [culture] is not simply a person who knows a good deal, for he may know very little, but a man who has obtained an accurate estimate of his own capacity, and of that of his fellows and predecessors, who is aware of the nature and extent of his relations to the world . . . , and who is at the same time capable of using his powers to the best advantage." Though Arnold might have found the emphasis on effort and discipline overly Hebraistic, to the liberal Americans culture most resembled religion (or at least the strenuous religion of their New England forbears) in this regard: it was less a source of reassuring comfort than a prod to continual striving.[29]

Still Colonists and Provincials in Culture

In theory, works of high cultural distinction humanized by reaching across artificial boundaries and erasing the superficial differences of nationality, class, and creed. Protestants and even agnostics could savor Dante, while Goethe spoke to those who might have never read German, let alone taken a grand tour of the Continent. The Greeks were the common property of all who came after them. Such high-minded convictions aside, it was nearly impossible for either Americans or Britons during the Victorian period to consider the imperatives of liberal culture apart from their national circumstances. The late nineteenth century saw men of letters in both countries intensify their focus on how literary production testified to national greatness. For Americans, this striving for a distinguished common culture became especially acute in the aftermath of the Civil War, when continuing cultural mediocrity seemed to imperil the power of the country's democratic example to inspire others. "To maintain ourselves," Lowell insisted in 1867, Americans had to "achieve an equality in the more exclusive circle of culture, and to that end must submit ourselves to the European standard of intellectual weights and measures."[30]

Specific concerns about American creative achievement tapped into a longer tradition. The Victorian liberals inherited from the generations of Cooper and Emerson a desire to vindicate American culture and American society's capacity to nurture true genius. The key problem of whether America was capable of achieving distinction in cultural matters involved a range of larger transatlantic anxieties about democracy, industrial capitalism, materialism, and the effects of cultural dissemination. Earlier sneers, while scathing, had often at least implied that greater cultivation would come in time, after the young republic had matured. Arnold's attack on Philistines reframed the issue by introducing a nagging suspicion that the cultural inadequacies of the United States might constitute not evidence of American "backwardness" but rather a sign of things to come across the world. The United States mattered to Arnold, as it had to Tocqueville, because both men sensed that it presaged Europe's future. While such a prospect alarmed European observers, the liberal Americans feared that at a time when Arnoldian devotion to culture was ascendant, the shortcomings in the cultural realm threatened to diminish the wider impact of the American example.[31]

Lowell feared that Americans' cultural shortcomings would extend foreign critics' unwillingness to practice "fair play" in assessing the United States. "So long as we continue to be the most common schooled and the least cultivated people in the world, I suppose we must consent to endure this condescending manner of foreigners towards us," he wrote in 1869. Two years earlier, Charles Eliot Norton had agreed with much of this diagnosis, writing to a British friend that while Americans were "still colonists and provincials in culture," the prospects for improvement provided grounds for optimism. "The war, if it has not made the nation more thoughtful, has made it more serious and capable of thought," Norton insisted. "There are indications, stronger now than ever before, that we shall not be forever content with the mediocrity of diffused intelligence, but shall [contribute] our part to the stock of thoughts and to advance civilization, not merely by the practical application to institutions of old principles, but by the discovery of new and fruitful truth."[32]

Norton's studied patience about the future typified a broader attitude. Doubts would be resolved in time, this cohort proclaimed, as Americans slowly realized their destiny as contributors to the life of the mind. Higginson, always a far more enthusiastic cultural nationalist than Norton, was particularly sanguine about the future. It hardly mattered whether the "full harvest" of American literature might be "postponed for another hundred years." What was clear was that it was "sure to come to ripeness at last." This postwar confidence signaled a willingness to await further developments, a commitment that in turn helped both men weather subsequent years of disappointment.[33]

The expected postbellum literary flowering did take time and effort, as many observers had predicted. Ever clearer signs of its appearance came, however, as the members of this cohort progressed through their adult careers and received aid from a slightly younger generation of men. The decisions made by Henry Adams, James T. Fields, Charles W. Eliot, and others to become "public moralists" on behalf of culture had arisen from the same interlocking set of New England institutions that had nurtured Norton, Lowell, Higginson, and Curtis. As the Cambridge circle achieved greater consolidation, it proved itself by incorporating newcomers. In fact, it subsequently lay much of its claims to national influence on this openness and ability to connect itself with the rest of the country more fully than had ever been the case in the antebellum years.

William Dean Howells of Ohio and Richard Watson Gilder of New Jersey served as the two most conspicuous examples of the New England incorporation of genius beyond its immediate orbit. Both of these talented men had made concerted attempts to gain entrée into the emerging northeastern literary establishment, and both were aided by the assumptions they shared with their elders about culture and politics. Howells's arrival in Boston in 1866 has since become a set piece of American literary history, as has his wartime Italian mission and his subsequent editorship of the *Atlantic* and then of *Harper's Monthly*. Howells's success as a "genteel eminence" by the late 1880s set a precedent for the inclusion of other newcomers, including Gilder, who aligned himself with the New England circle of Lowell, Norton, and Longfellow in the following decades. Gilder and his wife, the painter Helena De Kay, had already established themselves in the artistic milieu of Manhattan when they set out for a visit to Cambridge in 1876. The couple was hosted by the older Brahmin critics, who were clearly warmed by Gilder's experiences as a Civil War soldier (just as they had been by Howells's authorship of Abraham Lincoln's 1860 campaign biography). Beside a shared set of wartime convictions was an outlook on culture that bound this younger generation to their New England elders. Gilder no less than Howells had made personal friendships well before becoming initiated into the cultural and political precepts of the group of *Atlantic* contributors.[34]

By the 1880s, Howells and Gilder solidified their standing by taking control of the literary monthlies that came to play a decisive role in the popularization of a high literary culture among middle-class Americans. Howells tended to perpetuate forms and institutions already in existence and in the early twen-

tieth century capped several decades of tributes to George William Curtis by
assuming his "Easy Chair" column at *Harper's Monthly*. Gilder was more innovative as editor, even if he did not follow Howells in championing realism or in
risking controversial political stances, such as Howells had taken in defense of
the Haymarket anarchists. Gilder's continued New York residence separated
him more fully from the Boston establishment of Lowell, Norton, and the rest,
a circumstance that imbued Gilder's work in cultural journalism with the same
metropolitan sensibility that marked the political writing of E. L. Godkin's
Nation magazine. Gilder's path toward the sacralization of culture was also distinct from that of the Boston Unitarians, who consistently hearkened back to
William Ellery Channing's notion of "self-culture." Gilder's introduction to
literary publishing came not under the auspices of liberal Christianity but in
partnership with the staunchly evangelical Josiah Holland of *Scribner's Magazine*. Holland's unexpected death, shortly after the *Century* was launched in
1881, assured that Gilder would assume sole control of a magazine that was destined to be the period's most important cultural venue. Gilder quickly pared
back the Christian moralism offered by Holland and replaced it with a sense
of aesthetic morality in covering the expressive arts, offering regular political
commentary, and maintaining general civic uplift. The *Century* devoted more
attention to the visual arts than any other popular magazine of the period,
though it was best known for the unusually high quality of its literature, poetry,
history, and criticism. By 1887, the *Nation* could hail the rival publication as
"perhaps the most judiciously edited magazine in the world." [35]

The literary establishment nurtured by such liberal men of letters achieved
unprecedented power and scope by the 1880s. As Richard Brodhead has
pointed out, magazines such as the *Atlantic*, *Harper's Monthly*, the *Nation*, and
the *Century* "succeeded in gathering [their] own large audience around the
matter of serious writing" in the final two decades of the nineteenth century. In
the pages of these journals, distinguished work by Henry James, Mark Twain,
and Howells found the mass audience that had eluded earlier literary masterpieces created by Hawthorne and Melville. The critical achievement of this
period's literary establishment went beyond fostering such late-nineteenth-
century literary icons and assuring them a contemporary readership. What
mattered, Brodhead argues, was that the "literary institutions under gentry
control in the later nineteenth century succeeded in creating, it may be, the
closest thing to a coherent national literary culture that America has ever
had." [36]

This generation's successful establishment of "classic" American literature

involved the same Anglo-American dynamic that marked the wartime vindication of democracy and the emphasis on liberal reform of Gilded Age politics. In
fact, only with difficulty could these men have divorced their literary concerns
from an English tradition that reached back to Shakespeare and to Chaucer.
The typical critical stance was to identify authors who "have vindicated the
position of American letters in the literature of the language," as Curtis wrote
in a tribute to Oliver Wendell Holmes in the early 1880s. At times, the scope became even more expansive, as in Norton's 1867 evaluation of Emerson, which
presented him not as a representative American thinker but as a poet whose
verse ranked "among the universal classics." This critical position was characterized by a subtle interplay between the national and the cosmopolitan, which
could acknowledge Emerson's universal appeal while simultaneously appreciating how much he had done "to emancipate and nationalize American literature," to use Higginson's standard formulation.[37]

Lowell had been attuned to the intertwining of the national and international since the 1840s, and he continued in the late 1860s to explain both what
set American literature apart from the world and what knit it together within
the tradition of English letters. He realized in the aftermath of war how his
country had been "socially and intellectually moored to English thought, till
Emerson cut the cable and gave us a chance at the dangers and the glories
of blue water." Yet his enthusiasm for cultural independence was different
from earlier nationalist projects like the "Young America" movement, which
Lowell believed awarded special literary merit to Americans simply because
they were American. The intimate set of ties Lowell had formed within the
world of Anglo-American liberal culture in the 1850s and 1860s expanded his
perspective and convinced him that the surest sign of national maturity was
a willingness to accept the same critical standards for writers on both sides of
the Atlantic. In this context, Lowell either presented relatively harsh assess-
ments (Thoreau) or neglected American writers altogether (Melville, Whitman). Lowell's professed standard involved not so much the articulation of
national experiences as the capacity to enliven the incomparably rich English
language, which he considered the "noblest vehicle of poetic thought that ever
existed."[38]

Efforts to gain recognition for American literature began in these men's
backyards. Most of them saw it as a truism that the "foundations of our distinctive literature were largely laid in New England," as Curtis observed in 1882.
Despite later charges of insularity, Massachusetts alone had produced enough
literary breadth to furnish a variety of themes and to allow for various ways

of building up (or tearing down) the reputations of Yankee writers. Emerson's place as a great philosopher and essayist was secure by the time of the Civil War, and the inspiration of his earlier revolt became more and more a part of how this generation of liberal men of letters understood his influence. The first American novelist whom liberal critics helped to canonize was Nathaniel Hawthorne, soon to become the quintessential American classic. His elevation ran counter to these men's politics, since Hawthorne had not only maintained his antebellum ties to the Democratic Party but had provided the *Atlantic* one of that magazine's most skeptical complaints about the direction of the Republican-led effort during the Civil War. Curtis acknowledged what he considered Hawthorne's disappointing lack of civic judgment but concluded with the flourish that he had become "one of the most enduring facts of English literature." Hawthorne's growing postwar (and posthumous) allure overjoyed Lowell, a longtime Hawthorne enthusiast if never a confidante. "I don't think people have any kind of true notion yet what a master he was," Lowell wrote privately to James T. Fields in 1868. "Shakespeare, I am sure, was glad to see him on the other side."[39]

Hawthorne's Gilded Age reputation was burnished as well by the respect given him by liberal men of letters in England. Not long after Edward Dicey returned from the wartime United States, he featured a tribute to Hawthorne in *Macmillan's*. This effort prepared the way for Dicey's cousin, Leslie Stephen, not only to commission an essay on Hawthorne for the *Cornhill* but also to write and contribute a separate evaluation. Stephen's review, which was published late in 1872, noted Hawthorne's intense consciousness of living in the "most prosaic of all countries." "Was it not a thing to weep over," Stephen asked, "that a man so keenly alive to every picturesque influence, so anxious to invest his work with the enchanted haze of romantic association, should be confined till middle age amongst the bleak granite rocks and the half-baked civilisation of New England?" Seven years later, Henry James made a quite similar point when he drew attention to the absence of traditional romance in Hawthorne's American surroundings. Most scholars have since remembered James's famous discussion of American "absences" as an encapsulation of the continuing gap between Old and New World circumstances. Yet just as important was the fact that James's book elevated this New England writer into the series edited by John Morley to honor "English Men of Letters." Morley had earlier inducted Emerson into that pantheon by writing a biography of the New England sage.[40]

Not long after James inducted Hawthorne into Morley's English literary pantheon, Henry Wadsworth Longfellow drew forth an even more dramatic display of transatlantic appreciation. Lowell and Norton had a greater emotional investment in Longfellow's reputation, since they had known him at Harvard and in Cambridge, worked with him weekly on his Dante translations, and extolled the "sweetness and light" that he provided to readers on both side of the Atlantic. Soon after his death in 1882, a devoted British reader of Longfellow's poetry offered to donate his bust to Westminster Abbey's Poet's Corner, which had already become the unofficial pantheon for the English profession of letters. Despite some grumbling in the English establishment, the Longfellow memorial went up in the spring of 1884.[41]

Placing American poets within the sanctum of Westminster Abbey provided the climax of a broader campaign on behalf of Anglo-American literary harmony. As the American representative to London at the time, Lowell played a key role in this accord, as did the Liberal Party leader William Gladstone, who had already reached out in print to England's "Kin beyond the Sea." Gladstone's writings in the late 1870s set the stage for Lowell's mission, since Gladstone had hailed the American branch of the "English-Speaking Race" as worthy of inclusion in what Charles Dilke had called "Greater Britain." When Lowell was transferred from the Spanish mission to the Court of St. James's, he quickly became, as his biographer put it, "something of a public institution." His fame there made him an obvious choice to address the Wordsworth Society, dedicate a plaque at Westminster Abbey, and eulogize Dean Stanley within that sanctum of British literary culture. Lowell went beyond the literary establishment by serving as a pallbearer at Charles Darwin's funeral and by sharing insights with members of the Birmingham and Midland Institute and the London Workingmen's College (an audience well versed in Lowell's poetry thanks to Thomas Hughes's many lectures on the subject). Curtis argued that such public performances showed that "we too are Englishman" and that the respect given to Lowell as a writer and as an American constituted the clearest sign to date of "how closely what is best in America is related to the best in England."[42]

The warmth of feeling among men of letters did not mean the end of Anglo-American cultural tensions, of course. This fact became evident during Matthew Arnold's visit to the United States in this same period. As several scholars have detailed, Arnold planned a visit for the early 1880s after first engaging Lowell, Higginson, and sundry other American critics in print. In these discussions, Arnold mustered his full battery of social criticism to express his doubts about whether "lovers of the humane life" were really dominant in America, as a Boston newspaper had boasted in an article that also suggested that the

United States might provide Britain with a model for pursuing cultivation on a wide scale. Arnold applied the terminology he had deployed in the 1860s directly to the United States. "Whereas our society in England distributes itself into Barbarians, Philistines, and Populace," he wrote, "America is just ourselves, with the Barbarians quite left out, and the Populace nearly." The "inward" process of culture faced grave difficulties in the United States, he continued, given how wholly the country was given over to "machinery."[43]

Arnold disavowed any intent to disparage the United States and insisted that he was merely extending to new ground the battle against Philistinism begun in Britain. He professed to speak as a "friend" of America, maintaining that he was less interested in "holding a controversy" than in "holding a friendly conversation." The relatively muted response to his first essay on America bore out this contention, but a generally sour response followed during his fall 1883 tour of the country. Press reaction to Arnold's supposedly supercilious tone jeopardized the reputation of apostles of culture among the American public more generally, just as Carlyle's illiberal rants had in the wake of "Shooting Niagara." It was not hard to see how Arnold's fortunes and those of the cultural establishment became linked in the public mind. Men of letters in the United States were clearly intrigued by the attention he devoted to the New World in his several essays and in the three lectures before American audiences on "Numbers," "Literature and Science," and, most controversially, "Emerson." But the liberal Americans' response was more complicated than their general association with Arnold suggested and reveals the extent to which nationalist sentiment limited their cosmopolitan aspirations.[44]

Arnold's presence in the United States reduced the animosity felt by some American men of letters. Higginson led his sometime antagonist on a tour of Massachusetts schools and was charmed enough to be puzzled by the hostile public reception. In person, Arnold was not at all "uppish," Higginson recorded (though he added, in his patronizing way, that Arnold was maybe a bit "gauche" and "slow to comprehend"). Higginson found the English critic "very cordial and appreciative . . . as friendly as if up for office." But Arnold's speeches and writing were another matter, as the general tone of his reception in the press made clear. That Arnold's genuinely sympathetic if candid treatment of Emerson provoked controversy makes these nationalist limitations all the more obvious. Confessing painfully that Emerson could not be ranked among the first-rate poets, writers, or philosophers, Arnold claimed that the Sage of Concord had done something of even "superior importance" for a whole generation of Anglo-Americans: he had been a cheerful critic and

an indispensable guide for those who "would live in the spirit." Arnold understood Emerson's significance and value as an ideal cultural critic who could be
unsparing in his condemnation of society's faults but leavened his condemnation with an unshakable optimism and a faith that in "labour, righteousness,
and veracity" lay not only duty but "happiness."[45]

Higginson refused to tolerate all of Arnold's criticisms of American culture, mocking the Englishman for being "kind enough to stand on tiptoe upon
our lecture-platform and apply his little measuring-tape to the great shade of
Emerson." In a literary equivalent to waving the bloody shirt, Higginson compared Arnold's dismissal of American literature to Britain's refusal to support
the Union during its momentous crusade against slavery.[46] In London, Lowell
maintained a courteous if superficial correspondence with Arnold, praising his
essay on "Literature and Science," offering letters of introduction, and taking
a general interest in his American travel plans. But Lowell, too, often became
indignant at Arnold's comments, especially his discussion of Emerson, and
doubted "whether Matthew Arnold is quite capable (in the habit of addressing a jury as he always is) of estimating the style of one who conversed with
none but the masters of his mother-tongue." Norton alone seemed genuinely
comfortably with Arnold—the two had first met in the 1850s and had then developed a more familiar acquaintance during Norton's 1872 residence in London. These ties led him to arrange for the American printing of the "Emerson"
essay, which Norton, nearly alone among Americans, found to be a "large and
liberal piece of criticism."[47]

Curtis did not forge personal ties with Arnold until the critic's second American tour, which took place in 1886. But Curtis followed the Arnold phenomenon during the earlier period, and his remarks on the poet reached the large
readerships of *Harper's Weekly* and *Harper's Monthly*. In an 1882 "Easy Chair"
column, Curtis expressed pride that Americans did not reveal their earlier
sensitivity when exposed to Arnold's first biting commentaries, considering
it a sign of national maturity that the "sly thrusts of clever and agile literary
swordsmen do not provoke even a rejoinder, still less any ill feeling." When
the newspaper press turned its guns on Arnold in the winter of 1883–84,
Curtis asked his readers to step back and consider the larger pattern of Americans' "disposition to resent a little the coming of foreigners, and especially of
Englishmen, not to deliver lectures, but to lecture us." Arnold's visit was the
latest in a series that went back to Frances Trollope and that had continued
through the American tours of Dickens, Thackeray, and Herbert Spencer.
Echoing Lowell's comments about Dickens's criticism in the 1840s, Curtis

made the case for hearing such critics out. He argued that because they had raised similar objections to life in their own country, they could not simply be dismissed as carping snobs. Even an indignant Higginson agreed with this point, reminding readers that like earlier Old World critics, Arnold had "said nothing about Americans more unpleasant than [he] had previously said about [his] own countrymen; and why should we expect to fare any better?"[48]

At the same time that newsmaking tours such as Arnold's accentuated long-standing national hostilities and prejudices, the evolving character of trans-atlantic print was establishing new contours of Anglo-American culture. As the literary scholar Clarence Gohdes notes, the period between 1865 and 1885 witnessed the move of the United States from a net importer to a net exporter of periodical literature. By the early 1880s, Britain had more subscribers to the *Century* and *Harper's Monthly* than to any comparable magazine produced within that country. American writers and critics who spoke directly to British readers thus had far less stake in directing their attention toward visiting critics. Curtis used the same column that praised Lowell's English mission to draw attention to this trend and to reflect on how the "entry of the American magazine into English homes" had far greater significance than the example of any single individual. By 1884, Curtis was aware that his words did not reach merely an American audience (though this community of readers alone stretched from Mt. Khatadin in Maine past the Mississippi to the banks of the Columbia River). He also had readers in Canada, Kent, "King's Lynn," and even in Carnmavon. The scope of this audience prompted him to proclaim, "To all these far-scattered homes upon different continents, yet bound together by a common faith, language, traditions, and love of liberty, this Magazine comes with its monthly message of cheer."[49]

The consequences of such altered circulation patterns are hard to exaggerate. Though tens of thousands of new British readers were first drawn to the superior illustrations of *Scribner's*, *Harper's*, and the *Century* (which were known for having the most skillfully executed pictures on either side of the Atlantic), subscribers to these journals gained immediate access to future classics of American literature in the pieces that Mark Twain, Henry James, and William Dean Howells first serialized in the American monthlies. The prominence of British writers in the American press lagged, especially in the *Century*, where Gilder hoped to nurture "native" voices. He even risked his magazine's new foreign audience by launching a series devoted to the American Civil War, much to the displeasure of Edmund Gosse, then the *Century* agent in England. Gilder was resolute in the course. The *Century*'s Civil War material had po-

litical implications in hastening a southern "Road to Reunion" that coincided
with Mugwump support for the Democratic Party in politics. But the heightened interest in the Civil War also acknowledged the deep cultural well that
could be tapped, as Higginson sensed when he later commented that it was
"absolutely impossible to disentangle from the work of any but the very youngest of our living American authors that fibre of iron which came from our great
Civil War and the stormy agitation that led up to it."[50]

The enduring popularity of British literature in this era was hardly surprising, given how powerfully British books and writers had dominated the
literary marketplace for the entire century. Nor was it surprising, given their
experience during the liberal high tide, that American men of letters would
particularly welcome inclusion in a larger Anglo-American literary community. But neither their earlier and broader Anglophobia nor their cosmopolitan
literary internationalism ever left them. So while Higginson and others championed national writing, they also urged their home audiences to overcome the
provinciality of the Anglo-American tradition and to broaden ties with non-
English-speaking parts of the world. Lowell continued to root the modern literary tradition outside of England by putting Homer, Dante, Cervantes, and
Goethe alongside Shakespeare. The breadth of Norton's interests extended beyond Europe: he published a lengthy 1869 review that introduced American
readers to the Persian poet Omar Khayyám, whose *Rubaiyat* Edward Fitzgerald
had recently translated into English. This piece allowed Norton to note the
comparatively early flowering of Persian poetry (with Omar preceding Dante
by two hundred years) and to call attention to the similarity between the Persian poet's concerns and the "spiritual temper of our own generation." Modern readers would be attracted to Omar Khayyám, Norton wrote, since he was
a "sceptic, a free-thinker, no true believer, but a very thorn in the side of the
orthodox disciples of the prophet." Later in life, Norton similarly exhibited an
interest in Asian (especially Japanese) thought.[51]

Higginson's discomfort with an exclusively Anglo-American frame of reference led him to vindicate the superiority of cosmopolitanism in literature.
He reveled in the "interchange" of national literatures—where, for example,
the French embraced Jane Austen, the Swedes loved Bret Harte and Mark
Twain, and a leading American novelist such as Howells ranked the Russians
first. Longfellow, a "universal poet," should be judged within this expanded
literary environment, Higginson explained, noting that Longfellow's poetry
had been translated into "German, Italian, French, Dutch, Swedish, Danish,
Polish, Portuguese, Spanish, Russian, Hungarian, Bohemian, Latin, Hebrew,

Chinese, Sanskrit, Marathi, and Judea-German." Echoing Lowell's internationalism from the 1840s, Higginson contended that "there is no accident about art; what is great is great," no matter the national inflection. Though he was a less adept student of foreign-language literature than Norton or Howells, Higginson insisted that "we need the English culture, but we do not need it more evidently than we need the German, French, Greek and oriental." Lowell similarly had returned to his earlier literary internationalism shortly before his death, claiming that "literature tends more and more to become a vast commonwealth, with no dividing lines of nationality."[52]

Such tendencies resulted in a trend toward sanctioning a world literature and the communion of all men. "Above all nations is humanity," Curtis affirmed, borrowing a phrase repeatedly associated with Goldwin Smith. This stance would provide a refuge for Higginson and Norton in the mid-1890s, shortly after both Curtis and Lowell had died. Much to the regret of liberal men of letters, this decade witnessed the erosion of an earlier Anglo-American alliance of cultivated liberalism. Links between these two countries that had earlier emphasized law, representative government, literature, a tradition of individual rights, and fair play were overtaken by imperialism and the racialized "Anglo-Saxonism" of Kipling and Roosevelt. The pull of humanity, expressed through a truly international world of letters, would be one of many means to counteract the prevailing spirit of domination and conquest. The challenge looming at century's end was reestablishing the bearings of an America that had grown to world power and putting national ideals in conversation with a universalizing sense of shared humanity.[53]

A Passion for Diffusing

James Russell Lowell welcomed the 1885 opening of a new public library in Chelsea, Massachusetts, with a disarmingly basic question: "Have you ever rightly considered what the mere ability to read means?" Amid the high tide of the 1860s, Lowell might have framed his answer as a reflection on the debt that "modern republicans" owed to literacy or explained how the world of print sustained political discussion across a continental republic. On this occasion, however, Lowell's politics were relatively muted. He focused instead on how books opened the world of cultivation to all people, regardless of background or wealth. Reading, Lowell explained, amounted to nothing less than the "key which admits us to the whole world of thought and fancy and imagination."

Speaking from the perspective of a voracious reader (and temporarily putting aside his standing as an artist, critic, and public dignitary), Lowell explained how books provided "comfort and consolation," "refuge . . . from sorrow or misfortune," and simple "friendship" between a willing individual and the greatest chroniclers of the human experience. As the primary means of self-education and self-development, books assured intellectual independence and allowed people to continue their self-culture beyond formal schooling. "The better part of every man's education is that which he gives himself," Lowell insisted, conveying how the new Chelsea library would be a part of that ongoing process.[54]

Lowell's emphasis on the broad appeal of great writing was common among late-nineteenth-century cultural spokesmen. This "passion for diffusing, for making prevail, for carrying from one end of society to the other, the best knowledge, the best ideas of their time" made "men of culture," according to Matthew Arnold, the "true apostles of equality." Respect for the spiritual integrity of art required men of letters to transcend the prevailing conceptions of rank or allegiance, at least if applied in any narrow sense. As Arnold explained in *Culture and Anarchy*, cultivated "aliens" were guided "not by their class spirit, but by a general *humane* spirit, by the love of human perfection." With such socially transcendent tendencies came an evangelical responsibility to spread "sweetness and light" to what Arnold disparagingly termed the "raw and unkindled masses of humanity." This notion, for all its obvious condescension, was not disingenuous. Understanding Victorian intellectual life is scarcely possible without appreciating the quest for an expansive audience. What in later light seems to be an air of pomposity about such missions did not tarnish the program of broad cultural elevation for millions of middle- and working-class readers across the Anglo-American world. Avid reading was a widely shared predisposition, as was the Arnoldian quest to disseminate "from one end of society to the other, the best knowledge, the best ideas of [the] time."[55]

Americans naturally emphasized the disseminating aspect of this Arnoldian mission and sought its fullest articulation through their cultural stewardship. Their efforts to cultivate American society were carefully designed to achieve the maximum breadth of impact. Victorian men of letters understood that sustaining individual self-cultivation required institutions. Questions of canons and transnational networks constituted only the first steps in shaping an American literary establishment. Equally important were efforts made to create or to expand a range of more popular institutions (including libraries, reading groups, and museums) and to organize and establish more advanced scholarly endeavors (archaeological societies, research organizations, graduate programs). And, of course, a crucial part of this equation was the tremendous outpouring of new printed forms, which would make texts and authors increasingly available to a broad reading middle class.[56]

To saturate society with culture was to make a new generation as familiar with the life of the mind as with the rituals of American politics. Higginson's "Plea for Culture" explained in 1867 how art might even become as universal as electioneering. "Every American boy imbibes political knowledge through the pores of his skin," Higginson observed, noting that through "newspapers, schools, local caucuses," a boy was "expected to have mature convictions before he is fourteen." That the same child could grow up in the United States without a single meaningful exposure to art constituted nothing less than a national embarrassment. American culture could scarcely hope to match the achievements of democratic Athens until children had the same opportunities afforded the youths of the Greek city-states. "With its twenty thousand statues, with the tragedies of Aeschylus performed for civic prizes, and the histories of Herodotus read at the public games—a boy could not any more grow up ignorant of art [in Athens] than he could here remain untrained in politics." Future generations might best achieve Athenian civic virtue by recurring to the agora of political journalism. But achieving excellence in the arts required moving beyond politics and embracing the more humane aspects of public life.[57]

Efforts to disseminate "high culture" were not aloof from politics, as was clear in the inspiration that came with the opinion-shaping work done for the Union during the Civil War. Norton's labors for the New England Loyal Publication Society convinced him that although many Americans read only newspapers, the "higher education of the country finds little expression" in this source. "I have sometimes thought that were I an editor of a country paper," he mused in 1863, "I would print in each number of my paper some bit of literature of real excellence,—such for instance as one of Bacon's Essays, or a passage from Emerson, or some other writer of universal authority." At war's end, Norton recognized what might be an even more innovative form for popularizing such monuments of learning and wrote to the publishers of Beadle's Dime Novels to explain the "heavy responsibility" that they assumed by becoming the "instructors of a large portion of the community." The inexpensive editions they delivered might bring "good reading within the means of the whole people," Norton enthused, and thus become one of the "securest methods" of ensuring that the "intellectual and moral culture of the people [would] keep pace with the material progress of the nation." The publisher's lack of interest stymied Norton's plan to edit a series of "dime Shakespeares" in the 1860s, though the same spirit returned at century's end, when Norton edited a six-volume series of literary "readers" for young people. In the preface to this collection, which appeared in 1894–95, he noted that a "taste for good reading is an acquisition the worth of which is hardly to be overestimated." He promised prospective readers that they would soon "share in the common stock of the intellectual life of the race" and "have the door opened [to] all the vast and noble resources of that life."[58]

Norton's tenure at Harvard over the last quarter of the nineteenth century did not lead him to relinquish hopes for a broad national audience, though this position allowed him to translate his remarkable erudition into the progress of scholarship in several distinct fields, some of which, like medieval studies, he had a hand in pioneering. Norton considered his engagement with Harvard undergraduates a part of his larger quest to shape the national future. Rather than seeing these students as like-minded initiates, he forecast how such future leaders might develop an appreciation of art and literature that would lead to greater cultivation in their leadership. Those who would acquire wealth later in life might also be more willing than otherwise to sanction a hospitable place for the arts and the humanities. Such a view made sense given the philanthropy for the arts that this period witnessed and that had a direct result in unifying intellectual institutions such as public libraries and museums. Norton's entrepreneurial and organizational experience at the New England Loyal Publication Society had prepared him to conduct important cultural work in the last decades of the century, as he almost single-handedly brought to life such institutions as the Archaeological Institute of America, the Dante Society, and the American School of Classical Studies at Athens. His influence can be still seen around Boston in the enduring institutions he played a role in founding: the Fogg Museum at Harvard, the Museum of Fine Arts, and the Isabella Stewart Gardiner Museum.[59]

Norton's cultural activity took shape in national and even international contexts; the Archaeological Institute of America sent budding American archaeologists (including Norton's son) to Asia Minor, and his scholarship on medieval cathedrals and on Dante earned European acclaim. But as had been the case in the 1850s, when he founded the Cambridge Evening School, Norton was always attuned to the local. A new set of opportunities opened up after he began spending summers in the remote town of Ashfield, nestled among the hills of northwestern Massachusetts, in the 1860s. Ashfield became a microcosm of the larger liberal cultivation project, an effort to elevate the townspeople culturally and to invigorate their civic life. No sooner had he bought property there than he was writing to Godkin to send "two or three extra copies of this week's & next week's *Nation*" to share with the townspeople. Curtis soon joined Norton in a neighboring farmhouse, and together they inaugurated an annual event to raise money to build a library and to revive the town's deteriorating academy. The annual Ashfield Academy dinner became a veritable institution in the last three decades of the nineteenth century, attracting an impressive roster of speakers from among Norton's and Curtis's extensive network of friends, including Lowell, Godkin, Howells, George Washington Cable, William James, Josiah Royce, Mark Twain, William Graham Sumner, and Booker T. Washington, among others. By 1890, Curtis felt sure that the annual event had "liberalized and emancipated the people." The importance of this local exercise extended beyond the townspeople and their academy, as James Turner has argued. Every year, as national newspapers covered the event, "Ashfield stepped forward to exemplify to the nation America's own best principles" of liberal cultivation and democratic participation.[60]

Such local efforts worked in tandem with national endeavors, which depended on communication technology. Heightening American appreciation of the visual arts, for example, was arguably aided by innovations in print media even more than by the rise of urban museums. Technical improvement assured that *Harper's Monthly* and the *Century* would establish themselves as the best illustrated monthlies in the English language. Including appealing images was a way for such magazines to increase their marketability, of course, but financial returns constituted only part of their mission. Gilder's emphasis on the visual arts resulted from his appreciation for this area of expression, evident both in his marriage to a painter and his intimate friendships with many leading American artists. At the height of the magazine's influence in the late 1880s, Gilder commissioned the engraver Timothy Cole to furnish an "Old Masters' series" by traveling through Europe and copying Old World masterpieces for New World magazine audiences. To help convey the worth of these iconic images, the magazine commissioned essays by Cole and William J. Stillman (editor during the 1850s of the *Crayon*, where Norton first published the essays that became *Notes of Travel and Study in Italy*). These pieces bore a broadly educational rather than overtly critical emphasis, seeking to bring knowledge and interest to a large periodical-reading middle class that was unlikely to travel to Europe to see the original works of art.[61]

Despite such new projects, print dissemination remained primarily focused on fiction, poetry, history, and essays, the literary forms through which a liberal democratic culture seemed most likely to be created. "We need to go to Europe to see the great galleries," Higginson explained in 1867, and this judgment remained valid even after the *Century* whetted appetites to contemplate sculpture, painting, and architecture in the premier Old World museums. Books were fundamentally more accessible, since the "boy who reads Aeschylus and Horace and Shakespeare by his pine-knot fire" has "at his command the essence of all universities, so far as literary training goes." Lowell ventured a quite similar claim for the equalizing potential of print, commenting that membership in the "select society of all the centuries" resulted from a will to commune rather than from social status. (The Harvard-trained W. E. B. Du Bois later made a similar point about the inclusive nature of great literature in his famous aside that despite the American color line, "I sit with Shakespeare and he winces not.") For Lowell, the egalitarian logic applied as much to countries as to persons, as he discussed in his 1869 assault on British cultural pretensions. Europe's condescension toward its younger, American rival was willfully blind, he argued, since such claims were issued "as if libraries did not make all nations equally old in those respects, at least, where age is an advantage and not a defect." [62]

The print circuit contained great democratic potential in that it collapsed the distinction between readers and writers for those seeking to launch their careers as imaginative artists. Learning to write poetry and fiction involved a careful program of reading and experimentation, not the long apprenticeship characteristic of training in the plastic arts. Higginson was especially concerned with encouraging culture-minded "amateurs" to follow their inspiration toward written expression and publication. The most famous of these appeals came in Higginson's "Notes to a Young Contributor," written shortly before he entered the Union Army, where he assured hopeful writers that it did not matter if they came "to literature from a library, a machine-shop, or a forecastle" as long as they had "learned to work with thoroughness the soil" they knew. While this essay became one of Higginson's better-known works during his lifetime, it is now remembered primarily because of its impact on a reclusive female poet from Amherst, Massachusetts. After reading Higginson's essay at the outset of the Civil War, Emily Dickinson resolved to write directly to the author, send him her poems, and ask him if they "breathed." [63]

Higginson indeed believed they breathed, though he confessed that the "peculiar quality and aroma" of those poetic exhalations left him, even three decades after he first encountered them, "somewhat bewildered." Dickinson's choice of Higginson as "preceptor" and portal to the outside world was a curious one. Her letter initiated a decades-long relationship with the literary colonel that ended with the posthumous publication of her verse in multiple volumes as well as in the pages of the *Atlantic*, *Century*, and other periodicals. Their relationship reveals Higginson's genuine openness to fresh voices regardless of their provenance. He recognized in Dickinson's strange verse a "wholly new and original poetic genius," and his appreciation for her talent only increased with every passing decade. Yet Higginson did not quite know what to make of so original and fresh a voice, and in his uncertainty, he sought to temper it, though not to the extent some of his critics have claimed. Along with Mabel Loomis Todd, Higginson edited Dickinson's poetry for publication by standardizing her "peculiarities of grammar," regularizing her capitalization, and providing "clarifying" titles. But after the first volume had been received so well, going through six editions in six months, Higginson no longer felt compelled to edit, urging Todd, "Let us alter as little as possible now that the public ear is opened."[64]

As the Dickinson case suggests, although the liberal Americans' efforts at canon formation had some notable blind spots, they were also more wide ranging than many later scholars have acknowledged. This phenomenon is most obviously evident in their inclusion of women writers. Higginson championed the writing and talent of Margaret Fuller and Lydia Maria Child, to both of whom he professed his intellectual and moral indebtedness until the end of his life. Younger writers also received his praise and more often encouragement. He applauded the work of Harriet Prescott Spofford (who had been a student at his evening school in Newburyport), Helen Hunt Jackson, Charlotte Forten (whom he had known in Beaufort, South Carolina), and Louisa May Alcott, among others. In columns, reviews, and biographical studies, he called attention to the work of these and other writers. Toward the end of his life, he, Gilder, and Mark Twain worked to have Higginson's friend, Julia Ward Howe, elected as the first woman into the American Author's Club, an organization he had refused to join until it allowed women (recalling his effort to break the color line at the Town and Country Club some fifty years earlier). Beginning with the novels of his old friend, Elizabeth Gaskell, Norton also attended to the work of women writers. He prepared an edition of Anne Bradstreet's poetry (though he was underwhelmed by her verse), enjoyed the New England novelist Sarah Orne Jewett (a friend of his daughter, Sara), and became a friend and admirer of Edith Wharton, whom he found an "intellectual woman . . . of most unusual breadth of culture and depth of feeling."[65]

But the liberal critics devoted more attention to cultivating readers than to nurturing artistic work, another area in which they struggled with their critical role and their genuine interest in making texts alive and meaningful for other readers. Generating a love for books and reading was the primary means of cultivating American democracy, and this period's evaluation of literary greatness thus came to focus on a work's ability to draw forth a deeply personal response from each of its readers. The communion between a particular text and its reader was not merely the transmission of technical virtuosity or literary genius. The best writers invited readers to take an active role in creating a personalized set of meanings. Lowell explained this idea when he pointed out that a person who "reads most wisely" was he "who thinks everything into a book that it is capable of holding." Following this logic meant that it was the "stamp and token of a great book so to incorporate itself with our own being, so to quicken our insight and stimulate our own thought, as to make us feel as if we helped to create it while we read." Lowell's notion of an individually active and engaged kind of reading was only amplified by the fact that he delivered this address on *Don Quixote* not to a group of Harvard students but to an audience at the Workingmen's College in London. Lowell's insistence that "classics" continued to speak with an eternal timeliness drew an echo from Curtis, who shared his friend's respect for those books that were "as fresh and good to-day as they ever were." Summing up the prevailing opinion for readers of his "Easy Chair" column, Curtis concluded that "if a book is capable of becoming old-fashioned, it may be suspected that it is not one of the great and permanent books." (This critical view, ironically, condemned much of Curtis's work to obscurity during the twentieth century.)[66]

Fostering a popular appetite for literature took several distinct forms. In the postwar period, Curtis broadcast his cultural enthusiasm primarily through his "Easy Chair" column, though his earlier novels remained in print and continued to sell briskly. He developed an abiding affection for the regular "Easy Chair" feature of *Harper's Monthly*, which, as he proudly noted in 1872, "goes every month into thousands of homes and chats familiarly with a host of personally unknown friends and critics." The essays that made up this column mixed a purposeful eclecticism with a distinctly personal voice, more avuncular than authoritative. The basic form was self-consciously modeled on Joseph Addison's mid-eighteenth-century "Tattler" essays. Like this predecessor, the "Easy Chair" strove for a "comprehensiveness" conveyed in Addison's announcement that "I shall from Time to Time Report and Consider all Matters of what Kind soever that shall occur to Me."[67]

The "Easy Chair" left reviews of contemporary fiction to other *Harper's* writers, such as William Dean Howells, who for several years was in charge of the "Editor's Study" column. Curtis's running commentary instead concerned "minor morals and manners," the same general set of topics he addressed during a briefer stint as a columnist for *Harper's Bazaar*, a magazine explicitly directed toward female readers. Critical accusations that this coverage was overly light and unserious caused Curtis to insist that "no morals are properly minor, and manners are very closely related to morals." In practice, he hardly dealt with etiquette or the conventional forms of politeness but instead offered a wide-ranging set of observations on culture, the arts, and learning. These upbeat pieces clearly found an audience, and they proved as popular with his readers as the liberal reform program Curtis set forth as editor of the more politically engaged *Harper's Weekly*.[68] Recognizing the difference between his two outlets, Curtis explained how readers of the *Monthly* had a "common ground of interest in the Elysian fields beyond debate." Satisfying this thirst for unifying truths led him to reflect on the nonpartisan aspects of public life, which drew him toward college commencements, musical premiers, and similar cultural happenings. A slightly sharper edge marked his comments on Victorian worthies such as Thackeray and Carlyle, and his consistently worldly view of current events was clearly framed in liberal terms, broadly applied. If the "politician, the bigot, the controversialist" were banned from the magazine's pages, Curtis did not hesitate to discuss such figures. He speculated on strikes, wars, greed, and corruption, weaving these themes around the literary reminiscences that appeared in nearly every issue.[69]

Curtis demonstrated the value of developing a literary persona in achieving prominence within the Gilded Age cultural scene. In some ways, it was even more important for Higginson to develop this sort of distinctive voice, since he lacked a regular affiliation and thus needed a recognizable sensibility and personality to achieve his standing before readers. What united his newspaper writing (for the reform, prosuffrage press and liberal religious press), his columns (for the *Woman's Journal* and for *Harper's Bazaar*) and his literary work (at the *Atlantic Monthly*, *Scribner's*, *Harper's Monthly*, and the *Century*) was an avowedly personal, conversational tone that marked nearly everything he wrote. Even his literary histories focused less on texts than on his chance meetings, at times seeming more concerned with dropping names than with offering particular evaluations of literary merit. While this tendency diminished his critical legacy, it served during his lifetime to provide eager readers with an "inside view" of culture's inner sanctum. The two autobiographical accounts Higginson wrote late in life—both of which alternated between the dual themes of reform and literature—exemplified his tendency to compose his prose essays through the prism of his personal experiences.[70]

Higginson realized better than most of his contemporaries that biography was an especially suitable means of cultural dissemination, particularly when such studies focused on writers' lives. The exemplary nature of life stories helped to highlight the moral vision that made a person worth remembering (or "representative," in Emerson's sense of the word). As Lowell wrote in 1867, the "main interest in biography must always lie in the amount of character or essential manhood which the subject reveals to us, and events are of import only as means to that end." More than two decades later, he went further, noting "that precious and persuasive quality, style, may be exemplified as truly in a life as in a work of art." Leslie Stephen, whose long-term reputation would be linked to his role at the magisterial *Dictionary of National Biography* (which he began to edit in 1882), furnished the best example of a generation that understood biography as a kind of living, breathing ethics. These life stories constituted, as Noel Annan has pointed out, a "way of catching morality as it flies," providing a better means of treating principles and dilemmas than the abstract eighteenth-century method.[71]

Attending to the lived experiences of artists had the additional merit of lowering the threshold required for an appreciation of "serious" literature and culture. Launched by John Morley in the late 1870s, the English Men of Letters series (which, in spite of its name, included both Americans and women) sought to introduce distinguished writers to a broad reading public and presumably spark a corresponding interest in the work of such "greats." In addition to recruiting Henry James for the Hawthorne volume and writing the volume on Edmund Burke, Morley secured contributions from Goldwin Smith (on William Cowper), James Froude (on Bunyan), and Leslie Stephen (whose multiple contributions—on Johnson, Swift, Pope, Hobbes, and George Eliot —anticipated Stephen's immersion in the *Dictionary of National Biography*). Morley's success inspired an American Men of Letters series that eventually included two volumes by Higginson (on Margaret Fuller and Longfellow) and studies of Curtis and of Lowell that remain useful sources of information on these figures. A second English Men of Letters series in the early twentieth century drew yet another book from Higginson (devoted to the antislavery poet John G. Whittier) while a similar Great Writers collection prompted Goldwin Smith to join the 1890s upsurge of interest in Jane Austen.[72]

A variation of this popularized biographical form came in the "life and let-ters" format that proliferated during the late Victorian period. While such col-lections grew from earlier efforts to pay testimonial tributes to distinguished lives, Victorians such as Norton and Curtis altered the form in basic respects, consciously attempting to allow the subjects to speak for themselves through correspondence that would best suggest the overall sweep of a person's public life — at least to a certain extent. Edifying and instructional imperatives always outweighed any obligation to authenticity or honesty that twentieth-century readers and writers might prefer. The American Arnoldians worried that pro-viding too many intimate details might disrupt the study of public character that was most important, as a roiling debate over Carlyle's letters made clear. This notorious episode began with a posthumous biography by the British his-torian James Froude that included highly unflattering depictions of Carlyle's relationship with his wife. Norton threw himself into the resulting controversy with a greater ferocity and tenacity than most observers would have predicted, launching relentless assaults on Froude that helped to clarify Norton's ideal view of the relationship of private details to the public lives of artists. Nor-ton's distaste for mere literary "gossip" was shared more broadly by his fellow men of letters, who clearly wanted to present a more ennobling view of literary careers devoted to the search for larger truths.[73]

National histories, or the life stories of entire countries, provided another means of cultivating large audiences' tastes for inspiration, good writing, and a compelling set of narratives. In the early 1870s, Higginson began work in this area with a *Young Folks' History of the United States*, a book that sold two hun-dred thousand copies by distinguishing itself in the lucrative textbook market. As the centennial celebrations of 1876 sparked an upsurge of even wider inter-est in the revolution, Higginson began to craft a series of essays for the literary monthlies and then in 1885 gathered these in his profusely illustrated *Larger History of the United States*. Goldwin Smith devoted less attention to histori-cal studies than might have been expected after he left Cornell and ended his teaching and lecturing career. But while he never wrote his intended history of the English Revolution, he presented an *Outline of American History* in 1893, which sold well, brought a number of glowing reviews, and laid the basis for his presidency of the American Historical Association a decade later. A notice in the *Nation* termed Smith's work a "literary masterpiece, as readable as a novel, remarkable for its compression without dryness, and its brilliancy with-out any rhetorical effort or display." Smith's two-volume history of England followed in 1901, generating interest in both the United States and England.

The reception to each of these books caused him to reflect that a "history of the world in a single octavo volume" would be "one of the most saleable books I could write" even as he realized that at the age of eighty-one, he was too old to undertake what might have been his most successful piece of writing.[74]

Though the liberal Victorians were understandably gratified by the growing audience for their work, they worried that the proliferation of books meant that undiscerning readers might consume an inappropriate amount of the debasing along with the uplifting. Quantity of reading was less important than quality, they insisted, and some books might actually impede the process of self-cultivation. As Lowell explained in 1885, as "much variety of company" existed among books as among people, and the "mind sinks or rises to the level of its habitual society." Readers had to choose their books carefully if they wished to improve rather than simply divert their minds. Every book a reader opened had the potential to serve as a rung "in the ever-lengthening ladder by which we climb to knowledge," but this potential could be realized only if the individual chose the right books and read them in the right way. Self-culture relied on deliberate effort as much as any process of training and discipline. "Desultory reading, except as conscious pastime," Lowell continued, "hebetates the brain and slackens the bow-string of Will." So the "first lesson in reading well" would involve teaching readers "to distinguish between literature and merely printed matter." Empowered by this knowledge, readers could choose "such books as make us think, and read them in such a way as helps them to do so, that is, by endeavoring to judge them, and thus to make them an exercise rather than a relaxation of the mind."[75]

Lowell had identified a central dilemma of liberal culture in his analysis of reading habits: how to assure the quality of culture that was being disseminated in ever greater volume. Americans of the Gilded Age had access to countless books, periodicals, and libraries, but there was no guarantee they would choose appropriate reading matter or even take the disciplining process of self-culture as seriously as they should. As Frederic Harrison pointed out for British readers, a glut of print might be no different than scarcity if it kept readers from good books. The drive to spread culture throughout society would defeat the larger purpose if standards were lowered to achieve breadth. "There are few greater sins than the dissemination of second-rate literature," Norton had warned a friend in 1864. "Good poetry is rare, but its rarity is no reason for printing bad verse to take its place." He remained concerned with this central dilemma as he worked toward an understanding of how democratic individualism could be achieved only within the context of critical authority.[76]

There Is No Country Where Genuine
Criticism . . . Is More Needed

In the summer of 1865, Norton began his blistering description of "The Paradise of Mediocrities" in the United States on a relatively upbeat note, choosing to frame this topic with an affirmation of what was best in the American people. "We are quick to learn," he confided, "we are willing to be instructed, we desire to know." Defying foreign sneers, Norton even insisted that "our public is neither bourgeois nor philistine." The grounds for such optimism remained uncertain, however, because of the unhappy fact that "criticism as a fine art has indeed hardly been practiced among us, and there is no country where genuine criticism would be of more use, or is more needed." "Alas!," he continued, "shallow critics match shallow authors and shallow scholars, and men who know little are flattered by and misled by men who know still less." Without requiring greater rigor from America's thinking class, the possibilities remained dim for a culture that might be elevated at the same time that it was broadened.[77]

A year earlier, Norton had taken time out from campaigning for Lincoln's reelection to provide not just a stinging indictment of America's critical establishment but an explanation of what its shortcomings meant for the country. The American literary landscape was infested with a "swarm of bad critics" who were annoying in proportion to their numbers and were inflicting even greater injury "than their feeble natural powers would seem capable of effecting." The injury stemmed from the dishonesty at the heart of their book-reviewing enterprise. There seemed to be "scarcely a journal" to which an "intelligent" American could turn to get an accurate and judicious opinion of a book. While reviewers were perhaps directly responsible for the sorry state of reviewing, Norton insisted that publishers and the public also shared part of the blame for the absence of any critical standards.[78]

Norton's frustration with American criticism in the 1860s was hardly a luxury that only the privileged few could afford to take seriously. Such critical failings constituted an urgent national problem, as not simply the "lover of literature" but every "lover of his country" should realize. Writing amid a war that sought to vindicate American democracy, Norton connected the state of American criticism to the state of popular government itself. If the "success of democratic institutions depends on the intellectual and moral training of the people," Norton reasoned, and if "this training is greatly influenced by the character of the books afforded them," then by failing to hold literature and learning to a high standard, degraded and irresponsible criticism posed a direct threat to the country. The time had come, as with other institutions in crisis or under reform, for a "true, sound, learned critical spirit" to emerge. "The days in which we live," Norton warned, "are serious; they demand honesty of thought and life, honesty in literature and in manners." If "our critics" could not display honesty and simplicity, "what is to be expected of those whom they influence by their writings?"[79]

Norton's desire for a critical presence that might set and uphold the criteria of artistic merit sprang from the same impulse that committed him to the broadest possible diffusion of cultivation. Both aspects of this project — the vertical and the horizontal — emerged during the early years of the high tide, when liberals redoubled their efforts to prove that public life could be both broadly democratic and liberally cultivated. But cultural and intellectual matters posed something of a problem, for here was a realm where "majority rule" seemed to make little sense, where democracy, understood as a quantitative measure rather than as a qualitative spirit, might prove corrosive. Could popular taste, manifested through the literary marketplace by "'circulation,' 'sales,' and 'size' of audiences," ever provide a reliable guide to aesthetic worth? The liberal critics found such a proposition absurd. "Numbers in politics must always and should always be a strong argument," Godkin affirmed, but in "matters intellectual and aesthetic," mere popularity might prove "fatal to excellence and to originality." The challenge lay in diffusing without watering down, in making "the best" prevail, in Arnold's phrasing, while ensuring that it remain "the best."[80]

Godkin looked to a set of "institutes," vaguely modeled on the French Academy, as a way of establishing and organizing cultural excellence. Such an "Organization of Culture," as he had imagined shortly after the war, would help shield intellectual and aesthetic endeavors from the "passion and ignorance" of "mere numbers" and might work toward "infusing something like discipline and order into the most undisciplined and disorderly host in the world — the thoughtful classes of the U.S." Many of Godkin's contemporaries looked to less formalized groups such as the American Social Science Association. The literary pursuits of Higginson, Frank Sanborn, and other early participants in the association did not hinder their enthusiastic support for relating critical intelligence to a broad reform agenda. Such an organization had already provided a point of focus among liberal reformers in England. A similar effort to nationalize intellectual life in the United States seemed desirable at the precise time that the country's politics were being broadened and its constitutional order fundamentally changed.[81]

The emergence of America's first true research universities constituted the most significant and enduring aspect of postwar efforts to restructure knowledge and establish a national basis for intellectual life. It hardly took the war to point out this need, as was evident in the mounting calls during the late 1850s to establish college faculties, libraries, museums, and laboratories that would "enable us to dispense with Europe," as George William Curtis put it. Writing in 1858, Curtis realized that even the most rigorous American colleges were little more than "high schools conducted upon a monkish plan," unable to offer the same serious opportunities for learning available in Europe and especially in Germany. The urge to nationalize culture during Reconstruction focused more attention on this need than had ever previously been the case and did so at a moment when liberal Americans became ever more aware of the reforms being initiated by British liberals at Oxford and Cambridge. Higginson ventured a truism in 1867 when he baldly stated, "what we need is a university." Continuing to send students to Germany for advanced studies would perpetuate American backwardness, he warned, and it therefore became imperative to provide young scholars with opportunities in their own country to "go and study anything that kindles [their] enthusiasm, and find there instrumentalities to help the flame."[82]

These early calls for advanced American scholarship help to explain the enthusiasm that men of letters expressed for new schools such as Cornell University and Johns Hopkins University, which opened in 1868 and 1876, respectively. An even greater sense of exhilaration came from Harvard's transformation under the leadership of Charles William Eliot, however, especially as Eliot established himself as an important liberal ally in the campaign for clean government and for fostering Anglo-American understanding through friendships with Bryce, A. V. Dicey, and others. Shortly after Eliot's appointment as Harvard president in 1869, Norton (who was Eliot's cousin) wrote from Europe to congratulate him: "There is no institution in America which is of greater concern, if its development keep pace with the need." Eliot hardly needed such encouragement, immediately establishing what he had termed the "New Education," which would consist of an elective system in the undergraduate curriculum, a series of advanced programs in the professional schools, a dramatic expansion of the faculty, and a program to assure a stream of international visitors to Cambridge. Norton became one of Eliot's most important recruits, joining the faculty and overseeing a series of courses in art history in the early 1870s.[83]

As a member of the Harvard faculty, Norton grew ever more convinced of the role that Harvard and other "superior institutions of learning" played in American intellectual life. He described these rejuvenated universities as the "head-waters of the stream of education by which the general intellectual and moral life of the community is in large measure supplied and sustained." In 1890, Norton explained to readers of *Harper's Monthly* that the "last twenty-five years" had been a "period of transition" for Harvard, which had moved "from the traditional narrow academic system to a new, liberal, and comprehensive system, in which the ideal of an American university—a different ideal from the English or the German—had been gradually working itself out." Norton deemed that this work was "of greater importance to the nation" than any that "has been going on anywhere during this time." Its international impact, he contended, should be a source of "legitimate pride" for all Americans who cared about their country's standing in the wider republic of letters. In light of the college's many contributions, the school "deserves far greater popular attention than it has received, far greater popular support."[84]

For the university to be fully national in its reach, Norton and others recognized that access to its advantages needed to be increased. President Eliot implemented plans to nationalize the university. Norton encouraged efforts to minimize differences in wealth among Cambridge scholars. He bemoaned the "evil influence of wealth" on the student body and insisted that among the characteristics that would make Harvard truly "liberal" was that it "be open upon equal terms to all students of whatever race or social position." This inclusiveness extended, to some degree at least, to women's education as well. Norton taught frequently at the Harvard Annex (soon to become Radcliffe College), the developments of which Higginson chronicled frequently, along with those of other women's colleges both in the United States and in Britain, for the *Woman's Journal*.[85]

Other college-bred men of letters cheered the efforts to reform America's oldest college, often claiming part of the credit for this development. Curtis commented frequently on university reform despite his lack of formal college training, applauding the "protest of the American genius" against the "tradition and routine" that had marked the insular learning typical of antebellum academies. He believed that the best of the old had led to the new, reasoning that because "study and learning are in their very nature humanizing," the newest innovations had resulted from a "spirit which the university itself bred." Lowell likewise noted continuity amid dramatic expansion when he marked the 250th anniversary of Harvard College in 1886, using the occasion to plead for the "Humanities," which he hoped would "be maintained undiminished in their ancient right." While he agreed that President Eliot had done a great service by nurturing science and expanding the curriculum, Lowell was resolute that "those arts that were rightly called liberal" should remain at the center of its educational mission. He defined these fields not in disciplinary terms but according to their impact, singling out the areas of study that "kindle the imagination, and through it irradiate the reason," those that "manumitted the modern mind" and "in which brains of the finest temper found alike their stimulus and their repose, taught by them that the power of intellect is heightened in proportion as it is made gracious by measure and symmetry."[86]

The desire for continuity amid change was most evident in the connections men of letters made between university training and the development of the country's moral sense. Curtis made a typical argument in insisting that the "great function" of the American college was not merely "to impart knowledge, but to stimulate intellectual and moral life" and that these institutions provided Americans with the best available antidote to the period's materialism and greed. In 1890, he wrote that the "choicest revelation" of the university was "not that of the useful resources of nature, great and indispensable as that revelation is, but of the spiritual resources of man." Norton agreed, writing the same year that the "largest acquisitions of knowledge remain barren unless quickened by the imagination into vital elements of moral discipline and growth." The emphasis on the moral dimensions of higher education caused this cohort to view advanced research agendas in the humanities with some skepticism. The methods of experimentation, analysis, and quantification were inappropriate means of approaching art and literature, since these areas represented, as Higginson termed them, a "World outside of Science." Within his newer discipline of history, Higginson insisted that the necessary rigor of basing conclusions on primary sources was a less important goal than achieving narrative clarity and the graphic delineation of character.[87]

A "scientific" approach to works of the imagination revealed the potential hazards of pursuing letters within the context of the modern university. Inappropriately crafted research agendas or monkish retreat into academic institutions, this generation began to understand, threatened to eviscerate precisely what made great art and literature appealing. Lowell expressed particular disdain for the deadening approach he associated with German literary scholars, scoffing at the "supersubtleties of interpretation to which our Teutonic cousins,

who have taught us so much, are certainly somewhat prone." In an address he
delivered to the London Workingmen's College while serving as minister in England, Lowell explained the damage that resulted "when the obvious meaning
of Shakespeare has been written into Hegelese, by some Doctor of Philosophy
desperate with the task of saying something when everything had been already
said, and eager to apply his new theory of fog as an illuminating medium." Norton shared this dim view of what he called "American Germanized pedants"
working to "cumber the roads of the real Scholar" by becoming "hinderers instead of helpers of the progress of knowledge, while arrogating to themselves
the exclusive possession of the keys to it." In this sense, pedantry could become
a form of philistine scientism, detracting from the true goal of humanistic inquiry and doing so from within the citadels of culture themselves.[88]

Amid these concerns about the modern university's scientism and professionalism, most Victorian men of letters continued to pursue serious criticism
in other venues. Though they had in many respects moved far away from their
predecessors in the antebellum republic of letters, the members of this generation continued to submit even their most scholarly work to magazines and
to popular publishing houses rather than to air them within the confines of
the university or feature them in specialized journals aimed at fellow profes-
sionals. Such choices assured a constant tension between critical authority and
popular response. The interplay of detached judgment and popular engagement marked the prevailing critical mode for scholars such as Norton, who was
serious about his erudition as well as about his program of outreach.[89] Pursuing these dual objectives was difficult enough in works such as Norton's *Historical Studies on Church Building* or his contributions to scholarship on Dante
and John Donne. But the endeavor could become even more vexed when men
of letters brought their critical sensibilities to bear not just on art and literature but on the larger culture around them.

These critical efforts often spurred a backlash against those who presumed
to sit in judgment and find fault with the surrounding world. The *Nation* tried
to apply the highest criteria to both culture and politics, even while its contributors realized that they were establishing a reputation for being "too critical if
not cynical." Critics risked completely losing their audience if they presented
themselves too far above the fray, and the end result might be no different
from lowering standards to curry popular taste. In an article directed toward
American readers, Leslie Stephen noted that Matthew Arnold had hindered
his effectiveness through exactly this sort of off-putting stance as a "superior"

critic. "A man who is compelled to expose the gross errors of his own country should do it with some little air of vexation," Stephen explained, rather than "self-satisfaction." Criticism was "always more irritating in proportion to the serene self-content of the critic."[90]

Both Lowell and Curtis excelled at this mode of genial criticism, at placing demanding ideals before their audience but doing so in a way that encouraged rather than disparaged. Borrowing a distinction from Goethe, Lowell clarified that criticism was meant "not to criticize, but to understand." Good critics entered into sympathy with the object of their criticism and opened themselves up to different ideas and new perspectives. The critical spirit nurtured a "judicial habit" that ideally tended "to liberality of mind and hospitality of thought." Curtis echoed Lowell in acknowledging that criticism at its best constituted "not censure, but perception and appreciation." Yet understanding and appreciation did not imply acquiescence or accommodation. Criticism would not be worthy of the name if it simply left matters at that. Open-mindedness was an excellent thing, Lowell admitted, but "let us not confound liberality with indifference." Instead, let us insist on a "high standard, whether in life or literature," Lowell told his "fellow-students" in the pages of the *Century*, "and, however charitable we may be and should be to those who fall below it (unless it be our own case), let us not stupidly deny that they have fallen below it." Taking a page from the same rhetorical playbook, Curtis insisted that the voice of the "true critic" will be "friendly, unflattering, but full of sympathy, and the words that it speaks will be heard in the heart of the earnest artist, 'Friend, come up higher.'"[91]

If all of the liberal critics did not achieve (or even attempt) this amiable stance toward their audiences, they did collectively and routinely insist on the indispensability of the critic's role, particularly in America, where the frenetic pace and outward show of life required all the more the promptings to "come up higher." Curtis acknowledged a growing resistance to what he called the "leadership of educated men," whom opponents denounced as "prigs, pedants, and impracticables." But he distinguished "mere petulant scolding" from that "fair criticism" that "keeps the world rolling forward." While others often attacked cultural critics as "scolding old women" (gendered attacks that would only intensify when the liberal critics shifted their focus to corrupt politics and to late-century imperial adventures), Curtis thought that critics demonstrated "heroism and independence," traits more usually considered manly than womanly. "It is always very much easier to swim with the current than to stem it, and to join in the general chorus rather than sing alone," Curtis observed, thus adding moral courage to the battery of manly traits (discipline, training, and strenuosity) already articulated.[92]

Liberal Americans understood the larger role of the cultural critic in terms laid out in one of Arnold's crucial early essays, "The Function of Criticism at the Present Time." In reviewing this significant essay (published as the introductory chapter to his 1865 volume, *Essays in Criticism*), the *Nation* grasped the originality of Arnold's definition, which had extended the practice of criticism from literature to life itself and insisted that critics demonstrate honesty, creativity, and independence (what Arnold called "disinterestedness").[93] The *Nation* praised Arnold for placing "his rare gifts and acquisitions . . . at the conscious service of a truly noble purpose"—to "share with his fellows the pleasures of a higher and richer intellectual life" and to insist that his fellow Britons "become the children of the intellectual promise," matching their earlier achievements in political liberty and material success. American critics had hoped to do the same for their fellow Americans, who, amid the ersatz wealth of the Gilded Age, seemed overly focused on the here and now and forgetful of the elsewhere and always.[94]

As the American liberals looked around them in the 1880s and 1890s, Higginson's initial "plea for culture" seemed in one sense to have been answered. The late nineteenth century witnessed the establishment of an impressive set of institutions devoted to culture around the country: the Museum of Fine Arts in Boston, the Metropolitan Museum of Art in New York, the Art Institute of Chicago, the Carnegie libraries dotting the landscape. Universities had expanded and modernized, had opened their doors to women and (less widely) to African Americans, and had become national in reach. The self-appointed stewards of culture had attained greater authority than had earlier seemed possible, presiding over a remarkable set of periodicals that reached hundreds of thousands of readers. But in another sense (a sense that Arnold, with his dismissal of mere institutions, would have recognized), American public life seemed perhaps less rather than more cultivated by the end of the century. New wealth had done much for the external trappings of culture, but what about the internal growth of individuals, that development that "profits not the outer man"? The beautiful buildings, the well-endowed universities, the gilt-bound editions of "classic" writers: might they have done no more, Lowell asked, than "to put the Book of Life into a costly binding, and to know nothing of the nobler uses that are shut within it"?[95]

Norton tackled this difficult subject in one of his last sustained pieces of cultural criticism, an essay on "Some Aspects of Civilization in America" written for the recently founded magazine the *Forum*. Taking an Arnoldian view of his task, Norton produced an all-encompassing critique by examining American history, education, politics, manners, recreation, and foreign policy. Norton believed Americans should rightly be proud of the "splendid spectacle of material growth and well-being" that they exhibited at the end of a century that found them transformed from a "small, weak people" into one "of the greatest and most powerful nations that the earth has known." Sounding a familiar theme, however, he cautioned that it would be a mistake to confuse this material progress with moral progress. The latter had clearly not continued apace, and Norton's outlook was bleak. The passage of years had tempered the optimism he had expressed, even amid the "paradise of mediocrities," in the 1860s, and the essay was gloomier in tone than nearly anything else he wrote. Immigration seemed more threatening, schools were less edifying, the press more sensational. Ignorance, barbarism, and shallowness seemed rampant, equally in evidence among poor city dwellers and the affluent elites who thronged to the New York Horse Show. Even colleges such as Harvard had become nurseries of barbarism, as football had replaced learning as the most enthralling campus event. Everywhere, Norton saw developing an increased emphasis on things external rather than things internal. All in all, it was not a pretty picture, but echoing Arnold, he insisted that Americans see it for what it was: "to deny or to undervalue the forces ranged against civilization is to increase their power."[96]

Norton struggled (with mixed success) to be unsparing but not despairing. He sought to provide remedies, though their feebleness perhaps revealed the depths of his discontent more than anything. Amid the failures of a system of popular education that imparted information but ignored its students' imagination and sympathy and a press that did not engage its readers in serious discussion but sought to thrill them with sensational trivialities, Norton's earlier vision of a cultivated and active citizenry appeared naive. He all but relinquished any hope of rallying a collective commitment from the country at large. Both cultural matters and this period's politics revealed too little evidence of the idealism of the 1860s to put stock in this approach. What hope remained would be placed in the sole individual, who by pursuing personal betterment would take the first step toward greater virtue for the entire society. Those who demonstrated evidence of "exceptional service or exceptional ability" were less important for Norton than those who possessed the "plain virtues and common uprightness" that had come to seem in increasingly short supply. To bring these out, Norton called for "every right-minded man" to

"raise the level of his own intelligence, to keep his moral sense clear and un-
perverted, to use his influence in maintaining the simple ideals of private and
public virtue." These actions would assure that the "slow processes of self-
improvement" remained a central idea long after its articulation in the early
nineteenth century.[97]

Facing a bleaker future than he might have ever imagined thirty years earlier,
Norton suggested that the cultivation of individuals might redound to the
greater good. Just possibly, this spirit of humane learning would be "gradually embodied in public opinion" and would thereby set the United States on
a better course for the future. The end result could hardly be more important. The cause of cultivating virtue was, he summed up, nothing less than the
"secular fight, on the issue of which the happiness of mankind depends."[98]

The Politics of Liberal Reform

*The war that established our position as a vigorous nationality has also
sobered us. A nation, like a man, cannot look death in the eye for four years without
some strange reflections, without arriving at some clearer consciousness of the stuff it is
made of, without some great moral change. Such a change, or the beginning of it, no
observant person can fail to see here. Our thought and our politics, our bearing as a people,
are assuming a manlier tone. We have been compelled to see what was weak in democracy
as well as what was strong. We have begun obscurely to recognize that things do not go of
themselves, and that popular government is not in itself a panacea, is no better than any
other form except as the virtue and wisdom of the people make it so.*
James Russell Lowell, "On a Certain Condescension
in Foreigners," 1869

Over the last quarter century of his life, James Russell Lowell mulled over a
central question: Could Americans live up to their Civil War selves? Lowell
never forgot that when the Union had faced its supreme crisis, an inspired citizenry had followed steady leadership toward noble goals. In so doing, it had
vindicated the cause of popular government across the world. That such accomplishments could be repeated was doubtful, and Lowell at times even expected the United States to experience a period of steady political decline.
These moments of despair inevitably produced a gloomy eloquence that has
since marked Lowell's reputation and has by extension informed the most
familiar portrait of liberal reformers as a group. Lowell's biting poetry — which
gleefully sneered at the rings, corruption, and general shabbiness of the Gilded
Age — seals the case for his status as a disaffected malcontent. Here, it seems,
was a figure whose superior cultivation made him out of step with his country
and pessimistic about its basic direction.

The way that Lowell measured the uncertain future against a heady past was
hardly unique to the United States, nor did he lack his moments of recurrent
hope. A transatlantic frame helps to tease out how earlier commitments were

recast and how democratic reforms in both Britain and the United States were reevaluated after the high tide of the 1860s. Before the American Civil War was even a year old, Fitzjames Stephen, a "higher journalist" and the brother of Leslie Stephen, anticipated how the criteria would later shift when he insisted that the "great political problem of the day—a problem infinitely more important than all party questions put together"—was simply whether "increasing the power of the popular voice" would work to raise the "general tone of public life" and cause it to be "pervaded by a higher conception of the objects of national existence." Stephen feared that the "second half of the hopes of the original liberals" (elevating the quality of government) would be less "widely fulfilled" than the first (increasing the quantity of those entrusted with self-government). Democracy, he feared, would in practice coincide with a decline in political virtue, and liberals would thus deserve the scorn of posterity. They would realize that they had "inflicted upon mankind the greatest of all curses—a permanent degradation of human life."[1]

This was hardly a novel problem in the late nineteenth century. Like Stephen's "original liberals," John Stuart Mill had similarly wrestled with the competing goals of broadening political participation and ensuring political competence in his 1861 *Considerations on Representative Government*. What was novel about the late nineteenth century was the expansion of a mass-based party system on both sides of the Atlantic that required (and elaborated) new techniques of management. The number of voters increased dramatically during these decades through population increases in the United States and further expansion of suffrage in Britain, thus giving rise to the era of organizational politics replete with the machines, bosses, and wire pullers often associated with the Gilded Age. Confronted by these new realities, liberals shifted their focus slightly. While the idea of educative citizenship still informed liberal reform, liberals fastened their attention more squarely on the qualitative side of Fitzjames Stephen's equation, on the concern with elevation, competence, and intelligence.[2]

But if liberals on both sides of the Atlantic were increasingly dissatisfied with late-nineteenth-century politics, their complaints were typically leavened by a faith in the future and a conviction that Anglo-American governance would continue to set the standard for stable progress. Liberal men of letters demonstrated an unwavering belief in politics by continuing their involvement in public life, by understanding it as a necessary component of a larger cultivating mission, and by hailing it as what Lowell termed the "noblest exercise of man's intellect and the best training of his character." The postbellum criticism offered by liberal reformers was sharp, and it regularly conveyed the same uncompromising sense of duty that had motivated the group's earlier attacks on slavery and the expansionist war against Mexico. Yet for all the severity of these critiques, Gilded Age liberal politics was no more likely to breed withdrawal or alienation than did the cultural endeavors undertaken by these same intellectuals. In both spheres, the prevailing liberal stance was that of a "jaunty jeremiah" capable of combining harsh criticism with a measured expectation that political progress was more likely to be achieved in America than anywhere else in the world.[3]

The liberal political program was not as consequential as the initiatives that this cohort pursued in the cultural realm, but the long-term significance of such efforts remained quite impressive. Liberal reformers never became a true establishment in Gilded Age politics, in part because it is unclear whether that is what they truly desired. Their voices were heard and their criticisms were sometimes heeded by those closer to the machinery of governance. The liberals' critique of Gilded Age politics included many blind spots. Their inattention to many of the challenges presented by urban poverty, enduring racism, and the concentration of industrial power would cause "New Liberals" and Progressives of a later generation to belittle the earlier reform vision as overly timid and naive. Much of this critique of the Victorians' sins of omission is fair, as is the criticism that the style of politics they envisioned centered on middle-class individuals as normative citizens and thus ignored the needs of working-class Americans. As the liberal men of letters generalized from their situations and preferences, their political ideals could at times seem abstracted from the realities of power as well as narrowly class bound.

Where this generation of liberals focused their attention, however, they set the terms of subsequent debates and did so within the same broadly transatlantic framework that marked their efforts in literature and art. No group would be more important in insisting on a modern commitment to a critical, opinion-oriented press, on a broad engagement with public opinion, and on the need to rein in the flaws of a political system that regularly elevated partisan advantage over the pursuit of the common good. Their refusal to play by established political rules drew a fierce response from party loyalists, including most famously an assault on their sexuality. The liberal men of letters ignored such attacks, maintaining their lifelong belief in the "duty of the scholar to politics and the times," as George William Curtis had put it decades earlier. In updating the formulation in the 1890s, E. L. Godkin acknowledged both the unpopularity and the importance that accompanied the "duty of educated men in a democracy." That duty lay in criticism: in speaking unpopular truths, in calling to mind higher ideals, and in exposing perceived shortcomings. Detractors might (and did) mock critics as talkers rather than actors, but Godkin insisted that it was "talk—somebody's, anybody's, everybody's talk—by which [all] changes are wrought, by which each generation comes to feel and think differently from its predecessor." Liberal men of letters took such talk to a new level in the late nineteenth century, elaborating a striking role as critical voices in an expanding national democracy.[4]

A Sovereign to Whose Voice Everyone Listens

For "great multitudes" of people, George William Curtis explained in 1881, the "unfolding of their paper is the opening of their minds." Such was an apt image for the editor who considered *Harper's Weekly* a "lay pulpit" that allowed him to preach the gospel of liberal reform for nearly three decades. In seeking to sway hearts, open minds, and rally commitment with every issue of this weekly journal of politics and culture, Curtis vindicated reasoned, cosmopolitan, and morally informed discussion as the basis for civic engagement. A similar set of objectives animated the editorial work undertaken by E. L. Godkin at the *Nation* magazine, a journal that featured not just Godkin's writing but that of nearly the entire cohort of transatlantic liberals. These two New York weeklies were the most influential examples of the journalism of ideas elicited by the hide tide's insistence on an educative, print-based politics. The same spirit could be seen in the journalistic work undertaken by Thomas Wentworth Higginson and Goldwin Smith during the 1870s and 1880s and by Richard Watson Gilder's attempt to offer readers of the *Century* a vision of civic improvement that would complete the magazine's cultivating mission. The world of liberal political reform in the Gilded Age was, in sum, the world of magazines and newspapers.[5]

Across a range of editorial projects, liberal intellectuals expanded on their earlier efforts in the "higher journalism" and attempted during the last third of the nineteenth century to reach the same large literate audiences that they cultivated through their Arnoldian promotion of literature and art. Intellectuals with a literary bent had long guided the most respectable monthlies and quarterlies. This trend continued in the 1860s and 1870s with Lowell, Norton, and then Henry Adams editing the *North American* and John Morley and Leslie Stephen overseeing the *Fortnightly* and the *Cornhill*. But the high tide of democratic aspiration involved new ambitions as well, a broad urge to move beyond the relatively focused outlets that Higginson described, with only slight exaggeration, as "circular letters addressed by a few cultivated gentlemen to those belonging to the same club." The key challenge was to achieve a broad audience without reducing the critical rigor displayed by more select publications. Higginson, for one, believed that an increased readership was more likely to distill ideas into excellence than to water them down. "It is not until a man knows himself to be writing for a hundred thousand readers," he reflected, "that he is compelled to work out his abstrusest thought into clearness."[6]

Gilded Age liberal journalism developed from Civil War experiences and especially the success that Union publicists had achieved during their first campaign to influence a large cross-section of the American middle class. When Charles Eliot Norton proposed in 1865 that Curtis might edit a "liberal Weekly, of the most advanced kind" then being planned by former abolitionists, Curtis took the opportunity to evaluate what he had already accomplished through the direction of the wartime political department of *Harper's Weekly*. A wholly new paper attracted him, especially one that Norton insisted would be written in an elevated tone. But Curtis feared that the high aspirations for the proposed journal "would constantly tend to make it outrun the popular sympathy," thereby "limiting its circulation to those who need no conversion." He was also wary about leaving *Harper's* at the precise moment that he had become "perfectly free" to speak his mind on all major questions of the day. The magazine allowed him complete freedom and a stable position, but it also gave him access to a larger and more diverse audience than the new, more specialized weekly would likely reach. Curtis admitted to Norton that the illustrated and sometimes frivolous *Harper's Weekly* "is not altogether such a paper as I should prefer for my own taste," but its popularity represented a crucial part of why Curtis felt compelled to remain there. The "immense" circulation— more than 150,000 at the close of the war and destined to double yet again by 1870—was "among the class which needs exactly the enlightenment you propose," he reasoned, concluding that by staying put he could do the "very work" Norton suggested and "upon a much greater scale than in the form you suggest." In declining the editorship of the *Nation*, Curtis thus cleared the way for Godkin's subsequent career there.[7]

Until his death in 1892, Curtis used *Harper's Weekly* to publicize the liberal reform program to a sizable middle-class readership. The paper's success revealed the appetite that existed for a regular application of transatlantic liberalism to American politics. Norton never fully accepted Curtis's decision to stay at the popular weekly and as the two men grew ever closer continued to suggest other opportunities to his friend. Curtis each time refused, declining entreaties to enter politics as a candidate, to assume the editorship of a daily newspaper, or to accept the prestigious mission to England that had long been used to reward politically active men of letters. *Harper's Weekly* suited Curtis as well as Harvard would suit Norton, in large part because of what Norton deemed his friend's "peculiar sensitiveness to what might be called the atmospheric currents of popular opinion." In 1867, Norton had already taken his measure of Curtis as a political editor, explaining to Godkin that Curtis was "sensitive as a barometer to [public opinion], and the rise or fall of his mercury indicates coming changes. His principles are as firm & clear as the glass tube, but his feelings & his opinions as to modes of action & courses of policy vary with the popular weather. This makes him an excellent & useful political writer & actor in such a country as ours & at such a time as this."[8]

Norton's description of Curtis implicitly drew a contrast with Godkin, whom Norton successfully recruited as editor of the *Nation*. In his new position, Godkin came to place a greater value on his principles and convictions than on whether he could curry public sympathy or even respond to the movements of public opinion. While the *Nation*'s founders initially hoped that it would focus most of its attention on the former slaves and on the Republican Party's southern program, Godkin accepted the job while insisting that he conduct a "really independent journal, which does not work in harness, although it may keep certain ends in view." Despite a guarantee of editorial independence, his willingness to attack Radical Republican leaders in print and to veer beyond the confines of a freedmen's journal enraged many of the paper's original backers and entangled the paper in an early set of controversies. After engineering a change in ownership, Godkin committed himself to "playing for ultimate and not immediate influence and success" by printing incisive criticism and by cultivating an ideologically broader audience than people focused exclusively on the postemancipation South. He shared Curtis's concerns about addressing those already "converted" to the cause and defended his conduct to Norton by saying that "if anything was well understood at the outset, it was that the *Nation* was to discuss questions evenly and moderately, & not in the slangwhang abolitionist style, for the purpose of reaching a public which the other antislavery papers do not reach."[9]

Though the early months of the *Nation* were difficult, Godkin believed his course had been justified and that his inclusion of science and literature along with politics had created a genuinely new voice on the American public stage.

"The paper is doing well," he reported. "The public evidently appreciates it, & I know we are reaching a class of people . . . who listen to our views on political questions for the sake of the other things the paper contains." Godkin's sense of the *Nation*'s broad appeal meant something quite different than Curtis's commitment to a large-circulation paper, which would attract readers first with illustrations and light sketches and then draw them into a consideration of liberal political principles. The *Nation* hoped instead to cultivate a following by engaging in the same combination of high-minded seriousness and polemical tone that distinguished London sheets such as the *Spectator* and *Saturday Review*. Godkin sought influence not through popularity but through distinction and thus viewed his undertaking as an experiment in whether the "best writers in America" could get a "fair hearing from the American public on questions of politics, art, and literature through a newspaper." He of course hoped to make the *Nation* a success, but he measured that success in terms of force rather than circulation. He was less interested in assuring that great numbers of subscribers read the paper than in assuring that no influential figures could completely ignore its perspective. In many ways, his aspirations were realized, since the *Nation* played a role in shaping late-nineteenth-century public life that went well beyond its relatively limited circulation, which under Godkin's editorship never rose above twelve thousand.[10]

The emphasis that these two liberal journalists placed on independence and reason formed part of a more general postwar sensibility, as James Russell Lowell nicely captured in 1865 when he noted that "in peace, governments cannot, as in war, find strength in the enthusiasm and even the passions of the people, but must seek it in the approval of their judgment and convictions." In January of the following year, Curtis applied this diagnosis to the conduct of *Harper's*, speaking out against the "obsequious adulation" that marked much of the northern press's attitude toward President Andrew Johnson, who remained popular even with many Radicals of his party. The duty of journalists was not to lobby for a popular president's program or to rally enthusiasm for his leadership but simply to reveal to him the "tendency and state of public opinion." In this way, Curtis explained, papers could serve as critical intermediaries between the people and their elected leaders. He clarified his position in the next issue by criticizing what he considered do-nothing journalism, singling out those editors who believed that their duty ended simply with revealing the state of opinion and then declaring that that opinion was determined and immovable. This kind of fatalism shirked the most important duty of "honest journalism," which lay in "enlightening public opinion by ar-

gument." For what, Curtis asked, were free speech and a free press worth if
journalists and editors abdicated this educative and argumentative function?
He saw his mission as considerably more important and activist: demonstrating sensitivity to the stream of opinion but then endeavoring "to turn that current in the true direction."[11]

The internal struggle for control of the *Nation* made Godkin particularly
committed to editorial autonomy and made him wary of all forces that inter-
fered with the consistent articulation of principled ideas. Fighting to determine
the magazine's direction had exposed Godkin's barely concealed combative
personality, and this quality made him more willing than other liberals to bring
the language of conflict into the new period of peace. Early in 1866, he committed himself to freeing the new journal from any "party, sect, or body" and
vowed that the publication would "wage war upon the vices of violence, exaggeration, and misrepresentation by which so much of the political writing of
the day is marred." The "war" that he had in mind differed substantially from
that which had just concluded, of course, since it offered not bloodshed but
cool reason and a determination "to try principles by their weight in the scales
of judgment, . . . and to contribute something, week by week, to the sum of the
rational belief on which the community must live and grow." Though his rhetoric frequently overwhelmed his intentions, Godkin saw reasoned moderation
as the ideal editorial position in a democracy such as the United States. "Where
there is no standard of political opinion fixed by authority, supported by government, or made venerable by tradition, but where opinion, even on primary
questions, is, by means of debate and discussion, continually a-making, it is
of first moment that all political and social doctrines should be tried on their
merits by rational criticism." Such an approach was well suited to the passage
of the country "from the revolutionary stage to that of constructing." Forging
the basis of a republic set on a new course by war required "above all things
calmness, moderation, and a regard for the rights of all."[12]

Higginson's editorial work for the *Woman's Journal* never achieved the influence of *Harper's Weekly* or the *Nation* but nevertheless offered a telling example
of the moderately argumentative and always high-minded journalism that was
becoming a clear liberal style. Higginson's weekly column, which he conducted
through the early 1880s, contained flashes of the old abolitionist fire. One of
his early columns rallied support by declaring that "reform is a war in which
words are bullets" and advised feuding suffragists to "fire . . . at your opponents" rather than to take potshots at one another. Yet his tendency to compare
this woman's suffrage weekly to William Lloyd Garrison's abolitionist *Libera-*

tor constituted little more than a rhetorical flourish. Like more influential liberal editors, Higginson believed that violence was not always the most effective
motor of change and was thus committed to the fact that "in a republican government, the wind is popular conviction." The best way to rally broad support
in the aftermath of war was to replace the stern, caustic moralism of Garrisonian abolition with the same uplifting tone that Higginson was then perfecting as a popular writer of fiction, a literary reviewer, and a social commentator.
The change in tactics followed from the nature of the respective causes as much
as it marked a new postwar zeitgeist or a transformation in Higginson's career.
Abolitionists had fought a "barbarism wholly behind the age" and thus had
to "enlist people of conscience and action" to do what was self-evidently right.
By contrast, Higginson thought that winning the vote for women touched the
"finest and most subtle strings of the social organization" and thus marked a
"further step in evolution." Higginson's belief, which he shared with many of
his friends in the recently formed American Woman Suffrage Association, that
the disfranchisement of women was "less capable of dramatic treatment" than
the horrors of slavery convinced him of the need to "impress the public more
profoundly, perhaps, but less sensationally" than abolitionists had.[13]

The liberal publicists combined their postwar call for moderation with demands for heightened moral seriousness. Norton's sense of journalistic ethics
was especially well developed and formed a regular topic of discussion with his
friends in the press. His convictions had been shaped by his interaction with
hundreds of editors during his leadership of the New England Loyal Publication Society, which had introduced him to the shortcomings of most journalists. In the midst of this effort, Norton lectured Jonathan Baxter Harrison of
Indiana, "Moral cowardice is a common fault of editors. Pray avoid it. Fight
the majority when it is wrong. Be sure that the ground you stand on is firm on
right principle & then never mind who attacks you." Curtis and Godkin, who
repeatedly echoed Norton's stance, did as much as any figures in the generation to establish the equivalent of a professional code of conduct for journalism. Curtis offered his most systematic reflections on "Newspaper Ethics" in
his "Easy Chair" column in *Harper's New Monthly Magazine*. In these pieces,
Curtis struck his usual conversational tone in explaining the need for editors to
avoid potential conflicts of interest and unseemly attacks on opponents. Such
guidelines were anchored in his core sense that effective journalism depended
on a consistent set of editorial convictions, detached from self-interest and the
necessarily compromising pursuit of office.[14]

The liberal men of letters offered a notion of elevated journalism as an alternative to that pursued by other members of the "press gang." The sensational press pioneered by James Gordon Bennett's *New York Herald* drew much of their ire, and the Victorian liberals regularly attacked its selfish valuing of profit over progress and entertainment over argument as a betrayal of readers' trust. Of nearly equal concern was the overtly partisan press, which remained a force to be reckoned with despite the waning of its influence in comparison with the antebellum period. Newspapers that continued to identify themselves as the "'organ' of some party, or set, or clique," Godkin complained, bound their editors by "party associations, or obligations, or ambition, to be silent on a thousand subjects on which a true regard for the interest of the public would require [them] to speak." Even worse, these party sheets' regular attacks on their enemies caused readers to become inured to the routine criticism, with the end result that the government was exempted "from that most useful of all checks, — the vigilance of the opposition." Norton feared that such a press inhibited the growth of public spirit by encouraging a small-minded intolerance. "The want of independence & sincerity in our press both secular & religious," he wrote to Godkin, "has had the worst effect in nourishing the growth of partisan narrowness & sectarian bigotry."[15]

Liberals' sense of their role developed from the campaigns of several famous newspapermen to parlay their editorial reputations into success as candidates. This trend culminated during Reconstruction with Horace Greeley's 1872 run for president. The *New York Tribune* editor's attempt to bring northeastern intellectuals under the banner of "Liberal Republicanism" turned out to be a fiasco, hampered not just by the candidate's violation of the unofficial barrier between statesmanship and journalism but by doubts about his character and discomfort about his partnership with former Confederates. His dismal showing helped to further the developing liberal idea that public life worked best when the distinct separation of party politics and journalism was maintained. In the new practice of "educative" journalism, an editor who tried to win power for himself was not living up to his true calling. Far better for him to help citizens decide which candidate and which policies were worthy of their support than to cloud the issue with more personal aspirations.[16]

The press's ability to reshape and elevate American public life depended on men capable of acting as the "daily critic and guide, the creator and the voice of public opinion." As college men themselves, the liberals naturally came to view higher education as the ideal preparation for journalistic work. In his first lecture as a faculty member of Cornell University, Goldwin Smith noted that the "right education of the journalist" was as important for Americans as the "right education of princes is in a monarchical country." In "so journalistic a country," the public had much to learn from writers "raised by the subject of history and its cognate subjects" to "take in humanity" and thus find it "now too uncongenial" to "wallow in the mire of party fanaticism or of scurrilous personalities." Charles Francis Adams Jr., who shared Smith's interest in both history and liberal reform, made a similar point to Harvard's Phi Beta Kappa Society in 1873. In discussing the university's mission to cultivate a "taste for statesmanship" among its undergraduates, Adams downplayed the importance of "ordinary party politics" and the aim of "getting into power" through office. He called for his audience instead to aspire toward the "direction of the Periodical Press" and to careers in "honest, independent opinion, founded upon extensive study and superior knowledge." In an era of professionalization and expanding universities, such an attitude was hardly surprising.[17]

E. L. Godkin attempted to formalize the connection between universities and liberal journalism in 1870, when Charles W. Eliot offered him a post in Harvard's department of history. Lowell, Norton, and the rest of Godkin's inner circle urged him to resist the attractive offer, arguing that his departure would ruin the *Nation* at the precise moment it had demonstrated its potential to reshape American public life. Hoping to arrive at a compromise, Godkin asked Harvard's Board of Overseers whether he might keep his ties with the magazine and direct its affairs while teaching in Cambridge. When his request was denied, Godkin angrily explained that "one of the great uses of history is to furnish a key to contemporary problems." To deprive him or any other future faculty member of a prominent public role was akin to forbidding a "medical professor to attend a patient, or a chemist to analyze for judicial purposes." The university's shortsightedness, he continued, would perpetuate the reputation of the college professor as a "bookish monk, of whose opinions on the affairs of the world, nobody need take any account." Despite his plea, the overseers remained firm, apparently drawing a distinction between a weekly paper such as the *Nation* (which they feared would regularly distract a faculty member from his duties) and the presumably less demanding responsibilities of conducting the *North American Review*. This quarterly, begun on the Harvard campus, passed in the postwar years from the hands of Lowell and Norton to the Harvard historian E. W. Gurney and then to Henry Adams, who joined the history faculty shortly after Godkin formally declined Eliot's offer.[18]

In his dispute with the Harvard overseers, Godkin had invoked the example of Goldwin Smith as proof that collegiate duties would not suffer from faculty participation in political journalism. During the first stage of an unusually distinguished academic career at Oxford, Smith had indeed been a regular contributor to the *Saturday Review* and had established himself as one of the most frequent contributors to the *Edinburgh Review*, *Macmillan's*, and then the *Atlantic*. Yet in 1870, in the same year that Godkin chose the *Nation* over Harvard, Smith ended his academic associations, permanently leaving Cornell University for Toronto, where he would spend much of the next four decades writing for American, Canadian, and British audiences. His contribution to Canadian journalism was characterized less by liberal moderation (which Smith, as much as Godkin, always had to struggle to achieve) than by a steady dose of liberal cosmopolitanism. He telegraphed his outsider status as a non-native Canadian by adopting "The Bystander" as his favorite signature and by devoting nearly as much attention to British and American topics as Canadian ones. Enemies worked hard to discredit Smith by questioning his basic loyalties and by denouncing his belief that Canada's ultimate destiny required that it be annexed to the United States. Charges of Smith's disloyalty had already become common by the late 1890s, when his reputation as a dissenter was sealed by his outspoken opposition to the Boer War, an overwhelmingly unpopular stance during a wave of militant Canadian support of British imperialism.[19]

Smith's career in Canadian journalism after 1870 epitomized the transnational scope of Gilded Age liberal reform, though never in an entirely predictable way. His example remained useful for his American and British friends, who continued to invoke his authority and to recall the heroic stance he had taken during the 1860s. Yet his position in Canada made it increasingly likely that he would follow rather than influence American trends. This pattern was especially true of the inspiration he took from American political reform movements, and by the early 1880s, he was consciously modeling his independent journalism on that of Godkin and Curtis. What Canada needed, Smith wrote to Curtis, was "something besides the organs of the two machines." A paper that held aloof from party intrigue, he explained, might provide a "nucleus of opinion" for "advanced" positions such as his desire for Canada to be incorporated into the United States. Even though Smith never achieved the same influence in Canadian politics that Godkin and Curtis did within the United States, Smith's efforts remained consequential. More than any other figure, he made Canada a node on the circuit of high Victorian liberal ideas and thus brought his adopted country into a larger discussion of transatlantic reform. Writings that Smith had first published in the *Canadian Monthly*, the *Bystander*, and the *Toronto Week* drew widespread comment on both sides of the Atlantic, as did a continuing string of essays and reviews he published in the *Nation*, the *Atlantic*, and a remarkably broad spectrum of British periodicals.[20]

In contrast to the British cases of John Morley and James Bryce, both of whom served in Parliament, liberal journalists in North America typically avoided formal ties with government. Despite the comparatively delimited scope of Curtis, Godkin, Gilder, Higginson, and Smith, their magazines struck a cosmopolitan perspective that made them part of a recognizably transatlantic phenomenon. The worldliness of *Harper's*, the *Nation*, the *Century*, and Smith's series of Toronto journals and columns persuaded readers of the need to keep up with transatlantic happenings. *Harper's* followed international events and played a key role in providing middle-class Americans with images of seminal events such as the Paris Commune of the early 1870s. The *Nation* committed itself even more fully to domesticating European affairs for an American audience. Godkin enlisted such notable overseas contributors as Charles Eliot Norton (who sent letters during his extended foreign travels), Leslie Stephen, A. V. Dicey, and James Bryce. In so doing, Godkin realized that in addition to bringing the world to Americans, he brought the American scene to readers beyond U.S. borders. "To the outsider the newspaper press is the nation talking about itself," he wrote, adding that "nations are known to other nations mainly through their press" (a point borne out during the Civil War when Americans had taken such offense at the *London Times* and found relief in the *London Daily News*).[21]

One of the most important achievements of liberal journalism in the Gilded Age was its ability to forge a sense of community and to set an agenda for reform-minded men of letters on both sides of the Atlantic. *Harper's Monthly*, the *Atlantic*, *Scribner's*, and the *Century* combined their coverage of European and especially Anglo-American culture with a similarly transatlantic stance toward politics. Yet the magazine of choice for Victorian liberals was the *Nation*, which published the work of this entire cohort save Curtis, who stayed committed to publishing exclusively with the *Harper's* firm. Because the *Nation* provided principled responses to a select—though by no means narrow—readership, its stances toward particular issues were internalized by those brought within its orbit. Norton aptly summed up the *Nation*'s contribution in 1902 when he noted that Godkin had done "more than any other writer of his generation to clarify the intelligence and to quicken the conscience of the thoughtful part of the community in regard to every important political question of the time." The philosopher William James testified in a similar vein that Godkin was "to my generation . . . the towering influence in all thought concerning public affairs." James appreciated that the *Nation*'s impact traveled beyond the Harvard faculty lounge, commenting that Godkin's influence had "certainly been more pervasive than that of any other writer of the generation, for he influenced other writers who never quoted him, and determined the whole current of discussion."[22]

James's understanding of how the *Nation*'s relatively small circulation could guide the "whole current of discussion" typified Victorians' appreciation of the mysterious if indispensable phenomenon of public opinion. Invoking this force allowed Godkin, Curtis, and a few other strong voices to claim a role in American politics that was out of proportion with the number of readers directly exposed to the writers' appeals and arguments. Liberals' appreciation of their power to mold and shape public sentiment in its broadest terms had been immeasurably strengthened during the Civil War, when they had witnessed an apparently unwieldy democracy gradually developing its collective power toward progressive national ends. Union victory and the sweeping changes that immediately followed helped to remind liberals throughout the late nineteenth century that a national public not only existed but was capable of cultivation. The understanding of public opinion as a fixed entity, capable of careful management, would come to be considered as naive by twentieth-century successors such as Graham Wallas and Walter Lippmann whose notion of a "phantom public" constituted in part a critique of the Victorians' comparatively innocent faith in large-scale democratic elevation.[23]

Well before Wallas and Lippmann took up the problem of public opinion, the transatlantic liberals pondered the operation of this shadowy force within the context of American democracy. British writers subjected the phenomenon of American public opinion to the most sustained inquiry, both because they wrote as analytical outside observers and because the connection between public opinion and liberal governance in their country reached back to the early nineteenth century. The press certainly boasted that it was the "embodiment of public opinion," as Leslie Stephen noted in 1870, meaning that it "says very much what many hundreds of thousands of people are saying." Identifying himself as "a Cynic," Stephen punctured this rhetorical balloon, however, noting that the grand pronouncements of editors and journalists were "at best . . . the work of a few clever men a little in advance, it may be, of the general current of opinion, but compelled by the necessity of their position not to be too far in advance." If Stephen anticipated in some respects Lippmann's notion of a "phantom" public, he did not carry what might have been a radical critique to its logical conclusion. In marking the transfer of power from Parliament to newspapers as "our supreme rulers," candor required him to consider how this vague entity known as "public opinion" was "singularly capricious and uncertain, and easily diverted from the reformation of mankind to the settlement of an infinitesimal private dispute." Yet he concluded his diagnosis on a less "cynical" if still ambivalent note. For him, public opinion was no more and no less than an "incomplete and unsatisfactory piece of machinery which on the whole does rather more good than harm."[24]

Stephen no doubt realized that raising too many questions about a rationally formed public opinion would threaten the entire Victorian liberal project and call into question the democratic aspirations that had become a key component of liberal journalism. His cousin, A. V. Dicey, went further, questioning the extent to which "the people" in England would, through public opinion, ever actually "govern" however much they technically "reigned." Even James Bryce's classic text of transatlantic liberalism, *The American Commonwealth*, contained nascent doubts and unresolved tensions. Bryce, who was both a close associate of Stephen and Dicey and a crucial part of the Gilded Age network of transatlantic reformers, devoted considerable attention to "this vague, fluctuating, yet indeterminate thing we call public opinion." It was understandable that a book that distilled liberal perspectives on American politics into a systematic survey gave such attention to the theme of public opinion. Equally unsurprising was Bryce's conclusion that "in no country is public opinion so powerful as in the United States," a place where, in an inversion of Dicey's comment about England, Bryce contended that opinion not only "reigned but governed." Recognizing its simultaneous obscurity and power, Bryce offered a memorable formulation of opinion: "omnipotent yet indeterminate, a sovereign to whose voice everyone listens, yet whose words, because he speaks with as many tongues as the waves of a boisterous sea, it is so hard to catch."[25]

Moving from platitudes to analysis required Bryce to draw a number of key distinctions, which in turn forced him to articulate some of liberal journalism's unspoken assumptions and to reveal some of its deepest tensions. Like Stephen, Bryce fully acknowledged the less-than-rational nature of most opinion, which for nineteen out of twenty citizens was merely "passive" and based more on sentiment and impression than on reasoned conviction. He was quick to point out that this rule applied across society and was as true among the propertied as the working classes. (Indeed, according to Bryce, affluence often had an adverse effect on opinion by making men timid and closed minded, which explained the historic fact that "nearly all great political and social causes have made their way first among the middle or humbler classes.") Among the re-

maining one in twenty—the "active" opinion makers and leaders—the press
performed a variety of overlapping functions, serving "as narrators, as advocates, and as weathercocks." A babel of views sometimes resulted, producing
an "uncertain sound" that could be difficult to interpret. Bryce skirted this
issue simply by concluding that a "sovereign is not the less a sovereign because
his commands are sometimes misheard or misreported."[26]

But other difficulties attended the subject of opinion, and Bryce filled a chapter of his book with the reasons "public opinion fails" in America. If opinion
was difficult to ascertain, it was also "slow and clumsy" in grappling with large
problems and "overkindly and indulgent" in matters of governmental miscon-
duct and incompetence. While he discounted older fears of tyrannical majorities, he pointed to a certain "fatalism of the multitude" that he thought life in
a vast, decentralized, good-natured, and optimistic country such as America
tended to breed. This fatalism made dissent agonizingly difficult. The strength
of public opinion in America posed its own dangers. The majority's confidence
in its wisdom and power could make it impervious to criticism. Having grown
accustomed to "seeing nothing but its own triumphs, and hearing nothing but
its own praises," the nation could become arrogant, smug, and self-satisfied.
Bryce's dire picture revealed an acute need for principled statesmen and critics
with the duty to "resist and correct" rather than to "encourage the dominant
sentiment." A country where public opinion ruled needed a continual "succession of men like the prophets of Israel to rouse the people out of their self-
complacency, to refresh their moral ideals," and Bryce pointed thankfully to
the presence of a group of "instructed critics" who "exert a growing influence
on opinion through the higher newspapers, and by literature generally."[27]

American liberal editors such as Godkin and Curtis (whom Bryce no doubt
had in mind) were only slightly less systematic in considering the complexities of public opinion, and they too wrestled with the tension between liberal
instruction and popular participation. This tension (as evident in politics as
in literature and art) pervaded their understanding of opinion. "Somebody's,
anybody's, everybody's talk" was important in a democracy, as Godkin argued,
but he considered essential the elevated and rigorous talk that critics such as
himself provided. Liberals clearly appreciated the educative impact of their
journals and repeatedly noted that the "higher newspapers" gave readers the
tools to force those in power to serve the public good. The independent press
led the way with a regular engagement that modeled how reasoned and morally
informed judgments might be framed. Godkin summed up the liberal understanding of an educative press in 1879 when he praised contemporary news-

papers for furnishing something entirely new. Modern republicans benefited from what he called a "constant medium for argument, exhortation, criticism, and debate." This ongoing seminar would of course be conducted by "that class which inherits the world's best traditions of thought and conduct, and which before the invention of the newspaper could speak with but a muffled and indistinct voice."[28]

Yet in keeping with their notion of educative citizenship, liberals coupled the emphasis on their critical powers with a belief that ordinary citizens should be cultivated participants rather than instructed spectators. Opinion in America is not simply "made but grows," Bryce observed, developing from a "mutual action and reaction" of the opinion leaders and the citizenry. This regular interchange held great democratic potential, Godkin thought, possibly superseding the act of voting, which he believed had become a comparatively dull and empty ritual. Casting ballots, Godkin explained, occurred far too infrequently to convey the majority's deliberate policy choices, especially since elections tended to focus more on a candidate's character than on his proposed legislative agenda. A more active model of citizenship depended on what newspaper readers did outside the immediate context of campaigns. With echoes of Mill, Bryce affirmed that the "practice of freely and constantly reading, talking, and judging of public affairs with a view to voting thereon, rather than the mere possession of political rights, . . . gives to popular government that educative and stimulative power which is so frequently claimed as its highest merit." On this point Curtis also agreed, insisting that the vitality of American democracy depended on the newspaper that "goes into every house and reasons with every voter" about the most pressing matters of common national concern. In the hands of liberal practitioners, the press aspired to be more than a mirror of popular sentiment, a transmitter of information, or a schoolmaster: it was an incubator of active discussion capable of elevating the entire country's ability to think.[29]

Slackening the Bonds of Party Tyranny

In 1869, as a war-hero president tried to establish a new basis for national peace and stability, the young Henry Adams trained his eye on what he considered to be America's greatest postwar challenge. In an article for the *North American Review*, Adams explained that politicians were imperiling the common good in their willingness to "convert a sacred public trust into a private property." This familiar enough tendency had nearly always been a sign of ill health in the body politic. Adams knew of this tendency from his recent experiences in Europe, and he also drew from an awareness of belonging to one of the most important political families in American history. These perspectives convinced him that selfish graft was likely to prove fatal in a republic for the simple reason that the "inevitable effect of opening a permanent and copious source of corruption in the legislation must be that the people are undone."[30]

What most disturbed Adams was the rush for patronage with each new administration, which put the principles of party loyalty above those of collective virtue. As he knew all too well, the regular rotation of offices had deep roots, reaching back at least to the time when Andrew Jackson had driven Henry's grandfather from the presidency. Reforming the spoils system would be a lengthier process than the younger Adams expected, and before a decade passed, he relinquished his determination to combat the pervasive power of party leaders. "Politics have ceased to interest me," Adams wrote to a friend in 1876, despairing that since the "machine can't be smashed this time," he would leave "this greatest of American problems to shrewder heads than mine." Adams subsequently contributed to American public life through his masterful histories and his anonymous novel, *Democracy*, a damning sketch of Washington politics greeted enthusiastically on both sides of the Atlantic.[31]

Adams withdrew from public life just as civil service reform was coming into its own and a full decade before the Mugwump revolt showed the power of liberals' independence from party dictation. These crusades demanded a patience that most liberal intellectuals were willing to display. With their efforts, meaningful overhaul of federal patronage would be implemented in the 1880s and 1890s, though these measures resulted in a less complete restructuring than many reformers had hoped, mostly because the parties controlled the process. Historians have generally agreed that the campaign against the spoils system became the defining "totem" of late-nineteenth-century liberal politics and the central feature of the liberal campaign against party rule. Scholars have accordingly subjected this topic to greater scrutiny than most liberal endeavors.[32]

Despite this attention, the moral dimensions of this campaign have remained out of focus, as have the democratic possibilities that reformers identified as the primary rationale for their efforts. Time and again, liberals railed against partisan "tyranny" as the inversion of one of their most cherished principles — the importance of implementing policy through elevated and informed public discussion. George William Curtis summed up the reformist critique in 1880 when he lashed out at the "venal oligarchy within the party known as the machine." What he found most objectionable was the attempt of a narrowly self-interested political class to "usurp the original powers of the people."[33]

Curtis and his allies certainly noted that the spoilsmen's illiberal greed hampered government efficiency, lowered the quality of the federal workforce, and weakened administrative stability. But their central concern involved the threat to a politics centered on reasoning citizens. True party leaders, Curtis thought, should "lead by moulding and guiding the popular intelligence, by the sympathy of common conviction, by resistless argument and burning appeal." Instead, the new organizational politics of mass-based parties and the system of rampant patronage on which it thrived had given rise to "party bosses" who played a role that was nearly the exact opposite of liberals' ideal statesman or opinion-shaping editor, relying on blind loyalty, bribery, and apathy. Party bosses provided management, not leadership, Curtis maintained, and their "opinions, if they have any, upon the great public questions they cannot or do not express, and if they could express, nobody would care to hear." As long as leaders were unwilling to talk to the public about issues of real concern, Curtis lamented that the "people are ceasing to rule," discouraged from exercising their intelligence, reason, and judgment.[34]

The liberal response to this state of affairs involved efforts to diminish parties' hold over individual citizens and governments. Independent journalism represented one such effort, and Curtis and Godkin did not hesitate to use their pages to criticize Republicans. "If politicians must look after the parties," Lowell reasoned, "there should be somebody to look after the politicians." Who better than those already performing a critical function in the press? Liberals quickly moved on to more direct measures, especially the modification of individual voting behavior and the systemic attack on the spoils system, which Curtis described as the "heart of the machine." Curtis bore more responsibility than any other figure for making a vague discontent with overly partisan appointments into the basis of a broad reform movement. He registered support for civil service reform as early as 1867, when *Harper's Weekly* welcomed the first congressional legislation on the topic as a "radical and searching reform for which we believe the country is fully ripe." In a lengthy address before the American Social Science Association two years later, Curtis shared Henry Adams's sense that Ulysses S. Grant might make the reform of spoils the peacetime equivalent of the recent crusade for emancipation and equal rights. Such hopes initially seemed well founded, and Curtis received a presidential appointment to lead the first national civil service commission in 1871. A dispute two years later (after Grant had been safely reelected) caused Curtis to withdraw from this official position. For the rest of his life, the *Harper's Weekly* editor pursued reform by drawing popular attention to the issue and pressuring unwilling politicians to pass laws that voters eventually came to demand.[35]

Early setbacks and perceived betrayals caused Curtis and his liberal allies to monitor the regular maneuvering over the Republican Party's presidential nominating process. While monetary policies, the tariff, and the "southern policy" constituted part of the liberal calculus in judging the "soundness" of potential candidates for the presidency, the most important test was whether a politician was courageous enough to take on the spoils system. By this measure, liberals welcomed the Republican Party's 1876 selection of Rutherford B. Hayes, whose support for patronage reform prevented significant liberal defection to the Democratic nominee Samuel Tilden, who also ran as a reformer. In 1880, most liberals were relieved that the selection of James Garfield stymied the antireform Stalwarts' efforts to nominate one of their own. Reformers had no way of knowing that the new president would be killed during his first year in office; if they had, they certainly would have registered stronger objections to Chester Arthur's place on the ticket as vice president. Ironically, the public outcry over Garfield's assassination by a supposedly disgruntled office seeker pushed Arthur, an avowed spoilsman, to sign the Pendleton Act in 1883 and to inaugurate the first significant federal-level patronage reform.[36]

As reformers participated in internal Republican Party struggles, they worked with even greater vigor to rouse popular support. In their view, the "improvement of the Civil Service" was "emphatically the people's case, the people's reform" and thus needed, as Henry Adams had insisted in 1869, to be taken "directly to the people." Knowing that entrenched interests would ignore reform unless they faced significant pressure from without, both Curtis and Godkin regularly publicized abuses in New York, realizing that the "evils and the perils, the dishonor, the corruption, the degradation of the system" seemed to be "most fully displayed" in Manhattan. The two main targets were the Tammany Hall Democratic machine (a liberal nemesis since at least the Civil War) and the Republican machine run by Roscoe Conkling, whose corrupt use of patronage at the New York Customhouse Curtis made a special effort to expose. Despite such widely publicized efforts, most members of the political class scoffed at the "snivel service reform" and considered it, as E. L. Godkin noted a short time later, with "much mingled disgust and amusement." Reform became a truly popular issue only in the closing years of the 1870s, when defenders of the existing system suddenly realized that the larger public had begun to pay attention. As advocates of public deliberation and debate, liberals were thrilled by this development, and most shared Godkin's satisfaction that "discussion of the system may be said to have only just begun." They expected that after the issue was engaged, it would continue, since "without defense as well as attack discussion is not possible, and without discussion the public is never thoroughly informed on any political question." Godkin's experience and instincts told him that a critical opportunity was at hand: although "unanswered argument on either one side or the other has always something of the dryness and ineffectiveness of simple preaching," the sudden "clash of arms" seemed likely to "rouse the popular attention." [37]

As had been the case during war, bloodshed would be as powerful as words in leading the way to reform. Curtis insisted that the "solitary pistol shot" that fatally wounded President Garfield during the summer of 1881 was destined to be "like the slight sound amid the frozen silence of the Alps that loosens and brings down the avalanche." The president's martyrdom seemed to have "startled this vast accumulation of public opinion into conviction," and his death alone explained why suddenly on "every side thunders the rush and roar of its overwhelming descent, which will sweep away the host of evils bred of this monstrous abuse." When Curtis spoke the next year before the National Civil Service Reform League (a new group that he would lead for the next eleven years), he insisted that "except for a factional quarrel, produced wholly by the strife for patronage or spoils, the President would not have been murdered." By ignoring the clear insanity of Garfield's assassin, Curtis laid the responsibility for the president's martyrdom at the feet of his enemies, presenting reform as a means of avenging a loss that Americans consciously linked to that of Abraham Lincoln. [38]

By the time that the Pendleton Act became law, a younger generation had already joined the cause. A particular concentration of new liberal groups emerged in Cambridge and Boston, where the Massachusetts Reform Club was founded in 1882 by a cluster of men who had attended Harvard shortly before and during the Civil War. Moorfield Storey, an established lawyer and the former secretary to Charles Sumner, was the leading spirit in a cohort that included such figures as Henry Lee Higginson, Charles Francis Adams Jr., and, on a more sporadic basis, William James. Storey had first expressed a sense of generational responsibility in his 1866 Class Day address when he asked his fellow Harvard graduates, "Though others have won the victory, is there not something for *us* to do? If our country is worthy of dying for, is she not worth *living* for; and can we not serve by our lives as well as by our deaths?"

He charged his audience that "as educated men, and members of a generation before which important questions will come for decision, it behooves us to consider what our part in the work ought to be." Many of those whom he intended to rouse would see worthy challenges a decade and a half after peace.[39]

Clear links developed between the colleges and liberal reform, though these connections did not stem from any simple sense of social class or professional expertise. What William James would later term the "social value of the college-bred" was thought to result from the supposed tendency of university education to draw out traits of character, imagination, and perspective. In 1877, Curtis insisted that the "master passion" of contemporary political excess could be tamed only by "men made familiar by education with the history of its ghastly catastrophe" and that it was left to "men with the proud courage of independence" to "temper, by lofty action born of that knowledge, the ferocity of party spirit." Two decades later, Godkin insisted that an "intellectual outlook" made university graduates natural reformers and critics of the political status quo. A college education's "most marked effect" on graduates was "in raising their standards" and changing "their notions of how things ought to be done." Compared to most citizens, college graduates "expect a good deal more in the character and attainments of public men, and in the order of public business." That evidence of philistinism, intolerance, and even venality among college graduates abounded (and about which transatlantic liberals frequently complained) failed to modify this viewpoint.[40]

By calling for leadership by the college educated, liberal reformers opened themselves to charges of elitism. They responded to such attacks by presenting themselves as true democrats and insisting that civil service reform represented the latest effort to root out the persistently illiberal spirit of aristocracy. By singling out this aspect of the opposition, they reversed the terms that had been applied to their approach. Godkin had noted back in 1865 that opponents of reform would try their best to attack its leaders as " 'aristocratic' or 'monarchical' " and as " 'opposed to the genius of our institutions' or 'un-American.' " Efforts to show how precisely the opposite was true thus had an element of defense as well as offense. Lowell hit a common note in attacking spoils as the "most aristocratic system in the world." Patronage through party loyalty depended "on personal favor and is the reward of personal service," he further explained. As the political boss "built up and maintained" his power, he came ever closer to the "mediaeval robber baron" who was distinguished "by his freehandedness in distributing the property of other people." Bryce declared that

Europeans learning about the current workings of the American party system saw "in this new country evils which savour of Old World corruption, even of Old World despotism." His lengthy discussion of machines, spoils, wire pullers, and rings recalled life in "Russia under the czar Nicholas I."[41]

Liberal reformers also worked to transform their cosmopolitan perspective from a liability into an asset. Even amid the Anglophobia of the late 1860s, Curtis insisted that "if France or Germany or England opens a new path in physical or political science, we will walk in it. If they offer a new invention, we will test it. If they announce a new thought, we will consider it. If in any pursuit or art they propose another method than ours, and testing it, we approve, we will adopt it." Like later transatlantic progressives, Curtis considered it "blank barbarism to wrap ourselves in mere nationality and to suppose that we monopolize what is best and fairest in human nature." He and other reformers were simply being honest when they faced up to the question of British influence: they clearly modeled their plans on the bureaucratic reforms undertaken in the United Kingdom in the 1850s. As Anglo-American hostilities cooled, it became safer to delve into the particulars of this example. By 1880, the reformer Dorman Eaton wrote an entire book about the workings of the British bureaucracy and pursued an extensive argument about the suitability of the British merit system to the United States and its even more fluid society. Curtis signaled his approval by writing the introduction to Eaton's volume.[42]

As reformers neutralized such attacks, they also fashioned assaults that invoked the "good fights" of their youth. This effort led them repeatedly to recall where they had stood in the titanic struggles of the "slave-driving Democrats" against Republicans during the 1850s. The "fury" that entrenched partisans directed against postbellum liberal reformers was taken as proof of the reformers' righteousness, just as had been the case during the pre–Civil War years. The stronger the attacks from such sinister interests, the clearer it seemed that reform was destined to be brought to completion. Lowell emphasized that reformers' "moral purpose" set them apart from their enemies by showing how their relatively small numbers gave them the same disproportionate influence that the early abolitionists had enjoyed. Liberals claimed that the exalted aims of these two groups also resembled one another, since while antislavery workers had "emancipated the negro, we mean to emancipate the respectable white man." (The "disrespectable" were presumably either already free or undeserving of emancipation.) Carl Schurz, another leading opponent of the spoilsmen, similarly compared the unreformed patronage system to slavery and Mormon polygamy. Party excess was the third American "relic of barbarism," he explained in 1885, rising to "almost equal in rank" those vices that the Republican Party had combated in its earliest days.[43]

Liberal reformers realized that comparing the spoils system to slavery was hyperbolic, even if such rhetorical excess remained a central part of their public campaign. Modeling what became the key liberal reform on abolition recalled that the intrepid actions of a few had earlier produced the complete overthrow of a far greater national disgrace. The precise nature of who suffered from the patronage system was hazier than in the earlier struggle against bondage. Government workers were obviously not literally enslaved, even if they were victimized by a system that made "servility . . . safer than honest independence" and that destroyed public servants by working to "corrode their manhood and consume their self-respect." Curtis borrowed from his earlier abolitionist oratory in depicting the demoralized, cringing public servant. In 1869, he reported that in at least one case a government employee had literally worked himself to death to meet the donation required of him by party bosses. Given the rarity of such actual violence from the spoils system, it was easier to explain that the status quo demoralized free citizens who were not directly involved in the tyranny. By denying to "human nature" what Godkin called a "fair chance to improve," the structure of patronage was "so arranged as to afford strong encouragement to dishonesty of nearly every degree." Its "chief influence" was thus repeatedly "on the side of vice and immorality." The whole structure constituted an inversion of the central liberal ideal of "fair play" for all concerned, not just for the politically connected.[44]

While the comparison of spoils with slavery was grossly imprecise in every way, one chief distinction involved the different modes liberals offered in their pursuit of these two "emancipations." Few leading American reformers sought to overthrow the system of partisanship or civil service appointments altogether, and most accepted the need for high-level political offices that would allow the executive to translate his party's deepest convictions into policy. Publicizing abuses of party bosses thus constituted a call for reform rather than for revolution. Progress toward the goal of a better party system was to be monitored through piecemeal legislation and patterns of appointment rather than through a radical uprooting of basic institutions. This prevailing reformism represented a basic facet of the liberal approach to this period's politics, signaling liberals' general acceptance of party government as a legitimate way to assure democracy's large-scale operation. Godkin set the tone for this critique in 1865 when he explained that parties "stand in very much the same relation to opinion that the engine does to steam": "they furnish the machinery by which it is enabled to make its impression on society and government." "Much as they have been declaimed against," Godkin continued, parties had the capacity to "stimulate thought on political questions, by associating the spread of certain ideas with the honors and exultation of victory."[45]

American liberal reformers repeatedly agreed with Godkin that the goal should not be to banish parties but to restore their association with principles. Having watched the Whig Party collapse and the Free Soil and Republican Parties successively emerge to embody new or abandoned ideals, the liberal reformers believed in the necessity and importance of parties. The current system was debased not because of its inherent defects but because it was reducing elections to little more than a means of deciding which members of the political class would benefit from government appointments. Curtis was particularly eloquent on the benefits that had come with party action during decisive moments of modern history, when ideas, not interests, were at stake. "Associated, energetic, and organized action," Curtis explained in 1880, was the only way that "great public objects can be secured" and progress achieved. As proof of his contention, he reviewed party-sponsored measures such as Catholic emancipation and the Corn Laws of Great Britain and of course the success of the American Republican Party in securing emancipation and subsequent peacetime accommodation. Invoking such experiences allowed Curtis to conclude that the "progress of liberty" was the "history of party."[46]

While liberals insisted on the honesty and integrity of individual candidates, the main criterion for evaluating the legitimacy of a party measure was whether it was guided by shared ideas and principles and offered a clear stance on the major issues confronting the nation (though what—beyond corruption and a party system run amok—those issues were, liberal reformers did not always specify). As public issues changed, most reformers assumed that a restructuring of parties would follow and expected that a new organization would displace the Republicans in the same way that they had assured the demise of the Whig Party during the 1850s. For this realignment to occur, old issues that traditionally divided parties had to give way to what Norton called the "crystallizing forces" that would be "strong enough to draw together the nucleus of a new party." Scant evidence appeared in the 1870s and early 1880s that such a process would take place. The prospects of realignment changed with the passage of the Pendleton Act, which led to widespread anticipation that the old parties would be supplanted by new ones. The *Century* magazine explained that by aiming a blow at the heart of the status quo, reformers were helping "to break up the existing organizations" held together only by "traditions of the past, the power of organization, and the desire for the spoils of office." After the work of destruction was complete, there would emerge "new parties based upon principles and animated by ideas."[47]

Though there would be no shortage of third parties in the remaining decades of the nineteenth century, none would succeed in replacing the Democrats or Republicans. If expectations to the contrary went unfulfilled, liberal reformers nonetheless pointed with pride to their work in "slackening the bonds of party discipline" and in "making the expression of open dissent from party programmes respectable and common." Through this work, they believed they had reasserted the worth of the citizen as a morally autonomous and reasoning individual on whom democracy and party government ideally rested.[48]

Unable to Beget or Bear . . . Doomed to Sterility, Isolation, and Extinction

Liberal reformers challenged the "discipline" of parties most decisively and famously not with the formation of a new party or even with their civil service reform efforts. Instead, their defection from the Republican to the Democratic candidate during the 1884 presidential election marked the high point of their coherence and effectiveness as a group. The Mugwump bolt from the Republican nominee James G. Blaine that began in the summer of 1884 was in many respects quite predictable. Liberal reformers had distrusted Blaine for years and had repeatedly threatened to leave the party of Lincoln if it made this enemy of reform its standard-bearer. The Democratic nominee, Grover Cleveland, did not merely represent the lesser of two evils: he had already proven himself a key ally, leading efforts for civil service reform while serving as governor of New York. In spite of this choice of candidates, some leading liberals still had great difficulty abandoning the party with which they had come of age and from which they had drawn their mature political identity. Curtis had already hailed those who "scratched" unsuitable candidates from GOP ballots as the new "minute men in politics." A presidential election was different, however, for it involved considerably higher stakes. The Democratic Party's return to power could never just be about the top of the ticket, since with the removal of Republicans came the reemergence of some constituencies that liberals believed had repeatedly proven their illiberal tendencies.[49]

Few were as enthusiastic about the Mugwump movement as Thomas Wentworth Higginson, who had spent the preceding decade and a half immersed in cultural rejuvenation, religious radicalism, and the woman suffrage movement. In 1876, Higginson subtly shifted his priorities at the same time that he moved with his new wife and daughter from Newport to Cambridge, where he agreed to represent his district in the Massachusetts legislature. Having backed a number of Democratic issues during his terms in 1880 and 1881, he was ready for the 1884 bolt and for the thrill of rallying a new generation to action. Curiously for one who recurred more than nearly anyone else to the heady experience of Civil War (and especially emancipation), Colonel Higginson took the opportunity of the 1884 campaign to declare all war-related issues officially dead. Replying to those who accused him of making peace with white supremacists in the South, Higginson joked in 1884 that it would take a special, scientific-grade magnifying glass to "discern faint differences between the Republican and Democratic platforms" and that the real issues now centered on questions of "honesty and courage in public administration." Invoking his former experience as a commander of black troops and his well-known "sympathy with the colored people of the South," Higginson helped to inoculate the Independents and by extension Cleveland from charges of complicity with former Confederate Redeemers or of heedless abandonment of black southerners. "What is reconstruction worth," he had asked in 1876, "if the Government that you have reconstructed is not an honest one?"[50]

Over the course of the 1884 election, the Mugwumps insisted that the candidates' character was more worthy of discussion than the indistinguishable policies offered in the respective party platforms. Early attention to Blaine's shady past and his involvement in corruption was complicated late in the summer, however, by new reports of Cleveland's earlier sexual indiscretions. The story of the child that Cleveland had conceived out of wedlock threatened to dominate the race and caused liberals to clarify a key distinction between the claims of public and private virtue. Their defense of Cleveland turned on the matter of perspective and the conclusion that what appeared to be a single lapse of judgment hardly made Cleveland a "habitual profligate," as Norton explained in a letter to Lowell. Norton reported that Curtis was "much troubled" by the new development and conveyed that all three of these old friends shared concerns regarding how this sex scandal might "weaken the effect of the moral protest against Blaine with those who are incapable of discriminating between offences venial, & offences unpardonable in a public man." Norton feared that the "mass of Americans are so generally ignorant of the world that such a transgression is likely to be judged with a severity not too great, perhaps, as regards

private character, but too great in regards to fitness for public service." For the
rest of the campaign, Curtis never ceased to frame the issues in moral terms,
though he increasingly drew readers' attention to Cleveland's consistent performance of his "official" duties and his genuine concern for the public trust,
qualifications that implied that his moral courage was untarnished by his admitted personal failings.[51]

Attacks on the liberals' independence movement came early and often;
sneers about the "Sunday-school and lemonade politics" of Independents began even before Blaine received the Republican nomination. The withering
attacks led party regulars to term the independents "Mugwumps," an Algon-
quin word for "great chief" that their detractors used to ridicule the bolters'
pretensions (and that the reformers themselves quickly embraced). The fri-
volity of the party regulars' attacks masked the very serious concern that the
liberal revolt might determine the balance of power. Curtis welcomed the fact
of a narrowly divided electorate, since it would give real power to those he
self-consciously associated with an Arnoldian "remnant" in American politics.
Those who were willing to "disclaim party allegiance when it conflicts with
moral conviction" represented a minority, he was forced to admit, though such
had been the case in nearly every struggle for conscience. In a close contest,
a principled group of voters, despite its small size, was destined to determine
which candidate would reach majority status, especially in a state as evenly balanced as New York. The size of this uncommitted group was likely to increase
in 1884, Curtis maintained, since the policy differences separating Cleveland
and Blaine seemed relatively minor. Parties that no longer chose candidates
to "represent a definite policy upon imminent and commanding issues" assured that the debate would turn on "personal considerations and the spirit
and methods of administration."[52]

The image of "Sunday-school and lemonade politics" evoked priggish if
well-intentioned schoolmarms. While gendered imagery had long been a favored means of discrediting political enemies, the emasculating charges
worked particularly well against the liberal reformers, who were indeed trans-
gressing the rules of male partisan affiliation. The scorn for "long-haired men
and short-haired women," once hurled at abolitionists, was easily transferred
to liberal reformers, whose hair supposedly was not only long but peculiarly
parted in the middle. Some detractors portrayed the Mugwumps less as womanly than as perversely asexual. From the lips of the Kansas Republican Senator John Ingalls sprang the most memorable denunciation: these "political epi-
cenes" were "effeminate without being masculine or feminine; unable either

to beget or to bear." As members of a "third sex," they were "doomed to sterility, isolation, and extinction."[53]

If the liberal Mugwumps' refusal to play by the rules of partisan politics was irksome, their embrace of a self-consciously critical role also drew fire from regular partisans, as it had in cultural endeavors as well. The Republican Theodore Roosevelt would prove one of their most vociferous detractors, denouncing liberals as mere "parlor reformers," who, lacking "sinewy power," "made up for inefficiency in action by zeal in criticising." Another well-known New York politician with whom Curtis frequently sparred, Senator Roscoe Conkling, also objected to the critical pretensions of the liberal intellectuals: "Their vocation and ministry is to lament the sins of other people. Their stock in trade is rancid, canting self-righteousness. . . . They forget that parties are not built up by deportment, or by ladies' magazines, or gush."[54]

The Roosevelts and Conklings of the world had a point, not simply because Curtis and Higginson wrote for "ladies' magazines." Liberal political reform contained more than a whiff of self-righteousness, and the liberals plainly were criticizing rather than "acting," as Roosevelt would have understood it. But the liberals understood criticism—not simply carping but evaluating, judging, appraising—as a political and patriotic act of tremendous importance. Further, they believed that their course was "manly," by which they meant independent, honest, and courageous. Godkin emphasized the special moral courage it took to hold Republicans to account when they had controlled the executive office for more than twenty years and thus had come to consider their party as "the Government" and "to treat criticism of it as disloyalty to the country." In this context more than ever, Curtis suggested, critical speech constituted political action.[55]

In any case, the question of the Mugwumps' political "impotence" was muted by their success in November. The exact role that independents played in the election's outcome was less important than the sense they gained of themselves in backing the winner in a presidential contest for the sixth consecutive time. Their advocacy burnished their image overseas and caused many friends abroad to see a "growing disposition to quote and defer to intellectual and moral eminence."[56] After the narrow victory, Cleveland would more or less live up to reformers' expectations—meeting their general approval in the matter of appointments and proving himself even more reliably "sound" in conducting his domestic and foreign policy. Reformers continued to identify him primarily as a leader of character rather than as a formulator of policy, however, and gradually sensed that his greatest contribution was to extend Abraham

Lincoln's example as a self-taught genius of character. Near the end of Cleveland's first term, Lowell called him the "best representative of the higher type of Americanism that we have seen since Lincoln was snatched from us." Like the savior of the Union, Cleveland demonstrated a "manly simplicity of character and an honest endeavor to do all that he could of duty." His "courage to tell the truth to the country without regard to personal or party consequences" constituted a testament not just to himself or his supporters, however. The whole country should take pride, Lowell argued, since Cleveland had worked "to remind us that a country not worth telling the truth to is not worth living in, nay, deserves to have lies told it, and to take the inevitable consequences in calamity."[57]

Few prominent Mugwumps served in the Cleveland administration, though they considered themselves a crucial element within a governing coalition that also included the Democratic Party's more traditional constituencies of southern whites and urban politicians. A particularly close set of ties would be forged between Cleveland and Richard Watson Gilder, who came to rank the president as the "towering individuality of our own day." As editor of the *Century*, Gilder had been struck with the candidate's superb judgment during the 1884 campaign and wrote early in Cleveland's first term that "like Lincoln, he knows what the honest heart of the nation believes in and craves, and will have sooner or later." Though the *Century* continued to take a nonpartisan stance in advocating reform, Gilder publicized his frequent White House visits and his elevation as one of the president's trusted unofficial confidantes. Gilder served as a sounding board for Cleveland's public papers while also acting the tutor in reading passages from Bryce's *American Commonwealth* to Cleveland after his unsuccessful 1888 reelection bid. Relations between the two men were less intimate during Cleveland's second term, which ran from 1893 until 1897, but enough interactions occurred that Gilder wrote a reminiscence of Cleveland a short time after his death.[58]

The Cleveland years produced optimism among liberals and gave them confidence that Americans were at long last accepting the need for an elevated public life. In 1888, Norton observed to Goldwin Smith that "our politics seem on the whole in a better condition than they have been for a long time." Not only were the Republicans being split by "Blaineism," Norton explained, but "Cleveland's character and courage" were lifting the Democratic Party "out of the slough in which it had been wallowing ever since the war." Godkin explained to James Bryce that the election "closes the war period in American politics." With Cleveland in office, respectable northern voters had relinquished their "traditional dread of the Democrats," which would now be further removed by "active experiments" and by an imminent rise of new parties.[59]

Lowell marked this sense of renovation in a set of political statements encapsulating the stance of liberal men of letters toward politics in late-nineteenth-century America. These pieces represented Lowell's first extended political commentary since the early days of Reconstruction, which he had followed with a break from politics and an immersion in criticism and poetry. When he returned to civic life in 1876, he did so not only as a commentator but as a participant, serving first as a presidential elector in the disputed election and then as a diplomat during two separate foreign missions between 1877 and 1885. While these experiences sharpened Lowell's understanding of liberal politics, they prevented him from speaking publicly on partisan issues. If it was inappropriate for a diplomat to engage in campaigning in 1884, it was nearly impossible for him to oppose the party of the president responsible for his appointment. In private correspondence, Lowell adamantly supported the Independents' bolt, however, and he affirmed his standing as a Mugwump after the fact. In so doing, he established himself as perhaps the brightest star in the constellation of literary independents that included Higginson, William Dean Howells, and Mark Twain.[60]

Lowell's discussion of political independence in the late 1880s was part of what his biographer Martin Duberman has called a "summing up" of Lowell's accumulated experiences and insights. The cumulative quality of Lowell's late political essays was evident in his tendency to hearken back to particular moments in his life, whether this meant recollections of his Civil War admiration for Lincoln or the invocation of Lowell's poetic tributes to intellectual independence from the 1840s. During this final period of his life, Lowell distilled his views into a larger conviction that politics represented the "noblest exercise of man's intellect and the best training of his character." In taking stock of the postwar period, Lowell sought images that might best combine a critical assessment with a qualified faith in a brighter future. "Our politics call loudly for a broom," he insisted. "There are rubbish-heaps of cant in every corner of them that should be swept out for the dustman Time to cart away and dump beyond sight or smell of man." The way forward would come through the workings of democracy, which more than any "other method of conducting the public affairs of men" was "capable of sloughing off its peccant parts" through the "forces of life at once so intense and so universally distributed." Aiding the process would be those statesmen imbued with the same qualities that distinguished the world's greatest artists. "He seeks and finds in the moral world the weather-signs of the actual world," Lowell explained in setting forth his notion of the ideal political leader. "He strives to see and know things as they really are and as they are related to each other, as they really are and therefore always must be; his vision undeflected by the cross-lights of transitory circumstance, his judgment undisturbed by the clamor of passionate and changeful opinion."[61]

In his reach for the proper metaphor, Lowell was less interested in describing Gilded Age America than in dramatizing the need for urgent change. As in the antebellum period, he sensed that dire warnings were the best hope of forestalling further descent. Of all the dangerous tendencies of American life, the greatest threat was the country's complacency, which caused the same neglect of political duties evident before the salve of war recast the crisis of the 1850s. Lowell's favored solutions did not involve a renewed military conflict, and neither he nor any of the members of his cohort concluded that all would be right if only the right leaders were selected and the most enlightened policies adopted. Assuming that salvation lay in liberal cultivation, Lowell hailed the new fiercely independent journalism as a sign of hope and expressed an equally favorable opinion on the broadening of debate about the spoils system. Political shenanigans could not "bear discussion," he asserted, since the "good sense of the American people" meant that scrutiny would ultimately lead to radical change. In time, the conversion of individuals would lead to a broader commitment to reform. As he put it in his most substantial discussion of liberalism, "it was the individual that should and could be leavened and through the individual the lump. To reverse the process was to break the continuity of history and to wrestle with the angel of destiny."[62]

The emphasis that Lowell and his fellow liberals placed on the individual over the "lump" hardly represented an attempt to sanction atomistic selfishness. In many ways, it was exactly the reverse. In what was admittedly a middle-class, idealized view of politics, the liberals easily assumed that the best decisions would be made when principles that could be shared collectively were elevated over self-interest that had to be calculated in private. The liberal fixation on political ideas and on civic education valued individual thought for its ability to reach a shared consensus about what constituted the common good, not for how it might produce gain or loss in a more narrow sense. What held parties together, they believed, were individual voters who had reached the same conclusion through a process of individual reflection and the weighing of morality and of effectiveness. In the end, conscience mattered because it led to common action in pursuit of broadly defined national ends. This ideal of

Victorian liberalism thus constituted a far cry from the interest brokering that would define later progressive political coalitions or academic debates over political pluralism.[63]

The search for consensus that defined Victorian liberal politics would remain a part of American life. But it was not particularly well suited to the politics of the 1890s and the early twentieth century. The pressing economic and international challenges that arose during this period produced party polarization while sparking the radically populist People's Party, the biggest third-party movement since the 1850s. Few liberals saw this development in a positive light (though Higginson found many good points, including the income tax, in William Jennings Bryan's platform). When they turned once more to Grover Cleveland as their favored candidate in 1892 (or to the "gold Democrat," John Palmer, in 1896), the liberals emphasized the commitment to sound money and low tariffs over public rectitude. In such an environment, it no longer made sense to speak as if few real differences existed between the competing parties. As liberal reformers found their sense of earlier despair returning, they could still hearken back to the success of the independent movement as proof that something better might appear in the future.[64]

Men facing old age and the passing of their closest friends could set the heady days of 1884 alongside the defining epoch of the 1860s. In both these periods, they found larger meaning in their efforts to improve American politics. Godkin struck a typical note when he eulogized the "set of people known as the 'Mugwumps'" ten years after Cleveland's first election. He frankly acknowledged that these "men of cultivation" had been misunderstood as "dissatisfied, querulous people who complain of everybody and cannot submit to party discipline." Yet despite widespread "ridicule and abuse," those within the movement still believed in the "inestimable service" the Mugwumps had performed. Lowell sought to inspire future liberal reformers and thereby to avert Ingalls's dire prediction of neutered extinction by traveling to New York to help inaugurate the new headquarters of the New York Reform Club. With his longtime friend and ally, George Curtis, standing on the platform behind him in what would be their last public appearance together, the aging New England man of letters envisioned a permanent place for critics in American culture—critics who would insist "in season and out of season that we shall have a country whose greatness is measured not only by its square miles, its number of yards woven, of hogs packed, of bushels of wheat raised . . . but also by its power to feed and clothe the soul . . . a country whose very name . . . shall call out all that is best within us by offering us the radiant image of something better and nobler, and more enduring than we, of something that shall fulfill our own thwarted aspiration."[65]

The Political Interest of the World Is Centered in America

In the late fall of 1884, Goldwin Smith declared his pride in the victory his closest American friends had just won. Writing in his "Bystander" column for the *Toronto Week*, Smith hailed Grover Cleveland's election as a "triumph of administrative integrity and sterling worth over the arts of a brilliant but unscrupulous and untrustworthy schemer." He made sure to note the role of the Mugwumps (and especially of Curtis's *Harper's Weekly*) in the defeat of James G. Blaine, whom Smith condemned more for jingoism than for corruption or links with the spoilsmen. The "intrepid adherence to the cause of reform" shown by the independents guaranteed that for at least the next four years, the United States would pursue a "rational tariff," a responsible budget, and a "foreign policy of good sense and sound morality."[66]

Smith's commentary acknowledged that the American presidential election had a still wider impact, and he urged his Canadian readers to expand their focus beyond the future course of U.S. federal policy. In conveying this broader significance, Smith found it noteworthy though not terribly surprising to report that the 1884 presidential election had been "watched in England with an interest inferior only to that which it has excited in the United States and hardly less practical in character." What had happened in the American election, he assumed, would likely frame the upcoming battles between British Liberals and Tories, both groups that had grown accustomed to using events in the United States as a source of political maneuvering. There was no secret to why the politics of a distant country were so enthralling. As Smith explained, "everything which seems to betoken the success or failure of the Democratic experiment tells on politics in Europe, especially in England; and with greatly increased force since communication has become so much closer." He might have mentioned that he had been as important as any other single figure in this process, having spent the past two decades keeping Canadians, Britons, and Americans up to date about happenings beyond their own borders.[67]

Europeans had associated America with a democratic future at least since the writings of Alexis de Tocqueville in the 1830s. Both Mill and Carlyle had agreed (albeit in different ways) that the Old World could glimpse its political destiny by casting its gaze across the Atlantic. The appreciation of mutual interests and a common destiny among Anglo-American liberals became especially pronounced during the American Civil War and its aftermath. This sense of kinship outlived the high tide of the 1860s and was sustained by more than the strong ties of personal friendship. The American experience served British liberals as a constant point of reference that could shed light on the constitutional, political, and social dilemmas of popular government. Their closest American counterparts similarly drew inspiration from the British success in rooting out corruption and party excess. Political reformers in the United States also responded on an emotional level, taking immense satisfaction in the global attention to their national course. While disavowing the "old bombast" of earlier days, the *Century* was still happy to report in 1883 that the "political interest of the world is centered in America and awaits the realization of our destiny." The magazine followed its observation with a familiar liberal injunction for America to use this wider audience to live up to its promise and to "laboriously set to work to create an atmosphere about the minds of young men which will nourish a high ideal of political duty."[68]

Liberals realized that opponents of popular government would not be silenced by the Union's success in restoring federal authority and ending slavery. If illiberal voices were less likely to gloat about American volatility and its racist hypocrisy, they could still draw attention to other unseemly aspects of the country's politics and associate the "Americanization" of Britain with the graft and greed of party bosses. By 1867, James Bryce reported that the "lobbyists, caucuses, and wire-pullers" of the United States had become as damaging to the cause of democracy as the "instability of Athens, the corruption of Rome," and the "ferocity of the French Revolution." Bryce's contributions to the 1867 *Essays on Reform* disentangled the failings of the United States from the intrinsic nature of democracy, as did the pieces written by A. V. Dicey and Goldwin Smith. The credibility of such an analysis rested less on logic than on the experiences that leading university liberals had assembled in visiting the United States and gaining a familiar understanding of how the country managed its affairs. The British liberals' authority on American affairs only increased as the steady stream of visits to the United States continued throughout the 1870s and 1880s. British observers came to learn that a visit to Washington was not enough and that the true spectacle of partisan gamesmanship came in less familiar locales. At the 1870 New York state Democratic convention at Rochester, for example, Dicey and Bryce developed their lasting interest in the American party system.[69]

As with Dickens and Arnold, American liberals willingly accepted foreign attention to their political flaws and even expected that criticism from friends to provide a constructive prod comparable to that used to discredit American slavery. A short time after James Russell Lowell discussed "A Certain Conde-scension in Foreigners," he explained to his friend, Leslie Stephen, that fair-minded outside analysis could produce considerable benefits. After expressing a sense of despair about the "power of 'Rings' in our politics" and the rail-ings of antidemocratic leaders against America's "huge stock-jobbery," he in-structed Stephen, "Pitch into us on all these matters as you will. . . . [Y]ou will do us good. . . . [C]riticism—no matter how sharp if it be honest—is what we need." Several years later, Lowell realized that not all Americans shared his tolerance for foreign faultfinding. A poem that Lowell used to couch criticisms of American corruption in the voice of a sneering Briton brought a sharp nega-tive response and left Lowell with a reputation as a disdainful Anglophile for more than a decade.[70]

Transatlantic criticism traveled in both directions, especially in the early postbellum years, when the *Nation* and *Harper's Weekly* routinely amplified the Liberal Party's program of nationalizing and broadening British governance and weighed in on the growing crisis in Ireland. Norton offered a more substan-tive contribution when he wrote about British poverty and discussed the prob-lem of emigration for John Morley's *Fortnightly*. The tone and content of these pieces signaled that Norton was more interested in offering solutions than in merely cataloging others' shortcomings. The same was true of Godkin's com-mentary in 1878 about Britain's first American-style urban political machine. Godkin compared his perspective on the Birmingham "Caucus" with that of distant observers who read the debates of the French National Assembly in 1790. While he hoped for the best, he was ready to warn of potential peril and to provide advice about how Britain might avoid its own version of Tammany Hall.[71]

As the pessimistic tone of such back-and-forth commentary suggests, an un-deniable mood of liberal disillusionment crept in during the 1870s. This fol-lowed from a shared sense that the high-tide expansion of suffrage had not produced the political results that many observers had predicted. The Ameri-can Republicans who had campaigned for Grant were initially pleased with his superiority to Andrew Johnson, though controversies provoked by Grant's administration (especially during its second term) caused them to emphasize instead how far short he fell of Lincoln's example. In Britain, leaders chosen through expanded suffrage produced even greater disappointment, especially when John Stuart Mill was defeated in his campaign for the first postreform

Parliament. The lack of distinction in what John Morley called a "Chamber of Mediocrities" suggested that democracy might dampen the political hopes of the most "advanced" liberals. The programs enacted by the Liberal government in the early 1870s further alienated Morley, who was especially upset by the opening of the national educational system to what he believed to be sectarian religious influences.[72]

The political disappointments in Britain and the United States were minor compared to the upheavals that swept France in 1870 and 1871. As many scholars have noted, the specter of the Paris Commune established during this period cast a pall over discussions of democracy for the rest of the decade. American liberals expressed a less unanimous response to this dramatic turn of events than might have been expected, with Godkin taking the hardest line and Curtis couching his disapproval in his characteristically more temperate tone. Norton, who was in Europe at the time (and thus removed from the overbearing influence of Godkin's *Nation*) confessed that he found himself "greatly more in sympathy with what I conceive to have been the notions that inspired the sincere & self-devoted part of the Commune than the 'Nation' has been." Echoing the stance taken by his Positivist friend, Frederic Harrison, a leading British supporter of the Commune, Norton expressed admiration for the original ideals of the Commune and, perhaps with the ennobling sacrifices of the American Civil War in mind, frankly acknowledged the "necessity of occasional violent revolutionary action to remove deep-seated evils."[73]

Yet the radical claims issuing from this latest French Revolution were not the sort of democracy he and most of his larger liberal circle sought for their own country. The general reaction among middle-class opinion makers shaped a larger sense of foreboding as time passed. This anxiety was intensified by a set of subsequent crises that by the end of the decade included a severe economic depression, a string of political scandals, a prolonged crisis over the 1876 presidential election, intensified labor unrest, and mounting concern over how best to resolve the "southern question" of national Reconstruction policy.[74]

Further indication that the high tide had ebbed (or at least that it had succumbed, in Higginson's phrase, to a powerful undertow) came as several prominent liberals moved away from their earlier support of woman suffrage. Goldwin Smith's apostasy garnered the most attention, and he conveyed how much the political climate had altered when he acknowledged that he had "once signed a petition for Female Household Suffrage got up by Mr. Mill." While Smith's change of heart seemed to grow mainly from sentiment and assumptions about women's "true nature," Godkin, who had never been a warm supporter of woman suffrage, linked his opposition to a more general unease with the current practice of American democracy. "Doubling the number of votes to be influenced or managed in any community," he warned, would dangerously increase the functions of party bosses and machines. He could think of no more decisive argument than this against woman suffrage at a moment when the party system was already buckling under the weight of this organizational challenge.[75]

The clearest evidence of liberals' skepticism toward democracy in these years concerned their increasingly negative view of urban governance. The spectacle of revolutionary Paris coincided with a vigorous liberal campaign against the Tammany Hall corruption of Boss Tweed. In this context, it was a short step for many liberal theorists to suspect that large metropolitan centers might be ill suited for the universal suffrage that had been established across the country more generally. What would become Gilded Age liberalism's greatest flirtation with reaction emerged in the form of the bipartisan Tilden Commission, on which Godkin served. Appointed by New York Governor Samuel Tilden, the commission issued an 1877 report that proposed to limit participation in some specific municipal elections (though not those for mayor or alderman) on the basis of property ownership, a recommendation that could have been taken (and, via Godkin, quite possibly was) directly from Mill's *Considerations on Representative Government*.[76] This measure, which the Republican-dominated New York state legislature passed in 1877 but which failed to achieve passage by a second legislature and thus was never enacted, drew the qualified support of both the *Nation* and *Harper's Weekly*. Liberal participation revealed the limits to and ambivalences of this cohort's attitude toward democracy not as an ideal but as it was practiced in modern city government. Concerns about the just-emerging Birmingham Caucus formed yet one more cross-current that bolstered a transatlantic liberal consensus that democracy within large cities too often led to illiberal results.[77]

American liberal intellectuals were less united in their skepticism about democracy than many scholars have assumed, however. Explicit questioning of universal suffrage represented the exception rather than the rule, though both Charles Francis Adams Jr. and Francis Parkman (neither a liberal nor a reformer) did so.[78] Goldwin Smith's reversal on woman suffrage drew immediate fire from Higginson in the *Woman's Journal* as well as from their erstwhile ally John Elliot Cairnes in *Macmillan's*.[79] Further, at the same time that *Harper's Weekly* was supporting the partial restriction of the urban electorate in New York City, the magazine registered loud complaints about the intimidation of the black vote in the South. Curtis, Higginson, and others raised similar objections to the reactionary implications of a forum sponsored by the *North American Review* in 1879 that set out to consider whether the enfranchisement of the freedmen during Reconstruction had been a mistake. Parkman's vitriolic attack in the pages of the *North American Review* on women's rights and on the entire premise of democratic governance generated a considerable response, even if historians have taken Parkman's writing as symptomatic of a more general pattern of Brahmin democratic disaffection. The *Nation* argued that Parkman was out of step with the "optimism which has always been characteristic of American life." And even Godkin, never to be mistaken for a zealous democrat, expressed impatience with the one-sided, inaccurate, and intellectually lazy attacks that issued from the pens of democracy's critics in Britain. While Gilded Age America had plenty of enemies of democracy, the most hostile forces lay beyond the ranks of liberal reformers among those whom this group would have considered illiberal racialists, religious authoritarians, and the most doctrinaire advocates of laissez-faire.[80]

Most liberals stopped short of repudiating democratic principles for the simple reason that these men were not ready to overturn convictions formed during the 1860s. This lingering spirit of democratic reform was clear in Goldwin Smith's response in an 1879 address he provocatively titled "Is Universal Suffrage a Failure?" Smith opened this piece with a call for the "spirit of hope, not that of despondency," to "preside over reforms," though he focused much of his speech on the ways that American popular government had fallen short of its promise. Reiterating the tenets of Millian educative liberalism, Smith insisted on the need for literacy among potential voters and then explained the flaws of municipal government, the dangers of excessive party spirit, and the negative influence of an overly rancorous press. Yet in the end, Smith chose to conclude on a more hopeful note, urging the members of the current generation to keep their sense of perspective and put their energy toward reform rather than withdrawal or repudiation. Smith made his case (as he had in *Essays on Reform*) by drawing distinctions between the abuses of American government and its inherent tendencies.

When we have separated from American democracy that which is not an essential part of it; when we have made allowance for extraneous influences and temporary pressures; when we have distinguished curable defects in the machinery of the system from inherent and incurable vices; and when, having done this, we survey the actual condition, material and social, of the American people, a foreign observer, while he must believe that there is much need of reform, and while he follows with the eye of anxious sympathy the efforts of reformers, can see no reason for despair.

Smith also made sure to praise those who sought to "purify the republic" through a program of liberal reform. If the ever more vigorous campaign for virtuous government represented the "hardest of all political tasks," it was also by "far the highest," he insisted. Striving to perfect popular government "produced character nobler than has been produced by political effort of any other kind," and the results of this mission promised to be the "grandest, the happiest, and the most enduring that the political imagination can conceive."[81]

By maintaining their reformist hopes through the 1870s, transatlantic liberals assured themselves a role in the extended period of Anglo-American innovation the following decade. The success of the civil service reform movement in the United States inspired Goldwin Smith to consider a similar movement in Canada, despite his sense that the party system in his adopted country was comparatively weak. Reformers within the British Liberal Party pursued a still wider range of measures under the leadership of William Gladstone, who served as prime minister between 1880 and 1886. An additional expansion of suffrage in 1884 was understood as the completion of the work of the 1867 Reform Act. It extended to the countryside the same qualifications that the earlier act had established for towns (though with some 40 percent of men remaining without the vote, Britain was still a long way from universal manhood suffrage). Even greater transatlantic attention was focused on the Corrupt Practices Act passed a year earlier. Gilder's *Century* pointed to this measure in a plea to press forward with reform of city government outside of the qualifications for voting. The magazine hoped that Americans would follow the British precedent by limiting the amount of money candidates could spend on campaigns and by handing over to municipal governments rather than parties the responsibility for printing and distributing ballots.[82]

The *Century*'s transatlantic circulation helped to make it an important voice in nurturing and sustaining the liberal accomplishments made in Britain and the United States during the 1880s. The magazine's running series, "Topics of the Times," regularly drew out those tendencies of reform liberalism that seemed to bode well for the Anglo-American future. Gilder and the other writers of this feature reasoned that because "English political thinkers are studying American methods in order to find a way out of their difficulties," it might be appropriate "for us to borrow a leaf out of English experience in the conduct of our elections." In addition to emulation, this cosmopolitan frame was invoked as a lever of shame. The scandalous nature of American politics was on par with the earlier scandal of slavery, the magazine argued, allowing the "opponents of free government in Europe" to point to "abuses in our civil service as a natural result of republican government, and therefore as a condemnation of that government itself." Through the 1880s and into the 1890s, liberal editors visited this point about the international embarrassment of American politics, especially in the urban areas that continued to be run by party bosses and their machines.[83]

Anglo-American political reform never drew the same intensity of feeling during the Gilded Age that it had in the 1860s, and it fell short of the cultural ties that animated the transatlantic exchange of the 1880s. The age of Gladstone and Cleveland saw liberal publications such as the *Century*, *Harper's Weekly* and *Monthly*, and even the *Nation* devoting more attention to the shared literary heritage of Britain and the United States than to the pursuit of cleaner and more effective government. Lowell's mission to England clarifies this ordering of liberal priorities, since his most important pronouncements focused on the ties of language and art rather than on governance. Lowell no doubt realized that a more direct venture into politics would risk an inappropriate identification with the Gladstonian Liberals, whose views of politics remained closest to his. Near the end of his tenure, he made an exception to this pattern when he used an address on "Democracy" in Birmingham to laud the shared Anglo-American commitment to popular government. His liberal associates were thrilled by his effort, agreeing with Curtis that there was "probably no presentation of American ideas on government in its relation to the individual man or on the future of universal suffrage" that "was so complete and satisfactory." His staunch defense of the American model was no less important in revising Lowell's reputation for Anglophilia dating from the mid-1870s.[84]

Lowell's Birmingham address recast the genealogy of democracy by considering Christian egalitarianism and England's "government by discussion" as necessary preconditions for Lincoln's government "of the people, for the people, and by the people." This expanded framework allowed Lowell to stake out a systematic response to the most common arguments against democracy, especially its supposed leveling effect, its tendency to dampen individual excellence, and its threat to property interests. Some observers in his audience might have wondered about his closing consideration of socialism, which he termed the "practical application of Christianity to life" and suggested might have "in it the secret of an orderly and benign reconstruction." In this most controversial part of his speech, he had generally followed a line of argument presented to American readers of the *Century* by his friend, Thomas Hughes, just a few months earlier.[85]

Lowell delivered his Birmingham address with a clear awareness that he was standing before a foreign audience. Four years later, he recalled that he had "felt it incumbent on me to dwell on the good points and favorable aspects of democracy as I had seen them practically illustrated in my native land" and that he had hesitated while outside of his country to "discuss family affairs before strangers." This did not mean he had ever lost sight of democracy's flaws, however, and he returned to the role of the "jaunty jeremiah" when he returned to the United States. "Here among ourselves," he explained, "it is clearly the duty of whoever loves his country to be watchful of whatever weaknesses and perils there may be in the practical working of a system never before set in motion under such favorable auspices or on so large a scale." In taking time to address these issues, Lowell avowed that his interest lay not in discrediting democracy but in drawing attention to the abuses that "experience and thought will in due time rectify."[86]

By softening his criticism while abroad, Lowell demonstrated that liberals' cosmopolitanism never wholly transcended the context of national particularities and the complexities of national pride. Lowell had already learned, as had most of his friends, that Americans resisted political observations that they perceived as overly influenced by foreign perspectives or sympathies, especially when the topic under consideration was the challenge of democracy. As Godkin explained in 1896, "doubts about its future seem doubts about the future of the nation, which no lover of his country is willing to entertain lightly." Liberals accepted this belief as a powerful reality, even if their caution tacitly compromised their emphasis on open and free discussion. In the context of the late nineteenth century, Godkin was right to observe that "political speculation is somewhat discountenanced or discouraged in America by the excessive cultivation of what is called 'patriotism.'" The country's compulsion to glorify democracy rather than to expect greatness of it was "not unusual in a young people whose growth in wealth and numbers has been prodigious," Godkin concluded, though this tendency assured that the true problems of popular government would remain less appreciated in the United States than elsewhere.[87]

Deeply held national convictions limited the transatlantic dimensions of liberal reform while hampering any interrogation of popular government that did not begin with an affirmation. As a result of such powerful forces, the cosmopolitan tendencies of the 1880s achieved their greatest significance not in the public sphere but in the lively debate among intellectuals themselves. This theoretical exchange owed much of its energy to the shared perspective of British thinkers such as Morley, Dicey, Bryce, Harrison, and Smith and to the American advocates of civil service reform and political independence. Interest in America's example was never the exclusive preserve of these like-minded friends—one of the most interesting developments was what Dicey termed the "Americomania" of British conservatives. Tory fears about Great Britain's rapidly democratizing parliamentary system and its implications for the government of Ireland caused William Lecky and Henry Maine to express a newfound admiration for America's seemingly more stable constitutional structure even as they continued to pronounce their dread of democracy. These Tory intellectuals departed from earlier conservatives, who had emphasized the instability of governance in the United States, instead focusing on how an independent judiciary, a strong executive, and the federal division of sovereignty checked rapid innovation within the United States.[88]

Liberal Americans offered little response to this new chorus of Tory praise and continued to frame views in accord with British Liberal thought. Bryce, Morley, and Gladstone contributed ever more regularly to American publications, as did Dicey, whose developing alienation from democratic liberalism helped Godkin appreciate his relative faith in the future. Seeming to resist a similar pull toward reaction, Godkin shored up his association with the progressive tendencies of British political culture by preparing lengthy criticisms of both Maine and Lecky. These efforts called attention to the conservatives' misunderstanding of the United States and repudiated their instinctive hostility to the principle of equality.[89] Far better suited to the reformist outlook of most American liberals was Bryce's *American Commonwealth*, which appeared in 1889. Bryce's popularity among American liberals was predictable, since his extensive American travels had caused him to consult with dozens of men of letters. Nearly every part of his seminal book conveyed the influence of his network of American friends. His debt is especially evident in his discussion of public opinion, civil service reform, woman suffrage, and the workings of the American party system.[90]

The transatlantic liberals' scholarly interest in Anglo-American democracy led them to present the first serious discussions of the modern party system. Both Tocqueville and Mill had surprisingly neglected this topic, basing their diagnoses on the role of social forces and the shadowy realm of "public opinion." Late Victorian liberals' new appreciation for partisanship resulted from the relevance of this influence to their political situation. The American campaign to replace the spoils system with a more idea-oriented party system coincided with the emergence within the British Liberal Party of the Birmingham Caucus, which was most associated with the advent of urban machine politics. These two trends provided diametrically opposed signals about the destiny of modern popular government and introduced a basic uncertainty about whether democracy's future would be characterized more by ideas or by organization. The near simultaneous fracturing of seemingly stable parties—with the Mugwump bolt from Republicans in 1884 and the defection of the Liberal Unionists from Gladstone's Liberal Party in 1886—raised further questions about parties' efficacy as a democratic form.[91]

Goldwin Smith took distrust of parties to its logical extreme and by the mid-1880s was making the idea of a nonpartisan national state a key feature of his political commentary. Smith's hostility to partisanship had roots in his youthful identification with the Peelite Whigs, though this skepticism temporarily abated during his cooperation with the progressive wing of the Liberal Party during the high tide of the 1860s. Over the following two decades, Smith's views about parties became increasingly sour, as he witnessed the rise of the Birmingham Caucus (whose leader, Joseph Chamberlain, Smith detested), engaged in battles with Canadian party insiders and their allies in the Toronto press, and then, most importantly, became disgusted by Gladstone's partisan maneuvering on behalf of Irish Home Rule. While other Liberals such as A. V. Dicey followed a similar path toward antiparty positions, Smith produced a uniquely systematic critique, applying the same standard in measuring a party's legitimacy as Edmund Burke had in his famous remarks in *Thoughts on the Cause of the Present Discontent*. Like Burke, Smith insisted that organizing into political groups should be limited to instances when a pressing national interest existed and when objectives could be achieved only by concerted action. He insisted that the permanent party system in Britain and the United States constituted little more than a "bisection of human nature" that betrayed the fact that humanity was composed of "shades [that] melt indistinguishable into each other." As issues shifted and matters of pressing concern changed, so too should the alignments of thinking individuals. Only the straitjacket of previous party combinations prevented such a natural fluidity of alliances and aims.[92]

Smith's increasing suspicion of parties put him at odds with liberals in the United States, whose belief in a purified party system never really wavered. "In one thing I believe you and I differ," Smith wrote to Curtis in 1877. "I have no

faith in Party, now that the real dividing line, Slavery & Antislavery, is gone."
Sensing that the future depended on finding "some other way of working free
institutions," Smith expressed grave doubts about whether "with Party, you
will ever get Administrative Reform" since these organizations "cannot dispense with its bribery fraud." In some respects, Smith was correct in predicting
the difficulties of changing abuses of partisanship without dismantling what
Steven Skowronek has termed the "party state" of the late nineteenth century.
As both Skowronek and Mark Summers have argued, the Gilded Age partisan system was remarkably resistant to change even after reformers achieved
much of their agenda. For Smith, this inherent defect of parties led him to
imagine what sort of constitutional structures might sustain a national state
devoid of compromising party organizations. The remote possibility of such
basic change led him increasingly toward despair. By 1891, Smith complained
to Bryce, "How we are to get out of party government is a question which some
oracle will I hope in time answer. But out of it we must get if we do not mean
to come to grief."[93]

By fostering a discussion of alternatives to the party state, the transatlantic
dialogue about popular government helped American reformers reaffirm their
commitments and clarify their critique. In the midst of reviewing Lecky, Godkin revisited the problem of the party functionary and ended with a surprisingly neutral stance toward the party boss. Earlier democratic theorists had
failed, Godkin explained, to predict the rise of a figure who "does not speak,
who makes no public impression, who is not rich or eloquent or in any manner
distinguished, yet who leads the voters and holds legislation in the hollow of
his hand." In an earlier period, this analysis might have led Godkin to call for
the removal of a clearly parasitical presence from the democratic process. Yet
he chose another tack in 1896, acknowledging that the "new, unforeseen democracy" of millions of voters had produced the "necessity of organizing and
directing the suffrage" and even gave a certain legitimacy to the "intervention
of the boss and his assistants."

On the eve of the twentieth century, Godkin realized that reform might
never stop such men from managing large groups of citizens, especially given
the electorate's resistance to reasoned appeals issued through the conduit of
liberal journalism. One way to reform rather than replace party operators was
to prevent them from unduly influencing the nominating process, which he
thought should be restored as a democratic rite. The general electorate, Godkin also maintained, should be permitted to convey its will directly through

a process of initiatives and referenda. Such proposed measures offered admittedly imperfect solutions to the larger problem. But for Godkin, the alternatives—specifically, the complete absence of parties—seemed even worse.[94]

An Anglo-American commitment to constitutional, multiparty democracy persisted into the twentieth century, as did the two countries' mutual interest in each other's political systems (first expressed long ago in the proposal for a Harvard-Cambridge lectureship). Much would be altered by the "New Liberalism," which as a generational rebellion became the effective political equivalent of the literary modernist's assault on the genteel tradition. The Victorian roots of later transatlantic commitments would remain evident, however, and at times would even dominate the scene. Amid the Great War of the 1910s, James Bryce served as British minister to the United States during the administration of President Woodrow Wilson, who had been a theorist of legislative governance during the 1880s. The Churchillian vocabulary of World War II and the early Cold War also rested on the notion developed by late-nineteenth-century liberals that English-speaking peoples were united by their commitment to stable democratic progress.

The long rhetorical shadow cast by their generation would likely have pleased the post–Civil War liberal reformers. But they would not have taken for granted the liberal future of a "special relationship" between England and America. The 1890s bred a mood of greater pessimism than ever before, in large part because of an Anglo-Saxonism that sanctioned racialism, cultivated a martial spirit, and sought dominance through the illiberal office of empire. Beset by such troublesome developments on both sides of the Atlantic, liberals ended their lives with a gloomier outlook than ever before. Such despair did not, however, prevent them from issuing one final call for critical dissent.

Global Power and the
Illiberalism of Empire

*The Jingoes are still numerous and powerful and absolutely crazy. . . . An immense
democracy, mostly ignorant, and completely secluded from foreign influences, and without
any knowledge of other states of society, with great contempt for history and experience, finds
itself in possession of enormous power and is eager to use it in brutal fashion against
anyone who comes along, without knowing how to do it, and is therefore
constantly on the brink of some frightful catastrophe.*
E. L. Godkin to Charles Eliot Norton, December 29, 1895

Late in 1895, Anglo-American relations took a turn that shocked liberal men
of letters even as it confirmed some of their deepest anxieties. That December, Grover Cleveland's hostile message to Great Britain regarding its boundary dispute with Venezuela "fell like a thunderbolt out of the clear sky," as the
Mugwumps' favorite president unexpectedly threatened war if Britain would
not yield to America's supremacy in the Western Hemisphere. Liberals who
had looked to Cleveland as their best hope for better government were horrified
by his belligerent stance and realized that they bore some of the blame for the
worst Anglo-American crisis in more than thirty years. Charles Eliot Norton
reached out to Leslie Stephen (who was equally perplexed by this "hideous war-
scare") and tried to set the trouble in a broader context. Cleveland's jingoism
mattered less to Norton than the public applause the president received, which
showed the "manifest growth of a barbaric spirit of arrogance and of unrea-
sonable self-assertion" among the American populace. The uproar furnished
the best evidence yet that America was "beginning a long course of error and
of wrong." The country that had only thirty years earlier seemed destined to
lead the world toward progressive enlightenment on a broad scale now seemed
"likely to become more and more a power for disturbance and barbarism."[1]

James Bryce had ushered in the 1890s with a set of similar warnings about what he called an "Age of Discontent." His diagnosis extended well beyond the United States to encompass the fate of liberal reform on both sides of the Atlantic. In overtly transatlantic terms, he identified a mood not of "despondency, still less despair" but "merely discontent, that is to say, disquiet, restlessness, dissatisfaction with the world as this generation finds it." Bryce remembered that earlier transatlantic reformers had embraced change and had identified stagnation as the greatest enemy of human happiness. This earlier liberalism seemed worthier of praise than its later manifestations, since it had a "greater confidence in the speedy improvement of the world, a fuller faith, not merely in progress, but in rapid progress, a more pervading cheerfulness of temper than we now discern." Reformers of the 1860s high tide may have been naive, Bryce conceded, but they had clung to the commendable belief that liberty and reason would bring about the "speedy triumph of the good." Their efforts to place religion, politics, and culture on a more equitable basis took place "not as ends in themselves, but as means to larger and higher ends." Yet the promised moral transformation of individual citizens had not occurred, Bryce was forced to admit. What progress had occurred "has been less than was expected, and expected not by enthusiasts only, but by reasonable and cool-headed men thirty or forty years ago."[2]

Bryce, Norton, and their closest associates among the liberal men of letters saw the gathering sense of generational disillusionment rise to new levels during the last decade of the nineteenth century. At the heart of the problem lay a spirit of militarism that showed how badly the world had gone awry. Europe was on its way to becoming what Bryce described as a "vast camp," with national armies counted in the "millions rather than hundreds of thousands." The American public that welcomed an armed confrontation with Britain in 1895 showed that fevered preparations for war were only a matter of time for the United States. Such an outcome seemed even more likely after the wrenching economic depression of 1893, when some political and industrial leaders suggested that expansion of overseas markets might provide the best means of revitalizing the U.S. economy. What Bryce called Cleveland's "absurd" interpretation of the Monroe Doctrine during the Venezuela crisis seemed to bring the world's leading republic closer to a military conflict too many now considered a welcome opportunity. The president's "reckless appeal to dangerous passions" in this instance would bear fruit by 1898, when the United States got the fight it wanted by transferring its appetite for war away from Britain and onto the far weaker power of Spain. Two quick military campaigns established

American control in the Caribbean and the Pacific. These victories then set the stage for a prolonged and deeply embarrassing campaign that pitted U.S. forces against a Filipino insurgency fighting to establish a self-governing republic.[3]

Transatlantic liberals confronted the militarism and imperialism of the 1890s from the perspective of advanced age. Two of this cohort's most important figures had already passed from the scene by the time the United States went to war with Spain: James Russell Lowell had died in 1891 at the age of seventy-two, and George William Curtis followed a year later at age sixty-eight. Many who remained were moving into retirement (though the younger men, including Bryce, John Morley, and Charles W. Eliot, hung on for decades longer). Norton became an emeritus member of the Harvard faculty in 1898, while E. L. Godkin stopped editing the *Nation* at the end of the following year. Higginson grew increasingly retrospective, committing much of his energies to a varied series of reminiscences. But dwelling more and more on what he called the "Outskirts of Public Life" did not mean detachment. The call of duty continued to ring for public critics whose lives were nearing their final period of service.[4]

The twilight crusade against imperial aggression was a bitter experience, even if it provided a few compensations. Rallying one last time in dissent recalled the same invigorating stand for principle experienced during the days of the antislavery movement, of the postwar high tide, and of the 1884 Mugwump bolt. As in earlier episodes, the experience of transatlantic cooperation provided some satisfaction as well. The liberal confrontation with empire built on a "Gladstonian" tradition in foreign affairs that had established international relations as a suitable venue for expressing a broader Anglo-American tradition of reasoned moralism. The record of this partly fictive tradition in Britain was mixed, having prevailed over the jingoism of the 1870s only to be frustrated by the challenges of Ireland as well as of Egypt. By the end of the century, British Liberals who identified with Gladstonian principles of international restraint faced similar challenges of imperial overreach in Britain's controversial war against the Boers in South Africa. On both sides of the Atlantic, patriotic aggressiveness dulled the prospects of liberal reform. Such developments marked a period of genuine crisis for men who had devoted their lives to the belief that ideas and the cultivation of reason would triumph over force and the cultivation of hatred. As the twentieth century dawned, their countries seemed as much in need as ever of the transatlantic liberals' critical efforts.[5]

Subordinating Public Policy to Moral Law

In their late-century campaign against empire, intellectuals had at their disposal a full arsenal of ideas and experiences. Much of their hostility toward
territorial expansion was intuitive to them, if not to later observers. Many U.S.
observers (disassociating continental expansion from what they more narrowly
called "imperialism") believed that an imperial America was a contradiction
in terms and a repudiation of the country's 1776 struggle against colonialism.
Other elements of the anti-imperial critique were widely available to all learned
republicans, who regularly looked to ancient examples (particularly that of
Rome) to reflect on the follies of empire.[6]

The experiences and encounters that had marked these men's lives constituted an equally important ingredient of their critique of the 1890s. The dilemmas of world power had intermittently intersected with the liberal vision of
cultural renewal and domestic political reform. When these liberals addressed
foreign policy, they were as likely to follow debates roiling Victorian Britain as
to consider how the ever-more-powerful U.S. government was charting a new
diplomatic course.

American liberals had cut their anti-imperial teeth as young men. Fifty years
before the Venezuelan crisis, New England writers reacted to a similarly controversial period of national aggression by opposing the Mexican-American
War and condemning it as an iniquitous plot of a grasping slave power. James
Russell Lowell's efforts to deflate the high-flown patriotism of "manifest destiny" had even gained him international acclaim. In folksy Yankee dialect,
Lowell had ridiculed the country's hypocrisy and self-serving bluster.

> They may talk o' Freedom's airy
> Tell they're pupple in the face, —
> It's a grand gret cemetary
> Fer the barthrights of our race;

When at century's end the gap between noble professions and brutal practices
abroad reappeared, Lowell's *Biglow Papers* enjoyed a transatlantic resurgence
of popularity. Though Lowell was dead, his verse lived on and provided anti-
imperialists with their most effective counterpoint to the jingoistic poetry of
Rudyard Kipling and others.[7]

Lowell had hardly been alone in mounting a youthful protest against American aggression toward Mexico and against American expansion in general. Norton had worried in 1851 that all the "talk about 'manifest destiny,' 'natural

boundaries,' 'geographical extension,' and such other topics" revealed a depraved national character. Higginson went farther, joining other New England radicals in signing a protest denouncing the Mexican War as a "war of invasion" and as "one of the great crimes of modern history." He believed that the war was "dishonorable to our name and race" and represented the "forfeiture of our mission as a people." Such views were common among the Brook Farm perfectionists with whom George William Curtis spent the war years. While Great Britain's young university-based liberals were not particularly attuned to the war between the United States and Mexico, they did express disapproval of warmongering in voicing both opposition to the Crimean War and sympathy for the nationalist movements mounted by Hungarians and Italians against the Austrian empire.[8]

Such episodes from the distant past were not the only personal point of reference for anti-imperialists of the 1890s. Much had changed in the half century that separated 1846 from the turmoil that accompanied calls to construct an overseas empire. The intervening period gave liberals a measuring stick for what constituted a "good war" — the Union cause they passionately defended. That experience ensured that none of them would ever be pacifists. If liberals continued to believe that war was an "ugly thing," the circumstances of the fight against the proslavery rebellion demonstrated, as John Stuart Mill had stated, that even worse was the "decayed and degraded state of moral and patriotic feeling which thinks nothing *worth* a war." The danger lay not in military conflict itself but in allowing martial tendencies to become something more than means to an end. "Nations love military display," Goldwin Smith had cautioned Charles Eliot Norton at the end of the Civil War. The pomp of mass armies "flatters them with the consciousness of force, just in inverse proportion to their moral greatness" and perhaps "in inverse proportion to their real heroism."[9]

The transatlantic ties formed during the 1860s assured that Americans' understanding of war and international affairs evolved in the following decades in dialogue with British debates about that country's colonial empire. Mid-Victorian commentators engaged in a broad exploration of the political economy of empire while elaborating a universalizing criteria of "civilization" that could be used not only to justify conquest but also to undermine its legitimacy. Writers for the *Nation*, *Harper's Weekly*, and other similar publications articulated much of their opposition to earlier American expansion with that same amalgam of utility and morality that characterized the "Manchester School" associated with Richard Cobden, John Bright, Goldwin Smith, and (in the clearest example of transatlantic migration) E. L. Godkin. This school of thought emphasized the economic burden that colonies accrued and the domestic reform opportunities they squandered. These midcentury British perspectives emerged at the same moment that the earlier link between pro-slavery aggression and territorial acquisition was severed. When U.S. President Ulysses S. Grant—clearly no champion of slavery—attempted to acquire Saint Thomas and Santo Domingo in 1870, liberal intellectuals moved into uncharted territory by appealing to arguments first framed by their friends across the Atlantic. Norton lashed out at Grant's "curious ignorance of the simplest principles of political economy," while Curtis mocked the hypocrisy of the "very loud and active party" that masked its self-interest with the grandiose rhetoric of mission. In considering the proper response to the 1868 Cuban revolt, Curtis warned that "if now we wish for Cuban freedom merely that we may seize the revenues that Spain loses, our pretense of regard for the rights of independence and self-government becomes unspeakably ludicrous."[10]

Liberals connected their distrust of post–Civil War territorial expansion to their growing concerns about the corruption and intrigue of American party politics. Godkin framed his opposition to empire in an idiom that owed much to the key tenets of his adopted country's liberal reform movement. In 1872, the *Nation* editor grumbled that Grant's annexationist scheme had been pushed forward by a "ring of 'operators' . . . into whose hands the new state would fall immediately on its annexation, and whose activities and profits would surpass anything they have treated us to here." Curtis was just as upset that various "'rings' and 'pools'" had been formed in connection with what he considered a "vile job." He informed Norton, then sojourning in Europe, that Grant was "smitten with the desire of territorial extension as a national and administrative glory" and, with his eye on reelection, sought expansion as a party measure. Annexationist schemes represented yet one more instance of the rampant self-seeking and political opportunism that liberals feared might dominate the postwar era.[11]

Despite such opposition to Republican maneuverings, foreign affairs never became a defining party issue in late-nineteenth-century American politics. Even the anti-imperialists' attempts to make the 1900 presidential election a referendum on overseas expansion failed completely. The lack of clearly defined party stances at home perhaps heightened the American interest in British partisan political struggles, which became increasingly focused on the proper exercise of global power.[12] By the end of the century, liberal thought on the dilemmas of empire would depend less on a theoretical tradition of British anti-imperialism than on the riveting drama played out over two decades by leading Tory and Liberal statesmen. A transatlantic liberal perspective on foreign affairs ultimately emerged, elevating moral, cosmopolitan, and reasonable commitments over that dangerously illiberal form of jingoism that sought to cultivate the most selfish and irrational of all national passions. Like other aspects of the Victorian liberal connection, the American engagement with this transatlantic debate was more focused on containing the illiberal forces of reaction than on offering any single set of doctrines. The key moment in clarifying these alternatives came in the late 1870s with the battle between the Conservative Party leader Benjamin Disraeli (known as Lord Beaconsfield after 1877) and the Liberal Party leader William Gladstone (known to admirers as either the Grand Old Man or the People's William). These two political titans came to personify, for Americans no less than Britons, different understandings of Britain's role in the world.[13]

The story American readers followed in the pages of the *Nation, Harper's,* and other liberal periodicals bore an imprecise and uncertain relationship to reality. As had been true with coverage of the 1867 Reform Bill, this newer political narrative was in large part crafted by liberal participants in Britain and then further shaped by their liberal allies in the United States. If the historical realities were more complex, the liberal narrative was rather straightforward, and in it Disraeli came to personify the illiberalism of jingoistic excess. As such, he initially drew more attention from American observers than did Gladstone, who seemed likely to remain in retirement after having led the Liberal government through the early 1870s. Disraeli's second ministry between 1874 and 1880 raised the specter of a newly emboldened conservatism whose hold on power depended (at least from the view of his Liberal enemies) on his attempts to suppress the intellect and the moral bearings of a citizenry and instead to seduce supporters by the shallowest possible conception of national glory. The worship of force associated with his new brand of popular imperialism evoked for liberals the attitude of Thomas Carlyle in the 1860s. It came, then, as no surprise that after assuming office, Disraeli offered Carlyle a baronetcy in 1874. (Carlyle refused.) But although lacking Carlyle's redeeming features, Disraeli's ability to rally a majority and rule the country threatened to reshape the future rather than simply to hold progress at bay.

Most Americans did not immediately grasp Disraeli's potential for mischief, having formed their first opinions of him as a novelist and as a canny political strategist rather than as an imperialist. In neither of these first two areas were the liberal men of letters particularly impressed with "Dizzy."[14] One of James

Russell Lowell's first contributions to the *North American Review* in the 1840s had faulted *Tancred* (the last novel in Disraeli's Young England trilogy) for having "no characters . . . no dramatic interest, none of plot or incident." Later liberal consideration of Disraeli's novels showed a consistent disdain, calling attention to what Leslie Stephen termed their "fantastic" qualities that made ambiguity and mysteriousness a keynote. By the 1870s, the case against Disraelian fiction coincided with a more general liberal suspicion of his political maneuvering and supposed unscrupulous lack of principle. "His career is like one of his own novels," wrote Curtis in 1876. "It leaves the impression of gayety, artificiality, audacity, cleverness, low ideals, and a mock greatness." His reputation as a wily opportunist had been set through his role in the 1867 reform movement, when he turned what had begun as a Liberal measure into a party gain for the Conservatives.[15]

Disraeli's elevation to power in 1874 was greeted with ambivalence, even though Americans expressed no predictions about whether aggressive foreign policy would define his ministry. After Disraeli's first year in office, Higginson introduced the minister to American readers by mixing a generally disapproving tone with selective praise. Higginson drew attention to Disraeli's career as a self-made man, to his relatively pro-Union stance during the Civil War, and to a parliamentary eulogy to the martyred Lincoln that "certainly should give to Americans a permanent feeling of kindliness toward the statesman who made it."[16] Higginson failed (as did most other Americans) to mention Disraeli's famous 1872 Crystal Palace speech, in which he had signaled his vision of Britain's imperial destiny as well as the importance of empire to his party ambitions by tarring the Liberal Party with an unpatriotic, anti-imperial brush. The strategy of contrasting conservative nationalism against liberal internationalism had become central to his policy by 1876, when the newly named Lord Beaconsfield assumed his realpolitik stance amid the Turkish massacre of Bulgarian Christians and the ensuing "Eastern question." Disraeli's defense of "British interests" and aggressive stance toward Russia inspired working-class Tories to swear that "by jingo," they were ready for war if necessary. As the possibility of a new war in Europe loomed, "Beaconsfieldism" and its "jingo" policy became increasingly familiar terms for readers of the *Nation*, *Harper's Weekly*, and Curtis's "Easy Chair" columns in *Harper's New Monthly Magazine*. At a moment when urban democracy was already raising alarm among liberal reformers, this supposed "political alliance between upper-class Jingoism and its rowdy counterpart" constituted one of the most ominous signs of illiberal reaction among working-class voters. Both Goldwin Smith and George William

Curtis explained the specter in terms that American readers could appreciate, comparing the Tory alliance of the "snobs and the mobs" to the earlier partnership "between the Southern slave-owners and the rabble of Northern cities."[17]

Americans saw Disraelian imperialism in terms shaped by those liberal British men of letters who launched a counteroffensive in the *Fortnightly Review*, the *Nineteenth Century*, and in the rest of the liberal press. Frederic Harrison framed the issue for Americans, explaining that just as the "system of slavery prepares the slave-holding caste for any inhumanity that may seem to defend it," so too an "empire of subjects trains up the imperial race to every injustice and deadens them to any form of selfishness." He even predicted that "what slavery and the slave trade once were to our grandfathers here, what a slave industry and a slave society were to the Americans of yesterday, that empire is becoming to Englishmen to-day." Goldwin Smith explained that the New World was as likely to be threatened by this new reactionary trend as the Old World was. Just as Disraeli flattered the queen and urged her to don the trappings of empire, his counterparts in the Canadian Tory Party remained busy hyping the spirit of unthinking monarchism and hereditary privilege. According to Smith, the Conservatives merely served as a front for the still powerful British aristocracy that was rolling back liberal measures on both sides of the ocean by distracting attention from pressing domestic problems. Its main objective was to "divert the mind of the people from progress at home to aggrandizement abroad," thus identifying a strategy later scholars would dub "social imperialism."[18]

Not surprisingly, the liberal Americans looked to William Gladstone as the leader most likely to hold the "British conscience fast and firm against Jingo delirium." Despite his blunder on Confederate nationalism during the war, Gladstone had already drawn transatlantic admiration for his role in suffrage reform (particularly his 1864 "pale of the Constitution" speech) and for agreeing to arbitration as a means of settling the *Alabama* claims. His dramatic return to Liberal leadership in the late 1870s drew on new themes, none more prominent than his repudiation of Disraelian foreign policy while directly appealing in the pages of the *North American Review* to Americans as Britain's "Kin beyond the Sea."[19] In *Harper's Weekly*, Curtis made sure that a broad segment of the American middle class realized the gap between Gladstone's virtues and Disraeli's vices. "Lord Beaconsfield appeals to prejudice and jealousy and vague fear, Mr. Gladstone to reason," Curtis wrote in one issue. In another, he insisted that "if Beaconsfield is popular because he defends the stupidity of the nation, Mr. Gladstone is popular for a very different reason."

"Gladstone's England," Curtis insisted, more clearly resembled Americans' "'mother country' than the England of Disraeli." This regular (and familiar) series of dichotomies had its intended effect. Relying somewhat uncharacteristically on the popular racial formulations of the day, Curtis reported late in 1878 that Americans had a "very general feeling" that an "Englishman of Englishmen, like Gladstone, represents more truly the England of which we, as an English-speaking race inheriting the great English traditions are proud, than an essential alien like Disraeli."[20]

American liberals assessed Gladstone's leadership with the same criteria they applied to Abraham Lincoln's management of popular opinion during the Civil War. Both statesmen, the liberals thought, had achieved success by bringing out what was best in the people as a whole, thus rising above the illiberal demagoguery of Disraeli, Stephen Douglas, or Andrew Johnson. Curtis explained that Gladstone assaulted jingoism "without the slightest flattery of popular error or pandering to popular prejudice"; rather, he built support among the "most liberal, the most enlightened, the most liberty-loving and truly English Englishmen" and then brought the rest of the country to the right cause. In liberals' view, Gladstone's two key interventions exemplified a democratic appeal to moral principle. His pamphlet on the *Bulgarian Horrors* sold two hundred thousand copies during its first month of publication, was then reprinted in newspapers, and was finally revisited in mass meetings assembled throughout the country. Goldwin Smith cheered the "indignation meetings" that Gladstone's effort helped to spark, believing that "national morality, above all, must, in doubtful cases, be declared" by "the nation" rather than by "men in power." Gladstone's successful 1880 electoral campaign rested on an even broader (if controversial) appeal. Standing for election in his new constituency of Midlothian (in southeastern Scotland), Gladstone barnstormed the country giving speech after speech to enormous crowds that turned out to hear the Grand Old Man. The so-called Midlothian campaign inaugurated a new kind of popular electioneering in Britain, which Gladstone would repeat during subsequent elections (and about which Thomas Hughes and James Bryce, who faced new challenges in their political careers, would frequently complain in letters to their American friends). Historians continue to debate the precise nature and consequences of the Midlothian campaign, but Americans such as Curtis insisted that Gladstone elevated popular political debate by encouraging, in the words of a recent biographer, a "new and high standard of political awareness, discussion, and citizenship." Curtis clearly had this style of politics in mind when he praised Gladstone's appeals to the citizenry's reason and intelligence.[21]

Gladstone's distinctive vision of a liberal foreign policy became even more specific as his campaign against Disraeli continued. Gladstone at first presented his party simply as an opposition to the unacceptable Tories. By the time of his first Midlothian tour, he had distilled his foreign policy program into six "right principles" that he vowed would be at the center of his party's approach: good government at home; preservation to the nations of the world of the blessings of peace; the concert of Europe; avoidance of "needless and entangling engagements"; acknowledgment of "equal rights of all nations"; and an insistence that the "foreign policy of England should always be inspired by the love of freedom." His record as prime minister during the 1880s hardly lived up to these ideals, as his armed intervention in Egypt in 1882 made patently clear. His American supporters were quite willing to rationalize his departures from the ideal, however, and to insist that exigencies aside, he had not compromised the soundness of his underlying beliefs. These beliefs emerged from what Curtis had already termed the Liberal leader's "honest dealing in subordinating public policy to the moral law."[22]

Though Gladstone was becoming an increasingly divisive figure among British Liberals, his victory in 1880 assured the American liberal reformers that they remained on the right side of history and that the future belonged to an internationalist, moral foreign policy, which they instinctively embraced. At the height of Disraeli's influence in 1878, Godkin had feared that such might not be the case. With a considerable dose of pessimism, he imagined the day when observers would look back and wonder why the "real sources of English greatness" had been "sacrificed in a vain attempt to realize the gaudy dreams of a novel-writer, who had climbed into power as a rhetorician through the intellectual degeneracy of a party which had ceased to have anything behind it but wealth." Though a popular orator such as Gladstone was of course no stranger to "rhetoric," liberal American observers repeatedly contrasted the direct simplicity of Gladstone (who had preferred, refusing a peerage, to remain "Mr. Gladstone") with the artificial spectacle of Disraeli, who had not only become Lord Beaconsfield but had, on his own authority, bestowed the title empress of India on Queen Victoria. With this contrast, it was no wonder that in 1880, with the Liberal Party back in office and British integrity restored, Curtis forecast a hopeful transatlantic future. An appeal to common sense and moral principles had caused British voters to rise up and to show how an aversion to "melodramatic men and politics" had been bred in the "blood of the English race from which we are mainly sprung." Homegrown jingoes such as James G. Blaine should remember that "Americans have been always most effective when least sensational," Curtis wrote. But he added that the "sudden and complete prostration" of the Disraelian vision signaled something deeper to anyone bent on the building of empires. Not imperial expansion or martial splendor but Gladstone's blending of democratic discussion with a foreign policy grounded in moral principles represented the very best of what Anglo-Americans had to offer.[23]

Ireland Is England's Touchstone, as Slavery Was Ours

Gladstone's American reputation continued to improve during his second ministry. Most American liberals continued to believe that he was a responsible steward of imperial power, and even his use of force during the 1882 Egypt crisis did not tarnish this reputation. By 1887, Godkin marveled that "no living American, has as much hold as Gladstone on the American imagination today." By that time, the Grand Old Man had pushed the Liberal Party to adopt his most controversial and most ambitious measure. He was in the midst of a fight to solve the most intractable problems of empire—the persistent Irish demands for greater political autonomy and for social, economic, and religious justice.[24]

American liberal reformers' interest in the problem of Ireland was to be expected, though few scholars have examined their immersion in this issue. The historian Robert Kelley has noted its centrality more generally, writing that "as Algeria obsessed the world in the 1950s and Vietnam in the 1960s," so "Ireland drew all eyes in the 1880s." Godkin, Curtis, Lowell, and several of their British counterparts went beyond mere observation to become key public figures in the most sweeping attempt yet to moderate Anglo-Irish tensions. The Gladstonian campaign for Home Rule represented the Americans reformers' most important intervention in the public policies of a foreign country. In their attempt to shape solutions, the Liberals experienced as many losses as gains. The Irish question fractured the British Liberal Party, resulting in its dramatic fall from power in 1885 and a fatal splintering into Gladstonian and Liberal Unionist wings. Those members of the transatlantic liberal alliance most intimately involved experienced this fracturing more personally, as Ireland ruptured and realigned relationships and pitted Goldwin Smith, Matthew Arnold, and A. V. Dicey against E. L. Godkin, John Morley, and James Bryce. While the controversy tested the limits of transatlantic liberal unity, it also reaffirmed and extended the lessons of the 1870s about how illiberal tendencies and corruptions accompanied international power acquired through foreign conquest. As such, Americans in the 1880s came to learn that Ireland offered, as Morley had noted in 1860, a "microcosm of the whole imperial question."[25]

Americans had far more intimate links to the Irish controversies than to the struggles between Disraelian jingoism and Gladstonian moralism in the late 1870s. Liberal critics had followed the epic debate over jingoism to help readers understand how the world's preeminent military power managed its foreign affairs. The liberals' stake in the Irish question involved domestic American politics in a much more direct manner. By 1880, when the Irish American population reached over four million, the United States had already become an important fund-raising and organizational base for Irish insurgents. Some Britons believed that this growing immigrant population had formed the most disruptive aspect of the entire difficulty and remained the main stumbling block to a lasting peace. American liberals never shared such an evaluation, even if they readily conceded the frequent illiberalism of Irish Americans as a group, associating them with the racism of the Democratic Party, the religious authoritarianism of the Catholic Church, or the political corruptions of the urban machine. In this instance, however, ethnic politics was judged primarily for the difficulties it injected into international issues by betraying the liberal ideal of American public life based on reasoned discussion. The tendency of politicians in both parties to court the Irish vote assured that U.S.-English relations would worsen as long as candidates continued to outdo one another in "twisting the lion's tail." As long as Ireland remained in turmoil, the liberal pursuit of reasonable democracy would be stymied by continued appeals to deeply held grievances.[26]

Anglo-American tensions over Ireland had entered a new stage in 1866, when the Fenian brotherhood attempted an invasion of Canada from the United States. This sensational turn of events captured headlines and reversed the earlier transatlantic dynamic of experiencing internal guilt and expressing blame about "foreign intermeddling." Earlier northern American reformers had for decades been defensive and embarrassed by slavery and attempts to cast antislavery as a subversive foreign conspiracy. It was understandable that they would emerge from their civil war convinced that in overcoming their fatal flaw they had assured their country's reputation as a leading (if recent) exemplar of human rights. At the same moment, the British self-image as the world's arbiter of civilization was compromised by the intensification of an old problem. With sudden clarity, Curtis and others realized that "slavery was our touchstone, as Ireland is England's."[27]

Liberal reformers were quick to point out that the condition of Ireland undermined England's moral authority abroad and drew further attention to the gap between profession and practice in the world's leading representative government. E. L. Godkin, whose father had been an early advocate of Home Rule, insisted that the island's misgovernance had "for two centuries [been] the scandal and disgrace of Anglo-Saxon religion and politics. It has discredited English liberty and English politics all over the earth." With the tables turned, Americans could hardly resist noting that the eyes of the "whole civilized world" looked to England to solve its problems and not simply to point out the problems of others. The "intolerable preacher," who had long directed its gaze at the flaws of foreign countries, now suddenly was forced to "practice a little." The young university Liberals seemed capable of the self-scrutiny that the circumstances required. John Morley popularized Irish reform in the *Fortnightly*, while Goldwin Smith (who had published a leading study of Irish history in 1861) also continued to offer suggestions.[28]

Liberal Americans combined disapproval of the Fenians' violent methods with sympathy for the suffering of the Irish people and an acknowledgment of the legitimacy of Irish grievances. The established (Protestant) Church of Ireland and the disastrous land situation—the core issues of the 1860s and 1870s —clearly violated liberal notions of freedom of conscience and "fair play." "An actual religious and political equality and a change in the land tenure must be achieved," Curtis warned in 1866, "before Ireland can rest, or England either." American liberals throughout those two decades announced a direct stake in helping to solve the Irish crisis. Lowell explained to Thomas Hughes that "one of the worst diseases we have to cure in the Irish who come over here is their belief that the laws are their natural enemies." If Irish immigrants came over ill prepared for American self-government, they also formed, according to Curtis, a dangerous political class "whose favor has been sought in the most unscrupulous way and for the most disastrous ends." The key lay not in banning Irish immigrants or in depriving them of political power but in a long-term campaign to encourage peace and reconciliation between the Irish and the English.[29]

Basic reform of Irish difficulties seemed possible during the liberal high tide of the late 1860s. American reformers expected that this persistent challenge might finally be met in the same spirit of transatlantic progress that had begun with emancipation. The problem of Ireland lent itself to similar moral convictions that informed the liberal campaigns to expand the suffrage, to pursue color-blind justice in Jamaica, and to bring about a liberal Anglo-American rapprochement. Each of these goals rested on a shared understanding, which

Curtis pointed out in discussing the Irish question, that the "key-note of En-glish as of American liberalism—the secret of peace and welfare—is Justice." Gladstone's first government made good on the promise by disestablishing the Irish Church in 1869 and by passing a major Land Act in 1870. Liberals wel-comed these measures despite disagreements about whether they would be enough to assure the "fair play" that the Irish deserved.[30]

To build consensus, several observers hearkened back to Edmund Burke's late-eighteenth-century observations and pointed out that a thousand land-lords owned half the land and peasants had no stake in or security on the land they worked. Even critics of Home Rule such as Matthew Arnold agreed that although government in England and Scotland had been conducted in accor-dance with the wishes of the majority, government in Ireland "has been con-ducted in accordance with the wishes of the minority and of the British Philis-tine." Such a clear case of artificial privilege and a violation of "fairness" led Victorian liberals to qualify the right to property, normally considered a lib-eral first principle. Here John Stuart Mill had paved the way, with his increas-ingly radical calls for land reform in Ireland from the 1840s until his death in 1873. Ireland was one of the three main issues, along with parliamentary re-form and women's rights, to which he devoted himself while in Parliament. The younger liberals followed Mill in insisting that "there must be limits" to the rights of property. "A government cannot be expected to uphold for ever by force," Goldwin Smith wrote shortly after Gladstone's first Land Act in 1870, "that which, though in strictness legal, fills the country with disaffection, and places the nation in constant peril." Lowell similarly urged Thomas Hughes, "Give [the Irish] property (or a chance at it) in the land." Anything less would be a mere "palliative," Lowell concluded.[31]

The course of events seemed to brighten, and Smith noted with satisfaction that Liberal reforms had transformed the "pikes of '93" into the "Home Rule orations of '71." As reason and conciliation slowly replaced prejudice and coer-cion, American liberals had confidence that Gladstone knew that "statesman-ship depends on justice, not violence."[32] Yet such optimism was premature. It would not be long before a new cycle of violence and coercion ensued, and the "orations of '71" gave way to the dynamite, arson, and murder of the early 1880s. As economic conditions worsened and the eviction of tenants accel-erated, a powerful network of transatlantic support helped Irish insurgents mount a new violent campaign that appalled most liberals. Among the most spectacular aspects of this mounting crisis was the series of land wars that swept the countryside, the assassination of Lord Secretary Cavendish in Dublin's Phoenix Park, and threats made by Charles Stuart Parnell, the leading Irish advocate in Parliament, to drive Gladstone from office by aligning with the Tories. All the while, a new round of British repression—the Force Bills enacted by Gladstone—confounded American observers.[33]

James Russell Lowell suddenly found himself in the midst of the gathering storm when suspects in a dynamite bombing claimed American citizenship to avoid prosecution. As ambassador to Great Britain, Lowell expressed public dismay with the recent Coercion Acts and wrote to Gladstone to express shock at the "violent measures proposed for the Irish malady." He faithfully followed the State Department's instructions, though he privately thought the suspects' claims to citizenship were rather dubious and assured his British hosts of his continuing friendly attitude. Simmering suspicion about his Anglophilia made him an easy target of political invective back home. As negotiations dragged on, attacks on his patriotism and his unwillingness to stand up to the British made their way to the U.S. House of Representatives. Rumors of his recall swirled that summer, and it was unclear whether he would weather the most controversial period in his diplomatic career. By late 1882, having won the release of the suspects, Lowell's position seemed secure, even if attacks on his character and Americanness continued (attacks to which the Birmingham address on "Democracy" constituted at least in part a response). Those within his liberal circle took the assault to heart and experienced in a more direct way than usual the volatility and force of an emotionally aroused opinion at home.[34]

The same year that Lowell helped to avert a damaging Anglo-American diplomatic rupture, the problem of Ireland injected a new level of antipathy into the transatlantic community of liberal intellectuals. This heated internal dispute was sparked in the fall of 1882, when E. L. Godkin made a plea for Home Rule in the pages of the *Nineteenth Century*. Godkin used a British magazine both to reach an explicitly British audience and to move beyond the *Nation*'s usual approach, which had mixed a condemnation of violence and radicalism with hopes for eventual progress through varied Irish reforms. Godkin began his 1882 plea in the role of a constructive outside critic, explaining that "there are some things which are better seen at a distance than hard by."[35] Most of what followed did not concern the details of a proposed solution, however, since Godkin essentially endorsed the Home Rule position already associated with Parnell. Instead, Godkin devoted a considerable amount of attention to the reactionary anti-Irish bigotry that he believed afflicted all but a handful of the English. The inability of Englishmen to rise above their illiberal prejudices, Godkin concluded, constituted "one powerful cause of the growing repulsion to the English connection which one now sees among large numbers of Irish-men."[36]

Godkin's article had singled out Goldwin Smith's recent speeches on the Irish question as furnishing an especially egregious instance of a normally "fair-minded and liberal Englishman" proving incapable of rising above ir-rational prejudice. While visiting England earlier that year, Smith had mocked late-eighteenth-century Irish assemblies as "orgies of declamation, stimulated by the wine which [Irish politicians] drank in oceans." Despite later nostal-gia, Smith assured his audiences that this earlier "Home Rule" epitomized the worst misrule possible. During official legislative sessions, "everybody got drunk, everybody was in debt; even the highest functionary of the law was a duelist." Godkin (himself no stranger to abusive rhetoric) quoted at length from Smith's diatribe as evidence that the "depreciatory way of looking at everything Irish" had "become a habit of the English mind, even among en-lightened Liberals."[37]

What Godkin described as Smith's "Hibernophobic fury" became even more apparent over the next few years as the agitation for Home Rule intensi-fied. Smith's more balanced attention to Irish problems in the 1860s had given him enormous authority, and *Harper's Weekly* had regularly quoted him as a fair observer of conditions on the island.[38] But by the early 1880s, his tendency to isolate enemies and to excuse the faults of friends tarnished his reputation for fair dealing, even as his public rants and his stinging anti-Irish correspon-dence with friends such as Curtis and Norton grew more extreme. ("Avoided Ireland," a relieved Curtis assured Norton after one of Smith's visits.) Through a series of what Godkin dubbed "denunciatory" lectures, Smith seemed in-tent on working "to inflame the English hatred of the Irish." This was "dia-bolical work for an educated man," Godkin concluded, in that it cultivated the "mutual hate between people" rather than their common ability to reason.[39]

Smith's Hibernophobic fury developed in tandem with what would be a long and disreputable career as an anti-Semitic propagandist. His interest in this largely unrelated topic began when he attempted to excuse Russian atroci-ties against the Jews (thus continuing his support for this "Christian power" against the Turks and his distrust of Disraeli during the Eastern crisis). His criticism of the "tribal" and "anti-national" tendencies of Judaism (like Ca-tholicism) soon took on a life of its own in Smith's work and thus became one of the chief hobbies of his later career. Such fixations put him further outside the pale of the liberal circle, leading Bryce to share Godkin's alarm at the "most extravagant way" in which Smith discussed Ireland. Even A. V. Dicey, who agreed with Smith in opposing Home Rule, regretted that Smith had "lost his head & his judgment both about the Irish & also about the Jews."[40]

American liberal intellectuals drew a clear lesson from the uproar surrounding the Irish question. Smith's course, combined with the attacks on Lowell, revealed that imperial grievances could corrupt the morals and cloud the reason of everyone involved, assuring the degradation of the system's supposed beneficiaries as well as its victims. "It is so hard to get an idea into the skull of an Englishman!," Bryce (a Scotsman) had remarked to Godkin at the beginning of this public dispute. Godkin admitted that the Irish were "partly to blame" for the prejudices against them since their "rhetoric is too wild and extravagant." The plight of this long-oppressed group was ultimately understandable, however, since history had proven it nearly impossible "to agitate peacefully in a way to persuade another *people* holding the power." Even the "heavy contributions they make to the turbulence and crime of the United States" could be traced to British flaws, Godkin subsequently argued, since the "bad social and political training received at home" constituted the primary cause of the bad habits they brought to their adopted country.[41]

Smith's verbal assaults produced the ugliest split within a liberal alliance that was fraying more generally as Gladstone pushed the Liberal Party to adopt Home Rule as its preeminent issue in 1886. Curtis remarked to readers of *Harper's Monthly* that "even the most tranquil of Easy Chairs has been rocked a little by the universal storm of political excitement in Great Britain," adding that "since the days of Waterloo there has been nothing comparable to it." The crisis led to some poignant exchanges among longtime friends who had grown accustomed to agreeing with one another. Leslie Stephen, A. V. Dicey, Thomas Hughes, and Matthew Arnold joined Smith in dissent from Gladstone's policy, which Bryce, Morley, Harrison, and Godkin supported. Writing from the London Athenaeum (the preeminent club of the Victorian intelligentsia), Hughes reported to Lowell that a "rush of friends" had just interrupted him to discuss Irish affairs — "all Unionists . . . except Bryce who retired speedily." After an earlier interaction, Stephen had felt compelled to write of his continuing respect and fondness for Bryce lest the latter worry "that an old friend might be judging you harshly."[42]

But while divisive and in some cases even painful for the transatlantic liberals, the crisis over Irish Home Rule reinforced many liberal tenets. Smith's invective would turn out to be the exception that proved the rule. Despite strong disagreements (aired in public as well as private), liberals in both countries helped to foster an elevated debate that would distinguish the 1880s as, in one historian's words, a "time when the academic liberal ideal of the informed discussion of constitutional issues came close to realization."[43] Friendships provided an important means of assuring the civility that prevailed. Still writing in the pages of the *Nation* and corresponding warmly with his opponents, the Liberal Unionist A. V. Dicey committed himself to addressing this inherently volatile issue with "as much calmness as the merits or demerits of free trade." Such restraint seemed imperative in matters of foreign and imperial policy, when national pride and the suspicions of loyalty provoked a reflexive emotionalism that posed the greatest threat to critical and open discussion. Bryce explained in the preface to the *Handbook of Home Rule* that only a careful discussion could helpfully shape the debate that had already generated such "warm controversy." This volume included contributions from Bryce, Gladstone, Godkin, and John Morley, among others, and was among the primary ways that the Liberal Party tried "to elucidate by calm discussion and by references to history" its attachment to Home Rule. Despite strong disagreements with Bryce and Godkin, Dicey's articles for the *Contemporary Review* and the *Nation* also provided models of detached legal reasoning, so much so that Godkin described them (somewhat disparagingly) as approaching the issue from a "lawyer's point of view."[44]

In this context of civil debate, apart from the emotions of partisan wrangling, evidence of a liberal consensus even emerged around the principle of local self-government for the Irish. In the letter reaffirming his friendliness toward Bryce, Stephen also conceded that he "had long been for home rule in some shape." Matthew Arnold, traveling in America during the 1886 election that ousted Gladstone from power, was exasperated with what he considered the shallow and mistaken sense that "all Americans" supported the Liberal leader. Arnold thought in reality that Americans expressed vague support for Gladstone simply because he was the "only propounder of a scheme of local government," and Americans liked local government, a preference Arnold shared. The general civility among liberal intellectuals could be seen when what looked like a possible public flare-up between Arnold and Godkin (in the pages of the *London Times* and the *Nineteenth Century*) was quickly defused. Though they continued to disagree, within a year Arnold wrote to Godkin that he wished that the New York editor could represent Ireland in Parliament "instead of editing even so good a paper as the *Nation* at New York!" Though he supported Gladstone, Godkin too was not necessarily committed to any one specific policy of Home Rule. He simply wanted the British to give the Irish a stake in their governance and in the management of their affairs. "In this way," he asserted, "something like public opinion would be created in Ireland," as the people "would have been made to think on subjects, and would have learnt what was reasonable and practicable in politics."[45]

On this crucial question of local self-government, the example of American federalism and arguments from American constitutional history came to play a central role. Bryce and Dicey, in particular, loomed as the two opposing intellectual heavyweights on the topic and squared off in a series of articles, pamphlets, and books throughout the late 1880s. Indeed, Bryce's *American Commonwealth* had been completed between Gladstone's two unsuccessful attempts at passing Home Rule (in 1886 and 1892) and thus represented a direct intervention into that debate. Bryce devoted considerable attention to the workings of American federalism, showing that it effectively combined central coordination of foreign affairs with local autonomy in most day-to-day activities. Bryce did not have a monopoly on scouring American history or governance for precedents, however. Other Home-Rulers looked less to the structures of 1787 than to the events of 1776, warning that a similar revolution might come if the empire were not managed properly. Liberal Unionists who opposed Home Rule emphasized the northern resolve in 1861 to prevent the anarchic devolution of power presented by secessionists, while others still looked to southern Reconstruction for a parallel. Arnold told Godkin that he "would not exactly copy the United States," but he found attractive the kind of federal system that granted the postwar southern states local autonomy but no separate "Southern Congress."[46]

In basic political terms, the Gladstonian push for Irish autonomy proved a disaster. In sparking the defection of the Liberal Unionists, it brought about the demise of the Liberal Party in the late Victorian period and began two decades of nearly uninterrupted Conservative rule. This development was not as clear in the aftermath of the party's 1886 defeat, however, as it would be in hindsight. Many liberal observers expected that further reasoned discussion would ultimately vindicate Gladstone's position or lead to a more acceptable alternative. Curtis insisted that the Irish issue was no more likely to go away than the slavery issue had been when the Democrat Franklin Pierce was elected in 1852. Even though the English had become "sick and tired" of the topic, Curtis gave Gladstone credit for putting the issue on the agenda. The "Irish question is now fairly lodged in English politics, and it will be settled only when it is settled upon fundamental English principles of fair play," he predicted in 1889.[47]

Curtis would not live to see a second major push for Home Rule in the early 1890s. One can easily imagine how he would have reacted to the fact that Gladstone's measure this time around was opposed not by the voters (who had arguably grown more supportive of his policy) but by the House of Lords, which blocked the measure. From the American liberals' perspective, this outcome had a certain symmetry. Both aristocracy and imperial conquest constituted relics of the illiberal past, and their responsibility for having stymied reform was thus hardly surprising. The cause of the future still seemed clear enough, and looking toward it, American liberals could imagine both a further weakening of the Lords and a greater fairness toward Ireland. The key questions were simply how long these changes would take and what sort of effort would be required to overcome the embarrassing legacy of brutality and privilege.

America Has . . . Chosen the Path of Barbarism

The failure to pass Home Rule during the 1890s might have generated more attention from Anglo-American liberals had it not been eclipsed by the still more spectacular episode of Grover Cleveland's saber rattling over the Venezuelan boundary. This unexpected act of belligerence threatened much of what the transatlantic liberals had spent their adult lives trying to achieve. They instinctively realized the potential damage to the Anglo-American collaboration they had expended enormous energy to secure. Such a prospect made the idea of war between the two countries even more disturbing than had been the case thirty years earlier, when the Trent crisis nearly provoked a war.

The high stakes of Cleveland's message ironically presented new opportunities to transform a dangerous showdown into an unexpected liberal achievement. This unlikely turn of events resulted from the nature of Cleveland's chief demand, which was initially obscured by his strident language. He insisted that international arbitration be used to settle the boundary dispute between British Guiana and Venezuela that had simmered for decades. The notion of great powers defusing tensions through formalized interactions accorded with the foreign policy of Gladstonian liberalism. Here was an opening worth seizing once the parties looked past the strange fact that one of the future "judges" had threatened war unless the trial was commenced with his full participation.

British Liberals became the key figures in building support for an arbitration process in 1896 despite the fact that they had just suffered an electoral drubbing by Lord Salisbury's Conservative Party the year before. James Bryce's and John Morley's effectiveness as spokesmen for arbitration resulted from their long-standing identification with this approach toward international conflict.

Liberal interest in structured mediation had dated from the late 1860s, when Gladstone had presented the American *Alabama* claims before a Geneva commission. This move had popularized the idea that formal proceedings provided a progressive alternative to war and had encouraged Liberal Party leaders to institutionalize a national commitment to arbitration. The sentiment gained ground during the early 1880s, when the provocative journalist W. T. Stead had written to James Russell Lowell, then serving as minister to England, that an "Anglo-American bond" would be "among the probabilities of the future" that might be secured by a "permanent tribunal or Court of Conciliation & of Arbitration to which all disputes by diplomacy will be relegated for prompt & pacific settlement." While the initiative did not at first travel far beyond the columns of the *Pall Mall Gazette*, then edited by Morley, it gained some of the same prominence within advanced segments of Gladstonian liberalism as did Irish Home Rule.[48]

In 1896, British Liberals campaigned for a general arbitration treaty with a direct appeal to popular sentiment. They realized that while out of power, they could rally support for a measure that had already generated enthusiasm among radicals and workingmen's clubs. The advice from America (provided primarily through Godkin) was to move slowly, lest Cleveland be needlessly rewarded for his bellicose actions. But the Liberal Party, led by William Vernon Harcourt (a friend of the North during the Civil War), helped to pressure the Conservative government, while John Morley pushed the issue forward in a widely noted article insisting that an immediate crisis might open the way to "improving the rules of what is called international law." A cooperative Anglo-American response to Turkish massacres in Armenia cleared the way early in 1897 for the Olney-Pauncefote Treaty. This represented an important symbolic victory, even though the U.S. Senate failed to ratify the treaty and the British government had acted less out of principle than out of the need to resolve Anglo-American tensions to concentrate on the even more pressing affairs under way in South Africa. A short time after Cleveland's message, the so-called Jameson Raid had marked the first sign of British encroachments on the Boer republics, a development that would play a strong role in the later Anglo-American rapprochement.[49]

American liberal intellectuals welcomed the transatlantic agreement and even predicted that a new era of peace was at hand. Editors of the *Century* suggested that the "wild, flippant, and provincial talk about war" might be permanently banished by a system inspired by the universities, the commercial community, and other "sedate elements on both sides of the water." This effort to make war an "anachronism" represented a "great opportunity for the English-speaking race" to extend the specifics of its settlement and lead "mankind to the glorious destiny of peace." In a later issue of the same magazine, E. L. Godkin considered what he called the "Absurdity of War," attacking the notion that military combat constituted an "improver of character, or moral elevator of the whole community." Despite the current fixation on the invigorating results of war, Godkin insisted that combat between men was "no more human or rational than fights between animals" and insisted that war was the "one great trait of barbarism of the primeval world retained by modern nations." Godkin's only hope was that the mass armies then being raised in most European countries would dissuade armed conflict by assuring its unprecedented destructiveness.[50]

This brief moment of optimism helped liberals reassert the importance of a progressive Anglo-American tradition. They did so amid a more general embrace of Anglo-American partnership, a version of what others called "Anglo-Saxonism." A. V. Dicey made one of the most striking suggestions in his 1897 call for "citizenship for the whole English people." Dicey had parted ways with American liberals on the issue of Irish Home Rule and continued to disagree with them on questions of empire. But he maintained his admiration for the country he had first visited some thirty years earlier and thus sought to establish a legal basis that might institutionalize the "community of ideals" between the two countries most deeply committed to the "rule of law." Short of any such "reunion," a "moral alliance" between the two countries might serve as a worldwide force for peace, reason, and free trade.[51]

Trends that seemed only to foster an intensifying militarism compromised liberal hopes for an Anglo-American future without war, however. Doubts persisted about deep currents that shaped life in both countries at the close of the nineteenth century. These "illiberal" currents suggested that even the most effective treaty or movement for international cooperation would likely fall short. Sensational newspapers such as Joseph Pulitzer's *New York World*, William Randolph Hearst's *New York Journal*, and Alfred Harmsworth's *London Daily Mail* perhaps constituted the most disturbing phenomenon, especially to a set of liberals who had championed the press's role in fostering an educative democratic citizenship. In the United States, an inflammatory press had shown during the Venezuela affair how effectively it could "fan every spark of annoyance into a flame and cover violence and misrepresentations with the cloak of patriotism." In detailing the role of these journals, James Bryce believed that editorial excess was "as great a danger to peace" in modern societies "as the jealousies of kings and queens were in earlier centuries." Norton condemned this new breed of editors for having "sought and won a discreditable success by pandering to the baser tastes and dispositions of the community." The tendency had spread beyond the metropolitan dailies, he warned, so that the entire country was beset by journalists whose concern for "notoriety and profit" resulted in a "cynical indifference to public morality, to the obligations of truth, and the restraints of honor."[52]

E. L. Godkin, who had worked for decades to develop a principled journalism attuned to international comity, found the peril of the "yellow press" especially disturbing. These papers' growing tendency to "hurl defiance, heap abuse, and impute motives" about the leaders of other countries had made these publications a "constant danger to the amicable relations of great powers." The threat of sensational journalism was made all the worse by politicians' reckless abdication of their responsibility for wise deliberation. Shortly after the Venezuelan crisis had been resolved, Godkin lectured readers of the *Nation* that the "more Congress, too, refuses or fails to discuss the situation, the more incumbent on the press is it to step into the gap and take up the neglected work of the Legislation." Yet such a responsibility to facilitate discussion was the "last thing our press thinks of," given the fact that the "late excitement" proved that most editors would raise a "holler" that concluded that "anybody which made for war was wise and good" while "whatever anybody did that made for peace was asinine or corrupt, or English."[53]

American belligerence was fed by the mounting craze for violent sports, a topic that had vexed Norton as early as 1880. In that year, he had led a Harvard committee that tried to curtail undergraduates' growing enthusiasm for intercollegiate football, an enthusiasm that he feared cultivated barbarism in its most demoralizing form. Although Norton approved those athletic activities that developed "manly and vigorous health" — for example, rowing or hiking, which had enthralled his generation and drawn particular enthusiasm from Leslie Stephen, Bryce, and Higginson — he thought football fostered an "unhealthy excitement" and, worse, encouraged "getting the advantage of opponents by concealment, fraud, or violence if it cannot be won by legitimate means." Such an activity would perhaps not be too serious if confined to youth, but the immense popularity of college football revealed that the problem touched the whole society. Through its "hysteric applause" and "indifference to fair play," the larger community nurtured these "barbaric instincts of youth" and set a poor example. Was it any wonder that young Americans clung to a new, morally inferior, set of priorities than did their Victorian elders?[54]

Norton's qualms about undergraduate football comprised part of a broader

discussion of how this new craze for athletics affected American public life and
what ideals of "manliness" it promoted.[55] In a series of articles in the *Nation*,
Godkin compared college stadiums lined with stretchers for the wounded to
the "dueling field and the prize ring," concluding that "it may be laid down
as a sound rule among civilized people, that games which may be won by dis-
abling your adversary, or wearing out his strength, or killing him, ought to be
prohibited, at all events among its youth." Such a practice, Godkin concluded,
"cannot fail to blunt the sensibilities of young men, stimulate their bad passions, and drown their sense of fairness." The "athletic craze" that had begun
in the "leading colleges" infused the entire culture since "young gladiators"
drew "nearly as many spectators" as those who had "roared in the Flavian
amphitheatre" and had the same "moral influence" as the "Roman arena."
That Britain seemed just as drawn to violent sport only made matters worse.
Godkin's and Norton's extreme reactions were not echoed by all liberal intellectuals, some of whom actually shared an enthusiasm for the game that put them
closer to Theodore Roosevelt (among the era's most ardent fans). But even a
lifelong advocate of hiking, cycling, and gymnasium workouts such as Higginson worried that athletic pursuits had displaced intellectual ones at American
colleges. And no liberal approved when the serious business of making war was
conceived as a sporting contest writ large.[56]

The explosion of the American ship the *Maine* in Havana harbor brought
these larger trends to a head. The American liberals had sympathized with the
Cuban revolutionaries' desire to throw off Spanish rule and understood that
many Americans supported entering a war for this purpose. But the liberals
believed that diplomacy should be given time to work and that so momentous
a decision should not be made rashly, especially in response to an event such
as the *Maine*. In the wake of that stunning incident, the press rallied troops to
the cause as if generating enthusiasm for the latest sports match. The liberal
anti-imperialists saw the roaring applause of fans as a bitter contrast with the
eerie silence of citizens, as a public committed to victory abroad turned against
those daring to oppose or simply question the American "team." American liberals had noted a kind of silent or uncritical patriotism accelerating throughout the 1890s. As early as 1892, the *Century* had contrasted what it called the
"reasoning patriotism" of critical engagement and the "childish patriotism" of
ritualistic flag saluting. To Richard Watson Gilder, Lowell had embodied the
former, higher kind of patriotism, the only kind worth having, and the *Century* editor brandished a favorite couplet that was already becoming a liberal
mantra:

I loved her old renown, her stainless fame—
What better proof than that I loathed her shame?[57]

As discussion grew ever more constricted, Norton roused himself for another critical performance. He made the possibility of wartime dissent the theme of a speech to Harvard undergraduates in which he pled for the "rights of independent individual judgment and expression" as something of an outsider, since his earlier cultural criticism had already tainted his public image. Channeling his dear friend Lowell (as well as invoking the example of John Bright during the Crimean War), Norton insisted that democracy most needed dissent when it was in the midst of patriotic frenzy, "when the clamour of the fife and drum, echoed by the press and too often by the pulpit, is bidding all men fall in and keep step and obey in silence the tyrannous word of command." When actions were most likely to crowd out underlying ideas, it was the "duty of the good citizen not to be silent, and in spite of obloquy, misrepresentation and abuse, to insist on being heard, and with sober counsel to maintain the everlasting validity of the principles of the moral law."[58]

In titling his talk "True Patriotism," Norton clearly echoed the larger liberal view that national commitment had been vulgarized and reduced to the symbolism and ritual of flag devotion. Dissent under such circumstances became an end in itself, all the more important when the rest of the country was swept up in the frenzy of war. Newspapers, politicians, and random letter writers accused Norton of cowardice, effeminacy, and even treachery. The public uproar was probably intended to silence Norton, though in this it was a decided failure. A week after his widely publicized speech in Cambridge, a mass meeting at Boston's Faneuil Hall mobilized opponents of America's naval presence in Manila Harbor, which was the key to the Philippine archipelago and an early victory in the war with Spain. These two events in greater Boston laid the basis for the American anti-imperialist movement. Over the next several months, a coterie of celebrated writers, editors, and college professors launched an ongoing campaign for greater restraint in foreign affairs.[59]

The ominously silent patriotism of the 1890s hardly represented an isolated trend. For Godkin, the boss and the party system were as much to blame as the press, since one of the lessons Americans had drawn from such an illiberal example was "to despise and suppress discussion." This was a dangerous development, Godkin continued, because "deliberation" constituted the "salt of democracy; it is what keeps it democratic." To engage in such momentous issues without hearing all sides was precisely the opposite of democratic, and Godkin found it incredible that President William McKinley could consider the "applause of crowds at railroad stations" a legitimate substitute for open, candid discussion of his seemingly shifting war aims.[60]

Norton and Godkin were even more despairing in their private correspondence than in their public statements. Shortly after his Cambridge speech, Norton complained to Leslie Stephen that "America has rejected her old ideals, turned her back on her past, and chosen the path of barbarism." Godkin's faith was shaken not just in his adopted country but in the whole idea of a thinking and reasoning citizenry. Over the final years of his life, Godkin found increasingly compelling the writings of Gustave LeBon (whose *Psychology of Crowds* was translated into English in 1897), since they helped him explain the apparent hysteria and irrationality of the end-of-the-century mass public.[61]

The hopelessness that these friends expressed tinged their earlier convictions with an undeniable note of despair. Both Norton and Godkin became increasingly gloomy in looking back over reform careers approaching their close. "When I think of what I hoped from America forty years ago," Godkin wrote to Norton in June 1898, "and see what is coming, I see that we all expected far too much of the human race. What stuff we used to talk!" To William James, Godkin confided that he found it "most curious to see how the great lessons of Liberalism of my youth seem to be forgotten, & fairly decent men have been turned into roaring blatherskites." Norton suffered a similar sense of betrayal during the 1890s, writing to a friend, "I have been too much of an idealist about America, had set my hopes too high, had formed too fair an image of what she might become."[62] Norton's sense of isolation only deepened with the decline of his friends' health—Godkin suffered a debilitating stroke in 1900, while Leslie Stephen showed signs of frailty during the last meeting between the two men in 1901. Norton's state of mind suffered as well, however, since, as he explained to Goldwin Smith in 1902, he found the "heaviest burden of old age to be the disappointment, which these late years have brought, in steadily increasing measure, of the hopes for the advance of civilized man that we had some reason to indulge, up to perhaps twenty years ago."[63]

When compared to other liberal Victorians, Higginson expressed a deeper commitment to the future, even if he could hardly be unaffected by the trends that closed the nineteenth century. In 1897, Higginson's faith in turning American patriotism toward a more noble vision inspired him to compose a new national hymn that featured an appeal to peaceful virtues rather than the glories of war. Anticipating the sentiments expressed in his Cambridge neighbor William James's "The Moral Equivalent of War," Higginson celebrated the "heroic qualities" that war often nurtured—"endurance, courage, patient self-control, the readiness of sacrifice"—but he sighed for a time when "these great gifts" might "be trained in ordinary life, without paying for them the terrible price of human blood." Although he had warned against a hasty conflict with Spain, after the fighting began he tried to strike a tone of caution. In his regular column for *Harper's Bazaar*, Higginson argued that events had "simply concentrated, within a few weeks the change which was, at any rate, impending through influences of longer duration." He considered that larger economic and geopolitical forces had worked to "destroy the isolation of the United States, and to compel us, against our will, to become a world power." Before long, Higginson injected a greater sense of lament and caution into his musings: "Is it not written in the Book of Proverbs that he who meddleth with strife not his own is like him who taketh a dog by the ears?," he asked in the late summer of 1898. When the war in Cuba seemed over, he speculated that the people might engage in a sober second thought before taking actions that would result in a formal empire. "After all excesses, all disputes," he hopefully observed, the "contending American parties generally fix upon modes of policy which are not so extreme as was expected and choose for really high office men of character."[64]

Higginson learned the hard way that hopes for the return of reason were premature. No sooner had Spain surrendered to the United States then a Filipino insurgency led by Emilio Aguinaldo issued a plea for complete national independence. Writing in the *Nation*, Godkin realized how much this move changed the equation: "Having started out to give the inhabitants of Cuba their independence, we are now insisting that the inhabitants of the Philippine Islands, who had also revolted against Spanish rule, shall acknowledge our supremacy over them." The language of liberation that had proven adaptable in the war to release Cubans from the Spanish yoke was much harder to sustain in battling the Filipinos themselves. A newer justification for aggression would arise, resting instead on notions of duty, destiny, and racial stewardship. In the immediate future, what had been the problem of hasty war gave way to the problem of brutal conquest and empire. The liberal intellectuals responded as a group to what they saw as a deeply illiberal turn of events, standing ready to wage a concerted struggle against what they believed to be a perversion of America's mission to the rest of the world.[65]

Imperialism—the Great Moral Plague of Our
Time . . . on Both Sides of the Atlantic

Shortly before the 1900 presidential election, E. L. Godkin, Thomas Wentworth Higginson, and Charles Eliot Norton added their signatures to an "Address to Independent Voters" prepared by the American Anti-Imperialist League. Their appeal urged reformers of all stripes to look past minor differences and support William Jennings Bryan, the Democratic Party's challenger to President William McKinley. In lending aid to Bryan's presidential bid, liberal reformers conveyed in the clearest terms that this was no ordinary election, reminding voters that they might use the opportunity to reject the recent U.S. pursuit of empire on the far edge of the Pacific. As the league's address explained, the country entered the political season facing a "greater danger than we have encountered since the Pilgrims landed at Plymouth—the danger that we are to be transformed from a republic, founded on the Declaration of Independence, guided by the counsels of Washington, into a vulgar, commonplace empire, founded upon physical force."[66]

Along with the other signatories, the trio of aging liberal reformers appealed to earlier episodes of American history (while ignoring others) in their final collective engagement in national politics. Alongside the selective invocations of the distant past were echoes of these men's bolt from the Republican Party little more than a decade and a half earlier. A sense of common purpose and an overlapping set of figures linked the anti-imperialism of the late 1890s to the pro-Cleveland movement of 1884. As Higginson noted in 1899, each of the public rallies against the Philippine occupation "seemed like an old Mugwump meeting." The roster of Mugwump celebrities was also the same, with Mark Twain and William James heading the list of notable writers and scholars. George William Curtis's "Easy Chair" took antijingoistic ground after passing to the control of William Dean Howells in the fall of 1900. The posthumous influence of James Russell Lowell was even more pronounced, as opponents of imperial wars in both the United States and Britain repeatedly drew on the piety-deflating power of his Mexican War–era *Biglow Papers*.[67]

For all such echoes, the 1900 election marked a quite different moment in the history of liberal reform than the 1884 bolt had. Supporting William Jennings Bryan was not a result of liberals' enthusiasm for the candidate himself, and his nomination did not allow them the opportunity to extol the character of a steadfast leader. What drove most liberal intellectuals to his candidacy was their calculation that the Democrats represented the lesser of two evils. Any distaste

for Bryan and his illiberal crusade for free silver in the 1896 election paled next
to what they considered the contemptible course taken by McKinley, whose
invocations of "duty" while waging an aggressive war led Norton to compare
the president to the devil himself. Defeating a sitting president during wartime seemed the best means of changing an increasingly embarrassing military policy. When McKinley won easy reelection in November, the liberal crusade against jingoism received a dire though not fatal blow. What had become
an anti-imperialist movement continued to rally support and to publicize excesses. The liberals who kept up this fight in their old age realized, however,
that criticizing the war had placed them on the losing side of history, a position
to which they were unaccustomed, least of all in a presidential election. Between 1860 and 1896, Norton, Godkin, and Higginson had only once backed
the eventual loser, when they had campaigned for Cleveland (who later became
a two-term president) against Benjamin Harrison in 1892.

The liberals' century-end critique of imperial war was formulated within the
same transatlantic context that had shaped their entire post–Civil War careers.
This context only increased the bitterness, isolation, and gloom they experienced between 1898 and 1902. While it was bad enough to be marginalized at
home, even worse was the transatlantic rapprochement that during this period
made "Anglo-Saxon" domination of subject peoples its prevalent theme. There
were few better expressions of this new Anglo-American kinship than that set
forth by Edward Dicey in a widely noted 1898 article. Refocusing his attention on the New World for the first time since the 1860s (when he had visited
the United States and avidly supported the Union), Dicey praised Americans
for finally accepting the "destiny" assigned to them as Anglo-Saxons. Their
birthright was racial rather than national, Dicey contended, and their "desire
to extend the area of dominion" and the "wish to become a ruling power in
the world by the subjugation of weaker races" was a racial instinct, bound to
manifest itself eventually in the "Great Republic of the West," even if it had
been formerly "kept in abeyance." The moderation of the New England states
had given way at last to western exuberance, which Dicey believed should be
grounds for congratulation among Americans brave enough to embrace the
"hereditary policy" of true Anglo-Saxons.[68]

This flattery of American imperialists had its intended effect with those in
positions of power. On the brink of war with Spain, John Hay, the minister to
England, heralded this new imperial alliance by declaring that a "sanction like
that of religion . . . binds us to a sort of partnership in the beneficent work of
the world." America and England were, he continued, "joint ministers of the

same sacred mission of liberty and progress, charged with duties which we cannot evade by the imposition of irresistible hands." Countless newspapers and after-dinner speeches subsequently echoed these themes. Such effusions only increased after the United States turned its attention from "liberating" Cuba to subduing the newly acquired Philippine Islands. At the same time, Britons took up a similarly brutal suppression in South Africa. Despite Bryce's earlier prescriptions for reducing tension there, the Conservative ministry betrayed enthusiasm for a war sparked by the Boers' preemptive strike against British power. As both nations fulfilled their "duty" and achieved their "destiny" in different remote corners of the globe, Dicey, Hay, and other imperialists basked in what they took to be a family reunion.[69]

The American liberals were scandalized by such a conception of an Anglo-American alliance, though some irony attends their response. They too had hoped for an Anglo-American rapprochement based on Britain and America's common political characteristics and would have had little trouble imagining that such a rapprochement included a commitment to "liberty and progress," as Hay observed. Yet since the time of the Civil War, the liberals had conceptually bifurcated "England" into two entities: one hostile, aristocratic, and even tolerant of slavery and the other friendly, liberal, and decidedly opposed to slavery. Rooted in the shared experiences and commitments of the war and the postwar high tide, the binational partnership they had envisioned and for which they had worked was a consciously liberal one. The dichotomy had held steady in the intervening decades, manifesting itself (with at times some creative misreading by the Americans) in the debate over Governor Eyre's brutality in Jamaica, in the argument between Disraeli and Gladstone, and in the response to Ireland. An alliance between jingoes on both sides of the ocean represented then not simply a threat to the liberals' cultivating project but also an inversion of their highest ideals. Thirty years earlier, they would scarcely have imagined that Theodore Roosevelt, the first Harvard graduate to occupy the White House since John Quincy Adams, would happily take up a "white man's burden" at the invitation of the British, let alone that this occurrence would be hailed as a sign of transatlantic understanding. The press and the universities who supported such an illiberal imperial spirit did not simply fall short of their expected role in fostering liberal cultivation; they became the primary engine in initiating a reactionary worship of force and brutality. One bitterly poignant indication of how far matters had descended since the 1860s came with the 1902 establishment of a series of Oxford University scholarships set aside for Americans (as well as British colonists and Germans). The vision of racial supremacy and world mastery set forth by Cecil Rhodes could hardly have been farther from the mutual understanding that the liberals had hoped would emerge from Henry Yates Thompson's 1865 Cambridge Lectureship proposal.[70]

Having chosen the "wrong" England with which to enter into partnership, American imperialists were now leading the country into a betrayal of its historic ideals. Higginson had earlier warned that Britain was the "headquarters," "normal school," and "university extension system" of jingoism. "The trophies of Great Britain," he further explained, would "not allow [Henry Cabot] Lodge and Roosevelt to sleep."[71] The charge that in annexing the Philippines, America was repudiating precisely the qualities that had previously set it apart from its European peers became the most frequent complaint voiced by the liberal anti-imperialists. "All the evil spirits of the Old World which we trusted were exorcised in the New," Norton lamented, "have taken possession of [America], and under their influence she has gone mad." His Cambridge neighbor, William James, put it more graphically when he complained that Americans had "puked up our ancient national soul." The most complete expression of this theme came in a detailed historical oration by Charles Francis Adams Jr. (president of the Massachusetts Historical Society) that announced that American annexation of the Philippines would constitute a grave departure from the "tracks of our forefathers" and an admission that "we have outgrown the Declaration of 1776 and have become as wise now as Great Britain was then."[72]

Such contentions obviously drew on a familiar tradition of "American exceptionalism," that conception of national identity supported by a selective (and often providential) reading of history that sharply distinguished the New World republic from the Old World empires. From the first decades after the American Revolution, this distinction formed a crucial part of national identity, even if it was built on the denial of America's extensive continental empire and violent subjugation and removal of "darker races." By the late nineteenth century, "national exceptionalism" had become a commonplace if not uncontested national stance. Its familiarity, however, can prevent an understanding of the full thrust of the liberal anti-imperialist critique, at least two features of which bear highlighting. First, attention to the selectivity of the liberals' historical narrative should not obscure the exhortative and critical work they enlisted that narrative to accomplish. In the great tradition of the jeremiad, Norton, James, and their allies mobilized the moral force of the past (here as an imagined rejection of Old World imperialism) to criticize the present. Far

from a cause for triumph or celebration, as a blameless history might be expected to provide, "national exceptionalism" functioned here instead (as during the antislavery campaign) as yet another weapon in the liberals' critical
arsenal, a cudgel with which to beat back once again American complacency
and self-congratulation.[73]

Second, grouping the transatlantic liberals with other "national exceptionalists" overlooks the cosmopolitan and outward-looking nature of their reform
work in the previous three decades. The postwar high tide had been premised
on the belief that a wave of liberal progress was washing over the larger Atlantic world. The victorious American Union had of course been the lunar force
responsible for this tide, but the tide itself was not distinctively American and
the surf, liberals hoped, would reach all shores. Even once the ebb set in, the
international perspective remained. British and American liberals recognized
that they faced national variants of the same larger problems, studying each
other's responses and borrowing solutions when appropriate. On issues of electoral reform, the civil service, urban governance, education, the role of political
parties, journalism, and diplomacy, the transatlantic liberals had mined each
other's experiences and innovations throughout the final three decades of the
nineteenth century. A kind of internationalism had also infused their ideas
about culture, in their insistence that American authors and scholars contribute to the larger world of letters and in their efforts to place the *Rubaiyat*, the
Inferno, and *Hamlet* as well as the *Scarlet Letter* before American audiences.
Liberal internationalism was most obvious in the Victorian liberals' support for
arbitration and other mechanisms for cooperation (articulated in Gladstone's
"concert of Europe" principle back in the 1870s).[74]

Higginson struck this "national internationalist" tone in an 1899 *Harper's
Bazaar* column that inverted Thomas Paine's credo to announce, "Where Liberty Is Not, There Is My Country." This piece, which the Anti-Imperialist
League circulated as one of its most popular tracts, combined attention to the
Revolution of 1776 with recollections of American enthusiasm for European
revolts undertaken by the Hungarians, Italians, and Irish. Higginson point-
edly included the "nonwhite" examples of the Spanish Republics, considering
them a more accurate parallel to the contemporary campaign for Filipino independence. Even before war broke out, Higginson tried to chasten what he saw
as a growing attraction to imperialism by reminding his readers that the "test
of one's real love of liberty and of republican government is that one should
not believe them to be the destiny of a single race or language only, but of all
nations."[75]

The American liberals were not alone in seeing annexation and conquest of the Philippines as a departure from American ideals. The British writers most committed to Anglo-American liberalism were similarly pained to witness the U.S. response to the temptations of empire. For Goldwin Smith, the menace of imperialism assured his return to good standing within the circle of liberal reformers. His extreme response to the Irish question and his growing anti-Semitism had alienated him from his erstwhile liberal allies, but his dire reaction to transatlantic jingoism brought him back into contact with estranged friends such as Frederic Harrison, who agreed that those "struggling against the torrent" simply could not afford "to remain opponents." In reestablishing ties with Americans, Smith stressed echoes from the 1860s, explaining to Norton that the "party in England which is now luring [you] with a partnership in aggrandizement is identical with that which was your bitter enemy and the ardent friend of the slave power at the time of secession." Confronting the newest incarnation of a reactionary foe, Smith channeled his energy into writing on the British and American wars from the unique position of a lifelong student of anti-imperialism, in the process blending British, Canadian, and American perspectives.[76]

Bryce divided his time during the 1890s among lobbying for arbitration, building support for Irish Home Rule, and developing an idealized vision of U.S. foreign relations, a topic he had all but ignored in the *American Commonwealth*. In private, he expressed his dismay at the turn of events: "As an American of the old school, I am staggered, & indeed disquieted." He lamented that Americans were now "in for . . . tropical colonies, a great navy, and the whole programme of the European 'world powers.'" In public he put the matter more diplomatically, and with the credentials of a trusted friend and professional student of the American system, he responded to the endless requests for explanations of how the momentous shifts in U.S. diplomacy "present themselves to the mind of those English friends of America who love her almost as much as they love their own island." In the pages of the *Century*, the *North American Review*, the *Atlantic Monthly*, and *Harper's*, Bryce gently discouraged Americans from establishing colonies in the Pacific or the Caribbean, arguing that such acquisitions would not only make the now isolated United States vulnerable to foreign attack but more importantly would undermine "one of the noblest parts of her mission in the world." This mission, he thought, lay in presenting an "example of abstention from the quarrels and wars and conquests that make up so large and so lamentable a part of the annals of Europe." He urged his American friends to resist "that earth-hunger which has been raging among the European states" and to remain true to their "great and splendid mission."[77]

As Bryce's comments clearly suggest, the liberal anti-imperialists believed in a mission for the United States as much as the imperialists did. Norton's disgust that America had "chosen the path of barbarism" revealed his comfort speaking in the current idiom of evolutionary theories of social progress (which held that European and American societies had ascended out of the stages of savagery and barbarism to reach the height of civilization they enjoyed in the nineteenth century). The "civilized" supposedly had a responsibility, as a corollary of this view, to spread civilization to those still trapped in the earlier stages of savagery and barbarism. In the broadest terms, the transatlantic liberals would have agreed with this idea of a civilizing mission. Indeed, Norton and his liberal allies believed that they had already fought a war for civilization when they had put an end to southern savagery during the Civil War. The postwar liberal reform program could similarly be seen as an attempt to elevate civilization in their countries so that they could serve as a model for the rest of the world. Norton bristled at the suggestion that in opposing the war in the Philippines, he was abdicating this mission and instead encouraging the United States to withdraw inward. In an 1899 letter to an expansionist and former student, Norton explained that "it is not that we would hold America back from playing her full part in the world's affairs"; rather, "we believe that her part could be better accomplished by close adherence to those high principles which are ideally embodied in her institutions." By following what he had in 1865 called "American political ideas," Norton believed that the United States might have exerted the "influence of a great, unarmed and peaceful power on the affairs and the moral temper of the world." But by taking an illiberal path to world power, America had "lost her unique position as a potential leader in the progress of civilization, and has taken up her place simply as one of the grasping and selfish nations of the present day."[78]

Where Norton and other liberal anti-imperialists strongly disagreed with other missionaries of civilization was in questioning whether the Philippine-American war was an effective agent in that process. British liberals confronted that question with even greater urgency after their country entered a war against the Boer republics of South Africa late in 1899. Unlike the American anti-imperialist movement, opponents of the South African war tended to focus on the practice of empire rather than the mere existence of an empire (which had been well enough established as a fact of British history). But in spite of this major difference, liberals rhetorically paired these simultaneous

instances of imperial force. From Canada, Goldwin Smith warned of a "junc-
tion of American with British Jingoism for the purpose of aggrandizement,"
while Frederic Harrison agreed that the "prevalent Imperialism" had become
the "great moral plague of our time, it seems, on both sides of the Atlantic."
The apparent friendliness between British Tory jingoes and American hyper-
patriots began to appear increasingly shallow and self-interested. "You are
hated just as much as ever," a cynical Godkin wrote to Marion Bryce in 1899,
"and it is a common remark how the stumps would resound with denunciations
of your attack on the Boers, if we were not in the same business ourselves."[79]

While the onset of the wars in South Africa and the Philippines had generated controversy mainly among distinct segments of the population, the armed
forces' brutal conduct in these two conflicts laid the basis for a more thorough
opposition. In mounting this opposition, the transatlantic liberals confronted
squarely the question of civilizing missions and even of civilization itself. Smith
and others drew attention to the use of torture against prisoners and the campaign against noncombatants, which included the first official use of "concentration camps" to contain civilians, a "scorched earth" policy of razing
farms across the land, and mass killings in the Philippines. Recognizing that
such brutality exposed the hollowness of American professions of benevolence,
Charles Francis Adams Jr. cautioned that all " 'divine missions' and 'providential calls' " should be viewed in the "cold, pitiless light of history," where it
became clear that the "knife and the shotgun have been far more potent and
active instruments [in the process of civilizing] than the code of liberty or the
output of the Bible Society." Mark Twain would make this point to even more
devastating effect in his ironic "To the Person Sitting in Darkness."[80]

As the liberal critics exposed the harsh reality of waging war against an entire population, they revealed how this "new" imperialism was, its own rhetoric
to the contrary, no more noble than earlier conquests. Writing for the *Nation* in
1901, Smith explained that earlier tyrants such as Genghis Khan "did not talk
about the brown man's burden, or pretend, as the Jingoes do, to be enlarging
the realm of civilization by wholesale slaughter and arson." The lack of embarrassment in making "triumphal pyramids of heads" was matched, Smith
thought, in modern times by the "tolerable serenity" with which otherwise
"civilized" people greeted the "daily returns of Filipinos or Boers shot down."
The liberal anti-imperialists kept up a steady stream of critical outrage, demanding government and independent investigations into reported atrocities.
Godkin informed *Nation* readers that official dispatches hardly conveyed the
extent of "our savage war for the 'cause of humanity,' " but thousands of letters

from private soldiers written home every week told the "horrible truth with all the impressiveness of native eloquence." By employing the words "savage" and "barbaric" to attack American and British policy (and comparing the political leaders unfavorably with their medieval forbears), the liberal anti-imperialists both demonstrated the cynical hypocrisy behind claims of exporting civilization and, ultimately more troubling, implied that the gulf separating civilized and savage was perhaps not so great. In this light, civilization was clearly not a "birthright," not something certain nations inherited, but something they had to nurture constantly lest illiberal forces become overwhelming and trigger a process of regression.[81]

In puzzling through these disquieting thoughts, the transatlantic liberals shared information, kept up with one another's affairs, and corresponded frequently by mail. An added opportunity to exchange views came with a spurt of transatlantic travel during the most pronounced stage of jingoistic Anglo-Saxondom. Norton visited Britain in 1900 primarily to conduct business as John Ruskin's literary executor, though the short trip also allowed Norton to receive an honorary degree from Oxford and to visit in person, for a final time, Leslie Stephen and A. V. Dicey. Norton was saddened to find during what became his last transatlantic sojourn that the "same evil influences have been at work there as in America, and the same ill results—the materialization of the public temper, the vulgarization of society, and the increase of jingo militarism." Godkin looked more positively on the conditions of British public life, which he compared favorably with the United States during his extended visits there between 1900 and his death in 1902. In 1901, Higginson made his final trip to Britain, using the occasion proudly to declare his anti-imperialist convictions at the seat of global power just as he had in the republican United States.[82]

A reverse flow across the Atlantic at nearly the same time brought A. V. Dicey, James Bryce, Frederic Harrison, and John Morley to the United States, where they witnessed firsthand the way in which Americans responded to their country's new global stature. Norton tried to lure as many of these liberal visitors to Cambridge as possible, and he succeeded both in bringing Harrison to deliver a talk in 1901 and in assuring that Bryce would deliver the inaugural Godkin lectures in the fall of 1904. Harrison's visits were marked by a dark vision of what the future held in store. "Intellectually, spiritually, morally, socially," Harrison told a New York audience, the "close of the century, as contrasted with its prime, is to my eyes a picture blurred, darkened, and out of harmony and proportion." Looking about him in 1901, he found "not progress, but decadence," an abandonment of those high ideals that had animated his generation and that were most blatantly betrayed in the current struggles to extend domination to the farthest corners of the world.[83]

These late interactions encouraged a kind of perverse one-upmanship, a wrangling over which country was more demoralized, which war more illiberal. Bewailing the "folly of ignorance and rascality" of the U.S.-Philippine war, Godkin assured an equally outraged Marion Bryce, "You do not see a quarter of it in England." Similarly, Norton deplored the "misery we are working in the islands" and insisted to Harrison that "this war of ours is even more criminal, & in a profound sense more disastrous than the war in South Africa." Bryce drew a different conclusion in writing to Norton, pointing out that Britain's war was "as least as needless as yours with Spain, and morally in so far worse that it was undertaken from no feelings so natural as those which the condition of Cuba had excited." The American war had at least accomplished something positive in ridding Cuba of Spanish misrule, while the British war had instead "ended in the extinction of two free republics, one of them a model community." Bryce even found himself "tempted to regret Disraeli: what more could one say? He was after all not quite so sordid as the present leader of the gentlemen of England," Lord Salisbury.[84]

In diagnosing the illiberalism of the new imperialism, liberals emphasized that racism and racial thinking had grown worse than at any time since the Civil War. In asking black voters to support William Jennings Bryan in 1900, Higginson explained that overseas conquest had done more to bolster white supremacy than any other force. "Every day in the Philippines is already training our young American soldiers to the habit of thinking that the white man, as such, is the rightful ruler of all other men," he insisted, adding that the Republican Party of Lincoln had now made freedom a "matter of complexion." (Higginson severed his association with Bryan the following year over the Democrat's "utterly retrograde and mediaeval" stance on questions of race.) Not surprisingly, Higginson devoted more attention than most liberal reformers to this fin de siècle eruption of racism. Speaking out on the cause of racial justice helped him to sustain a continuing identification with his abolitionist past and his experience as one of the first commanders of black troops during the Civil War.[85]

Higginson condemned racial presuppositions even when they appeared within his circle of transatlantic acquaintances. His friendly relationship with James Bryce was strained (though not disrupted) by Bryce's increasing emphasis in the 1890s on the inferior capacities of the world's "darker races" for self-government. After reading one of the Scotsman's essays addressed to an American audience in 1899, Higginson sternly warned Bryce that "you express very dangerous doctrine in implying that one race is to be the judge for another whether it is fitted for the suffrage." The immediate result of such a doctrine would be further imperial aggression and an encouragement to deprive justice to downtrodden populations such as the Irish, Higginson continued. "So soon as we undertake to decide which races are backward, Democratic government is weakened." He then dramatized the intellectual poverty of racial theorizing by noting that "until the recent strange revival of Anglicanism here, three Americans out of four regarded England as 'a backward race!'" [86]

Other liberals joined Higginson in debunking the idea of Anglo-Saxon racial superiority. Goldwin Smith ridiculed what he called the "mystical fancies about destined preeminence of race" that had been, in his opinion, "invented to sanction conquest" (though he continued to cling to a few such "fancies"). Godkin had previously done battle with Anglo-Saxonism, defending the Irish from the charge that their reckless violence demonstrated their incapacity for self-government. All peoples, Godkin had written then, including "Anglo-Saxons[,] resort to somewhat the same methods under similar circumstances," and he pointed to the postwar behavior of southern whites as proof of this claim. Indeed, the U.S. South furnished the most damning evidence against Anglo-Saxon superiority. Southerners represented the purest Anglo-Saxon "stock" in the country, liberal critics pointed out, and look how "civilized" their region was. In an article written shortly after Sam Hose's brutal mutilation in Georgia, the *Nation* described the situation as "simply a descent into barbarism by a people who pretend to be civilized, and, not only that, but are pretending to spread civilization." [87]

U.S. involvement in a war across the Pacific helped liberals to reconsider what had been their conventional geography of race. They gradually moved away from their earlier tendency to consider questions of race mainly by evaluating the relationships between former masters and slaves in the American South and across the Caribbean. Alongside the difficulties in the Philippines, attention was soon drawn to a wholly different site of racial difference in the example Japan provided of "nonwhite" capabilities. If American and European intellectuals evidenced a broad vogue for Japan in the late nineteenth century, not all commentators linked this period's "discovery" of Asian culture to the prospects for race in the next century. Such was Higginson's approach, however, and he held up the Japanese success in working out that country's destiny as a way to argue that growth through self-cultivation should apply to the Filipinos and, for that matter, to all humans. Norton voiced much the same expectations with a comparable accent on what later generations would call pluralism. He was drawn to the Japanese example by his friendships with Harvard students from that country, which further convinced him that civilization was a "relative term" and that it was not "as white people are apt to assume a possession exclusively theirs." Norton's comparative appreciation of Western civilization led him to suggest that the East might be an even better setting for cultivating human values. To a former student from Japan he wrote, "We have as much to learn from the East as you of the East have to learn from the West, and I am not sure but that the lesson the East has to teach is the most important."[88]

Norton's and Higginson's interest in the Far East prepared them to greet the 1905 Russo-Japanese peace treaty as the dawning of a brighter day. As the last American members of the liberal cohort, they had taken little satisfaction in the end of "hostilities" in the Philippines in 1902. They realized that the pall of empire remained as long as U.S. troops constituted the primary source of authority there. Yet when war between Russia and Japan began in 1904, Norton found himself hoping that part of the "Oriental race" might achieve terms "which shall admit of the natural development of [Japan] and of her assuming that hegemony in the East which she seems capable of holding." The true conclusion to the dispiriting episode of hyperjingoism came with the peace initiatives taken by President Theodore Roosevelt, a prime mover in America's 1898 imperial adventures. In negotiations held at Portsmouth, New Hampshire, the United States brokered peace rather than spread war, and the true victors were the "self-respectful and subtle Japanese," who seemed to have gained the "diplomatic no less than the moral victory," Norton thought.[89]

If liberals in their old age found themselves casting their gaze toward the far Pacific, the transatlantic ties still mattered most in the end. Norton acknowledged the strange sense of kinship between British and American liberals that was born of shared experiences and ideas in a series of letters that he wrote during the final years of his life. In 1905, he reached out to Goldwin Smith, explaining that "seldom as we have met & infrequently as we have written to each other during the past forty years, we are not far apart as the end of life draws near." Norton knew he had a receptive audience when he explained that the "bitterest disappointment which life has brought to me has been the failure of the hopes in regard to this country & the progress of man here in independent & republican America, — the hopes which were so bright even when we first knew each other." These dampened hopes were the "worst blow that modern civilization has had, perhaps a mortal blow," and he was left with the question, "Is our modern civilization worth saving?" If it were not, "how may the break up of the old order be accomplished with least disaster & misery?"[90]

Disappointment was not the same as despair. Norton refused to forget the hopes that had been buoyed during the liberal high tide. Later that year, in the wake of the Portsmouth treaty, he again wrote to Smith, striking a different tone: "We have lived through a period of the world's history of surpassing interest & enormous change. But we have seen only the beginning of the mightiest revolution in human affairs, and we shall have to quit the stage in the very middle of a most entertaining scene. I, however, shall not be sorry to go, though my curiosity as to what is about to happen may never be satisfied."[91]

The world had grown much closer by the first decade of the twentieth century than had seemed possible eighty years earlier, even if it had not grown more reassuring in the process. Given the high hopes and the stark disappointments, some sense of alienation among liberals was all but inevitable. But as Norton's interactions with Goldwin Smith revealed, doubts remained tempered by a faith that things might again be set right. Something seemed thoroughly American about the quest to retain optimism amid such bitter setbacks. James Bryce identified this trend in one of his last letters to Norton. In 1907, during yet another of Bryce's trips across the Atlantic, he noted in passing that "here in America more than any where else one finds the pendulum of one's mind continually swinging to and fro." The future was as murky to the Briton, who would live for another decade and a half, as to his New World friend Norton, who died thirteen months later. Until the end, a battle continued within even the most disillusioned liberal souls. As they considered their lives, their moment, and their legacy, they found themselves as if by instinct cycling repeatedly between what Bryce identified as the competing sentiments of "depression and faith."[92]

Epilogue

On May 12, 1911, a bright spring day, eighty-eight-year-old Thomas Wentworth Higginson was laid to rest in Mt. Auburn Cemetery. The fact that he had outlived nearly all his contemporaries meant that here would be no assemblage of Victorian liberal lights at the ceremonies that honored him. Without the presence of James Russell Lowell, George William Curtis, or Charles Eliot Norton (whose passings Higginson had noted in 1891, 1892, and 1908, respectively), others tried to assess his legacy. Six African American soldiers played an important role by carrying Higginson's casket, which was draped with an old regimental flag of the First South Carolina Volunteers, up the hushed aisles of the First Parish Church in Cambridge. This poignant acknowledgment was accompanied by a stream of commentary concerning Higginson's antislavery activities, his defining Civil War service, and his various late-nineteenth-century reform positions. As tributes to the old colonel trickled out over the following weeks in the *Nation*, the *Atlantic*, *Harper's Bazaar*, and the *Woman's Journal*, readers were also reminded of his literary output and his efforts to reach a national middle-class reading public.

In the realms of literature, reform, and national culture, much had clearly changed between Higginson's entry into the world and his exit. The year he was born witnessed the publication of James Fenimore Cooper's first "Leatherstocking Tale" and the proclamation of the Monroe Doctrine. In the year he died, Randolph Bourne had just begun his undergraduate studies at Columbia College, the African American artist and activist James Weldon Johnson was busy writing his *Autobiography of an Ex-Colored Man*, and 146 people were killed when a fire broke out at the Triangle Shirtwaist Factory. By 1911, the "Victorian era" was already a relic of the past. A generation was putting its stamp on what Britons termed the Edwardian period and what Americans would remember as the Progressive era. The sense of discontinuity with the past seemed perhaps clearest in the emergence of literary modernism, a development that Leslie Stephen's daughter (and Lowell's goddaughter), Virginia

Woolf, noted in her oft-quoted pronouncement that "On or about December 1910, human character changed."[1]

The modernism that Higginson barely lived to witness would not be kind to the liberal Victorians as a group. Their reputation suffered acutely in the decades immediately following their deaths. They would find themselves ridiculed—or, perhaps worse, ignored altogether—by their political and literary intellectual successors. The young moderns so effectively discredited their Victorian predecessors that they turned the adjective into a term of contempt. By 1920, for intellectuals in Greenwich Village and Bloomsbury, "Victorian" had become synonymous with priggishness and conventionality. The American Victorians would meet their match in George Santayana, who, two years after Higginson's death, derided these exemplars of the "genteel tradition." The British Victorians would be similarly lampooned by Lytton Strachey, who devastatingly skewered their piety and hypocrisy as entirely inappropriate for the twentieth century.[2]

Two figures who successfully bridged the Victorian and modern eras, the philosopher William James and his brother, the novelist Henry James, left a detailed set of comments about their elders, revealing a complicated set of relations, alternately tender and hostile. William expressed indebtedness to Godkin's *Nation* for his "whole political education," praised Lowell's "singularly boyish cheerfulness and robustness of temperament," and chatted easily with Norton in letters and visits to Shady Hill. Henry echoed William's views, describing Lowell as "wonderfully simple & genial . . . and expressively kind to me" and finding himself moved by the "quite touchingly beautiful and human" portrait of Lowell that emerged from the letters Norton collected and published in 1893. Yet the Jameses also expressed exasperation with their elders. William yawned over the "perfect *bog* of reasonableness" that was Bryce's *American Commonwealth*, complained of the "entirely needless priggishness of [Matthew Arnold's] tone," and called Norton's posing "as a great man, and [being] taken so seriously while about it, . . . one of God's best ironical strokes." Henry surely offered the most evocative characterization, describing A. V. Dicey and his wife as "good, but decidedly too ugly, useful information-ish, grotesque-Oxfordish, poor-dinnerish, etc." (Bad dinners were a particular transgression in the James family: William also complained of a woefully scanty meal with the Nortons at Shady Hill.)[3]

The complaints about Spartan meals and useful information suggest that what most irked a younger generation of intellectuals was the Victorians' austere earnestness. Twentieth-century intellectuals were far less captivated by notions of "duty," "character," and "honor," mouthed so frequently by the critical generation of the Civil War. Curtis's 1856 "The Duty of the American Scholar to Politics and the Times" may have served as a bracing charge to educated men of his generation, but by the second decade of the twentieth century, such a plea sounded hopelessly oratorical and archaic to young intellectuals such as Walter Lippmann and Randolph Bourne who were concerned with immediate experience and democratic vitality.

The moderns were not wrong in their judgment of the liberal Victorians. There was plenty about them to exasperate anyone, especially those who did not share their common experiences. What the twentieth century would come to see as their well-meaning but empty rhetoric was at times disconnected from reality. Indeed, the failure of so many Victorian liberals to back up their pretty words with action rendered such utterances hollow in the eyes of later observers. But if later modernist intellectuals were not quite wrong, they were surely too sweeping in their judgment. As might be expected of young people, their historical imagination was underdeveloped, and they could never see Higginson, Norton, Curtis, and Lowell as anything but the crotchety old men they had become at the end of their lives. Such indifference is hardly surprising — in fact, all young intellectuals may need to take such a stance toward their elders, at least initially. But if the young moderns had cared to look harder, they might have experienced a faint shock of recognition at the group of restless and ambitious literary men who, in the 1840s and 1850s, wrestled with how best to establish themselves as upstart writers and critics of mainstream society. They might also have appreciated the momentousness of the age the Victorians had worked to shape. It is still hard to appreciate how the end of slavery, the future of democracy, the existence of a nationalized middle-class reading public, an established place for critical dissent, and the power of the United States in the world had hung in the balance in the second half of the nineteenth century.

The historical insensitivity of the young intellectuals has had lasting effects, and we have largely remained captive to the modernist and Progressive view of the late nineteenth century, relying on this snapshot in the place of a fully realized portrait. The result has been an impoverished understanding not only of them but of ourselves as well. Now, as the dust of nearly a century has settled and the high ambitions of the moderns and Progressives have also gone largely unrealized, we can consider both generations historically and see that the moderns offered too blanket a dismissal, used too blunt a weapon to attack their predecessors. For all the Victorians' limitations — whether measured in terms of will, empathy, or vision — their contributions to American cultural and intellectual life can be denied only by doing violence to the historical record. In fact, far from being as outdated as the moderns once thought, these men anticipated several of the moderns' concerns and even in many ways represent "our [own] contemporaries," in Charles Taylor's phrase.[4]

Removing the refracted lens of the early twentieth century can cast new light on several features of the late-nineteenth-century liberal men of letters. Rather than the insular and blinkered provincials of the prevailing caricature, the members of this generation emerge as nineteenth-century cosmopolitans. Their cosmopolitanism, to be sure, was always limited by their insecure place in a European world still largely skeptical about if not hostile to the American "experiment." Yet as we have seen, these men were well traveled and well read, attentive to and willing to make use of lessons learned from other countries and time periods. Speaking for the group, Godkin expressed impatience with the "general belief that we are a peculiar or chosen people to whom the experience of other people is of no use."[5]

This cosmopolitanism and awareness of the world around them not only mitigated exceptionalist tendencies in the Victorian liberals' thought (an occupational hazard for nearly all nineteenth-century American men of letters) but even nudged them close to historicist or relativist notions of culture and civilization that would become dominant in the twentieth century. Higginson's 1897 attack on immigration restriction, for example, clearly anticipates some of the themes in Bourne's much better known "Transnational America," written nearly two decades later. Higginson argued that all Americans had been immigrants at one point or another and that American society had always been in flux. "We err in assuming that any one race monopolizes all the virtues," Higginson wrote, "or that the community only suffers with each importation." Further (and, again, like Bourne), Higginson took a double swipe at northern intolerance and southern white supremacy when he observed that the most violent and lawless segments of the population were not new immigrants but Anglo-Saxons living in "those portions of the Union least touched by foreign immigration." Higginson's perverse relish at debunking notions of Anglo-Saxon supremacy might well have provided a model for the "white-moustached, well-dressed . . . old Union soldier" who in James Weldon Johnson's 1912 novel argued for the non-Anglo-Saxon origins of nearly every achievement of civilization. As this fictional relic of the Civil War cautioned, "racial supremacy is merely a matter of dates in history."[6]

The comparative progressiveness of Higginson's racial views would be the key to his "rediscovery" during the 1960s, as scholars concerned with tracing out the antislavery tradition turned to his example. His wartime *Atlantic Monthly* essays on slave rebellion and resistance reappeared in 1969, while his *Army Life in a Black Regiment* became a central nineteenth-century text, appearing in no fewer than seven different editions between 1961 and the early twenty-first century.[7]

Might the time be ripe for a reexamination of the liberal Victorians' more general critical project? Though discussions of democracy today have a far more populist inflection, the liberal understanding of democratic politics and particularly of the educative nature of citizenship may be more germane at the outset of the twenty-first century than was ever the case during the twentieth. The liberals' distrust of parties and of an overweening partisanship that limits political options clearly resonates today when fewer and fewer Americans register a party affiliation and when Americans increasingly lavish praise on "maverick" politicians. The liberals' notorious attack on the spoils system, though often misunderstood by historians, revealed a concern that the party system had created a dangerous nexus between spoilsmen and an industrial plutocracy that has certainly not ceased to be a problem even a century after the first legislative attempts to police "clean government" and disinterested public service.

These conditions make the liberal's normative vision of critical citizenship as relevant now as during the high tide of the post–Civil War 1860s. The liberal ideal of democratic politics attempted to combine unprecedented inclusiveness (of African Americans and women) with the elevation of the individual voter as a reasoning civic participant capable of thinking for himself or herself. Victorian liberals' attention to public opinion as the crucial force that must be molded or nudged along put them on the cutting edge of political thought. Later democratic realists called into question the liberals' faith in this amorphous power, pointing to the voters' ignorance and irrationality. But more recent attempts by political theorists to elaborate a discursive or communicative model of politics echo (unconsciously) the Victorian emphasis on speech and discussion as precisely the things that make, in Godkin's phrase, democracies democratic. In an era when only about 50 percent of Americans turn out to vote in presidential elections and much of the media seems set on thwarting rather than facilitating meaningful discussion, we might do well to reinvigorate the Victorians' insistence on the "stimulating" effect of civic participation as well as on democratic discussion. Though their normative ideal of citizenship may seem either naively optimistic or overly austere, it bespoke a respect for voters as reasoning individuals far removed from the current trends of endless "spin" or deceptive "frames."[8]

The faith in ordinary readers grew from the liberal Victorians' insistence on what the philosopher, critic, and public intellectual Richard Rorty calls the "inspirational value of great works of literature." Even at those moments when reform and political movements occupied the bulk of their energies, Higginson, Lowell, Norton, and Curtis never relinquished their standing as literary men. In this capacity they developed their conviction that works of art and literature could and should be universally shared. As was true of their political reform, this cultural outlook extended both horizontally and vertically, democratizing access to "great books" and working to secure a place for the wheat amid the constant chaff thrown up by the mass market. To this end, they pioneered "middlebrow" efforts at diffusion and mediation—both attempting to make texts available and serving as intermediaries between the classics of "Western culture" and a broad reading public. Twentieth-century critics and publishers would build on these (often unacknowledged) earlier efforts and launch a variety of publication series intended to appeal to a range of brow sizes. Most recently, the media mogul Oprah Winfrey has taken up this middlebrow project, with some controversy, insisting that ordinary Americans—high school graduates, homemakers, television viewers—might share her sense of reading as a transporting and enriching experience.[9]

Victorian liberals applied the same sensibility in contemplating the U.S. role in the larger world, an area where their vision seems similarly to have self-evident relevance. A very different international situation prevails during our own day, when we can look back over the horrific wars of the twentieth century and the military actions taken in the aftermath of the September 11, 2001, terrorist attacks. While the idea of a "special relationship" between Britain and the United States may seem the most enduring of the Victorian efforts in foreign affairs, we should recall the nature of the alliance liberal Victorians hoped to bring about—one based not simply on shared language, ethnic origins, or even historical experience but on principle and specifically on principles of justice and "fair play" that require discussion and elaboration. As the liberals' experience in the 1890s revealed, the preservation of such principles was not assured merely by the fact of an alliance.

The liberal conviction that reason and thoughtful discussion must always have a place in the conduct of foreign policy remains a vital legacy, as does their example of voicing criticism amid the clang of hyperpatriotism. From Lowell's *Biglow Papers* to Norton's "True Patriotism" and Higginson's "Where Liberty Is Not, There Is My Country," the liberal Victorians forged a model of liberal opposition. In so doing, they carved out an institutional space (in the

various periodicals they edited and to which they contributed) and provided
moral legitimacy for engaged dissent. Their insistence on the need for a critical or "reasoning" patriotism—a lesson we have continually to relearn—thus
ranks among their most lasting contributions.[10]

What united the Victorians' endeavors in these three areas—educative politics, democratic culture, and a critical stance toward the nation's foreign policy
—was their notion of liberal cultivation. And perhaps here the Victorians remain most clearly our contemporaries. The notion of the self that underlay Victorian liberal cultivation had infinite powers and faculties that might be drawn
out and developed. Selves were moral and rational beings, engaged citizens,
dutiful members of communities, sympathetic participants in a cosmopolitan
and transhistorical world of human aspiration, imaginative readers and observers, and much more. To recover this strand of Victorian liberalism moves
us far away from the caricature of nineteenth-century liberalism as either an
atomistic possessive individualism or a negative freedom of the unencumbered
self. Recognizing the robustness of this older liberalism might help us to en-
rich our own.

Notes

Abbreviations

AtMo	*Atlantic Monthly*
AVD	A. V. Dicey
CEN	Charles Eliot Norton
CEN Papers	Charles Eliot Norton Papers (bMS Am 1088.2), Houghton Library, Harvard University, Cambridge, Mass.
CFA	Charles Francis Adams Jr.
CWE	Charles W. Eliot
CWJSM	John Stuart Mill, *Collected Works of John Stuart Mill*, 33 vols. (Toronto: University of Toronto Press, 1972–91)
ELG	E. L. Godkin
ELG Papers	E. L. Godkin Papers (bMS Am 1083), Houghton Library, Harvard University, Cambridge, Mass.
FH	Frederic Harrison
GS	Goldwin Smith
GS Papers	Goldwin Smith Papers, Olin Library, Cornell University, Ithaca, N.Y.
GWC	George William Curtis
GWC Papers	George William Curtis Papers (bMS Am 1124), Houghton Library, Harvard University, Cambridge, Mass.
HA	Henry Adams
HNMM	*Harper's New Monthly Magazine*
HW	*Harper's Weekly*
JB	James Bryce
JB Papers	James Bryce Papers, Bodleian Library, Oxford University, Oxford, England
JRL	James Russell Lowell
JRL Papers (A)	James Russell Lowell Papers (bMS Am 765), Houghton Library, Harvard University, Cambridge, Mass.
JRL Papers (B)	James Russell Lowell Papers (bMS Am 1483), Houghton Library, Harvard University, Cambridge, Mass.
JRL Papers (C)	James Russell Lowell Additional Papers (bMS Am 1484), Houghton Library, Harvard University, Cambridge, Mass.
JRL Papers (D)	James Russell Lowell Additional Papers (bMS Am 1484.1), Houghton Library, Harvard University, Cambridge, Mass.
JSM	John Stuart Mill
LS	Leslie Stephen

MA   Matthew Arnold
MHS   Massachusetts Historical Society, Boston
NAR   *North American Review*
NELPS   *New England Loyal Publication Society Broadside*, Rare Book
            Collection, Wisconsin Historical Society Library, Madison
RWG   Richard Watson Gilder
RWG Papers Richard Watson Gilder Papers, New York Public Library, Rare Books
            and Manuscripts Division, New York, N.Y.
TWH   Thomas Wentworth Higginson
TWH Papers Thomas Wentworth Higginson Papers (MS Am 1162.10), Houghton
            Library, Harvard University, Cambridge, Mass.
WJ   *Woman's Journal*

Introduction

1. TWH, "Tribute to Professor Norton"; later republished in slightly amended form as TWH, "Ruskin and Norton"; see also TWH, "CEN," 129–30. In earlier eulogies, CEN had similarly emphasized the "Americanism" of GWC and JRL, friends who in talent and manners clearly ranked with the best of the "Old World of to-day" but who found inspiration not in the "lingering exclusive spirit of chivalric superiority" but in the "larger, more generous, modern spirit of democratic society" (CEN, "JRL," *HNMM*, December 1892, 846).

2. Even these dramatic differences obscured some important similarities between TWH and CEN, especially in devotion to education and culture. Each man founded and ran an evening school for working people (CEN in Cambridge, TWH in Newburyport), each wrote for the important fledgling periodicals *Putnam's Monthly* (in New York) and the *Atlantic Monthly* (in Boston), and each began an intellectual journey that would take him increasingly far away from the organized religion of his father.

3. Both Blodgett, "Mugwump Reputation," and David Hall, "Victorian Connection," have similarly reminded us that even crusty old men were once young and energetic. The frozen-in-time view emerges in such works as Sproat, *Best Men*; Tomsich, *Genteel Endeavor*; Levine, *Highbrow/Lowbrow*. Biographies that treat a whole life are better suited to the dynamism of change over time and acknowledge the significance of expectation, disappointment, and memory. See especially Duberman, *JRL*; Edelstein, *Strange Enthusiasm* (which is much better on the antebellum and war periods than on the remaining fifty years of TWH's life); James Turner, *Liberal Education*.

4. CEN's comments quoted in "The Unitarian Convention at Springfield," *New York Evening Post*, undated clipping in CEN Papers, Cyc 1014F; Menand, *Metaphysical Club*, x. The full quotation reads, "For the generation that lived through it, the Civil War was a terrible and traumatic experience. . . . To some of them, the war seemed not just a failure of democracy, but a failure of culture, a failure of ideas."

5. For an evocative description of the worldview and intellectual bearings of this social-

intellectual type, see David Hall, "Victorian Connection"; for the British, see Collini, *Public Moralists*, chapter 1.

6. Although changes were beginning, the characteristics that brought the transatlantic liberals together — shared notions of civic duty, intellectual aspiration, and political commitment — remained heavily gendered in the mid–nineteenth century. Women, however, were responsible not simply for emotional sustenance but also for shaping some of these liberals' most deeply held convictions (as in the case of TWH's fiancée, Mary Channing, who introduced him to the radical and intellectual world surrounding Concord) or aiding their literary careers (as in the case of LS, who married William Makepeace Thackeray's daughter and eventually took over his role as editor of the *Cornhill*). Further, these men carried on rich and significant correspondence with female friends (especially with each other's wives), from which much of the evidence in this book is drawn.

7. LS to CEN, May 10, 1873, in Maitland, *Life and Letters*, 234–35. On the importance of male friendships, especially in literary and public circles, see Crain, *American Sympathy*; Julie Ellison, *Cato's Tears*; Yacovone, "Abolitionists."

8. Out of historiographical convention more than historical authenticity, I have chosen to identify these figures by the anachronistic term "intellectual." On various Anglo-American models of publicly influential scholars, see Collini, *Public Moralists*; Knights, *Idea of the Clerisy*; Raymond Williams, *Culture and Society*; Landow, *Elegant Jeremiahs*; Holloway, *Victorian Sage*; Sacks, *Understanding Emerson*. The American liberals came into contact with JSM at a propitious moment when he had entered on what Collini identifies as the critical phase of his career as a public moralist; see Collini, *Public Moralists*, chapter 4.

9. TWH, "A Plea for Culture," *AtMo*, January 1867, 29–37. On the comfortable social location of the even less alienated Victorian British intellectuals, see Kent, *Brains and Numbers*; Harvie, *Lights of Liberalism*; Collini, *Public Moralists*.

10. The subject of these liberals' "manliness" is fascinating and complex; it crops up in this volume but deserves to be treated at greater length. Although Victorians invoked the word "manly" with numbing frequency, as did their contemporaries, that ubiquity should not obscure differences in meaning, both from our own day and within the nineteenth century. As Donald Yacovone has argued in another context, "Americans accepted no single definition of manhood" but rather "displayed a variety of phases or styles of masculinity which sometimes blurred gender distinctions in ways that would disturb contemporary Americans" ("Abolitionists," 86). Attending to this variety and blurring is particularly important in the case of the transatlantic liberals, whose manliness was repeatedly called into question. As northeastern, European-oriented reformers and scholars, they bumped up against a host of gendered associations. Their involvement and stances in three discrete arenas of public life particularly opened them up to charges of effeminacy: literary culture, anti-spoils reform politics, and dissent on foreign policy. However, the liberals adhered to an ideal of manliness that persisted throughout their lives and provided a counterlanguage of criticism. For broad treatments of nineteenth-century manliness, see Filene, *Him/Her/Self*; Rotundo, *American Manhood*; and the essays in Carnes and Griffen, *Meanings for Manhood*, and Mangan and Walvin, *Manliness and Morality*. For discussions specific to the late nine-

teenth century, see Bederman, *Manliness and Civilization*; Townsend, *Manhood at Harvard*; Hoganson, *Fighting for American Manhood*. On the disagreements that can lurk behind seemingly consensual concepts, see Rodgers, *Contested Truths*.

11. Important exceptions include David Hall, "Victorian Connection"; James Turner, *Liberal Education*. Rodgers, *Atlantic Crossings*, 4–5, contrasts histories that seek comparisons with those that seek connections. For transatlantically framed studies of other intellectual groups, see, for example, Kloppenberg, *Uncertain Victory*; Kelley, *Transatlantic Persuasion*; O'Brien, *Conjectures*; James Turner, *Without God*.

12. MA, *Culture and Anarchy*, 48. Channing's importance is explained in Daniel Howe, *Making the American Self*, 131–35. Levine, *Highbrow/Lowbrow*, presents an influential understanding of culture as a possession rather than a process. More attuned to prevailing Victorian self-understandings are Bender, *New York Intellect*; Daniel Howe, *Making the American Self*; Jonathan Rose, *Intellectual Life*. A separate strand of Romantic cultivation, associated particularly with Coleridge and by extension the German concept of *Bildung*, is discussed in Raymond Williams, *Culture and Society*.

13. GWC, "Fair Play for Women," in *Orations and Addresses*, 1:230; CWE to Booker T. Washington, September 7, 1906, CWE Papers, Harvard University Archives, Cambridge, Mass.

14. Carlyle, *Shooting Niagara*, 23.

15. This idea is, of course, from Isaiah Berlin's classic essay from the 1950s, "Two Concepts of Liberty" (in *Four Essays*, 118–72), which remains a standard citation. See the excellent corrective in Urbinati, *Mill on Democracy*, especially 158–72. Caricatured treatments of "orthodox" liberal political economy abound but are perhaps best associated with the midcentury works of MacPherson (*Political Theory*) and Hartz (*Liberal Tradition*). Scholars have been arguing against this misperception for years; see most recently Drescher, *Mighty Experiment*; Sklansky, *Soul's Economy*.

16. JSM as "doyen" in Burrow, *Crisis of Reason*, 152. A generation-long scholarly reassessment of JSM brings his emphasis on self-development into focus. The groundwork for this renewed appreciation began in 1972 with the thirty-three-volume edition of his *Collected Works* and culminated with Capaldi, *JSM* (2004), the first full-scale biography in fifty years. Other important interventions include Dennis Thompson, *JSM*; Collini, *Public Moralists*; Ryan, *J. S. Mill*; Biagini, "Liberalism and Direct Democracy"; Urbinati, *Mill on Democracy*. The few attempts to identify Millian strands of American liberalism include Keller, *Affairs of State*; Parrington, *Main Currents*.

17. On the enormous topic of liberalism's history, see especially Burrow, *Liberal Descent*; Burrow, *Whigs and Liberals*; Kloppenberg, *Virtues of Liberalism*; Dorothy Ross, "Liberalism." For the British uses of the term, see Vincent, *Formation*; Parry, *Rise and Fall of Liberal Government*; Biagini, *Liberty, Retrenchment, and Reform*.

18. GWC, "The Case of Ireland," *HW*, April 21, 1866, 243; CEN to ELG, January 1, 1866, ELG Papers.

19. Burrow, *Whigs and Liberals*, 5. On political languages, see also Skinner, "Meaning and Understanding"; Pocock, *Politics, Language, and Time*; Collini, Winch, and Burrow, *That Noble Science*; Rodgers, *Contested Truths*.

20. Even as classically liberal a theorist as JSM could rely on an eclectic mixing of political vocabularies when necessary, as when he supported a proposal for electoral reform in the 1850s by explaining that it would be "in the best sense of the word, Conservative, as well as, also in the best sense, liberal and democratic" (JSM to Edwin Chadwick, December 20, 1859, in *CWJSM*, 15:654–55). Kloppenberg, "The Virtues of Liberalism," in *Virtues of Liberalism*, 21–37, has noted the blending of different traditions, specifically republicanism, liberalism, and Christianity, in early American political thought. Gerstle, "Protean Character," makes a similar point about the need for historical specificity when discussing twentieth-century liberalism. For attempts to restore some of liberalism's historical richness and expansiveness among political theorists, see Rosenblum, *Another Liberalism*; the essays in Rosenblum, *Liberalism and the Moral Life*, especially Okin, "Humanist Liberalism"; Kateb, "Democratic Individuality"; Rosenblum, "Pluralism and Self-Defense."

21. Whitman, *Democratic Vistas*, 3. Despite this historical overlap, I realize that liberals need not be democrats and that democrats need not embrace the liberal principles of the cultivating Victorians who are the subjects of this book. For more on the connections and tensions between liberalism and democracy, I have drawn from Fishkin, *Democracy and Deliberation*; Barber, *Passion for Democracy*; Judis, *Paradox*; Zakaria, *Future of Freedom*.

22. Because these critical Americans were not original thinkers and are not canonical figures, recent scholars of "discursive democracy" have not shown interest in them. But the recent attention to JSM, whose vital understanding of democratic participation the reformers largely elaborated, certainly suggests their relevance. See especially Urbinati, *Mill on Democracy*. For theories of discursive democracy, see, for example, Habermas, *Between Facts and Norms*; Benhabib, "Liberal Dialogue"; Benhabib, "Toward a Deliberative Model"; Gutmann and Thompson, *Democracy and Disagreement*.

23. For the relationship between dissent and engagement, see Walzer, *Company of Critics*; Lasch, *True and Only Heaven*; Lasch, *Revolt of the Elites*.

Chapter One

1. GWC, "The Duty of the American Scholar to Politics and the Times," in *Orations and Addresses*, 1:14.

2. Ibid., 1:35. The gulf separating Buckminster and GWC could be marked by their different attitudes toward John Milton, whom Buckminster denigrated and GWC cherished as a model of the "true scholar." On Buckminster, see Daniel Howe, *Unitarian Conscience*, 174–80. Buell has rightly pointed out that Emerson's performance—in the Phi Beta Kappa speech and elsewhere—placed him in a much broader "nonparochial" tradition of Victorian sages who contended "against their own philistine adversaries" (*Emerson*, 45–46). See also Milder, "American Scholar."

3. All quotations are from Emerson, "American Scholar," 65, 63, 67; see also Sacks, *Understanding Emerson*.

4. [Oliver Wendell Holmes], "The Autocrat at the Breakfast-Table," *AtMo*, November 1857, 56. Anne Rose, *Victorian America and the Civil War*, has argued for the importance

of vocation to this generation of elite Americans, contending that work provided a major source of fulfillment and absorbed most of the task of self-definition that earlier generations had found in religion. For the broader pattern in British Victorianism, see Houghton, *Victorian Frame of Mind*.

5. For the centrality of "character" to Victorian thought, see Collini, *Public Moralists*, especially chapter 3.

6. TWH, *Unitarian Autumnal Convention*, 11–12. The most thorough source on TWH remains Edelstein, *Strange Enthusiasm*; see also the extensive discussions in Leach, *True Love and Perfect Union*; Looby's introduction to TWH, *Complete Civil War Journal*. On this period as an era of reform, see Tyler, *Freedom's Ferment*; Davis, *Ante-Bellum Reform*; Walters, *American Reformers*; Higham, *From Boundlessness to Consolidation*; Mintz, *Moralists and Modernizers*.

7. TWH to Louisa Higginson, April 1845, November 1844, quoted in Edelstein, *Strange Enthusiasm*, 58, 56.

8. TWH, *Cheerful Yesterdays*, 92; Edelstein, *Strange Enthusiasm*, 38. TWH's fiancée, Mary Channing, was a member of the influential Channing family that included the brothers Walter Channing, the dean of the Harvard Medical School and pioneer of obstetrics; Edward Tyrell Channing, the Boylston Professor of Rhetoric who taught literary and oratorical style to two generations of Harvard students (TWH included); and William Ellery Channing, the famed liberal Unitarian minister. The younger generation included Ellery Channing, who married Margaret Fuller's sister, and Mary Channing, who married TWH in 1847. See Broaddus, *Genteel Rhetoric*.

9. TWH, *Cheerful Yesterdays*, 92; Mary Higginson, *TWH*, 43. TWH's abandonment of literature for the ministry was more protracted than this narrative conveys. After enrolling in the Divinity School in 1844, he dropped out to pursue literary aspirations, reenrolled in the fall of 1846, and graduated in the spring of 1847. For a fuller discussion of his doubts and decision, see Edelstein, *Strange Enthusiasm*, 53–67.

10. TWH was following a common pattern, just beginning to give way, of college men who went through, in Buell's words, a "scribbling phase" (*New England Literary Culture*, 58) before settling down to a more practical career. The tension between self-absorption and public duty formed the central theme in TWH's postbellum novella, *Monarch of Dreams*, where the protagonist's increasingly solipsistic concern with his unconscious imagination causes him to miss out on the one great event of his era, a civil war. TWH's book of memoirs, *Cheerful Yesterdays*, mentions neither the high heels nor the bust of Hebe.

11. Mary Higginson, *TWH*, 71. TWH joined Channing, Clarke, and Parker in signing a circular protesting the Mexican War, published in the *National Anti-Slavery Standard* and reprinted in Philip Foner and Winchester, *Anti-Imperialist Reader*, 1:24–25. On Unitarian notions of duty and distrust of intense egotism, see Daniel Howe, *Unitarian Conscience*; Grodzins, *American Heretic*.

12. Mary Higginson, *TWH*, 97. "Manly" (and its nominal cognate, "manliness") reappears constantly in the writings of not only TWH but also GWC, JRL, and CEN as a descriptor at once significant and trite. Though its meanings could vary in subtle and surprising ways with each usage, in most contexts to be manly meant to be independent, coura-

geous, straightforward, honest, and self-restrained. TWH's emphasis on action and daring makes his usage the most gendered (in that it relied most heavily on "womanly" as its conceptual opposite) of the four men. The others more typically contrasted manliness with immaturity (boyishness) and brutishness (nonhumanness). For a thoughtful discussion of the word's meanings in the British Victorian context, see Collini, *Public Moralists*, chapter 5.

13. For Emerson, see Henry Smith, "Emerson's Problem"; Gougeon, *Virtue's Hero*; Strysick, "Emerson, Slavery, and the Evolution of the Principle of Self-Reliance." TWH never begrudged Emerson his insistence on solitude but made clear that his respect for the Concord sage depended on Emerson's commitment to abolition and reform. TWH vociferously contested posthumous charges of Emerson's aloofness from reform and insisted that he was a fellow toiler in the antislavery field. See TWH's review for the *Nation* of Oliver Wendell Holmes Sr.'s biography and his article on "Emerson as the Reformer" in the 1903 *Boston Advertiser*, both of which are discussed in Gougeon, *Virtue's Hero*, chapter 1.

14. TWH, "Clergy and Reform" (1847), reprinted in TWH and Meyer, *Magnificent Activist*, 324–31. This speech was originally published in the *Christian World*. TWH reprinted it again in 1851 as a series of newspaper columns in Newburyport. He borrowed from Novalis the notion of an antagonism between the clergy and the thinking class. The supposed "anti-institutionalism" of New England reformers informed Elkins, *Slavery*, and Fredrickson, *Inner Civil War*, though each established a polarity that has obscured as much as it has revealed. A corrective appears in Anne Rose, *Transcendentalism*.

15. Channing, *Self-Culture*, 31, 28. To Channing (and TWH), engaging in dutiful reform did not detract from individual development but was an important route to it: "The moral and religious principles of the soul, generously cultivated, fertilize the intellect. Duty, faithfully performed, opens the mind to Truth, both being of one family, alike immutable, universal, and everlasting." On the tension between self and society throughout a later period of American history, see McClay, *The Masterless*.

16. TWH, "Dr. Dewey's Lecture," *Daily Evening Union*, December 19, 1850.

17. On force, see Houghton, *Victorian Frame of Mind*, 196–217. More recent discussions of Victorian manliness include Mangan and Walvin, *Manliness and Morality*; James Adams, *Dandies and Desert Saints*; Collini, *Public Moralists*, chapter 10; Hilton, "Manliness"; Collini, "Manly Fellows."

18. TWH, "Saints and Their Bodies," TWH, "Gymnastics," and TWH, "Barbarism and Civilization," all published in *AtMo* in the late 1850s and then collected and republished in TWH, *Out-Door Papers*, 1–30, 131–76, 105–30. TWH believed the "invalidism" of American women to be a perversion of human nature and a false understanding of civilization. He sought to contradict the common "impression that cultivation and refinement must weaken the race. Not at all; they simply domesticate it. Domestication is not weakness" (TWH, "Barbarism and Civilization," in *Out-Door Papers*, 125–26).

19. TWH to JRL, January 23, 1848, JRL Papers (D); TWH, *"Man Shall Not Live by Bread Alone,"* 9, 8. Though the Free Soil Party failed to win, it made an impressive showing in its first campaign, outpolling the Democrats in Massachusetts as well as New York and Vermont. On the "American 1848," see Wilentz, *Rise of American Democracy*, chapter 20.

20. TWH's evening school in some ways constituted a forerunner to the end-of-the-

century settlement movement that brought college men and women into contact with working-class adults. While he originally advertised his intent to accommodate 50 students, 150 showed up the first evening. See "The Evening School Meeting," *Newburyport Daily Evening Union*, November 25, 1850; "Evening School Notice," *Newburyport Daily Evening Union*, November 29, 1850; "Evening School—New Arrangement," *Newburyport Daily Evening Union*, December 6, 1850. Edelstein, *Strange Enthusiasm*, 124, states that the school's attendance reached as high as 400. For a similar evening school in Cambridge, see James Turner, *Liberal Education*, 106–7.

21. TWH, *Mr. Higginson's Address*; Von Frank, *Trials*.

22. TWH, "Last Words before the Election," *Newburyport Daily Evening Union*, November 9, 1850. TWH explained, "We reverence law so much, that we would be fined and imprisoned rather than attempt to escape from it." Though he became increasingly radical in the late 1850s, his advocacy of northern disunion might be seen in similar terms—as a defensive move to protect northern institutions rather than an abandonment of law, society, or institutions. Higham, *From Boundlessness to Consolidation*, makes a similar point about the antislavery movement in the 1850s.

23. TWH, *New Revolution*, 8.

24. TWH, "Physical Courage," *AtMo*, November 1858, 50–51, reprinted in *Out-Door Papers*, 31–52.

25. Ibid. TWH's obsession with physical activity in the 1850s is addressed in Edelstein, *Strange Enthusiasm*; Leach, *True Love and Perfect Union*, 305–7; Blanchard, *Oscar Wilde's America*, chapter 1. For the wider context of force in the Brown circle, see Stauffer, *Black Hearts*; David Reynolds, *John Brown*.

26. On midcentury literary culture, see, for example, Faust, *Sacred Circle*; Lewis Simpson, *Man of Letters*; Bender, *New York Intellect*; Widmer, *Young America*; Ostrander, *Republic of Letters*; Buell, *New England Literary Culture*; Charvat, *Literary Publishing*.

27. Duberman, *JRL*, 31. Duberman's excellent account can be supplemented, at least for the antebellum period, by Leon Howard, *Victorian Knight-Errant*; Hale, *JRL and His Friends*.

28. JRL to G. B. Loring, November 15, 1838, in JRL, *Letters*, 1:33. Though JRL had spent some time with Emerson while rusticated at Concord, JRL had mocked the "Divinity School Address" in his Class Poem, which occasioned a lengthy letter asking Emerson's forgiveness; see JRL to RWE, September 1, 1838, JRL Papers (A). For a full discussion of the incident, see Duberman, *JRL*, 28–29. On the precariousness of a literary life in New England, see Daniel Howe, *Unitarian Conscience*, chapter 7; Buell, *New England Literary Culture*, chapter 3. On Coleridge and Carlyle, see Gross, *Rise and Fall*; Raymond Williams, *Culture and Society*.

29. Duberman, *JRL*, chapter 2.

30. JRL, "The Plays of Thomas Middleton," *Pioneer*, January 1843, 32; JRL, "The Function of the Poet," in *Function*, 4, 7, 9.

31. JRL to Charles F. Briggs, February 18, 1846, in JRL, *Letters*, 1:104; JRL, "Stanzas on Freedom," in *Complete Poetical Works*, 55.

32. "It is a very hard thing in society, as at present constituted, for a male human being (I do not say for a man) to avoid being a slaveholder," JRL wrote. "I never see Maria mend-

ing my stockings . . . without hearing a faint tinkle of chains." "Yet how avoid it," he asked, quickly dismissing any thoroughgoing reform, "Maria laughs when I propose to learn darning" (JRL to Charles F. Briggs, February 18, 1846, in JRL, *Letters*, 1:105). JRL's zeal for women's rights sharply diminished in later years.

33. JRL to Sydney Gay, June 16, 1846, in JRL, *Letters*, 1:114; JRL, "On the Capture of Fugitive Slaves near Washington," and "The Present Crisis," in *Complete Poetical Works*, 82, 67–68; Wood, *Poetry of Slavery*, 559. See also JRL, *Anti-Slavery Papers*, made up of his contributions to the *Pennsylvania Freeman* and the *National Anti-Slavery Standard*.

34. JRL, "The Biglow Papers," in *Complete Poetical Works*, 167–217. The full rhyme reads: "I'd an idee thet [Mexicans] were built arter the darkie fashion all, / An' kickin' colored folks about, you know, 's a kind o' national." On the popularity of the *Biglow Papers* in Britain, see Wood, *Poetry of Slavery*, 558.

35. JRL, "The Prejudice of Color," in *Anti-Slavery Papers*, 1:16, 18–19. See also JRL's "Ethnology" and "Sympathy with Ireland," both in *Anti-Slavery Papers*, 2:25–32, 1:100–107. JRL realized that even exceptional individuals would always be burdened by prejudice, as they could never "quite attain that quiet unconsciousness so necessary to a full and harmonious development." Lowell's antiracialism was qualified by his certainty that white America represented a "higher civilization" from which African Americans inevitably benefited ("The Prejudice of Color," in *Anti-Slavery Papers*, 1:22). The Town and Country Club was a more radical, less exalted precursor to the Saturday Club. On the plot to have Douglass admitted, see TWH to JRL, July 5, 1849, JRL Papers (A); JRL's response, quoted in Duberman, *JRL*, 185.

36. JRL, "Ethnology," in *Anti-Slavery Papers*, 2:25.

37. Quotations from JRL's "The Present Crisis" and "On the Capture of Fugitive Slaves" appear in *Complete Poetical Works*, 67–68, 82.

38. JRL to Sydney Gay, March 17, 1850, JRL to C. F. Briggs, March 26, 1848, both in JRL, *Letters*, 1:178, 125. JRL continued to view the most radical abolitionists as a "body of heroic men and women, whom not to love and admire would prove me unworthy of either of those sentiments, and whose superiors in all that constitutes true manhood and womanhood I believe never existed," and he defended Garrison against his critics as "a great and extraordinary man" who simply had become so used to being right when "all the world was wrong" that, "like Daniel Boone, he moves away as the world creeps up to him, and goes farther into the wilderness" (JRL to Sydney Gay, June 16, 1846, JRL to C. F. Briggs, March 26, 1848, both in JRL, *Letters*, 1:112, 125).

39. JRL to C. F. Briggs, March 26, 1848, in JRL, *Letters*, 1:125.

40. JRL, "Pseudo-Conservative," in *Anti-Slavery Papers*, 2:197–203; JRL, "The Present Crisis," in *Complete Poetical Works*, 68.

41. JRL to Charles F. Briggs, August 8, 1845, in JRL, *Letters*, 1:93. Emerson had made a similar point in "Self-Reliance." JRL's commitment to antislavery could at times seem almost incidental, as if the struggle against oppression were as important as eradicating the source of oppression itself. "I do not value much the antislavery feeling of a man who would not have been abolitionist even if no such abomination as American Slavery ever had existed," he wrote in 1846 (JRL to C. F. Briggs, February 18, 1846, in JRL, *Letters*, 1:105).

Such a man, JRL believed, would no doubt be insensitive to all the other forms of tyranny and oppression that existed in society.

42. JRL, "A Fable for Critics," in *Complete Poetical Works*, 145; JRL to CEN, August 28, 1865, JRL to C. F. Briggs, January 23, 1850, both in JRL, *Letters*, 1:348, 173.

43. JRL and R. Carter, *Prospectus of the Pioneer, a Literary and Critical Magazine*, reprinted in Sculley Bradley, Introduction. Requiring surgery and treatment for his eyes in New York City, JRL attempted to edit the monthly by mail. When he finally returned home, he learned that the publishers had gone bankrupt before he could cash even their first check, saddling him with a debt he would need years to pay off (Duberman, *JRL*, 44–53). See also Sculley Bradley, introduction.

44. JRL, "Nationality in Literature," *NAR*, July 1849, 199, 200, 202. This piece also noted that "the Stamp Act . . . scarcely produced a greater excitement in America than the appalling question, *Who reads an American book?* "; see Tocqueville, *Democracy in America*, 471, 256; Trollope, *Domestic Manners*, 76–77, 285; Dickens, *American Notes*, 248. For a good summary of foreign criticism, see Wiebe, *Self-Rule*. For the Young Americans' literary nationalism, see Ziff, *Literary Democracy*; Widmer, *Young America*.

45. JRL, "Nationality in Literature," *NAR*, July 1849, 210, 209. See also JRL, introduction to the first issue of the *Pioneer*, January 1843, 1–3.

46. JRL, review of Dickens, *Pioneer*, January 1843, 45.

47. JRL to CEN, May 22, 1857, JRL Papers (A). For detailed discussions of the *Atlantic*'s founding, see Duberman, *JRL*, 162–82; M. Howe, *"Atlantic Monthly"*; Sedgwick, *Atlantic Monthly*, chapters 1–2.

48. Statement of editorial purpose, *AtMo*, November 1857.

49. On political slant of the *Atlantic* under JRL, see Duberman, *JRL*, 139.

50. TWH, *Cheerful Yesterdays*, 85. More detail about GWC's youth appears in Milne, *GWC*; Cary, *GWC*; GWC, *Early Letters*.

51. GWC to Sarah Whitman, quoted in Milne, *GWC*, 29. His brother, Burrill, recalled first hearing Emerson speak in 1835, when Burrill was thirteen and George was eleven.

52. Burrill Curtis to CEN, January 5, 1893, GWC to Julia Curtis, December 31, 1848, both in GWC Papers.

53. Cary, *GWC*, 48.

54. Milne, *GWC*, 71.

55. Mott, *History of American Magazines*, 2:419; "Introductory," *Putnam's*, January 1853, 1–3; Emerson to GWC, quoted in Milne, *GWC*, 65. See also Bender, *New York Intellect*, 164–68; Widmer, *Young America*. GWC lost a considerable sum of money in the *Putnam's* venture and was as hard-pressed to repay loans as JRL had been in facing debts incurred from the *Pioneer*.

56. *London Athenaeum*, quoted in Milne, *GWC*, 58; CEN to Arthur Hugh Clough, July 7, 1854, in CEN, *Letters*, 1:113; JRL to Charles F. Briggs, August 21, 1845, in JRL, *Letters*, 1:100. JRL explicitly contrasted his and GWC's experiences in 1854, saying, "I really do not care for anybody's opinion but my own—good opinion I mean—and, thank God! I have never got that yet. Of course, I should like popularity if I could get it—the grapes are not sour; on the contrary, no one can enjoy more heartily than I do the sweetness of Curtis's,

who is eating them now with the bloom on, pulpy and full of sun" (JRL to Charles F. Briggs, JRL, *Letters*, 1:210–11). Over in England, JSM had read and enjoyed GWC's travel writing; reading a letter of GWC's during the Civil War, JSM asked, "Is he the same Curtis who wrote a book — a clever one I remember it was — about Egypt?" (JSM to John Elliot Cairnes, July 29, 1864, in *CWJSM*, 16:949).

57. GWC, "Thackeray in America," originally published in *Putnam's* in June 1853, reprinted in GWC, *Literary and Social Essays*, 135.

58. GWC, *Nile Notes*, 134; GWC to George Curtis, March 15, 1851, GWC Papers.

59. GWC to George Curtis, March 15, 1851, GWC Papers; GWC, *Potiphar Papers*, 1.

60. GWC to CEN, September 15, 1859, GWC Papers; [W. D. Howells], "GWC," *NAR*, July 1868, 108; CEN to Arthur Hugh Clough, February 4, 1855, in CEN, *Letters*, 1:118–19; GWC, "Patriotism," in *Orations and Addresses*, 39.

61. On the influence of Shaw family, see Cary, *GWC*, 102–3; Milne, *GWC*, 84–86; Foote, *Seeking the One Great Remedy*.

62. Godwin, "GWC," 30. Godwin's experience with John O'Sullivan's *Democratic Review* had provided an earlier model for combining politics and literature in one periodical, as Widmer reveals in *Young America*. For more on *Putnam's* politics, see Bender, *New York Intellect*, 164–68.

63. GWC quoted in Milne, *GWC*, 24; "Editorial Notes," *Putnam's*, November 1854, 561. See also "Our Parties and Our Politics," *Putnam's*, September 1854, 2–16; "American Despotisms," *Putnam's*, November 1854, 524–32.

64. GWC to Daniel Ricketson, August 13, 1884, GWC Papers. Writing in 1902, Howells explained that "humanity was above the humanities" for GWC. Howells acknowledged the usefulness of GWC's subsequent political reform career but could not help regret that one who had been such an important voice in the 1840s to men of Howells's age had not devoted his literary talents "wholly to the beautiful, and let others look after the true" (*Literary Friends*, 110–11).

65. GWC, "The Duty of the American Scholar to Politics and the Times," in *Orations and Addresses*, 8.

66. FH, "CEN," in JRL, *Among My Books*, 314. James Turner, *Liberal Education*, 111–12, explains CEN's genius for friendship based on his generosity, curiosity, and tolerance for disagreement (both morally and politically). See also the incisive discussion of CEN in Duberman, *JRL*, 194–95. On CEN's centrality to late-nineteenth-century Anglo-American intellectual interactions, see David Hall, "Victorian Connection."

67. CEN, *Letters*, 1:11–12. On Andrews Norton, see Daniel Howe, *Unitarian Conscience*, especially 15–16, 189–92, 264–66; James Turner, *Liberal Education*, 22–27; Habich, "Emerson's Reluctant Foe"; TWH, "The Road to England," *AtMo*, October 1899, 521–29.

68. For even earlier efforts to establish a cosmopolitan New England clerisy, see Lewis Simpson, *Man of Letters*; Habich, "Emerson's Reluctant Foe." *Sartor Resartus* was originally published in serial installments in *Fraser's Magazine* in 1833 and 1834. It did not appear in book form in Britain until 1838, two years after its Boston publication. For details of the work's American publication history, see Jackson, "Reader Retailored."

69. Appleton quoted in Duberman, *JRL*, 194; CEN on GWC in CEN, *Letters*, 1:68. For

a detailed itinerary and discussion of CEN's trip abroad, see James Turner, *Liberal Education*, chapter 3.

70. CEN to Francis J. Child, April 22, 1851, in Francis J. Child Papers, Houghton Library, Harvard University, Cambridge, Mass.

71. CEN, *Considerations*; GWC to CEN, May 28, 1853, GWC Papers; *Putnam's*, June 1853, 692–93; JRL to CEN, January 9, 1854, JRL Papers (A). Godwin's review noted that "a little work called 'Considerations . . .' is well intended, and well written—clear in its statements and arguments, and elevated in tone; but the author has not pondered his subject as deeply as he ought to have done, and by taking for granted often what it was incumbent on him to prove, lays himself open to the most damaging replies."

72. CEN, *Considerations*, 119. Among the contemporary reviews that stressed CEN's conservatism was that of a British writer who called the book "anti-American," "anti-republican," and "distantly civil" to liberty while "downright hostile to equality and fraternity" ("Distantly Civil to Liberty," unsigned, undated clipping, CEN Papers, Cyc 1014 F RH147). A similar evaluation, though expressed in admiring terms, can be seen in the unsigned review for the *Southern Quarterly Review*, January 1855, 253–67.

73. CEN, *Considerations*, 59–60, 53, 79–80, 20. For discussions that ignore CEN's call to reform, see, for example, Fredrickson, *Inner Civil War*, 31–32; Tomsich, *Genteel Endeavor*, 64–66.

74. CEN, "St Nicholas and Five Points," *Putnam's*, June 1853, 509–12; CEN to F. J. Child, January 22, 1855, CEN Papers. In "Dwellings and Schools for the Poor," *NAR*, April 1852, 464–90, CEN wrote of English model houses and included woodcuts of one in London.

75. James Turner, *Liberal Education*, 53–54, 97; CEN to "My Dearest Mother," November 16, 1850, in CEN, *Letters*, 1:73; CEN, "The Manchester Exhibition," *AtMo*, November 1857, 33–46; CEN, *Notes*; CEN, *New Life*. Discussions of Pre-Raphaelite art within CEN's circle can be seen in GWC, "The Lounger," *HW*, October 8, 1859, 642–43; JRL to CEN, [1856], in JRL, *Letters*, 247–48; and throughout the short-lived *Crayon* magazine, edited by William J. Stillman.

76. John Bradley and Ousby, *Correspondence*, 21; James Turner, *Liberal Education*, 134–35; Stein, *John Ruskin and Aesthetic Thought*.

77. CEN's reflections on his father were written shortly after the latter's death; see CEN, *Letters*, 1:84. For CEN's enthusiastic response to *Origin of Species*, see CEN to Elizabeth Gaskell, December 26, 1859, in CEN, *Letters*, 1:202.

78. CEN, "'La Prime Quattro Edizione' of Vernon," *AtMo*, May 1860, 628–29; CEN, *Notes*.

79. JRL, "Notes of Travel and Study in Italy," *AtMo*, May 1860, 630; James Turner, *Liberal Education*; Henry James, "CEN," in *American Essays*, 118–30.

80. Arthur Hugh Clough to "Miss Smith," [December 26, 1852], in Clough, *Correspondence*, 2:353; James Turner, *Liberal Education*, 113–14, 119–20; CEN to Mrs. Gaskell, February 7, 1860, in CEN, *Letters*, 1:204–6; CEN to Mrs. Gaskell, June 2, 1860, CEN Papers.

81. For CEN's marriage to Sedgwick, see James Turner, *Liberal Education*, 172–76.

Chapter Two

1. CEN, "American Political Ideas," *NAR*, October 1865, 564; CEN to GWC, March 9, 1863, in CEN, *Letters*, 1:263.

2. JRL to C. F. Briggs, May 11, 1861, in JRL, *Letters*, 1:310; TWH to Louisa Higginson, April 17, 1861, quoted in Edelstein, *Strange Enthusiasm*, 243; GWC to [Jane] Norton, June 11, 1862, in Cary, *GWC*, 155.

3. TWH, "The Ordeal by Battle," *AtMo*, July 1861, 89–90.

4. ELG quoted in ELG, *Life and Letters*, 1:219; HA to CFA, July 17, 1863, in Ford, Adams, and Adams, *Cycle*, 2:47.

5. CEN, *Letters*, 1:197.

6. CEN to Mrs. Edward Twisleton, December 13, 1859, in CEN, *Letters*, 1:201; [CEN], "The Public Life of Captain John Brown," *AtMo*, March 1860, 378–81.

7. CEN to Arthur Hugh Clough, December 6, 1859, CEN to Mrs. Edward Twisleton, December 13, 1859, both in CEN, *Letters*, 1:196, 199–200; CEN to Meta Gaskell, August 19, 1860, CEN Papers. For the wider context, see Drescher, "Servile Insurrection"; Stauffer, *Black Hearts*; David Reynolds, *John Brown*.

8. CEN, *Soldier*, 5, 7, 12, 13.

9. CEN, "The Advantages of Defeat," *AtMo*, September 1861, 360. CEN made similar comments in a letter to GWC, convinced that Americans not only deserved but needed a defeat such as Bull Run "to deepen conviction and make the true end of the war . . . plain to the whole people" (August 1, 1861, CEN Papers). He repeated this sentiment throughout the crisis, explicitly linking suffering to emancipation: "The harder the war for us the better it is for the negro" (CEN to GWC, April 16, 1863, CEN Papers). See also, for example, CEN to Henry Bellows, October 12, 1861, Henry W. Bellows Papers, MHS; CEN to GWC, May 11, 1862, CEN Papers. Fredrickson and others curiously neglect this connection to emancipation, seeing only a hard-boiled praise of suffering; see Fredrickson, *Inner Civil War*, 74; Sproat, *Best Men*, 17.

10. TWH, "Visit," 60–72. Throughout his life, TWH remained concerned with the proper understanding of Brown's raid, even though TWH's interpretation, as Edelstein shows, changed over time (*Strange Enthusiasm*, 221–36). He wrote to an assistant editor at the *Century Magazine* in 1887 to disagree with the characterization of Brown that appeared in the *Century's Encyclopedia of Modern History*. Full of inaccuracies and "twaddle," the entry on Brown was "so diluted as to be unreadable," TWH complained (TWH to Robert Underwood Johnson, August 23, 1887, *Century* Manuscripts, Huntington Library, San Marino, Calif.).

11. *Call for a Northern Convention*, 1857, circular signed by TWH, among others, TWH Papers.

12. TWH, "The Ordeal by Battle," *AtMo*, July 1861, 94; GWC, "American Doctrine of Liberty," in *Orations and Addresses*, 1:120. TWH's articles on black resistance were collected and published in 1889 as *Travellers and Outlaws*. GWC's comments reflect a broader "romantic racialism" that sought, in some ways, to combat antiblack racism by turning racial caricatures on their head and representing the "black race" in an overtly Christian

idiom, emphasizing their gentleness and meekness and contrasting it to the aggressive and arrogant "white race." See Fredrickson, *Black Image*; Bay, *White Image*; Furstenberg, "Beyond Freedom and Slavery," which charts how black resistance was part of the debate over African Americans' capacity as republicans.

13. CEN to Mrs. Edward Twisleton, December 13, 1859, in CEN, *Letters*, 1:201; GWC, "Stephen A. Douglas," *NAR*, October 1866, 511.

14. JRL to Charles Nordhoff, December 31, 1860, in JRL, *Letters*, 1:308–9; TWH to JRL, November 22, 1859, JRL Papers (A). TWH thought the silence on Brown was "unworthy of the originally bold attitude of the Atlantic" and volunteered to write something himself, though he feared that the "magazine could hardly shoulder me." JRL admitted that "editorially, I am a little afraid of Brown" but asked TWH for something nonetheless (JRL to TWH, October 24, 1859, in JRL, *Letters*, 1:298–99). While TWH seems not to have offered anything, JRL did print CEN's mixed review of James Redpath's *The Public Life of John Brown* in March 1860.

15. JRL, "Self-Possession vs. Prepossession," *AtMo*, December 1861, 769. For a similar search for a silver lining in Lincoln's apparent lack of greatness, see CEN to GWC, October 2, 1861, in CEN, *Letters*, 1:243–44.

16. JRL to CEN, September 20, 1861, JRL Papers (A); JRL to Miss Loring, May 29, 1854, in JRL, *Letters*, 1:212; CEN to Henry Bellows, October 12, 1861, Bellows Papers; CEN to GWC, October 12, 1861, CEN Papers. Like JRL, CEN called for emancipation as early as August 1861, contradicting assertions (made by Fredrickson, *Inner Civil War*, and elsewhere) that he became an abolitionist only after emancipation.

17. CEN to Mrs. Edward Twisleton, December 13, 1859, CEN to A. H. Clough, December 6, 1859, both in CEN, *Letters*, 1:201, 197; JRL, "Villa Franca, 1859," in *Complete Poetical Works*, 324, originally published as "Italy, 1859," *AtMo*, December 1859, 738. CEN's admiration for the power of Brown's words formed the basis of his critical review of Redpath's biography. There was only one way "in which his life could be properly told,—and that was, to allow him, as far as possible, to tell it in his own words" ("The Public Life of Captain John Brown," *AtMo*, March 1860, 378). Though this cohort was ambivalent about the use of force, its members found much to praise in war itself. Nothing else could so successfully bring out admirable traits of patience, endurance, and courage in citizens and elevate them above the "ignoble round of petty cares and selfish interests," according to CEN ("Our Soldiers," *NAR*, July 1864, 173).

18. [CEN], "The Irrepressible Conflict," quoted in George Smith, "Broadsides," 299; GWC, "Editor's Easy Chair," *HNMM*, October 1862, 709.

19. CEN to GWC, March 5, 1861, December 5, 1861, March 8, 1862, all in CEN, *Letters*, 1:219, 246, 252; [CEN], "Abraham Lincoln," *NAR*, January 1865, 20–21.

20. CEN to GWC, September 3, 1863, in CEN, *Letters*, 1:263. For a tribute to the Gettysburg Address, see CEN, "Our Soldiers," *NAR*, July 1864, 204. Meta Gaskell sent CEN the quotation from F. D. Maurice about the Second Inaugural Address and the Bible, which CEN repeated in a letter to ELG (October 1, 1865, ELG Papers). Such sacred comparisons are hardly surprising with this particular address. See White, *Lincoln's Greatest Speech*.

21. GWC to CEN, March 6, 1862, GWC Papers; [CEN], "Abraham Lincoln," *NAR*, Janu-

ary 1865, 20–21; JRL, "Abraham Lincoln," in *Writings*, 5:183. JRL's piece was originally titled "The President's Policy" and appeared in the *NAR*, January 1864, 234–61.

22. JRL, "Abraham Lincoln," in *Writings*, 5:183, 192; JRL, "Commemoration Ode," in *Complete Poetical Works*, 344.

23. JRL, "Abraham Lincoln," in *Writings*, 5:195, 199, 206–7. Crosby and Nichols, the *NAR*'s publishers, used Lincoln's letter as an advertisement for the newly refurbished quarterly, much to JRL's horror at so blatant a "puff." JRL remained proud of his relatively early (January 1864) appraisal of Lincoln's statesmanship. He (somewhat) mockingly defended his primacy in 1887 when, in response to a question by RWG on the authorship of the *NAR* article, JRL wrote back, "one of our Boston papers said the other day that Emerson did [Lincoln] justice first, but after his murder. In this case, I am inclined to be jealous of my thunder" (JRL to RWG, January 21, 1887, JRL Papers [A]).

24. CEN to Mrs. Edward Twisleton, December 13, 1859, in CEN, *Letters*, 1:199. While all three men strongly admired Lincoln, none lapsed into hero worship. Lincoln was important because of what he stood for: "In himself, notwithstanding his unwearied patience, perfect fidelity, and remarkable sagacity, he is unimportant; but as the representative of the feeling and purpose of the American people he is the most important fact in the world" (GWC, "The Election," *HW*, November 19, 1864, 738).

25. CEN to Jonathan Baxter Harrison, March 20, 1864, CEN Papers.

26. JRL, "The Pickens-and-Stealin's Rebellion," in *Writings*, 5:91, originally published in *AtMo*, June 1861, 757–63; TWH, "The Ordeal by Battle," *AtMo*, July 1861, 89–90.

27. GWC, "Editor's Easy Chair," *HNMM*, October 1862, 709.

28. On the connection between public opinion and emancipation, see, for example, Davis, *Problem of Slavery*; Drescher, "Public Opinion"; Bonner, *Mastering America*, chapter 3.

29. Parry, *Rise and Fall of Liberal Government*, traces the centrality of public opinion in Victorian governance back to the 1820s. See also Schmeller, "Importance of Having Opinions."

30. Duberman, *JRL*, 238, 263, 438 n. 13.

31. JRL to J. L. Motley, July 28, 1864, in JRL, *Letters*, 1:335.

32. GWC to CEN, September 18, 1859, GWC Papers; GWC, "Political Infidelity," in *Orations and Addresses*, 1:126; CEN to Meta Gaskell, August 30, 1862, CEN Papers; GWC to CEN, June 18, 1862, in Cary, *GWC*, 155. On *Harper's Weekly*, see Mott, *History of American Magazines*, 2:469–87. GWC's elevation was part of a general trend of growing antislavery influence in the wartime press; for a survey, see McPherson, *Struggle for Equality*.

33. CEN to Meta Gaskell, January 26, 1863, CEN Papers. For more on CEN's wartime endeavors, see James Turner, *Liberal Education*, chapter 7.

34. CEN to Jonathan Baxter Harrison, July 2, 1863, CEN Papers; CEN to GWC, January 30, 1863, in CEN, *Letters*, 1:259; CEN to John Bright, May 8, 1863, John Bright Papers, British Library, London, England; CEN to J. M. Forbes, February 6, 1863, September 25, 1863, both in CEN Papers. See also George Smith, "Broadsides"; CEN, Thayer, and Endicott, *Report*.

35. ELG to Charles L. Brace, January 7, 1862, in ELG, *Gilded Age Letters*, 6. For biographical information on ELG, see ELG, *Life and Letters*; Armstrong, *ELG: A Biography*.

36. CEN to F. L. Olmsted, January 24, 1864, CEN Papers; ELG, *Life and Letters*, 226; Armstrong, "Freedmen's Movement."

37. CEN to Aubrey de Vere, December 27, 1864, in CEN, *Letters*, 1:281; CEN to George Perkins Marsh, February 2, 1864, George Perkins Marsh Papers, University of Vermont Library, Burlington. "Norton was the real editor," JRL readily confessed some twenty years later, "and I only a name" (JRL to RWG, February 7, 1887, JRL Papers (A); see also JSM to John Elliot Cairnes, April 2, 1864, in *CWJSM*, 15:16). On the refurbished *NAR*, see David Hall, "Higher Journalism"; James Turner, *Liberal Education*, 187–93.

38. TWH's journals reveal a tortured process of assertion and sublimation throughout the first year of the war that had clear sexual overtones: "My present duty lies at home. . . . [L]et me swallow down all rebellious desires and philosophically use the opportunities and enjoyments I have. Perhaps good may yet come from this enforced abstinence" (journal entry, August 15, 1861, in Mary Higginson, *TWH*, 207–8). For a discussion of TWH's struggle over military service, see Edelstein, *Strange Enthusiasm*, 247–57; TWH, *Complete Civil War Journal*.

39. CEN to GWC, March 30, 1863, CEN Papers. "Negro Spirituals" appears in TWH, *Army Life*, chapter 9, a fascinating work of both folklore transcription and literary criticism. The best examination of TWH's wartime writing is Looby's introduction to TWH, *Complete Civil War Journal*.

40. Howard Mumford Jones, introduction, xi.

41. TWH, *Harvard Memorial Biographies*, 1:v.

42. Ibid., v–vi. See also Fredrickson, *Inner Civil War*; Peter Hall, *Organization of American Culture*.

43. CEN to GWC, June 24, 1865, in CEN, *Letters*, 1:268; JRL, "The Pickens-and-Stealin's Rebellion," in *Writings*, 5:84; Lincoln, *Lincoln*, 304.

44. JRL, "Abraham Lincoln," in *Writings*, 5:180–81; Tocqueville, *Democracy in America*, 224.

45. [GWC], "The Real Contest," *HW*, September 6, 1862, 562; [GWC], "Why Immigration Increases," *HW*, May 23, 1863, 322. The willingness to subject democracy to experimental proof was similar to British thinkers' approach regarding Caribbean emancipation, as set forth in Drescher, *Mighty Experiment*.

46. [GWC], "The Election," *HW*, November 19, 1864, 738; JRL, "McClellan or Lincoln," in *Writings*, 5:163. On the challenge of this election, see Hyman, "Election of 1864"; Paludan, *People's Contest*, 245–57.

47. CEN to Jonathan Baxter Harrison, March 20, 1864, CEN Papers; JRL, "McClellan or Lincoln," in *Writings*, 5:173. GWC campaigned more openly for Lincoln by serving as a delegate to the National Convention in Baltimore, by writing the official letter of renomination to President Lincoln, and then by giving speeches for his election almost daily throughout the fall of 1864. He even received the Republican nomination for Congress—marking his only run for political office—though he knew he had no chance of election in heavily Democratic New York City; see Cary, *GWC*.

48. [CEN], "Immorality in Politics," *NAR*, January 1864, 105–28.

49. [GWC], "The Election," *HW*, November 19, 1864, 738; CEN to Aubrey de Vere, December 27, 1864, in CEN, *Letters*, 1:282.

50. TWH, "The Ordeal by Battle," *AtMo*, July 1861, 95; JRL, "The President's Policy," *NAR*, January 1864, 259; CEN to ELG, March 5, 1864, March 11, 1864, both in CEN Papers. ELG's resulting article dissected American "Constitution worship" ("The Constitution and Its Defects," *NAR*, July 1864, 117–46). On changing American attitudes toward the Constitution, see Paludan, *Covenant with Death*; Vorenberg, *Final Freedom*, 107–12, 185–97.

51. [CEN], "American Political Ideas," *NAR*, October 1865, 564. For JSM's approval, see JSM to CEN, November 24, 1865, in *CWJSM*, 16:1119.

52. [CEN], *NELPS* 74.

53. CEN to Frederick Law Olmsted, January 24, 1864, CEN Papers.

54. On Brahmin martyrdom, including James's well-chronicled memory of the young Lowell couple, see Fredrickson, *Inner Civil War*, 158; Menand, *Metaphysical Club*, 74–75; Waugh, *Unsentimental Reformer*; Bundy, *Nature of Sacrifice*.

55. JRL, "Memoirae Positum: R. G. Shaw," in *Complete Poetical Works*, 337–39. A line from the poem would be engraved on the famous Shaw Memorial in Boston, unveiled in 1897. In a letter to Sarah Shaw (August 28, 1863, in JRL, *Letters*, 1:327), JRL admitted that the "best verse falls short of noble living and dying" and explained, "I would rather have my name known and blest as his will be, through all the hovels of an outcast race, than blaring from all the trumpets of repute." This is among the several suggestions that Shaw's antislavery convictions were as important as Brahmin self-sacrifice, the factor stressed in Fredrickson, *Inner Civil War*, 152–56.

56. TWH, "Do Americans Hate England?," *NAR*, June 1890, 90. During the war, TWH was more aloof from transatlantic tensions than most of his associates, a consequence of having fewer personal ties with British figures. Late in 1861, he wrote to his mother that while he found it "galling that [foreigners] should say such things of us," he was sure that foreign critics would "unsay them when disproved" (August 23, [1861], in TWH, *Letters and Journals*, 157).

57. The British response to the Civil War has generated an enormous scholarship. The interpretive evolution can be traced in the correspondence of HA and his family; in the Progressive Era Ephraim Adams, *Great Britain*; and in Jordan and Pratt, *Europe and the American Civil War*. A selection of more recent studies of public opinion includes Mary Ellison, *Support for Secession*; Blackett, *Divided Hearts*; Duncan Campbell, *English Public Opinion*.

58. GWC to CEN, August 19, 1861, GWC Papers; GWC, "English Hate," *HW*, December 6, 1862, 771.

59. JRL, "Self-Possession vs. Prepossession," *AtMo*, December 1861, 765; GWC, "Editor's Easy Chair," *HNMM*, December 1861, 125; [GWC], "A New Literature," *HW*, May 10, 1862, 291.

60. JRL, "Self-Possession vs. Prepossession," *AtMo*, December 1861, 766; JRL, "Mason and Slidell: A Yankee Idyll," *AtMo*, February 1862, 269; JRL, "Biglow Papers: Second Series," in *Complete Poetical Works*, 232.

61. [CEN], "England and America," *NAR*, April 1865, 339; [GWC], "Why Immigration

Increases," *HW*, May 23, 1863, 322; [GWC], "Why Is England Our Enemy?," *HW*, January 4, 1862, 2–3. On this understanding of America's world role, see McPherson, "Whole Family of Man"; Davis, *Slavery and Human Progress*.

62. Earl of Shrewsbury quoted in Ephraim Adams, *Great Britain*, 282; *London Times* quoted in Annan, *LS*, 52. On the pro-Confederate sympathies of British conservatives, see Bellows, "Study of British Conservative Reaction"; Blackett, *Divided Hearts*; Behm, "Through Imperial Eyes," chapter 3; Dubrulle, "We Are Threatened with . . . Anarchy and Ruin."

63. Gaskell, *Letters*.

64. Ruskin to CEN, February 10, 1863, August 6, 1864, both in John Bradley and Ousby, *Correspondence*, 75, 80; Ruskin's views on slavery from the last of his "Four Essays on Political Economy" are quoted in John Bradley and Ousby, *Correspondence*, 76.

65. Thomas Hughes to JRL, June 15, 1861, JRL Papers (A). See also the 1864 Hughes speech reprinted in Hughes, "Thomas Hughes"; Thomas Hughes, "Peace on Earth," *Macmillan's*, January 1866, 200. Hughes wrote the *Macmillan's* article after spending the last year of the war collecting information about the heroism of and sacrifice borne by America's "best blood" in the "great war for freedom." The piece focused on the losses borne by the extended Lowell family.

66. GWC, "John Bright *versus* John Bull," *HW*, March 22, 1862, 178. On French liberals, see Walter Gray, *Interpreting American Democracy*. On JSM during the war, see also T. Park, "JSM, Thomas Carlyle, and the American Civil War"; Collini, *Public Moralists*. From within Britain, HA similarly recognized JSM's prominence, calling him a "mighty weapon of defense for our cause in this country" (HA to CFA, February 13, 1863, in HA, *Letters*, 1:330).

67. [GWC], "An English Critic," *HW*, March 15, 1862, 163; JSM, "The Contest in America," *Fraser's* 65 (February 1862): 259; JSM to J. L. Motley, September 17, 1862 in *CWJSM*, 15:797. See also JSM's 1873 *Autobiography*, which recalled that the American war was "destined to be a turning point, for good or evil, of the course of human affairs for an indefinite duration" (in *CWJSM*, 1:266).

68. GWC, "Gladstone upon the War," *HW*, May 24, 1862, 322; GWC to CEN, June 26, 1862, GWC Papers; GWC to J. E. Cairnes, November 16, 1862, John Elliot Cairnes Papers, National Library of Ireland, Dublin.

69. GWC to J. E. Cairnes, March 12, 1863, Cairnes Papers. For an extended discussion of Cairnes, see Weinberg, *John Elliot Cairnes*; Davis, *Slavery and Human Progress*, 244–58. JSM's correspondence with Cairnes (*CWJSM*, vol. 16) reveals the extent to which both men followed and engaged in debates over the American Civil War.

70. Thomas Hughes to JRL, February 18, 1864, JRL Papers (A). On LS's visit, see Maitland, *Life and Letters*, 105–29; Annan, *LS*, 52–57.

71. Thomas Hughes to JRL, February 18, 1864, JRL Papers (A); LS, *The "Times"*; Maitland, *Life and Letters*. LS asked JRL to be Virginia's godfather (or, as the agnostic preferred, to stand in "quasi-sponsorial relation" to her) (Annan, *LS*, 56).

72. JSM to J. L. Motley, January 26, 1863, in *CWJSM*, 15:828; GS, *Does the Bible Sanction American Slavery?*; [GWC], "Our Friends in England," *HW*, November 7, 1863, 706; CEN to GWC, October 18, 1864, in CEN, *Letters*, 1:281. On GS, see GS, *Selection from GS's*

Correspondence; Wallace, *GS*, 27–41; Phillips, *Controversialist*. For CEN's public estimate of GS, see [CEN], "GS," *NAR*, October 1864, 523–39; [CEN], "England and America," *NAR*, April 1865, 331–46.

73. GS to CEN, in GS, "Letters"; CEN, "England and America," *NAR*, April 1865, 343. In addition to CEN's two *NAR* pieces that mention GS, CEN publicized his new friend's writings and lectures in *NELPS* 60, 211, 216, 221, 222, and commissioned a review (by Sidney G. Fisher) of GS's *Does the Bible Sanction American Slavery?* that appeared in *NAR*, January 1864, 48–74.

74. GS, "England and America," *AtMo*, December 1864, 766.

75. GWC, "Our Friends in England," *HW*, November 7, 1863, 706.

76. [JRL], "The President's Policy," *NAR*, January 1864, 248. Disraeli's 1845 novel, *Sybil*, was subtitled "The Two Nations" and described a major gulf separating England's rich and poor.

77. JRL, "The President's Policy," *NAR*, January 1864, 248. This section was deleted when the article was reprinted as "Abraham Lincoln" in *Writings*, 5:177–209.

78. JRL to Sarah B. Shaw, [June 8, 1861], JRL Papers, MHS; JRL to CEN, January 1865, JRL to LS, April 10, 1866, both in JRL, *Letters*, 1:343–44, 358–64; JRL, "On a Certain Condescension in Foreigners," in *Writings*, 3:248. In a footnote, JRL made sure to except the late Arthur Hugh Clough, Thomas Hughes, and LS, "the most loveable of men," from his general censure of Englishmen.

79. JRL to CEN, "Morrow of St. Ulysses," April 1865, JRL Papers (A); JRL, "The Rebellion: Its Causes and Consequences," in *Writings*, 5:152.

Chapter Three

1. "The Great Festival," *Nation*, July 6, 1865, 5; "Eighteen Hundred and Sixty-Five," *Nation*, January 4, 1866, 6.

2. JSM to RWE, August 12, 1867, in *CWJSM*, 16:1307.

3. GWC, "Our Foreign Friends," *HW*, April 22, 1865, 243.

4. GS to CEN, July 26, 1865, in GS, "Letters," 120. The direct causal connection GS made between events in the United States and politics in Great Britain has not been universally accepted by historians, though most recent historians tend to ascribe at least some influence to it. On this debate, see, for example, Gertrude Himmelfarb, "Politics and Ideology: The Reform Act of 1867," in *Victorian Minds*, 333–92; Allen, "Civil War," 77–96; Harvie, *Lights of Liberalism*, chapter 6; Kent, *Brains and Numbers*, 33–38; Biagini, *Liberty, Retrenchment, and Reform*, 258.

5. "The Great Festival," *Nation*, July 6, 1865, 5.

6. Gerlach, *British Liberalism*, 5–13.

7. HA to CFA, November 21, 1862, in HA, *Letters*, 1:316; John Morley, "Young England and the Political Future," *Fortnightly Review*, April 1867, 491. See also the pairing of these statements in Kent, *Brains and Numbers*, 37–38.

8. HA explained, "In England the Universities centralize ability and London gives a field.

So in France, Paris encourages and combines these influences. But with us, we should need at least six perfect geniuses placed, or rather, spotted over the country and all working together" (HA to CFA, November 21, 1862, in HA, *Letters*, 1:316).

9. For Comtism, see Kent, *Brains and Numbers*; for liberal attraction to national liberation, see Harvie, *Lights of Liberalism*; Biagini, *Liberty, Retrenchment, and Reform*; Finn, *After Chartism*. The American liberals under consideration here only rarely invoked Comte, though other Americans did. See Harp, *Positivist Republic*.

10. JRL to "Miss Norton," October 14, 1870, JRL to CEN, August 28, 1870, JRL to Thomas Hughes, October 18, 1870, all in JRL, *Letters*, 2:63–64.

11. CEN, journal entry, April 12, 1873, in CEN, *Letters*, 1:475–76; LS to CEN, May 10, 1873, in Maitland, *Life and Letters*, 234. LS's full dedication reads, "I venture to dedicate this book to you in memory of a friendly intercourse never, I trust, to be forgotten by me; and in gratitude for its fruitfulness in that best kind of instruction which is imparted unconsciously to the giver" (LS, *Essays on Freethinking*).

12. CEN to Meta Gaskell, May 22, 1868, CEN Papers, explains his confidence in the course of Reconstruction, while CEN to ELG, June 8, 1869, ELG Papers, characteristically explains, "I have tried in vain all winter to find a convinced Tory,—a man who read history, had travelled, & preserved his faith in Toryism as the system by which the world should be regulated. But there seems to be no such character. The Conservatives have nobody of distinct political principles; they are simply well off & desirous to remain so, conservative by position & by birth."

13. ELG to CEN, December 4, 1867, in ELG, *Gilded Age Letters*, 116; CEN, journal entry, November 23, 1872, in CEN, *Letters*, 1:432; FH, "CEN," in FH, *Among My Books*, 316–17.

14. TWH, "The Road to England," in *Contemporaries*, 348–73; TWH, *Letters and Journals*; TWH, "Literary London Twenty Years Ago," in *Cheerful Yesterdays*, 271–97; TWH, "Literary Paris Twenty Years Ago," in *Cheerful Yesterdays*, 298–325.

15. Thomas Hughes to JRL, September 20, 1865, JRL Papers (A); Thomas Hughes to JRL, "New Year's Eve" 1870, JRL Papers (B); Mack and Armytage, *Thomas Hughes*, 139–42. JRL was interested in Hughes's "mutual enlightenment scheme" but doubted that any comparable committee in the United States would have the intended effect: "our people are so sensitively jealous just now that I fear it might arouse opposition of an ignorant sort, and do more harm than good" (JRL to Thomas Hughes, February 7, 1871, in JRL, *Letters*, 2:69–70).

16. Details of Thompson's travel appear in his diary, which has been reprinted as Henry Thompson, *Englishman*, 42, 44, 66.

17. Henry Yates Thompson letter, American Lectureship, 1865–66, File, University Library, Cambridge University, Cambridge, England. William Gladstone echoed Thompson's sentiment a decade later, writing in the *NAR*, "For the political student all over the world it will be beyond anything curious as well as useful to examine with what diversities, as well as what resemblances, of apparatus the two great branches of a race born to command have been minded, or induced, or constrained, to work out, in their sea-severed seats, their political destinies according to their respective laws" ("Kin beyond the Sea," *NAR*, September–October 1878, 181–82).

18. Open letter from Edward Dodd, American Lectureship, 1865–66, File. Martin, "Cambridge Lectureship," 23, identifies Dodd as a "local vicar and fierce opponent." Other opponents objected to Harvard on religious grounds. H. R. Bailey, a fellow at St. John's, wondered if the other members of the Cambridge Senate were aware that Harvard "as far as it professes any form of Religion, is distinctly Socinian, or, if Americans prefer the term, Unitarian": "Emerson, the Pantheist, was trained" there (open letter from H. R. Bailey, American Lectureship, 1865–66, File).

19. Open letter from H. R. Bailey, American Lectureship, 1865–66, File; Martin, "Cambridge Lectureship," 24. The *Cambridge Chronicle* declared, not implausibly, that the proposal amounted "to a wish to indoctrinate in the youth of the governing classes a love for democratic principles and democratic institutions" (quoted in Martin, "Cambridge Lectureship," 24).

20. JRL to LS, April 10, 1866, in JRL *Letters*, 1:360; LS to JRL, February 23, 1866, in Maitland, *Life and Letters*, 176–78; CEN to ELG, March 23, 1866, ELG Papers; CEN, "The American Lectureship at Cambridge, England," *Nation*, April 12, 1866, 457–59; [GWC], "Editor's Easy Chair," *HNMM*, May 1866, 801.

21. CEN, "The American Lectureship at Cambridge, England," *Nation*, April 12, 1866, 457–59.

22. [CEN], "Justice to the Blacks the Interest of the Nation," *NELPS* 74; [CEN], "Review of George Livermore," *AtMo*, August 1863, 263–64.

23. [GWC], "Shall We Cut Off Our Noses?," *HW*, June 28, 1862, 402; GWC, "The Good Fight," in *Orations and Addresses*, 1:152.

24. JRL, "The Prejudice of Color," in *Anti-Slavery Papers*, 1:16; TWH to JRL, July 5, 1849, JRL Papers (A); Duberman, *JRL*. Frederick Law Olmsted and Henry Bellows also worked, through the Union League Club, to end segregation in northern transportation.

25. JRL to CEN, August 1858, in JRL, *Letters*, 1:283–84; CEN to JRL, September 5, 1858, called Buckle's denial of the "influence of race" one of his "hasty and ill-considered generalizations" (CEN, *Letters*, 1:194). Broader discussions of Victorian ethnology can be found in Menand, *Metaphysical Club*; Horsman, *Race and Manifest Destiny*; O'Brien, *Conjectures*. Other Victorian Britons saw Buckle's reluctance to apply racial determinism to distinctive European "stocks" as holding "Germanic" thought in check, as Mandler, "'Race' and 'Nation,'" explains.

26. [Thomas Carlyle], "Occasional Discourse on the Negro Question," *Fraser's* 40 (February 1849): 670–79; JSM, "The Negro Question," in *CWJSM*, 21:85–95. For more on midcentury attitudes toward race, slavery, and freedom, see Drescher, *Mighty Experiment*; Catherine Hall, "Competing Masculinities"; Holt, *Problem of Freedom*. On Carlyle, see Levy, *How the Dismal Science*; Wood, "Anatomy of Bigotry"; Behm, "Through Imperial Eyes."

27. GWC, "Paying Colored Soldiers," *HW*, November 28, 1863, 755; CEN to GWC, April 16, 1863, GWC to CEN, March 30, 1863, TWH to CEN, June 28, 1863, CEN to Elizabeth Gaskell, April 23, 1863, all in CEN Papers.

28. Cairnes to Sarah Shaw, May 2, 1863, June 21, 1863, in Weinberg, *John Elliot Cairnes*, 162–66; JSM to Henry Fawcett, August 24, 1864, in *CWJSM*, 15:877.

29. GWC, "The Freedmen," *HW*, May 14, 1864, 306; GWC, "Our Duty to the Freedmen," *HW*, January 6, 1866, 2–3.

30. TWH, "Fair Play the Best Policy," *AtMo*, May 1865, 625–26.

31. On TWH and confiscation, see *Nation*, May 9, 1867, 366; [GWC], "Easy Chair," *HNMM*, March 1888, 635 (which notes that "Fair Play has prevailed over ecclesiastical hatred and over personal slavery and what are called the new questions—corporate power, monopoly, capital, and labor—are only new forms of the old effort to secure fair play"). Other invocations of this terminology appear in "The Essence of the Reconstruction Question," *Nation*, July 6, 1865, 4–5; GWC, "Fair Play for Women," in *Orations and Addresses*, 1:215–38. For British Radical uses of the phrase, albeit in a vastly different context, see McWilliam, "Radicalism and Popular Culture."

32. [GWC], "The Troubles in the West Indies," *HW*, December 2, 1865, 754. On the Eyre controversy, see Semmel, *Jamaican Blood*; Bolt, *Victorian Attitudes to Race*; Lorimer, *Colour, Class, and the Victorians*; Holt, *Problem of Freedom*.

33. [CEN], *NELPS* 298; JRL, "The Seward-Johnson Reaction," in *Writings*, 5:319; [GWC], "The Lesson of Jamaica," *HW*, January 5, 1867, 3.

34. JRL, "Mason and Slidell: A Yankee Idyll," *AtMo*, February 1862, 270; [GWC], "The Lesson of Jamaica," *HW*, January 5, 1867, 3; [ELG], "The Week," *Nation*, July 12, 1866, 22. JRL's verse quickly entered the liberal lexicon; CEN supported "negro citizenship" in 1865 with a passing reference to "all men up say we" (CEN to ELG, February 24, 1865, ELG Papers).

35. GS, *Civil War*, 72; GS to CEN, July 26, 1865, December 16, 1865, January 6, 1866, March 27, 1866, all in GS, "Letters." GS quoted in [GWC], "The Horrors of Jamaica," *HW*, December 30, 1865, 819.

36. [LS], "England," *Nation*, February 28, 1867, 172–73. For the impact of the Eyre case on British intellectuals, see Kinzer, Robson, and Robson, *Moralist in and out of Parliament*, 184–217; Harvie, *Lights of Liberalism*, 126–27; Catherine Hall, "Economy of Intellectual Prestige"; Kent, *Brains and Numbers*, 25–26. Semmel, *Jamaican Blood*, 118, points out that scientific men largely opposed Eyre, while literary men generally supported him.

37. *Saturday Review* quoted in Lorimer, *Colour, Class, and the Victorians*, 178; JSM, *Autobiography*, in *CWJSM*, 2:281; [LS], "England," *Nation*, December 27, 1866, 522. See also Iva Jones, "Trollope, Carlyle, and Mill"; Catherine Hall, "Economy of Intellectual Prestige"; Catherine Hall, "Competing Masculinities."

38. [GWC], "Tennyson and Governor Eyre," *HW*, November 24, 1866, 739; [ELG], "Popular 'Leaders,'" *Nation*, November 1, 1866, 351–52; [ELG], "The Week," *Nation*, October 4, 1866, 263.

39. Thomas Carlyle, "Shooting Niagara, and After?," *Macmillan's*, August 1867, 319–36.

40. [ELG], "The Week," *Nation*, August 29, 1867, 163; [ELG], "Thomas Carlyle," *Nation*, September 5, 1867, 194–95; JRL, "Carlyle," in *Writings*, 2:95.

41. [ELG], "Thomas Carlyle," *Nation*, September 5, 1867, 194–95; JRL, "Carlyle," in *Writings*, 2:95; [GWC], "Carlyle vs. the Human Race," *HW*, September 7, 1867, 562.

42. [GWC], "Carlyle vs. the Human Race," *HW*, September 7, 1867, 562. That ELG felt something important was at stake is clear from the fact the *Nation* ran an extended conversa-

tion about Carlyle in its pages, including two lengthy articles in response to two letters from J. F. Kirk (September 5, 1867, 195–96, September 19, 1867, 237–39). See [ELG], "Thomas Carlyle," *Nation*, September 5, 1867, 194–95; [ELG], "Thomas Carlyle's Influence," *Nation*, September 19, 1867, 235–36. For Carlyle as a pivotal figure in British imperialism, see Catherine Hall, *Civilising Subjects*; Catherine Hall, "Competing Masculinities." Curtis's dismissal of Carlyle's cynicism as "impotent" was an easy and familiar way to discredit an opponent (and one to which Curtis himself was often subjected), but the subject of Carlyle's sexuality became a lively one in later years. See Broughton, "Impotence, Biography, and the Froude-Carlyle Controversy"; Broughton, *Men of Letters*.

43. For the failure to grant former slaves meaningful political power outside the United States, see Eric Foner, *Nothing but Freedom*, 3, 23–24, 46. On the Second Reform Act, see Machin, *Rise of Democracy*; Parry, *Rise and Fall of Liberal Government* 207–17; Catherine Hall, McClelland, and Rendall, *Defining the Victorian Nation*.

44. [LS], "England," *Nation*, July 2, 1868, 8.

45. JRL, "Reconstruction," in *Writings*, 5:230; JRL, "Scotch the Snake or Kill It?," in *Writings*, 5:260. See also [GWC], "The Blacks and the Ballot," *HW*, May 20, 1865, 306; CEN to ELG, February 24, 1865, ELG Papers.

46. JRL, "The Seward-Johnson Reaction," in *Writings*, 5:310–11.

47. TWH, "Fair Play the Best Policy," *AtMo*, May 1865, 622; [CEN], "American Political Ideas," *NAR*, October 1866, 551, 562–63; GWC, "The Soldier's Monument," in *Orations and Addresses*, 3:51–53.

48. CEN to ELG, October 4, 1865, ELG Papers (discussing Connecticut voters' rejection of black suffrage); JRL, "Reconstruction," in *Writings*, 5:237; JRL, "The President on the Stump," in *Writings*, 5:279.

49. [GWC], "Stephen A. Douglas," *NAR*, October 1866, 511–12, 517; JRL, "Seward-Johnson Reaction," in *Writings*, 5:291. During the war, GWC had called Douglas the "representative politician of an era which had apparently lost all faith in ideas" ("The American Doctrine of Liberty," in *Orations and Addresses*, 1:116).

50. Thomas Hughes to JRL, September 20, 1865, JRL Papers (B); John Elliot Cairnes, "The Negro Suffrage," *Macmillan's*, August 1865, 335–36; Gasparin, *Reconstruction*, 27. Although liberal Americans noted the contributions of French liberals such as Gasparin and Laboulaye during and immediately after the war, members of the two groups developed no personal relations and American interest in the French rather quickly ceased.

51. JSM to Henry Fawcett, February 5, 1860, JSM to Moncure D. Conway, October 23, 1865, both in *CWJSM*, 15:672–73, 1006. The latter letter includes an interesting exchange between JSM and Wendell Phillips, who objected to JSM's insistence on a literary requirement for the vote. "Does [JSM] not remember that for four men out of five, education does not come from books? Does he suppose there was no education in the world before printing was invented? . . . The mass of men have their faculties educated by work, not reading." JSM responded (via Conway), "It is very true that intelligence, and even a high order of it, may be formed by other means than reading, and even (though, I think, rarely) without the aid of reading: but not, I think, intelligence of public affairs, or the power of judging public men." JSM's concession on black suffrage represents an interesting and rare modification

of the "discourse of competence" that Kahan, *Liberalism*, has recently demonstrated was a central (and defining) feature of nineteenth-century European liberalism.

52. CEN to ELG, January 9, 1865, ELG Papers; ELG to CEN, February 28, 1865, April 13, 1864, both in ELG, *Gilded Age Letters*, 21–22, 27.

53. Voters in three northern states (Connecticut, Minnesota, and Wisconsin) rejected referenda on black suffrage in 1865; see McPherson, *Ordeal by Fire*, 501–2. On debates within the Republican Party, see Wang, *Trial of Democracy*, chapter 1.

54. CEN to ELG, April 14, 1865, ELG Papers; ELG to CEN, April 13, 1865, in ELG, *Gilded Age Letters*, 28; James Turner, *Liberal Education*, 201.

55. ELG to CEN, October 12, 1864, February 28, 1865, both in ELG, *Gilded Age Letters*, 15, 23.

56. For discussion of these essays, see chapter 5. See also [ELG], "The Democratic View of Democracy," *NAR*, July 1865, 111. Collini, *Public Moralists*, 60–90, has demonstrated the centrality of "altruism" to the Victorian language of liberalism.

57. [ELG], "The Tyranny of the Majority," *NAR*, January 1867, 205, 226–27.

58. Preface to *Essays on Reform*, v. GS, "The Experience of the American Commonwealth," in *Essays on Reform*, 217–38, extended several themes first offered in "The Philosophy of the Cave," *Macmillan's*, June 1866, 81–96. See also LS, "On the Choice of Representatives by Popular Constituencies," in *Essays on Reform*, 85–126. For background, see Harvie, *Lights of Liberalism*.

59. JSM, *Considerations on Representative Government*, in *CWJSM*, 19:390. Dennis Thompson, *JSM*, has labeled these two criteria "participation" and "competence." My reading of *Considerations on Representative Government* has been influenced by Thompson as well as by Biagini, "Liberalism and Direct Democracy"; Urbinati, *Mill on Democracy*; Miller, "Mill's Civic Liberalism."

60. JSM, *Considerations on Representative Government*, in *CWJSM*, 19:403–4. On the question of whether JSM was "really" a democrat, see works cited in n. 59, which represent a revision of mid-twentieth-century interpretations of JSM as a proponent of "elite rule." Proportional representation has been picked up from time to time as a way to ensure minority representation, both ideologically (as JSM imagined) and (more recently) racially. Cohen, *Reconstruction*, discusses the "administrative mandate" among turn-of-the-century social scientists, but the extent to which her subjects were influenced by JSM's proposals on this front is unclear. But JSM was not a proto-Fabian and did not imagine investing bodies of elites with unchecked power to legislate on behalf of the many. The Commission of Legislation, which he quickly abandoned as impractical, was conceived as narrowly technocratic and wholly accountable to Parliament.

61. JSM, *Considerations on Representative Government*, in *CWJSM*, 19:399–401; Dennis Thompson, *JSM*; Urbinati, *Mill on Democracy*; Miller, "Mill's Civic Liberalism"; Held, *Models of Democracy*; Capaldi, *JSM*. On the reception of JSM's political works, though not *Considerations on Representative Government*, see Nicholson, "Reception and Early Reputation."

62. AVD, "The Balance of Classes," in *Essays on Reform*, 67–84; JB, "The Historical Aspect of Democracy," in *Essays on Reform*, 239–78.

63. [GWC], "The Vote upon the Constitutional Amendment," *HW*, June 18, 1864, 386–87; [GWC], "The Revolution in England," *HW*, June 15, 1867, 370; GWC to CEN, May 6, 1867, GWC Papers. GWC followed the British debates in part as a means of preparing for his role as delegate to the New York state constitutional convention.

64. JSM to Parker Pillsbury, July 4, 1867, JSM to CEN, November 24, 1865, both in *CWJSM*, 15:1289, 1119; Kinzer, Robson, and Robson, *Moralist in and out of Parliament*; GWC, "The Right of Suffrage," in *Orations and Addresses*, 1:192–93; Ellen DuBois, *Feminism and Suffrage*, 171.

65. GWC, "The Right of Suffrage," in *Orations and Addresses*, 1:181–213; Pugh, "Limits of Liberalism"; Ellen DuBois, *Feminism and Suffrage*.

66. JSM, "The Exclusion of Women from the Franchise," in *CWJSM*, 28:91–93. See also Kinzer, Robson, and Robson, *Moralist in and out of Parliament*, 113.

67. [CEN], "Female Suffrage and Education," *Nation*, August 22, 1867, 152. See also [GWC], "More Light!," *HW*, March 31, 1866, 195; ELG, "The Democratic View of Democracy," *NAR*, July 1865, 117.

68. Parry, *Rise and Fall of Liberal Government*, 216.

69. [CEN], "Female Suffrage and Education," *Nation*, August 22, 1867, 152; See also [GWC], "More Light!," *HW*, March 31, 1866, 195; [ELG], "The Democratic View of Democracy," *NAR*, July 1865, 117.

70. [GWC], "The Suffrage and Education," *HW*, February 27, 1869, 131; [ELG], "Educational Tests," *Nation*, February 18, 1869, 125–26; CEN to ELG, March 6, 1869, ELG Papers.

71. JRL, "Reconstruction," in *Writings*, 5:230; CEN to John Andrew, January 19, 1867, John A. Andrew Papers, MHS; [GWC], "The Suffrage and Education," *HW*, February 27, 1869, 131. GWC had made the same point immediately after the war in "Ignorance as a Political Disability," *HW*, June 10, 1865, 354–55.

72. "The Week," *Nation*, August 22, 1867, 142–43; GS to CEN, July 26, 1867, in GS, "Letters." Both of these pieces noted that John Bright was looking primarily to "intelligent artisans." On debates over the Second Reform Bill, see Parry, *Rise and Fall of Liberal Government*; Biagini, *Liberty, Retrenchment, and Reform*; Kahan, *Liberalism*.

73. John Morley, "Young England and the Political Future," *Fortnightly Review*, April 1867, 491; Catherine Hall, McClelland, and Rendall, *Defining the Victorian Nation*.

74. [ELG], "The Democratic View of Democracy," *NAR*, July 1865, 117–18.

75. Ibid., 117. In *Considerations on Representative Government*, JSM insisted that all voters know how to "read, write, and I will add, perform the common operations of arithmetic." He did not see this restriction as particularly onerous because he coupled it with a demand for universal education, reasoning that those who failed to qualify would only have their "own laziness" to blame. In an ideal world, JSM continued, suffrage would also be contingent on some rudimentary knowledge of geology, geography, and world and national history, but "these kinds of knowledge" were probably not generally accessible anywhere but in the "Northern United States" (*CWJSM*, 19:470–72).

76. Keyssar notes that the Gilded Age attraction to literacy restriction was based less on a liberal emphasis on reading than on these measures being "ideologically more palatable" than a property or taxpaying requirement in the North and West and a means that white

southerners used to skirt the requirement for racial neutrality in the Fifteenth Amendment (*Right to Vote*, 142). The most cited portraits of liberals as hostile to democracy are Sproat, *Best Men* (emphasizing ELG's 1865 stance); McGerr, *Decline of Popular Politics*.

77. [ELG], "The Democratic View of Democracy," *NAR*, July 1865, 117; ELG to Henry Bellows, February 4, 1867, in ELG, *Gilded Age Letters*, 100; "The Essence of the Reconstruction Question," *Nation*, July 6, 1865, 4–5; [GWC], "More Light!," *HW*, March 31, 1866, 195. ELG revealed that political participation lay at the center of his concern when he told CEN that "all voters ought to know how to read at least—not a bit of the Constitution or the Lord's Prayer—but a piece of the newspaper of the morning of election day" (April 13, 1865, in ELG, *Gilded Age Letters*, 28). Like JSM, the American liberals coupled any such proposal for a literacy requirement with demands for universal compulsory education. See, for example, [CEN], "Female Suffrage and Education," *Nation*, August 22, 1867, 152.

78. [ELG], "Educational Tests," *Nation*, February 18, 1869, 125–26.

79. [ELG], "The Democratic View of Democracy," *NAR*, July 1865, 118; JRL, "Scotch the Snake or Kill It?," in *Writings*, 5:180, 243–45. In contrast, he expressed a wartime sense that there was "no more insidious treachery than that of the telegraph," which was capable of sending "its electric thrill of panic along the remotest nerves of the community" ("Abraham Lincoln," *NAR*, January 1865, 180).

80. ELG "Popular 'Leaders,'" *Nation*, November 1, 1866, 351–52; see also CEN to Frederick Law Olmsted, January 24, 1864, CEN Papers.

81. [GWC], "Editor's Easy Chair," *HNMM*, June 1866, 118–20. GWC pointed out that Carlyle's assault on "government by talk" had begun in 1850 ("Editor's Easy Chair," *HNMM*, October 1885, 798). Carlyle urged "silence" in his 1866 "Inaugural Address at Edinburgh," from which GWC quoted (Carlyle, *On the Choice of Books*).

82. Recent work on JSM has drawn out his emphasis on discursive or communicative politics. Collini, *Public Moralists*, chapter 4, discusses JSM's understanding of his seat in Parliament as simply a larger and higher-profile platform than his more typical venues. Biagini, "Liberalism and Direct Democracy," traces the Athenian origins of JSM's view of representative government, which allowed him to fuse republican and liberal elements. Urbinati, *Mill and Democracy*, offers a compelling discussion of JSM's "agonistic" politics, with its preference for "talking" (associated with Athens) over "acting" (associated with Sparta). See also Kinzer, Robson, and Robson, *Moralist in and out of Parliament*, a helpful study of JSM's parliamentary career. For an admission about JSM's lack of oratorical skills, see LS, "England," *Nation*, September 13, 1867, 214, though this opinion was not universally shared.

83. ELG, "The Prospects of Political Art," *NAR*, April 1870, 398–420.

Chapter Four

1. TWH, "Literature as an Art," *AtMo*, December 1867, 745; TWH, "A Plea for Culture," in *Atlantic Essays*, 6, 21, first published in *AtMo*, January 1867, 29–38. For a response to TWH's article, see "A Plea for Culture," *Nation*, February 21, 1867, 151–52.

2. TWH, "A Plea for Culture," in *Atlantic Essays*, 6, 18, 20. For studies that empha-

size cultural retreat rather than engagement, see Tomsich, *Genteel Endeavor*; Levine, *High-brow/Lowbrow*.

3. See, for example, the declaration, in the first issue, that "one principle of *The Nation* is to promote and develop a higher standard of criticism" ([ELG], "Critics and Criticism," *Nation*, July 6, 1865, 10).

4. Stefan Collini, introduction to MA, *Culture and Anarchy*, ix; DeLaura, *Hebrew and Hellene*; Coulling, *MA and His Critics*.

5. GWC, "Easy Chair," *HNMM*, October 1884, 797.

6. MA, *Culture and Anarchy*, chapter 3.

7. Ibid., chapter 4. I have relied here on Collini's helpful discussion of MA in both the introduction to MA's *Culture and Anarchy* and *Arnold*.

8. TWH, "Americanism in Literature," *AtMo*, January 1870, 231. For Fuller's use of "Philistine" in the *Dial*, see TWH, "The Equation of Fame," in *Studies in History and Letters*, 277.

9. TWH, "Literature as an Art," *AtMo*, December 1867, 745; TWH, "Plea for Culture," in *Atlantic Essays*, 9. On the ambiguity at heart of the Arnoldian notion of culture, see Raymond Williams, *Culture and Society*, 126–29.

10. "MA," *Nation*, April 19, 1888, 316. On this point, see David Hall, "Victorian Connection." While Paul DiMaggio coined the phrase "sacralization of culture," it is often most closely associated with Levine. Neither scholar attends to the religious context of the late-nineteenth-century cultural endeavors. See DiMaggio, "Cultural Entrepreneurship in Nineteenth-Century Boston: The Creation of an Organizational Base"; Levine, *Highbrow/Lowbrow*, 85–168.

11. TWH, *Things Old and New*, 15.

12. Ibid., 15, 19; LS, "Religion as a Fine Art," in *Essays on Freethinking*, 63–64; CEN to JR, October 8, 1869, in John Bradley and Ousby, *Correspondence*, 175. See also TWH, "Scripture Idolatry" and "The Sympathy of Religions," both in *Studies in History and Letters*, 318–59.

13. CEN to J. B. Harrison, March 19, 1865, August 15, 1865, both in CEN Papers. On Victorian agnosticism, see James Turner, *Without God*; Lightman, *Origins of Agnosticism*. On CEN, see James Turner, *Liberal Education*. The Free Religious Association is discussed in Persons, *Free Religion*; Leigh Schmidt, *Restless Souls*.

14. LS, *Essays on Freethinking*; CEN to Frederick Law Olmsted, July 24, 1881, CEN Papers; Lightman, *Origins of Agnosticism*, 149–50; James Turner, *Without God*.

15. JRL to LS, May 16, 1874, May 27, 1874, in JRL, *Letters*, 2:125, 127; JRL to CEN, January 1, 1874, JRL Papers (A); JRL, "The Cathedral," in *Complete Poetical Works*, 349–60. Critics have made similar points about the self-conscious and cerebral as opposed to immediately emotional quality of JRL's and MA's religious poetry; see, for example, Duberman, *JRL*, 244–45; Collini, *Arnold*, chapter 3.

16. Wallace, *GS*, 211–25. For more on GS's discomfort with the agnostic label, see CEN to GS, January 31, 1905, CEN Papers.

17. JSM, "Inaugural Address at St. Andrews," in *CWJSM*, 21:251. JSM and MA had more in common when it came to views of culture and self-improvement (though JSM's great fear

was stagnation, not "anarchy"). See Robson, "Civilization and Culture," 347–48; Alexander, *MA and JSM*. Moreover, despite obvious differences, both FH's positivism and MA's culture constituted manifestations of a similar nineteenth-century ethical humanism; see Vogeler, "MA and FH." For more on the controversies surrounding the publishing history of *Culture and Anarchy*, especially FH's rebuttal and MA's subsequent response, see Coulling, *MA and His Critics*.

18. JR to CEN, September 12, 1869, in John Bradley and Ousby, *Correspondence*, 172; JRL to LS, April 29, 1873, in JRL, *Letters*, 2:95–97. CEN's interest in reaching out to Ruskin and other British aesthetes coincided with the end of the war, as can be seen in CEN to Dante Gabriel Rossetti, March 21, 1865, Ms. Facs d. 273, Bodleian Library, Oxford University, Oxford, England.

19. ELG and others who were closest to JSM never forgave Carlyle's actions during the 1860s, as is clear in ELG, "Carlyle's Political Influence," in *Reflections and Comments*, 287–94.

20. CEN, journal entry, March 23, 1869, CEN to Miss E. C. Cleveland, June 7, 1869, both in CEN, *Letters*, 1:322–25, 338–39.

21. LS to Oliver Wendell Holmes Jr., January 24, 1873, LS to JRL, July 14, 1871, both in Maitland, *Life and Letters*, 231, 228. JRL's vague response professed a similar admiration for Carlyle: "I quite agree with you about Carlyle, and perhaps was harder on him than I meant, because I was fighting against a secret partiality" (JRL to LS, July 31, 1871, JRL, *Letters*, 2:74). LS wrote an appreciation of Carlyle for the *Cornhill* after his death in 1881 but subsequently published a more critical piece on "Carlyle's Ethics" in *Hours in a Library*, 2:286–94.

22. TWH, "Carlyle's Laugh," *AtMo*, October 1881, 463–66; RWE to CEN, February 23, 1870, in CEN, *Letters*, 1:340–41. TWH suggested a fuller reconciliation than seems possible in reporting the great interest that Carlyle took in the former slaves and even (improbably) his concession that the ballot had been necessary to secure their freedom.

23. GWC, "Easy Chair," *HNMM*, April 1881, 787.

24. Alexander, *MA and JSM*; David Hall, "Victorian Connection," also pair their intellectual leadership.

25. MA, *Culture and Anarchy*, 62. See also Rubin, *Making of Middlebrow Culture*, 2–15.

26. Channing, *Self-Culture*, 17; CEN, "Intellectual Life in America," *New Princeton Review* 6 (November 1888): 324; TWH, *Hints*, 26. Raymond Williams, *Keywords*, 87–93, explores the etymology of "culture," which he terms "one of the two or three most complicated words in the English language."

27. CEN to Jonathan Baxter Harrison, October 2, 1863, CEN Papers; JRL, "Shakespeare Once More," in *Writings*, 3:32. CEN's phrase, predating by a year MA's similar usage in his essay on "The Function of Criticism at the Present Time" (*National Review*, November 1864, 230–51; reprinted in *Culture and Anarchy*, 26–52), is significant and revealing of the common transatlantic concern with culture in the mid-nineteenth century. James Turner, *Liberal Education*, 257–58, provides an interesting discussion of the differences between Arnoldian and Nortonian ideas of culture, with the latter taking a more historicist form.

28. MA, *Culture and Anarchy*, 43; ELG, "Chromo-Civilization," *Nation*, September 22, 1874, 202.

29. ELG, "Chromo-Civilization," *Nation*, September 22, 1874, 202.

30. JRL, "A Great Public Character," in *Writings*, 2:279. Collini, *Public Moralists*, 342–74, offers a suggestive perspective on the development of literary studies in England (a topic that lies beyond this book's scope).

31. Longfellow, "Defense of Poetry," *NAR*, January 1832, 56–79; JRL, "Nationality in Literature," *NAR*, July 1849, 196–215.

32. JRL, "On a Certain Condescension in Foreigners," in *Writings*, 3:251; CEN to Meta Gaskell, October 28, 1867, CEN, *Letters*, 2:297. GWC did not wait until the postwar period to predict a cultural renaissance, declaring in 1862 that the "great rebellion will produce a literature" ("A New Literature," *HW*, May 10, 1862, 291).

33. TWH, "A Plea for Culture," in *Atlantic Essays*, 19.

34. Brooks, *New England*, 68–74.

35. JRL to RWG, December 15, 1875, in JRL, *Letters*, 2:152–53; *Nation*, September 28, 1887, 265. The Christian influence remained present in the *Century*'s Social Gospel leanings. For more on RWG and the *Century*, see Bender, *New York Intellect*, 208–16; John, *Best Years*.

36. Brodhead, "Literature and Culture," 472–73. See also Henry May, *End of American Innocence*, part 1; Bender, *New York Intellect*, chapters 4–5.

37. GWC, "Holmes," in *Literary and Social Essays*, 234; [CEN], "Mr. Emerson's Poems," *Nation*, May 30, 1867, 430–31. TWH, "The New World and the New Book," in *New World*, 8. On Emerson's international appeal, or "nonparochialism," see Buell, *Emerson*, 47–58.

38. JRL, "Thoreau," in *Writings*, 1:366; JRL, "Shakespeare Once More," in *Writings*, 3:2. See also JRL, "Emerson the Lecturer," in *Writings*, 1:349–60. Although unimpressed with Thoreau personally, JRL recognized his literary originality to some extent. See Duberman, *JRL*, 169–72.

39. GWC, "Longfellow," in *Literary and Social Essays*, 196; [GWC], "The Works of Nathaniel Hawthorne," *NAR*, October 1864, 539–57; JRL to James T. Fields, September 7, 1868, in JRL, *Letters*, 1:405. Here JRL echoed Melville's comparison of Shakespeare and Hawthorne in "Hawthorne and His Mosses." Duberman, *JRL*, 487–89, helpfully discusses the Lowell-Hawthorne relationship, while Brodhead, *School of Hawthorne*, 51–63, provides the key account of Hawthorne's Gilded Age acclaim.

40. Edward Dicey, "Hawthorne," *Macmillan's*, July 1864, 241–46; LS, "Hawthorne," in *Hours in a Library*, 1:160, 166; Henry James, *Hawthorne*. Morley initially tried to secure JRL to write the biography (John Morley to JRL, November 7, 1877, JRL Papers [C]).

41. CEN to JR, November 2, 1877, in John Bradley and Ousby, *Correspondence*, 401; Gohdes, *American Literature*; "America in Westminster Abbey," *Nation*, November 9, 1882, 397–98.

42. W. E. Gladstone, "Kin Beyond the Sea," *NAR*, September–October 1878, 179–213; JRL, *Writings*, vol. 6; Thomas Hughes to JRL, August 7, 1886, JRL Papers (A); [GWC], "Easy Chair," *HNMM*, December 1884, 165–68. GWC's Anglophilia emphasized not only that Britons and many Americans shared a "common" stock, religious traditions, and lan-

guage but also that both countries cherished the "same great forms of freedom" and were "engaged in a lofty and friendly rivalry to develop those forms to the utmost for the benefit of humanity" ("Easy Chair," *HNMM*, November 1882, 960). A decade later, JRL received his own place in Westminster Abbey—a memorial window.

43. MA, "A Word about America," *Nineteenth Century*, May 1882, 684. LS noted the applicability of MA's cultural criticism in the United States, ascribing MA's greater reputation in the United States than in Great Britain to the fact that the "ugly side of middle-class mediocrity" was more pronounced in America (*Studies*, 2:110).

44. MA, "A Word about America," *Nineteenth Century*, May 1862, 689-96. The American literary establishment's response to MA is addressed in Raleigh, *MA and American Culture*; Coulling, *MA and His Critics*; DeLaura, "MA and the American 'Literary Class.'"

45. TWH to sister, November 28, 1883, in TWH, *Letters and Journals*, 323; MA, "Emerson," in *Discourses in America*, 202. MA here specifically contrasted Emerson and Carlyle, declaring Emerson's "work more important than Carlyle's." Carlyle's temper (by his own admission "dyspeptic, solitary, [and] self-shrouded") had "cut him off from hope," MA explained, echoing JRL's opinion from the 1860s, which rendered Carlyle's worldview too austere to aid humanity.

46. TWH to sister, November 28, 1883, in TWH, *Letters and Journals*, 323-24; TWH, "A Cosmopolitan Standard" and "On Taking Ourselves Seriously," both in *New World*, 46, 36-37. Even after MA's death, TWH continued to attack him, chiding him for the "ignorant pity" he bestowed on JRL as the American poet left England for home: "Mr. Arnold never in his life had one glimpse of what America is to an American" ("Lowell's Closing Years in Cambridge," in *Book and Heart*, 52). TWH's mixed opinion of MA was more than reciprocated. In a letter written to his daughter in 1887, MA called TWH a "rather terrible person" and a "vain goose" (MA to Lucy Charlotte Arnold Whitridge, November 15, 1887, in MA, *Letters*, 6:319-20).

47. JRL to James B. Thayer, in JRL, *Letters*, 2:275-76; CEN to ELG, November 17, 1883, ELG Papers. See also DeLaura, "Matthew Arnold and the American 'Literary Class.'"

48. MA, *Letters*, 6:191; [GWC], "Easy Chair," *HNMM*, November 1882, February 1884, October 1884; TWH, "The Trick of Self-Depreciation," in *New World*, 206. RWG also found cause for national pride in the initially subdued response to MA's criticisms; see RWG to JB, May 23, 1882, RWG Papers.

49. [GWC], "Easy Chair," *HNMM*, December 1884, 165-68; Gohdes, *American Literature*, 47-70.

50. RWG to Gosse, quoted in Herbert Smith, *RWG*, 75-80; John, *Best Years*; TWH, "On Literary Tonics," in *New World*, 67. On the politics of Civil War memory, see Blight, *Race and Reunion*. RWG's enthusiasm for the "Battles and Leaders" series (which Blight rightly sees as part of a white-dominated "reconciliationist" tradition) should not be conflated with the *Century*'s wider coverage of the sectional conflict and Civil War. Though the magazine published local-color artists such as Joel Chandler Harris, it was open to more serious discussions of slavery (from Frederick Douglass in its inaugural issue) of abolitionism (especially its symposium on John Brown) and of postwar race relations (most notably in the liberal critique of George Washington Cable). While the magazine's contents provide the best

evidence of its relative liberalism in matters of race, helpful overviews appear in Herbert Smith, *RWG*; John, *Best Years*.

51. JRL, "The Five Indispensable Authors," *Century*, December 1893, 223–24; [CEN], "Les Quatrains de Kheyam," *NAR*, October 1869, 565; James Turner, *Liberal Education*.

52. TWH, "A World-Literature," *Century*, April 1890, 923–24; TWH, *Henry Wadsworth Longfellow*, 5; TWH, "Americanism in Literature," in *Studies in History and Letters*, 227; JRL, "Poetry and Nationality," in *Function*, 144.

53. [GWC], "Easy Chair," *HNMM*, December 1884, 165–68. On Anglo-Saxon racialism, see Anderson, *Race and Rapprochement*.

54. JRL, "Books and Libraries," in *Writings*, 6:84, 83.

55. MA, *Culture and Anarchy*, 110, 79; Jonathan Rose, *Intellectual Life*. MA added that such apostles were to make knowledge accessible by divesting it of all that was "harsh, uncouth, difficult, abstract, professional, exclusive," by bringing it "outside the clique of the cultivated and learned."

56. On institution building, see DiMaggio, "Cultural Entrepreneurship in Nineteenth-Century Boston: The Creation of an Organizational Base"; DiMaggio, "Cultural Entrepreneurship in Nineteenth-Century Boston, Part II"; Peter Hall, *Organization of American Culture*; Garrison, *Apostles of Culture*; James Turner, *Liberal Education*, especially chapters 11–13.

57. TWH, "Plea for Culture," in *Atlantic Essays*, 15–16.

58. CEN, "CEN on Dime Novels"; CEN to Jonathan Baxter Harrison, October 2, 1863, CEN Papers; preface to the "Heart of Oak Books," quoted in CEN, *Letters*, 2:199.

59. James Turner, *Liberal Education*, especially 277–319, provides an excellent discussion of the staggering array of CEN's scholarly and institutional innovations.

60. CEN to ELG, October 19, 1866, ELG Papers; GWC to CEN, July 31, 1890, GWC Papers; James Turner, *Liberal Education*, 209–10, 280, 324–25.

61. John, *Best Years*, 139.

62. TWH, "The New World and the New Book," in *New World*, 16; JRL, "Books and Libraries," in *Writings*, 6:84; W. E. B. Du Bois, "Souls of Black Folk," 284; JRL, "On a Certain Condescension in Foreigners," in *Writings*, 3:248–49. On Du Bois at Harvard during the liberal Victorian heyday of the 1880s, see Lewis, *W. E. B. Du Bois*, chapter 5.

63. TWH, "Letters to a Young Contributor," first appeared in *AtMo*, March 1862, 401–10, and then in *Atlantic Essays*, 69–92, and *Hints on Writing and Speech-Making*, chapter 1; some of the same spirit can be seen in the later advice provided in TWH, "Literature as a Pursuit," *Critic* 47 (August 1905): 163–67. TWH published this letter from Dickinson (dated April 1862) in "Emily Dickinson's Letters," *AtMo*, October 1891, 444.

64. TWH, "Emily Dickinson's Letters," *AtMo*, October 1891, 444; [TWH], "Recent Poetry," *Nation*, October 15, 1891, 297; TWH, "An Open Portfolio," *Christian Union*, September 25, 1891, 392. Efforts to put the Dickinson issue in broader perspective can be seen in Wells, *Dear Preceptor*; Mazurek, "I Have No Monarch"; Edelstein, "Emily Dickinson"; Edelstein, *Strange Enthusiasm*, 343–52.

65. TWH to Julia Ward Howe, 1906, February 7, 1907, TWH Papers; CEN to William James, June 1, 1901, James Family Papers, Houghton Library, Harvard University,

Cambridge, Mass. See also TWH, *Margaret Fuller Ossoli*; the essays on Child and Jackson
in TWH, *Contemporaries*, 108–67. In addition to these biographical studies, TWH wrote
countless essays for the *WJ* on women's intellectual endeavors. See, for example, "American
Women in Literature," November 23, 1872; "Literary Aspirants," June 21, 1873; "Intellectual Cinderellas," March 28, 1874; "The Intercollegiate Literary Association," January 16,
1875; "The Feminine Element in Literature," February 17, 1877. On CEN's relationship
with Wharton, see also James Turner, *Liberal Education*, 403–4.

66. JRL, "Don Quixote," in *Writings*, 6:123; GWC, "Editor's Chair," *HNMM*, June 1875,
138. JRL's emphasis on the role of readers here recalls Whitman's comments in *Democratic
Vistas*. On the eternal freshness of the classics, see Garry Wills, "There's Nothing Conservative about the Classics' Revival," *New York Times Magazine*, February 16, 1997; Rorty, "On
the Inspirational Value of Great Works of Literature," in *Achieving Our Country*, 125–40.

67. [GWC], "Easy Chair," *HNMM*, March 1872, 613; [GWC], "Easy Chair," *HNMM*,
April 1887, 821.

68. [GWC], "Easy Chair," *HNMM*, September 1875, 593–98. GWC's "Manners on the
Road" column ran in *Harper's Bazaar* for several years in the 1870s. GWC later recalled that
those "little essays" were concerned not with the "fashions in clothes and personal behavior so much as the whole conduct of life" ("Easy Chair," *HNMM*, April 1887, 821).

69. [GWC], "Easy Chair," *HNMM*, May 1875, 908.

70. The popularity of GWC and TWH are discussed in Hubbell, *Who Are the Major American Writers?* The autobiographies were TWH, *Cheerful Yesterdays*; TWH, *Part of a Man's
Life*.

71. JRL, "A Great Public Character," in *Writings*, 2:287; JRL, "Our Literature," in *Writings*, 6:224; Annan, *LS*, 300–316.

72. Kijinski, "John Morley's 'English Men of Letters.'" Gross, *Rise and Fall*, 107, notes
of Morley's collection, "No comparable series has ever come so close to attaining the rank
of a traditional British institution."

73. GWC, *Life and Letters*; James Turner, *Liberal Education*. CEN was comparatively
clumsy in more strictly biographical accounts, such as a sketch of Longfellow, which spent
pages and pages describing New England before turning to the poet. A helpful discussion
of the sensational controversy between CEN and Froude—a subject on which nearly every
liberal Victorian weighed in—appears in Broughton, *Men of Letters*.

74. Haultain, *GS*, 174. The *Nation* review from 1893 appears in the promotional material
in the back of these volumes.

75. JRL, "Books and Libraries," in *Writings*, 6:85.

76. FH, *Choice of Books*, 9–15; CEN to J. B. Harrison, March 20, 1864, CEN Papers. On
this dilemma, see also Brodhead, *School of Hawthorne*, chapter 3; Garrison, *Apostles of Culture*; Rubin, *Making of Middlebrow Culture*, chapter 1.

77. CEN, "The Paradise of Mediocrities," *Nation*, July 13, 1865, 43–44.

78. [CEN], "Notices of Gillett's Huss," *NAR*, July 1864, 270–71. ELG made the same
point in "Critics and Criticism," *Nation*, July 6, 1865, 10–11.

79. [CEN], "Notices of Gillett's Huss," *NAR*, July 1864, 270.

80. [ELG], "Organization of Culture," *Nation*, June 18, 1868, 486–88.

81. Thomas Haskell, *Emergence of Professional Social Science*; Dorothy Ross, *Origins of American Social Science*; Goldman, "Exceptionalism and Internationalism." On the British Social Science Association, see Goldman, *Science, Reform, and Politics*; Heyck, *Transformation of Intellectual Life*.

82. [GWC], "A University," in "The Lounger," *HW*, April 17, 1858, 243; TWH, "A Plea for Culture," in *Atlantic Essays*, 6. American liberal responses to British university reformers can be tracked in GS, "University Education," *Journal of Social Science* 1 (June 1869): 24–55; Hugh Hawkins, *Between Harvard and America*.

83. CEN to CWE, December 18, 1869, CWE Papers, Harvard University Archives, Cambridge, Mass.; ELG, "Universities in Politics" and "The Hopkins University," both in *Reflections and Comments*, 164–73. On CWE, "New Education," see the article he published shortly before his appointment as president, in *AtMo*, February 1869, 203–20.

84. CEN, "Harvard," 4, 23, 24. As with American literature, the liberal critics thought the ideal university would be both distinctively American and confidently international in its reach. As president, CWE regularly invited foreign notables to lecture at Harvard, attempting (unsuccessfully) to persuade William Gladstone to use his temporary "retirement" from politics to give a course of lectures on political economy in 1878. More successful efforts came in bringing AVD, JB, FH, and William Morris to Cambridge. See CWE to W. E. Gladstone, July 27, 1878, Gladstone Papers, British Library, London, England; CWE to Morris, February 12, 1894, CWE Papers.

85. CEN, "Harvard," 24. A sample of TWH's columns in the *WJ* includes "What Harvard Gives and Refuses," October 18, 1872; "Sex in Education," November 8, 1873, November 15, 1873; "Vassar College," November 22, 1873, November 29, 1873; "Smith College," November 7, 1874; "Wellesley College," November 28, 1874; on British colleges, see "Girton College," December 14, 1878; "Newnham Hall," December 28, 1874. Though he devoted a great deal of attention to women's education, TWH's daughter did not go to college (Edelstein, *Strange Enthusiasm*, 393).

86. [GWC], "Easy Chair," *HNMM*, September 1871, 619; JRL, "Harvard Anniversary," in *Writings*, 6:160. Four years earlier, MA had attempted both to make room in his cultural world for science and to maintain a privileged space for the "humane letters" therein in his 1882 Rede Lecture at Cambridge, which JRL, then in London, wrote to praise (MA, "Literature and Science," *Nineteenth Century*, August 1882, 216–32; MA to JRL, August 11, 1882, in MA, *Letters*, 5:223). For American use of the "humanities," see Veysey, *Emergence of the American University*, 180–250; James Turner, *Liberal Education*, 320–45, 368–92; Winterer, *Culture of Classicism*, 110–32.

87. GWC, "Easy Chair," *HNMM*, April 1890, 800; CEN, "Harvard"; TWH, "A World outside of Science," in *Book and Heart*, 28–40. TWH's efforts as a historian remained largely unaffected by that discipline's academic professionalization, despite his willingness to gather copious primary sources in his documentation of slave rebellions for the *Atlantic Monthly*. For his reliance on an earlier conviction that good history was that made "graphic" by the "imaginative power," see *Part of a Man's Life*, 46. A similar stance toward exhaustive research that was not distilled into clear prose can be found in GS's regular disparagement of academic history.

88. JRL, "Don Quixote," in *Writings*, 6:122; CEN to ELG, December 31, 1901, ELG Papers. JRL was not always so dismissive of German learning and even compared it favorably to English and American criticism in "Shakespeare Once More" (in JRL, *Writings*, 3:1–94). TWH urged a formalist approach to the study of literature, "quite apart from all national limitations," and asserted that formal literary principles were "something apart from the laws of science or invention or business, and not less worthy than these of lifelong study" ("A World-Literature," *Century*, April 1890, 923).

89. See James Turner's important discussion of CEN's scholarly development, which represented an advanced but not specialized mode of erudition and research and "*not* . . . a middle course between popular culture and disciplinary specialism" (*Liberal Education*, 337–45).

90. CEN to ELG, July 26, 1872, ELG Papers; [CEN], "Notices of Gillett's Huss," *NAR*, July 1864, 271; [LS], "Political Situation in England," *NAR*, October 1868, 549. No connection necessarily existed between professionalization and public withdrawal, as CFA revealed in his 1901 presidential address before the American Historical Association, when he urged the association to time its public meetings in accordance with presidential elections. In this way, the newly associated historians might be able to frame issues, place matters in proper context, and otherwise provide useful perspective for the American electorate. See CFA, "An Undeveloped Function," in *Lee at Appomattox*, 274–338.

91. JRL, "Criticism and Culture," *Century*, February 1894, 515–16; GWC, "Easy Chair," *HNMM*, July 1886, 308–14. Though TWH engaged in a regular series of "friendly" evaluations, he also punctured the mystique of literary criticism in essays such as "The Equation of Fame" and "The Literary Pendulum," both in *New World*, 88–96, 213–20.

92. GWC, "The Leadership of Educated Men," in *Orations and Addresses*, 3:334; [GWC], "Easy Chair," *HNMM*, February 1887, 475–82. On gender and culture, see Douglas, *Feminization*; Lears, *No Place of Grace*; Duffy, "Gender of Letters"; Butler, "Mugwump Dilemma," chapter 4.

93. By disinterestedness, MA did not mean neutrality or objectivity but a fierce independence. The "bane of criticism," he thought, was that "practical considerations cling to it and stifle it." "Our organs of criticism are organs of men and parties," he complained, and loyalty to them came before the "place of mind" (MA, "The Function of Criticism at the Present Time," in *Culture and Anarchy*, 37).

94. "Mathew [*sic*] Arnold's Essays," *Nation*, July 6, 1865, 25.

95. JRL, "Criticism and Culture," *Century*, February 1894, 515–16. On cultural philanthropy, see DiMaggio's two essays on "Cultural Entrepreneurship"; McCarthy, *Noblesse Oblige*.

96. CEN, "Some Aspects of Civilization in America," *Forum* 20 (1896): 641–51. CEN's hand-wringing over immigration was fairly uncharacteristic for him, as he (like JRL, TWH, and CWE) remained aloof from the nativist attitudes of many of his peers. See Tomsich, *Genteel Endeavor*; Solomon, *Ancestors and Immigrants*. On college sports, see Townsend, *Manhood at Harvard*.

97. CEN, "Some Aspects of Civilization in America," *Forum* 20 (1896): 641–51.

98. Ibid.

Chapter Five

1. Fitzjames Stephen, "Liberalism," *Cornhill*, January 1862, 70–84. Fitzjames Stephen perhaps held a skeptical attitude toward democratic liberalism in part because, unlike his brother, Leslie, Fitzjames did not enjoy transatlantic ties. For more on his stance, see Lippincott, *Victorian Critics*.

2. Dennis Thompson, *JSM*, offers an excellent discussion of JSM's commitment to the two (at times competing) principles of participation and competence. On "organizational politics," see Keller, *Affairs of State*; Summers, *Party Games*. On European liberals' perennial concern with "competence," see Kahan, *Liberalism*.

3. JRL, "Tariff Reform," in *Writings*, 6:182. Brownell, *American Prose Masters*, 185, labels JRL a "jaunty jeremiah."

4. ELG, "The Duty of Educated Men in a Democracy," in *Problems of Modern Democracy*, 223. GWC had revised his earlier "scholar" formulation along similar lines, delivering a commencement address at Union College in 1877, "The Public Duty of Educated Men," reprinted in *Orations and Addresses*, 1:262–85. The change in terminology suggests the process of professionalization under way in late-nineteenth-century America. While few might continue to recognize themselves as "scholars," all college graduates (or autodidacts, like GWC) could identify as "educated men."

5. GWC, "New York and Its Press," in *Orations and Addresses*, 1:299; Kent, "Higher Journalism"; David Hall, "Higher Journalism."

6. TWH, "The Shadow of Europe," in *New World*, 30. TWH was specifically discussing the relatively small circulations of British periodicals.

7. GWC to CEN, April 26, 1865, in Cary, *GWC*, 195.

8. CEN to ELG, February 1, 1867, CEN Papers. CEN added that GWC was "not a statesman of the first class,—of whom there are none in America just now—but one the [*sic*] first of the second class."

9. ELG to CEN, July 27, 1865, August 16, 1865, both in ELG Papers. Edited versions of these two letters appear in ELG, *Gilded Age Letters*, 41, although the passages that convey ELG's reflections on his opinion-shaping role are omitted.

10. ELG to Frederick Law Olmsted, May 5, 1865, in ELG, *Gilded Age Letters*, 31. ELG and CEN, however, fretted constantly about the "heaviness" of the *Nation* ("We want more entertaining matter," ELG to CEN, June 30, 1865, in ELG, *Gilded Age Letters*, 37). For circulation figures, see Mott, *History of American Magazines*, 3:331–56.

11. JRL, "Reconstruction," in *Writings*, 5:234; [GWC], "Sycophancy," *HW*, January 20, 1866, 35; [GWC], "The Press and Public Opinion," *HW*, January 27, 1866, 50. Hampton lays out the several different typologies of Victorian journalism, like the "reflective" and "instructional" functions GWC combined here, in *Visions of the Press*.

12. ELG, "The Newspaper and the Reader," *Nation*, August 10, 1865, 165–66; ELG, "Personalities in Politics," *Nation*, September 27, 1866, 251–52; "Prospectus," *Nation*, January 4, 1866, 30–31.

13. TWH, "Turn Your Guns on the Enemy," *WJ*, November 19, 1870; TWH, "Short Cuts," *WJ*, April 22, 1871; TWH, "Immediate, Unconditional Emancipation," *WJ*, Decem-

ber 16, 1871; TWH, "The New Year," *WJ*, January 3, 1874; TWH, "Less Sensational," *WJ*, February 6, 1875. On the split among suffragists, see Ellen DuBois, *Feminism and Suffrage*.

14. CEN to J. B. Harrison, August 14, 1863, CEN Papers; similar advice presented in CEN to ELG, October 4, 1865, ELG Papers; GWC, "New York and Its Press," in *Orations and Addresses*, 1:303, 311; GWC, "Newspaper Ethics," reprinted in *Ars Recte Vivendi*, 93-136.

15. [ELG], "The Profession of 'Journalism,'" *Nation*, July 17, 1873, 37-38; [ELG], "Opinion-Moulding," *Nation*, August 12, 1869, 127, 126; [ELG], "The Democratic View of Democracy," *NAR*, July 1865, 130; CEN to ELG, January 1, 1866, ELG Papers. See also [ELG], "Editorial Perspective," *Nation*, January 27, 1870, 54-55. On the partisan press in this era, see McGerr, *Decline of Popular Politics*, 14-22; Summers, *Press Gang*.

16. On Greeley, the liberals, and the 1872 election, see Summers, *Press Gang*, 237-55; Sproat, *Best Men*, 81-87. The transatlantic context of educative journalism is best appreciated by comparing McGerr, *Decline of Popular Politics*, 69-106, with Hampton, *Visions of the Press*, 48-74.

17. GS, "The Study of History: A Lecture Delivered before the Cornell University," *AtMo*, January 1870, 44; CFA, *An Address Delivered at Cambridge*. On literary professionalization, see Bledstein, *Culture of Professionalism*; Wilson, *Labor of Words*; Schudson, *Discovering the News*. On universities, see Veysey, *Emergence of the American University*; Winterer, *Culture of Classicism*.

18. ELG to E. W. Gurney, August 4, 1870, ELG to CWE, August 5, 1870, August 25, 1870, all in ELG, *Gilded Age Letters*, 151-55. Related letters (including details about the possibility of ELG delivering college lectures on political economy at Cornell in 1867 and at Yale in 1872) are included in ELG, *Life and Letters*, 58-70; ELG, *Gilded Age Letters*, 147-55. Similarly, in 1872, when John Morley expressed interest in the professorship of political economy at University College, London, a position recently vacated by John Elliot Cairnes, JSM and Helen Taylor Mill urged him not to give up his role at the *Fortnightly*, believing that he could "exercise a wider influence through [the *Fortnightly*] than you could do through the Professorship" (JSM to John Morley, May 11, 1872, in *CWJSM*, 17:1892; the editorial note states that the paragraph from which this quotation is taken "is in Helen Taylor's hand and bears her initials").

19. GS's sense of his role can be seen in [GWC], "Mr. GS and the Canadian Press," *HW*, June 25, 1881, 407; GS to GWC, December 3, 1885, GS Papers. For a broader view, see Wallace, *GS*; Phillips, *Controversialist*.

20. [GWC], "The Bystander," *HW*, January 24, 1880, 51; [GWC], "The 'Bystander,'" *HW*, January 6, 1883, 3; GS to GWC, July 8, 1884, December 3, 1885, both in GS Papers. GS's contributions to the British journals are listed in Houghton, *Wellesley Index*, and his articles for the *Nation* appear in Daniel Haskell, *The Nation*. The GS Papers contain a comprehensive list of all GS's writings.

21. [ELG], "The Political Crisis in England," *Nation*, September 13, 1866, 212-13; Kent, "Higher Journalism"; Katz, *From Appomattox to Montmartre*.

22. CEN to LS, June 3, 1902, in CEN, *Letters*, 2:322; William James to Henry Lee Higginson, February 8, 1903, in William James, *Letters*, 2:182.

23. Lippmann, *Phantom Public*; Wallas, *Human Nature*. On these two figures, see Steel, *Walter Lippmann*; Wiener, *Between Two Worlds*.

24. "A Cynic" [LS], "Our Rulers—Public Opinion," *Cornhill*, March 1870, 288–98; AVD, "Some Aspects of Democracy in England," *NAR*, October 1883, 317–26. On the "discovery" of public opinion in Liberal Britain, see Parry, *Rise and Fall of Liberal Government*.

25. JB, *American Commonwealth*, 2:929.

26. Ibid., 913, 938, 930.

27. Ibid., 1010, 921. JSM had, of course, also insisted on protecting (and even nurturing) the expression of unpopular and minority opinions in one of his most famous treatises, *On Liberty*.

28. ELG, "The Duty of Educated Men in a Democracy" [1894], reprinted in *Problems of Modern Democracy*, 199–223; [ELG], "The Future of the Newspaper," *Nation*, June 26, 1879, 432–33; see also [ELG], "The Mystery of the Newspaper," *Nation*, August 12, 1875, 104–5; ELG, "The Newspaper Side of Literature," *Century*, May 1888, 150–51.

29. JB, *American Commonwealth*, 2:938, 915, 1013; GWC, "New York and Its Press," in *Orations and Addresses*, 1:308.

30. HA, "Civil Service Reform," *NAR*, October 1869, 443–75.

31. I have laid out HA's abbreviated career as a liberal reformer in Butler, "Investigating the 'Great American Mystery,'" 95. JB was among the many British reviewers of HA's novel ("Some Aspects of American Public Life," *Fortnightly Review*, November 1882, 634–55).

32. Sproat, *Best Men*, identifies this issue as a group "totem"; Hoogenboom, *Outlawing the Spoils*, remains the definitive overview. Among more recent works, see Cohen, *Reconstruction*; Beckert, *Monied Metropolis*, which view reformers' motives with skepticism. Tucker, *Mugwumps*; Summers, *Party Games* attend more closely to the period's rampant party corruption as the primary aim of reform efforts. Along with Summers's *Party Games*, Skowronek's *Building a New American State* explains the obstacles any meaningful reform controlled by the parties would face.

33. GWC, "Machine Politics and the Remedy," in *Orations and Addresses*, 2:154.

34. Ibid., 154. Much of this view is echoed in [RWG], "The Political Education of the People," *Century*, September 1884, 784.

35. JRL, "The Place of the Independent in Politics," in *Writings*, 6:213; [GWC], "Reform of the Civil Service," *HW*, March 2, 1867, 130; GWC, "Civil Service Reform: An Address Delivered before the American Social Science Association in October, 1869," in *Orations and Addresses*, 2:21–28; Hoogenboom, *Outlawing the Spoils*. TWH even found a way to connect civil service reform to the cause of women's rights, arguing that the current spoils system discriminated against female civil servants and that they would benefit from a system of competitive examinations. "Every woman should, for the sake of her own sex, be a civil service reformer" ("Woman and Civil Service Reform," *WJ*, November 12, 1881).

36. Sproat, *Best Men*, 70–141; Hoogenboom, *Outlawing the Spoils*.

37. HA, "Civil Service Reform," *NAR*, October 1869, 459; GWC, "The Reform of the Civil Service," in *Orations and Addresses*, 2:80; GWC, "The Progress of Reform," in *Orations and Addresses*, 2:235; ELG, "The Civil Service Reform Controversy," *NAR*, April 1882, 379–95. In discussing the "fatalism of the multitude" and the "failures" of public opin-

ion, JB had argued that "to catch and to hold the attention of the people is the chief difficulty as well as the first duty of an American reformer." He singled out civil service reform as one instance where "a few enlightened citizens from the Eastern states" had succeeded in persuading their fellow citizens and forcing politicians to pass "appropriate legislation" (*American Commonwealth*, 2:1008, 977).

38. GWC, "The Spoils System and the Civil Service," in *Orations and Addresses*, 2:175; GWC, "A Year of Reform," in *Orations and Addresses*, 2:203.

39. Moorfield Storey, "Public Duty of College Men, Harvard Class Day Oration, 1866," Moorfield Storey Papers, MHS. On the "second generation" of liberal reformers, see Blodgett, "Mugwump Reputation."

40. James delivered his address on "The Social Value of the College Bred" in 1907 at Radcliffe College before publishing it in *McClure's* in 1908. It was then reprinted in his 1911 volume, *Memories and Studies*, 309-27. See also GWC, "The Public Duty of Educated Men," in *Orations and Addresses*, 1:273; ELG, "The Duty of Educated Men in a Democracy," [1894], reprinted in *Problems of Modern Democracy*, 199. Though he would certainly never doubt the importance of a college education, JB was considerably more circumspect about the necessary connection between education and advanced public opinion. The educated man, he wrote, "is apt to underrate the power as well as the worth of sentiment," and his education "sometimes fills him with a vain conceit of his own competence which closes his mind to argument and to the accumulating evidence of facts" (*American Commonwealth*, 2:913).

41. [ELG], "The Democratic View of Democracy," *NAR*, July 1865, 125; JRL, "The Place of the Independent in Politics," in *Writings*, 6:214; JB, *American Commonwealth*, 2:898. See also [GWC], "Does Civil Service Reform Create an Aristocracy?," *HW*, January 4, 1873, 836; ELG, "The Danger of an Office-Holding Aristocracy," *Century*, June 1882, 287-92; [RWG], "Republican Institutions and the Spoils System," *Century*, August 1884, 627-28. Mark Twain, a frequent liberal ally, drew this parallel to humorous effect in *A Connecticut Yankee in King Arthur's Court* (1889), especially in the chapter on "Competitive Examinations."

42. GWC, "Civil Service Reform," in *Orations and Addresses*, 2:26; Eaton, *Civil Service*. On transatlantic borrowing in matters of the civil service, see Titlow, *Americans Import Merit*. The willingness of liberal reformers to embrace foreign experience anticipates the attitude of the Progressives depicted in Rodgers, *Atlantic Crossings*.

43. GWC, "Machine Politics and the Remedy," in *Orations and Addresses*, 2:158; JRL, "The Place of the Independent in Politics," in *Writings*, 6:201; Carl Schurz, "The Great Reform," *Boston Advertiser*, December 12, 1885, clipping in Moorfield Storey Papers, Library of Congress Manuscripts Division, Washington, D.C.

44. GWC, "The Relations between Morals and Politics, Illustrated by the Civil Service System," in *Orations and Addresses*, 2:123; GWC, "Civil Service Reform," in *Orations and Addresses*, 2:17; ELG, "Commercial Immorality and Political Corruption," *NAR*, July 1868, 264; [RWG], "The New Abolition," *Century*, January 1894, 470. TWH offered an interesting reflection on reformers' tendency to claim the mantle of antislavery in "The Succession of Reforms," *WJ*, October 26, 1878.

45. [ELG], "The Democratic View of Democracy," *NAR*, July 1865, 120–21.

46. GWC, "Machine Politics and the Remedy," in *Orations and Addresses*, 2:145–46. Summers, *Party Games*, corrects the conventional though incorrect assumption that Independents/Mugwumps were hostile to parties per se.

47. CEN to GWC, January 28, 1875, CEN Papers; [RWG], "The Effect of Civil Service Reform upon Parties," *Century*, May 1883, 151–52. CEN persisted in hoping for a replacement of the Republican Party, as seen in CEN to GWC, October 31, 1874, March 5, 1883, CEN to JRL, July 3, 1880, CEN to Frederick Law Olmsted, July 22, 1880, all in CEN Papers.

48. ELG, "The Duty of Educated Men in a Democracy," [1894], reprinted in *Problems of Modern Democracy*, 120.

49. GWC, "Machine Politics and the Remedy," in *Orations and Addresses*, 2:159. Summers, *Rum, Romanism, and Rebellion*, provides helpful information about the liberal revolt and pays special attention to GWC's role in the 1884 campaign.

50. TWH, *Young Men's Party*; TWH, *Cheerful Yesterdays*, 350–51; Edelstein, *Strange Enthusiasm*, 330. TWH plainly had a great deal of ambivalence about Reconstruction and was uncertain about what stance he should take ten years after the war. He had declared the major problems of Reconstruction solved when, "with the tolerably suspicious eyes of an abolitionist," he revisited South Carolina in 1877 and marveled at the progress the former slaves had made in just over a decade. Most of his old soldiers, he claimed, owned their own land, and he was happy to report that he saw "pictures from the illustrated papers on the wall, and the children's school-books on the shelf" (TWH, "Some War Scenes Revisited," *AtMo*, July 1878, 1–9). He had, however, acknowledged just a year earlier that outrages such as the 1876 Hamburg massacre "instantly postponed for at least four years all those fine questions of civil service reform." Ultimately, by 1884, he had decided that federal support for the local Republicans was doing more harm than good, claiming he did not want "to see [black southerners] forever employed as mere pawns in the game that political parties are playing" (TWH, "Miss Forten on the Southern Question," *WJ*, December 30, 1876; TWH "The Moral from South Carolina," *WJ*, May 5, 1877). Edelstein, *Strange Enthusiasm*, 319–35, provides a detailed account of TWH's vacillations.

51. CEN to JRL, August 1, 1884, JRL Papers (A); [GWC], "Grover Cleveland," *HW*, October 18, 1884, 179–96.

52. [GWC], "The Nomination," *HW*, May 17, 1884, 310; [GWC], "The Remnant," *HW*, July 12, 1884, 443; [ELG], "The Independent Organization," *Nation*, November 20, 1884, 432; [RWG], "Republican Institutions and the Spoils System," *Century*, August 1884, 627–29. Summers, *Rum, Romanism, and Rebellion*, 179–86, explains the meaningful differences that divided Democrats and Republicans in 1884 and concludes that liberals willfully minimized the significance of these contrasting positions.

53. *Congressional Record—Senate*, March 26, 1886, 2786. Historians have perpetuated such gendered imagery, with the standard study of liberal reformers depicting their "impotent dismay" at political corruption and their inclination to step "daintily into the stream of party politics" and "impatiently command all other swimmers to quit the water" (Sproat,

Best Men, ix, 276). On gender and political discourse, see Hofstadter, *Anti-Intellectualism*; Baker, "Domestication of Politics"; McGerr, "Political Style"; Hoganson, *Fighting for American Manhood*; Edwards, *Angels in the Machinery*.

54. Roosevelt, *Autobiography*, 89; Conkling, *Life and Letters*, 540.

55. For Mugwumpery as manly, see, for example, [GWC], "The Nomination," *HW*, May 17, 1884, 310. TWH, for one, was completely unruffled by the attacks on reformers' manliness, happily conceding that reformers—from abolitionists to civil service reformers—were often "manly women and womanly men." "The highest types of each sex," he explained, echoing Margaret Fuller and his own youthful self, "have in them something of the other" ("Manly Women and Womanly Men," *WJ*, December 9, 1882). TWH, however, was not averse to more conventional kinds of gender baiting, at least not when it came to Walt Whitman and Oscar Wilde, two men he refused to recognize as manly (TWH, "Unmanly Manhood," *WJ* February 4, 1882).

56. JB to ELG, February 6, 1886, ELG Papers.

57. JRL, "Tariff Reform," in *Writings*, 6:184–85. For another comparison of Lincoln and Cleveland, see CEN to Frederick Law Olmsted, March 5, 1885, CEN Papers.

58. RWG to Edward Eggleston, August 1888, RWG to W. C. P. Breckinridge, June 24, 1885, both in Rosamond Gilder, *Letters*, 225, 132; RWG to JB, March 28, 1889, JB Papers.

59. CEN to GS, June 16, 1888, GS Papers; ELG to JB, November 20, 1884, JB Papers.

60. Duberman, *JRL*, chapter 15.

61. Ibid., 352; JRL, "Tariff Reform," in *Writings*, 6:181–99; JRL, "The Place of the Independent in Politics," in *Writings*, 6:190–221. Duberman, *JRL*, chapter 15, thoughtfully discusses JRL's late writings.

62. JRL, "Tariff Reform," in *Writings*, 6:181–99; JRL, "The Place of the Independent in Politics," in *Writings*, 6:190–221.

63. For the prevalent confusion on this issue, compare Tomsich, *Genteel Endeavor*, which emphasizes the "organic" quality of liberal reform, with Sproat, *Best Men*, which suggests a starker individualism than existed. Montgomery, *Citizen Worker*, offers a penetrating analysis of the class limitations of what CFA called "Individuality in Politics."

64. TWH expressed support for the income tax in a letter to JB (March [3], 1897, JB Papers).

65. ELG, "The Duty of Educated Men in a Democracy," [1894], reprinted in *Problems of Modern Democracy*, 120; JRL, "The Place of the Independent in Politics," in *Writings*, 6:190–221; extensive newspaper coverage labeled "Address on Politics before the New York Reform Club," JRL Papers (A).

66. GS, "Bystander," *Toronto Week*, November 13, 1884, in GS Papers. On liberals' distaste for Blaine's "spread-eagleism" and "peremptory" tone in foreign affairs while secretary of state, see, for example, [GWC], "The Administration and South America," *HW*, February 11, 1882, 82.

67. GS, "Bystander," *Toronto Week*, November 13, 1884, in GS Papers. For an earlier assessment of English interest in the U.S. presidential election, see GS to GWC, November 1876, GS Papers.

68. [RWG], "The Outlook for Statesmen in America," *Century*, June 1883, 307.

69. JB, "The Historical Context of Democracy," in Guttsman, *Plea*, 169. See also Gerlach, *British Liberalism*; Ions, *JB and American Democracy*; Kent, *Brains and Numbers*; Harvie, *Lights of Liberalism*.

70. JRL to LS, April 24, 1869, in JRL, *Letters*, 2:25–27; JRL, "The World's Fair, 1876," *Nation*, August 5, 1875, 82.

71. CEN, "The Poverty of England," *NAR*, July 1869, 122–54; CEN, "On Emigration," *Fortnightly Review*, August 1869, 189–99; [ELG], "The Caucus in England," *Nation*, September 5, 1878, 141.

72. Sproat, *Best Men*; Von Arx, *Progress and Pessimism*. On the Forster Education Act of 1870, which Morley opposed, see Parry, *Rise and Fall of Liberal Government*, 237–38. His distrust of government support for religious education had its closest American counterpart in the campaign against public funding of Catholic schools, a movement placed in its proper transatlantic frame by McGreevy, *Catholicism and American Freedom*.

73. CEN to ELG, November 3, 1871, ELG Papers. In this extraordinary letter, CEN acknowledged that "capital seems to me to have an unfair advantage over labour" and that the principles of self-interest and relentless competition had come "pretty nearly to a deadlock." The length and thoroughness of his letter suggests the unease provoked by disagreement with the imperious ELG. FH's articles on the Commune appeared in the *Fortnightly*. CEN wrote to praise them and to urge FH to have them published separately as a pamphlet and circulated to the "whole English-speaking newspaper press" in Britain and America (CEN to FH, August 6, 1871, FH Papers, British Library of Political and Economic Science, London School of Economics, London, England).

74. Katz, *From Appomattox to Montmartre*; Eric Foner, *Reconstruction*; Painter, *Standing at Armageddon*; [GWC], "The Commune and the Republic," *HW*, July 1, 1871, 594–95; CEN to GWC, December 25, 1870, CEN Papers; CEN to FH, August 6, 1871, FH Papers; CEN to ELG, November 3, 1871, ELG Papers.

75. GS, "Female Suffrage," *Macmillan's*, June 1874, 139–50; ELG, "The Real Problems of Democracy," *AtMo*, July 1896, 6. See also [ELG], "Woman Suffrage in Michigan," *Nation*, May 14, 1874, 311–13. GS and ELG (in the 1874 article) both made much of JSM's supposed peculiarity in matters of marriage and sexuality and especially of his estimation of his wife, Harriet Taylor, found in his recently published *Autobiography* (1873; in *CWJSM*, 1:193–99). That his oddly rational relationship with and intellectual overestimation of Harriet clouded his judgment and explained his attachment to the "crotchet" of woman suffrage became an axiom among Victorian intellectuals on both sides of the Atlantic.

76. [GWC], "Voting in Cities," *HW*, September 29, 1877, 758–59; Quigley, *Second Founding*, 145–59; Beckert, *Monied Metropolis*, 221–23; Beckert, "Democracy in the Age of Capital." With particular reference to some unspecified "great towns" in the northern United States, JSM strongly argued that "representation should be co-extensive with taxation, not stopping short of it, but also not going beyond it." "Those who pay no taxes, disposing by their votes of other people's money, have every motive to be lavish and none to economise." He sought to reconcile this view with universal suffrage by insisting on a very low threshold

of taxation that would "descend to the poorest class" (JSM, *Considerations on Representative Government*, in *CWJSM*, 19:471–72). This would ensure the poor both a stake in the city and voice in its management, which JSM insisted was the ideal scenario.

77. [ELG], "The Caucus in England," *Nation*, September 5, 1878, 141. For other liberal views on the failure of democracy in urban settings, see Dorman Eaton, "Municipal Government," *Journal of Social Science* 5 (1869): 1–35; Simon Sterne, "The Administration of Cities," *International Review* 4 (1877): 631–46; Rhodes, *History*, 6:411; AVD, *Lectures*, 160. [GWC], "The Rights of Tax-Payers," *HW*, April 7, 1877, 263, acknowledged the consistency of making state finance as well as city finance a matter for a restricted electorate but explicitly rejected a retreat from universal suffrage on the state level and implicitly disavowed such a retreat on the national level (undoubtedly because of his commitment to black suffrage). Quigley, *Second Founding*, 157, misconstrues this article both by misreading the phrase "general government" (which he incorrectly changes to " '[national] government,' " when it refers to state government) and by mistaking arguments that GWC cited (and then debunked) as representations of GWC's views. A reading of the full article makes GWC's meaning quite clear: "The State expenses must be regulated by the general Legislature, which must also determine the rights of all the citizens, and the rules for the general government, and which must therefore be the representative of the whole population."

78. CFA, "The Protection of the Ballot in National Elections," *Journal of Social Science* 1 (1869): 91–112; Francis Parkman, "The Failure of Universal Suffrage," *NAR*, July–August 1878, 1–20; Francis Parkman, "The Woman Question," *NAR*, October 1879, 303–22. There is currently no general history of antidemocratic thought in Gilded Age America, though an examination of the topic is long overdue. For an overview of the legislative attempts to restrict suffrage, see Keyssar, *Right to Vote*.

79. TWH, "GS in England," *WJ*, July 4, 1874; J. E. Cairnes, "Woman Suffrage: A Reply," *Macmillan's*, September 1874, 377–88. The debate continued when ELG defended GS in the pages of the *Nation*, October 15, 1874, 251, and TWH objected to the terms of ELG's defense in the *WJ* (TWH, "A 'Truth,' " *WJ*, October 24, 1874). In 1882, TWH again took GS to task for his "vehement attack on Woman Suffrage" in an article on American politics (GS, "The Machinery of Elective Government," *Nineteenth Century*, January 1882, 126–48; TWH, "Mr. GS on the Family," *WJ*, February 11, 1882).

80. Eugene Lawrence, "The Conspiracy against Freedom," *HW*, December 16, 1876, 1011; [GWC], "Friends of the Negro," *HW*, March 8, 1879, 183; "Notes," *Nation*, July 18, 1878, 42–44; ELG, "The Real Problems of Democracy," *AtMo*, July 1896, 2–4.

81. GS, "Is Universal Suffrage a Failure? A Lecture Delivered before the Citizens of Ithaca," *AtMo*, January 1879, 71–83. For a succinct and helpful comparative discussion of European and British liberals' emphasis on the "competence" of the electorate, see Kahan, *Liberalism*.

82. GS to GWC, March 31, 1881, in GS Papers; [JB], "England.—The Progress of Democracy," *Nation*, February 12, 1885, 134–36; [RWG], "Reform in Municipal Government," *Century*, July 1887, 470. On suffrage, see Kahan, *Liberalism*, 134–36. For the 1880s British quest for "clean government," see Machin, *Rise of Democracy*, 88–105; Parry, *Rise and Fall of Liberal Government*.

83. [RWG], "Republican Institutions and the Spoils System," *Century*, August 1884, 627–28; [RWG], "The Voting Power of Ignorance," *Century*, March 1887, 806–7; see also [RWG], "A Word to the Friends of America Abroad," *Century*, November 1881, 146; [RWG], "Further Electoral Reform," *Century*, February 1890, 633–34.

84. [GWC], "JRL," *HW*, June 20, 1885, 388. No less a committed democrat than John Dewey found JRL's Birmingham address particularly stirring. See Dewey in Menand, *Pragmatism*, 195.

85. JRL, "Democracy," in *Writings*, 6:7–37; Thomas Hughes, "Trades-Unionism in England," *Century*, May 1884, 126–34.

86. JRL, "The Place of the Independent in Politics," in *Writings*, 6:194–95.

87. ELG, "The Real Problems of Democracy," *AtMo*, July 1896, 11.

88. AVD, "Americomania in English Politics," *Nation*, January 21, 1886, 52–53; AVD, "Can the English Constitution Be Americanized?," *Nation*, January 28, 1886, 73–74. See also AVD, "An English View of American Conservatism," *Nation*, April 15, 1880, 282–83; "An Observer" [AVD], "The Effect of American on English Politics," *Nation*, January 20, 1898, 45–46; for an overview, see Tulloch, "Changing British Attitudes." For more on the relationship between Ireland and fears of democracy, see Von Arx, *Progress and Pessimism*.

89. ELG to JB, October 17, 1887, in ELG, *Gilded Age Letters*, 359: "Charles Norton and I used at one time to have such gloomy talks over the future of modern society late at night in his library that the story got about Cambridge that the dogs used to howl in sympathy with us, but we were I think never as gloomy as Dicey, and we saw the fun of it at intervals, which I am afraid he does not." See also ELG, "An American View of Popular Government," *Nineteenth Century*, February 1886, 177–90; ELG, "The Real Problems of Democracy," *AtMo*, July 1896, 1–13. Among the scattered positive invocations of Maine, see [RWG], "Constitutional Amendments," *Century*, April 1889, 950–51.

90. Of his reliance on ELG, JB wrote to his friend, "I should have liked to say in the Preface how much more I am indebted to you than to any other source for the views I have formed, both to your letters and talks and to the Nation articles, but thought it would be more prudent not to do so because all the set of people whom you have been battling against all these years would at once lay hold of the statement and say (not without truth) that I was reproducing the Evening Post and Mugwumpism" (October 22, 1888, ELG Papers). See also the letters between TWH and JB on woman suffrage, the chapter on which JB contemplated asking TWH to write (JB to TWH, February 2, 1887, November 30, 1887, March 20, 1888, all in TWH Papers). For other informants, see Tulloch, *JB's "American Commonwealth."*

91. Tulloch, *JB's "American Commonwealth"*; Pombeni, "Starting in Reason."

92. GS, "Decline of Party Government," *Macmillan's*, August 1877, 298–306; GS, "The Organization of Democracy," *Contemporary Review* 47 (March 1885): 316–33; GS, "Burke on Party," *American Historical Review* 11:1 (October 1905): 36–41.

93. GS to GWC, August 26, 1877, GS to JB, May 7, 1891, both in GS Papers; GS, "The Machinery of Elective Government," *Nineteenth Century*, January 1882, 126–48. Support for GS's skepticism about parties reforming themselves can be found in Skowronek, *Building a New American State*; Summers, *Party Games*.

94. ELG, "The Real Problems of Democracy," *AtMo*, July 1896, 6.

Chapter Six

1. CEN to LS, January 8, 1896, in CEN, *Letters*, 2:236–37; LS to CFA, January 1, 1896, in Maitland, *Life and Letters*, 444.

2. JB, "An Age of Discontent," *Contemporary Review* 59 (January 1891): 14, 15, 20.

3. JB, "British Feeling on the Venezuelan Question," *NAR*, February 1896, 145–54; JB to ELG, January 24, 1896, ELG Papers. See also ELG to JB, January 9, 1896, JB Papers. The economic motivations of late-century imperialism are stressed in LaFeber, *New Empire*; William Williams, *Tragedy*. Ninkovich, *United States and Imperialism*, emphasizes cultural concerns, especially a commitment to "civilization."

4. TWH, "The Outskirts of Public Life," *AtMo*, February 1898, 188–200.

5. Kelley, *Transatlantic Persuasion*, conveys the emphasis on international affairs within Gladstonian liberalism and also stresses its transatlantic scope. I take the phrase "cultivation of hatred" from Gay, *Cultivation*.

6. A supposed distinction between the "natural" U.S. continental expansion and Britain's overseas colonial acquisitions was more or less taken for granted by Americans and Britons alike in the nineteenth century. That such a distinction depended on a willful amnesia about Native American conquest and the invasion of Mexico is perhaps as obvious as it is important to acknowledge. As I have explained elsewhere, the terms "anti-imperialist" and "anti-imperialism" are vexed and misleading, but because they dominate the contemporary debates, I have opted to keep them (Butler, "Liberal Victorians"). See also Amy Kaplan, "Left Alone with America," in *Cultures of U.S. Imperialism*, edited by Kaplan and Pease, 3–21; Kramer, "Empires, Exceptions, and Anglo-Saxons."

7. JRL, *Biglow Papers*, in *Complete Poetical Works*, 182. For earlier New England attitudes toward territorial growth, see Varg, *New England and Foreign Relations*.

8. CEN, *Considerations*, 131; "Protest of the Church of the Disciples," January 21, 1847, in Philip Foner and Winchester, *Anti-Imperialist Reader*, 24–25; Harvie, *Lights of Liberalism*; Finn, *After Chartism*.

9. JSM, "The Contest in America," in *CWJSM*, 21:125–42; GS to CEN, in GS, "Letters," 125. Nathaniel Hawthorne had made a similar point in the skeptical wartime essay that had so astounded the liberal Unionists ("Chiefly about War-Matters," *AtMo*, July 1862, 43–62).

10. CEN to GWC, December 25, 1870, CEN Papers; [GWC], "Cuba," *HW*, April 10, 1869, 226; [GWC], "St. Thomas and St. Domingo," *HW*, April 16, 1870, 242. On the Manchester School view of limited empire, see Thornton, *Imperial Idea*; A. Taylor, *Trouble Makers*; Michael Howard, *War and the Liberal Conscience*; Porter, *Critics of Empire*. On ELG, see Armstrong, *ELG and American Foreign Policy*. For a broader view of Reconstruction-era expansionism (which brought Alaska and St. Thomas under U.S. control), see LaFeber, *New Empire*; Charles Campbell, *Transformation*, 16–19.

11. ELG quoted in Beisner, "Thirty Years"; GWC to CEN, May 3, 1870, GWC Papers. GS noted the partisan maneuvering in British foreign affairs as well, complaining in 1878 that the Conservative government could expect the support of the whole people only during what it considered national crises by "dropping for the time its party character, and

suspending everything like party warfare and party moves" ("A Word for Indignation Meetings," *Fortnightly Review*, July 1878, 92).

12. British liberals also paid attention to American developments, with GS commending the United States for resisting the "most tempting morsel" of Santo Domingo and bringing to an end the "territorial rapacity" driven by slaveholders (GS, "The Policy of Aggrandizement," *Fortnightly Review*, September 1877, 316; GS, "The Expansion of England," *Contemporary Review* 45 [April 1884]: 533).

13. The contest between Disraeli and Gladstone, specifically over the "Eastern question," became one of the "great set-pieces of Victorian history" and functioned "as a prism for the refraction of national and international attitudes" (Matthew, *Gladstone*, 16). On Disraeli and Gladstone as "cult figures," see T. A. Jenkins, *Parliament, Party, and Politics*, 23–24; on the contemporary tendency to personify foreign policy debates specifically in the competing personas of Disraeli and Gladstone, see Durrans, "Two-Edged Sword." See also Eldridge, *England's Mission*; Cain, "Radicalism, Gladstone, and the Liberal Critique"; Shannon, *Gladstone and the Bulgarian Agitation*.

14. Liberal (and nonliberal) assaults on Disraeli often had a hint of anti-Semitism, and sometimes (as in the case of GS) much more than a hint. The Tory leader's Jewish ancestry, though he had been baptized in the Church of England, provided an obvious subtext for comments about his "Oriental" flair for melodrama and spectacle, his "alien" status in England, and his characterization (in, for example, the pages of *Harper's*) as an "adventurer," a "wizard," a "coxcomb," a "dandy," a "Sybarite," and a "sphinx" (Wohl, "Dizzi-Ben-Dizzi"). JRL, who served as minister to Spain through much of Disraeli's controversial ministry, sympathized with the prime minister in part because of what JRL perceived as a popular prejudice; see JRL to CEN, August 2, 1878, JRL to Thomas Hughes, November 17, 1878, both in JRL, *Letters*, 2:222, 233; for the broader context of JRL's peculiar fascination with European Jewry, see Duberman, *JRL*, 305–10.

15. [JRL], "D'Israeli's *Tancred, or the New Crusade*," *NAR*, July 1847, 201–25; LS, "Mr. Disraeli's Novels," *Fortnightly Review*, October 1874, 430–50; CEN to James Baxter Harrison, August 6, 1878, CEN Papers; [GWC], "Easy Chair," *HNMM*, November 1876, 931–36; [GWC], "Gladstone and Disraeli," *HW*, February 21, 1874, 170; TWH, "Recent Essays," *NAR*, July 1879, 106.

16. TWH, *English Statesmen*, 54–61. Disraeli's sympathies during the American Civil War were not in actuality so clear, as noted in Gerlach, *British Liberalism*, 51. Among the earliest treatments of the Tory penchant for expansion appeared in "England's 'Imperial Instincts,'" *Nation*, March 23, 1876, 192–93.

17. For "by jingo" song, see Cunningham, "Jingoism"; GS, "A Word for Indignation Meetings," *Fortnightly Review*, July 1878, 95. Nearly a decade earlier, in response to Disraeli's maneuvering on the Reform Bill, GWC had already noted that Disraeli's cultivation of the "lowest part of the population" resembled the alliance between "Southern slave lords and Northern immigrants" ("English Politics," *HW*, July 4, 1868, 418). For a detailed discussion of the politics of the Turkish-Bulgarian crisis, see Shannon, *Gladstone and the Bulgarian Agitation*.

18. FH, "Empire and Humanity," *Fortnightly Review*, February 1880, 45–46; GS, "Canada and the United States," *NAR*, July 1880, 22; GS, "The Policy of Aggrandizement," *Fortnightly Review*, September 1877, 305. The term "social imperialism" was popularized by the British political economist J. A. Hobson and later used by V. I. Lenin, as explained in Semmel, *Imperialism*.

19. W. E. Gladstone, "Kin beyond the Sea," *NAR*, September–October 1878, 179–213. The way GWC and other liberal Americans associated Gladstone with democracy, through his expansive "pale of the Constitution," often overlooked his actual skepticism and ambivalence about universal suffrage.

20. [GWC], "The Question of War," *HW*, May 25, 1878, 406; [GWC], "Beaconsfield and Gladstone," *HW*, April 3, 1880, 211; [GWC], "Stupidity," *HW*, January 24, 1880, 51; [GWC], "Beaconsfield's Dangerous Game," *HW*, December 14, 1878, 986–87. See also [GWC], "The Tory Attack on Mr. Gladstone," *HW*, July 13, 1878, 547; [GWC], "English Politics," *HW*, March 13, 1880, 163; [GWC], "Gladstone's Famous Victory," *HW*, April 24, 1880, 258; and the regular commentary in 1878 and 1879 in GWC's "Easy Chair" columns. The *Nation*'s treatment of Gladstone was always much less effusive than *Harper's*, stemming perhaps from the ambivalence of at least two of its British contributors, LS and AVD, who were always more skeptical of the Grand Old Man than either ELG or JB, another contributor. For the larger context of Gladstone's appeal to the United States, see Parrish, "Gladstone and America."

21. [GWC], "The Question of War," *HW*, May 25, 1878, 406; GS, "A Word for Indignation Meetings," *Fortnightly Review*, July 1878, 89; H. C. G. Matthew (on Gladstone's new style of politics) quoted in Biagini, *Liberty, Retrenchment, and Reform*, 414, 392–95. See also Matthew, *Gladstone*, 59–60; Matthew, "Rhetoric and Politics"; Biagini, *Liberty, Retrenchment, and Reform*, 392–95. Making use of firsthand accounts of working men studying Gladstone's speeches, Biagini has argued (following Matthew) that Gladstone "managed to square the circle of reconciling mass democracy with the values of the traditional liberal ethos of a politically conscious and actively critical citizenry."

22. GWC, "Editor's Easy Chair," *HNMM*, June 1884, 151; ELG, "What Will Mr. Gladstone Do with Egypt?" *Nation*, 1882, September 21, 1882, 236. On Gladstone's foreign policy in practice during his second ministry, see Biagini, "Exporting 'Western & Beneficent Institutions.'"

23. ELG, "England and Russia," *Nation*, February 14, 1883, 61; [GWC], "Our Foreign Policy," *HW*, January 7, 1882, 2. The liberal Americans were far from objective, but Colin Matthew has provided at least partial confirmation of their perceptions of difference, explaining that "Tories in general distrusted the concept of politics based on rationality" and that "they perceived the growing significance of symbol in politics," while Liberals "had the need, even the craving, for public discussion of issues, actions, and programmes" ("Rhetoric and Politics," 51).

24. ELG to JB, October 17, 1887, JB Papers.

25. Kelley, *Transatlantic Persuasion*, 229. CEN's and TWH's engagement in the Irish agitation, despite the former's friendship with the Irish poet Aubrey De Vere and the latter's cooperation with Irish Americans in Massachusetts politics, amounted to little more than

noncommittal expressions of sympathy: "The Fates are certainly very cruel to Ireland" (CEN to Aubrey De Vere, November 5, 1890, CEN Papers).

26. O'Grady, *Irish-Americans*, 35; Pletcher, *Awkward Years*.

27. [GWC], "Mr. Gladstone and Ireland," *HW*, April 23, 1870, 259. Earlier, GWC had drawn another analogy: "If we are told that we don't understand the situation, and that nobody but an Englishman can, we shall remember that Americans used to say precisely the same thing about slavery; and their foreign friends proved to be the wiser when they said the situation could not endure" ("The Aspect of Ireland," *HW*, December 28, 1867, 819).

28. [GWC], "The Tragedy of Ireland," *HW*, December 15, 1866, 786; [ELG], "The Collapse of Home Rule in Ireland," *Nation*, November 21, 1878, 314; [GWC], "Mr. Gladstone and Ireland," *HW*, April 23, 1870, 259. Comparison between American slavery and British misgovernment of Ireland littered liberal writings after the war. JRL had drawn an analogy in the 1840s as a way of criticizing the antiabolitionism of Irish American agitators: "We should like to have any American favorer of Irish rebellion explain to us the moral distinction between Ireland and South Carolina. . . . All that we ask of the friends of Ireland is that they should be consistent, and make no chromatic distinctions between whites slaves and black" ("The Irish Rebellion," in *Anti-Slavery Papers*, 2:132–34). See also JRL, "Sympathy with Ireland" in *Anti-Slavery Papers*, 2:100–107.

29. JRL to Thomas Hughes, July 18, 1870, in JRL, *Letters*, 2:258–59; [GWC], "England in Ireland," *HW*, November 14, 1868, 723; ELG to JB, May 28, 1886, in ELG, *Gilded Age Letters*, 340–41. GWC lamented not only that the Irish formed a large and "imperfectly instructed foreign element in our politics" but also that their presence had provoked a "vehement and imposing protest in the form of an 'American' party," which was "essentially un-American in its principle and tendency."

30. [GWC], "The Case of Ireland," *HW*, April 21, 1866, 243: "The population is energetic, self-reliant, and asks only for just government and fair play for industry."

31. MA quoted in John Morley, "MA," reprinted in Morley, *Nineteenth Century Essays*, 354; GS, "The Irish Question," *Contemporary Review* 21 (March 1873): 517; JRL to Thomas Hughes, July 18, 1870, in JRL, *Letters*, 2:258–59. On JSM and Ireland, see Holt, *Problem of Freedom*; Steele, "J. S. Mill and the Irish Question," 216–36; Zastoupil, "Moral Government"; Kinzer, "J. S. Mill and Irish Land"; Kinzer, Robson, and Robson, *Moralist in and out of Parliament*.

32. [GWC], "The Case of Ireland," *HW*, April 21, 1866, 243; GS, "The Irish Question," *Contemporary Review* 21 (March 1873): 518; [GWC], "A Great Public Question," *HW*, January 8, 1881, 18.

33. GWC had expressed his dismay over one of Gladstone's earlier coercion acts in "Mr. Gladstone and Ireland," *HW*, April 23, 1870, 259. See O'Day, *Irish Home Rule*, 58–91.

34. JRL to W. E. Gladstone, November 17, 1880, Gladstone Papers, British Library, London, England; O'Grady, *Irish-Americans*; Pletcher, *Awkward Years*. Duberman's thorough examination of the relevant diplomatic sources absolves JRL from most of his critics' charges and demonstrates his instrumentality in winning the release of the American suspects (*JRL*, 322–30). ELG defended JRL yet went even further in a private letter to JRL than the United States was willing to go in disagreeing with British policy. See [ELG], "The Irish-

American 'Suspects,'" *Nation*, March 30, 1882, 264–65; [ELG], "Aliens and Natives under the Irish Coercion Act," *Nation*, April 27, 1882, 353; [ELG], "Mr. Lowell and the Irish," *Nation*, May 25, 1882, 438; [ELG], "The Reasons Why Mr. Lowell Should Be Recalled," *Nation*, June 1, 1882, 457; ELG to JRL, April 24, 1882, in ELG, *Gilded Age Letters*, 282.

35. ELG, "An American View of Ireland," *Nineteenth Century*, August 1882, 175–92. This claim became one of the central points in the ensuing controversy. ELG had sent his article to JB, asking him to place it, and en route it somehow received the title "An American View of Ireland." To this, GS instantly objected, terming ELG an "Irish Nationalist who showed the usual hostility of his party to Great Britain." ELG in turn balked at this characterization, as he had lived in the United States for more than twenty years and claimed to have provided one of the most balanced journalistic voices on British affairs there. GS's "shabby trick," ELG wrote to JB, was intended to get "rid of a disagreeable critic by appealing to English prejudice" (October 27, 1882, in ELG, *Gilded Age Letters*, 291). JB expressed a similar point about Americans' greater objectivity on this contentious issue in "England and Ireland," *Century*, June 1883, 249.

36. ELG, "An American View of Ireland," *Nineteenth Century*, August 1882, 175–92. ELG's conversion to Home Rule—and its consequences for his views on Irish Americans and on the limits of reason in political discourse—is a fascinating story that is too complex to delve into here. It can be pieced together through his extensive periodical contributions and his correspondence, especially with JB, in ELG, *Gilded Age Letters*; JB Papers; and ELG Papers.

37. ELG, "An American View of Ireland," *Nineteenth Century*, August 1882, 175–92; GS, *Conduct of England*, 16; GS, "Parliament and the Rebellion in Ireland," *Contemporary Review* 41 (May 1882): 890–97.

38. ELG to JB, February 16, 1886, in ELG, *Gilded Age Letters*, 338; [GWC], "A British Confederacy," *HW*, July 16, 1881, 455; [GWC], "The Irish Situation," *HW*, November 12, 1881, 754–55; [GWC], "Ireland," *HW*, June 3, 1882, 338; [GWC], "Michael Davit," *HW*, June 24, 1882, 386–87.

39. GWC to CEN, May 9, 1887, GWC Papers; ELG to the editor of the *New York Daily Tribune*, May 6, 1884, clipping in JB Papers. See also GS, "Great Britain, America, and Ireland," *Princeton Review*, November 1882, 283–305; GS, "Why Send More Irish to America," *Nineteenth Century*, June 1883, 1–3.

40. GS, "The Jewish Question," *Nineteenth Century*, October 1881, 494–515; GS, "Can Jews Be Patriots?," *Nineteenth Century*, May 1878, 875–87; JB to ELG, October 28, 1882, AVD to ELG, December 29, 1882, both in ELG Papers. For another contemporary comment on GS's anti-Semitism, see Isaac Besht Bendavid, "GS and the Jews," *NAR*, September 1891, 257–71. See also Phillips, *Controversialist*.

41. JB to ELG, August 18, 1882, ELG Papers; ELG to JB, September 15, 1882, in ELG, *Gilded Age Letters*, 288–89; ELG, "American Home Rule," *Nineteenth Century*, May 1886, 801.

42. [GWC], "Easy Chair," *HNMM*, September 1886, 638; Thomas Hughes to JRL, January 30, 1887, JRL Papers (A); LS to JB, June 15, 1866, JB Papers. On the rift among liberals,

see also Harvie, *Lights of Liberalism*, 218–32; Harvie, "Ideology and Home Rule"; Roach, "Liberalism."

43. Harvie, "Ideology and Home Rule," 299.

44. AVD, "Home Rule from an English Point of View," *Contemporary Review* 42 (July 1882): 66–86; [JB], "Editor's Note," in *Handbook of Home Rule*, 3; ELG, "A Lawyer's Objections to Home Rule," in *Handbook of Home Rule*, 129–54.

45. LS to JB, June 15, 1886, JB Papers; MA to editor of the *London Times*, July 24, 1886, MA to Jane Martha Arnold Forster, June 13, 1886, both in MA, *Letters*, 6:310–11, 160; ELG, "An American View of Ireland," *Nineteenth Century*, August 1882, 184, 186. ELG continued by arguing that if the Irish learned to settle their grievances at the polls, they would no longer settle them "with blunderbusses from behind hedges." Though he supported Home Rule, he quickly pointed out that "if Ireland were independent tomorrow, it's about the last place in Europe in which I should care to take up my abode" (ELG to JB, June 7, 1882, in ELG, *Gilded Age Letters*, 284).

46. MA to ELG, October 3, 1887, MA to editor of *London Times*, July 24, 1886, in MA, *Letters*, 6:310–11; ELG, "American Home Rule," *Nineteenth Century*, May 1886, 793–806. According to JB's biographer, Gladstone had first suggested the topic of studying American federalism (Tulloch, *JB's "American Commonwealth,"* 68–79). See also Hernon, "Use of the American Civil War." This debate echoed an earlier one during the Civil War, when CEN and GWC objected to John Elliot Cairnes's comparison of the Confederate states with the American colonies. GWC instead imagined the Confederate South as Wales. On British interest in federalism more generally, see Bell, *Building Greater Britain*.

47. [GWC], " 'Sick' of Home Rule," *HW*, November 9, 1889, 890. See also GWC, "Poor Ireland," *HW*, December 27, 1890, 1002–3. On the Liberal Party's demise, see Parry, *Rise and Fall of Liberal Government*. As Parry points out, this episode further hurt the Liberals by sticking them with the unpopular reputation of being soft on empire.

48. Stead quoted in Gerlach, *British Liberalism*, 79; the letter was sent after the *Pall Mall Gazette* had printed a similar plea, perhaps written by Stead. Gerlach, *British Liberalism*, 214–16, explains that Gladstone remained aloof from the arbitration movement.

49. John Morley, "Arbitration with America," *Nineteenth Century*, August 1896, 320–37; Boyle, "Venezuela Crisis." On the Olney-Pauncefote Treaty, see Perkins, *Great Rapprochement*, 26–29. As ambassador to the United States, JB negotiated another arbitration treaty with Secretary of State Philander Knox in 1911, but it too failed to pass the Senate. See Ions, *JB and American Democracy*, 233.

50. "Anachronism of War," *Century*, March 1896, 790–91; ELG, "The Absurdity of War," *Century*, January 1897, 468–70. RWG cautioned ELG about a complete condemnation of war, fearful that such a position might tarnish the example of the American Civil War; see ELG to RWG, October 26, [1896], in ELG, *Gilded Age Letters*, 484.

51. AVD, "England and America," *AtMo*, October 1897, 441–45. AVD returned to the United States in 1898, staying with CEN at Shady Hill. Though the two increasingly disagreed on matters of empire, CEN wrote to LS, AVD's cousin, that "he and I find ourselves in close agreement on most questions; while in regard to most matters of opinion, our judg-

ments so nearly coincide that there is little chance for discussion" (October 22, 1898, in CEN, *Letters*, 2:275). On Anglo-Saxonism at the end of the century, see Anderson, *Race and Rapprochement*; Kramer, "Empires, Exceptions, and Anglo-Saxons." On ideas about federation more generally in Victorian political thought, see Bell, *Building Greater Britain*.

52. JB, "British Feeling on the Venezuelan Question," *NAR*, February 1896, 145-50; CEN, "Some Aspects of Civilization in America," *Forum* 20 (1896): 641-51. On the rise of yellow journalism, see Linderman, *Mirror of War*, 148-73. For changes in the press generally, see Wilson, *Labor of Words*, 17-39; Schudson, *Discovering the News*. For the British "New Journalism" associated with Harmsworth, see Hampton, *Visions of the Press*.

53. ELG, "The Newspaper and Diplomacy," *NAR*, May 1893, 579; [ELG], "The Function of Discussion," *Nation*, February 20, 1896.

54. CEN, "Some Aspects of Civilization in America," *Forum* 20 (1896): 641-51; Townsend, *Manhood at Harvard*.

55. On ideas about manliness at the end of the century and the newer fascination with masculinity, see Bederman, *Manliness and Civilization*; Higham, "Reorientation of American Culture"; Dubbert, *Man's Place*; Rotundo, *American Manhood*; Townsend, *Manhood at Harvard*. For British developments, see Catherine Hall, "Competing Masculinities"; Mangan and Walvin, *Manliness and Morality*.

56. [ELG], "Football Again," *Nation*, November 30, 1893, 406; ELG, "The Athletic Craze," *Nation*, December 6, 1893, 422-23. TWH expressed to President Eliot a concern that the rise in college sports had contributed to a decline in intellectual prestige. Scholars and thinkers no longer seemed to gain any "reputation in the general community and next to none in the university" in the 1890s: "The athletes take it all" (March 28, 1896, CWE Papers, Harvard University Archives, Cambridge, Mass.).

57. [RWG], "What Is Patriotism?," *Century*, August 1892, 630. RWG also urged the practice of a more "imaginative" patriotism, a kind of civic awareness of the larger consequences and meaning of one's behavior in light of true American values ([RWG], "Patriotism and Imagination," *Century*, January 1898, 476). Before the outbreak of war, this article had specifically protested corrupt politics and southern lynching as acts lacking in civic and moral imagination. JRL couplet comes from "An Epistle to GWC," in *Complete Poetical Works*, 390.

58. CEN, "True Patriotism," in CEN, *Letters*, 2:267.

59. The northern liberals represented only one part of a particularly unwieldy and otherwise divided coalition. On the "movement" (to the extent that it was one), see Beisner, *Twelve against Empire*; Tompkins, *Anti-Imperialism*; Welch, *Response to Imperialism*. Hoganson, *Fighting for American Manhood*, provides a good discussion of how debates over gender inflected anti-imperialism.

60. ELG, "Come and Let Us Reason Together," *Nation*, November 10, 1898, 344. CFA made a similar case in CFA to JB, May 31, 1900, JB Papers.

61. CEN to LS, June 24, 1898, July 8, 1899, both in CEN, *Letters*, 2:270, 284; ELG to CEN, July 1, 1899, in ELG, *Gilded Age Letters*, 520.

62. ELG to CEN, August 4, [1898], in ELG, *Gilded Age Letters*, 507; CEN to Sam G. Ward, March 13, 1901, in CEN, *Letters*, 2:303.

63. CEN to ELG, February 9, 1893, ELG Papers; CEN to GS, February 20, 1900, CEN Papers.

64. TWH, "Sound Forth Again the Nation's Voice," *WJ*, May 29, 1897; TWH, "War at Last," *Harper's Bazaar*, May 7, 1898. TWH's other relevant writings for *Harper's Bazaar* include "Wars and Rumors," April 16, 1898; "A New World Power," June 11, 1898; "The Die Is Cast," July 16, 1898; "Ships and Rafts," September 3, 1898.

65. [ELG], "Our Savage War 'for the Cause of Humanity,'" *Nation*, April 20, 1899, 288.

66. *Springfield Republican*, October 22, 1900, reproduced (with list of signatures) in Philip Foner and Winchester, *Anti-Imperialist Reader*, 461–63. The address took this quotation from a speech Senator George Hoar of Massachusetts had made the previous year.

67. Harrington, "Literary Aspects of American Anti-Imperialism," provides a wealth of information on writers during the imperial crisis. Many of those involved also compared their actions in this episode to those during the Civil War, as when William James sent ELG "a word of thanks and a bravo bravissimo for your glorious fight against the powers of darkness. I swear it brings back the days of '61 again, when the worst enemies of our Country were in our own borders" (December 24, 1895, ELG Papers).

68. Edward Dicey, "The New American Imperialism," *Nineteenth Century*, September 1898, 501. Dicey may have wanted to claim expansion as a racial instinct, but his article also enumerated several social and political reasons for the rise in imperial sentiment, including the growth of cities and the increase of class conflict—in short, the "same social difficulties which have long perplexed European statecraft." On the competing claims of national destiny and racial destiny, see Kramer, "Empires, Exceptions, and Anglo-Saxons." On Anglo-Saxonism more generally, see Anderson, *Race and Rapprochement*; Martellone, "In the Name of Anglo-Saxondom"; Hitchens, *Blood, Class, and Nostalgia* (tracing the tendencies through the twentieth century).

69. Hay quoted in Charles Campbell, *Anglo-American Understanding*, 125; Perkins, *Great Rapprochement*, 87.

70. "The White Man's Burden" was, of course, the title of a poem by Rudyard Kipling, addressed to all of the United States (via *McClure's*) and not strictly to Roosevelt, who would not reach the White House until two years after its publication. ELG had nothing but scorn for Kipling's imperial poetry, dismissing him as a "pernicious, vulgar person . . . the poet of the barrack-room cads" (ELG to Louise Dawson, December 23, 1899, in ELG, *Gilded Age Letters*, 529). See also TWH, "The Poets and the Conquerors," *Harper's Bazaar*, June 10, 1899, 479. On the original terms of the Rhodes trust, see Kenny, *History*; Schaeper and Schaeper, *Cowboys into Gentlemen*.

71. TWH, "School of Jingoes." TWH's point here anticipates the line of inquiry Ernest May suggested in his "speculative essay," *American Imperialism*.

72. CEN to LS, June 24, 1898, July 8, 1899, both in CEN, *Letters*, 2:270, 284; William James to G. F. Hoar, May 11, 1900, in William James, *Letters*; CFA, *"Imperialism,"* 11, 20–21. Mark Twain drew a similarly sharp contrast in his scathing "To the Person Sitting in Darkness," *NAR*, February 1901, 161–76.

73. Liberals were only intermittently selective in their American history and often pointed out how far Americans had fallen from their ideals in their treatment of Native

Americans and African Americans. Kramer, "Empires, Exceptions, and Anglo-Saxons," portrays liberal anti-imperialists as "national exceptionalists" (in contrast to the "racial exceptionalists" who imagined a common Anglo-Saxon imperial destiny). The history and meaning of "exceptionalism" are quite complex and variable, though the concept often gets flattened out by a failure to distinguish between different kinds of exceptional thinking. In addition to Kramer's, the most important recent discussions include Rodgers, "Exceptionalism"; Dorothy Ross, "Liberalism and American Exceptionalism"; Thomas Haskell, "Taking Exception to Exceptionalism." For a thoughtful discussion of James's critical "cosmopolitan patriotism," though one that grossly mischaracterizes JRL's view, see Hansen, *Lost Promise*, chapter 1.

74. Though Rodgers, *Atlantic Crossings*, treats them as antithetical, cosmopolitanism and exceptionalism are not necessarily incompatible, as Dorothy Ross points out in "Liberalism and American Exceptionalism." On the significance of Gladstone's principle of cooperation for liberal international thought, see Michael Howard, *War and the Liberal Conscience*, 56–60.

75. TWH, "Where Liberty Is Not, There Is My Country," *Harper's Bazaar*, August 12, 1899; TWH, "The Dream of the Republic," in *Book and Heart*, 101–2. TWH's internationalism in no way diminished his fairly consistent Anglophobia. See, for example, TWH, "The Cant of Cosmopolitanism," in *Book and Heart*, 110–16; TWH, "Partiality to All Alike," *Harper's Bazaar*, November 12, 1898.

76. FH to GS, January 27, 1900, in GS, *Selection from GS's Correspondence*, 340; GS to CEN, November 22, 1898, GS Papers. The return of friendly feeling between GS and ELG is noted in ELG to JB, March 18, 1901, in ELG, *Gilded Age Letters*, 542. GS tried to check his anti-Semitism, but it appeared in his comments about the questionable British identity of the Jewish outlanders in the Transvaal on whose behalf the South African war was allegedly waged. See, for example, GS, *In the Court of History*.

77. JB to RWG, September 9, 1898, RWG Papers. JB published articles about imperialism in at least a half dozen American periodicals, and his response is more complex than I have conveyed here. While he made his personal opposition to American colonial expansion clear (in "The Armenian Question," *Century*, November 1895, 150–55; "The Policy of Annexation for America," *Forum* 24 (1897): 385–95; "Some Thoughts on the Policy of the United States," *HNMM*, September 1898, 609–18; "British Experience in the Government of Colonies," *Century* 57, March 1899, 718–29), his views are more ambiguous in "The Essential Unity of Britain and America," *AtMo*, July 1898, 22–29.

78. CEN to Charles Waldstein, November 18, 1898, CEN to Sara Norton, February 8, 1899, both in CEN, *Letters*, 2:280, 290–91. Ninkovich, *United States and Imperialism*, emphasizes the basic similarities between imperialists and anti-imperialists. Eldridge, *England's Mission*, makes a similar point about shared commitments to a civilizing mission among Britons who otherwise disagreed on matters of imperial policy. Cain, "Radicalism, Gladstone, and the Liberal Critique," reinforces this view specifically across the Disraeli-Gladstone divide.

79. GS to Hertz, October 29, 1900, in GS, *Selection from GS's Correspondence*, 364; ELG to

JB, November 18, 1899, in ELG, *Gilded Age Letters*, 526–27; GS, "Imperialism in the U.S.," *Contemporary Review* 75 (May 1899): 628; Noer, *Briton, Boer, and Yankee*. CFA echoed ELG's cynicism in a public address on the new Anglo-Saxon rapprochement: "We, in America, were inclined to sympathize strongly with the rebels of South Africa; but we now have rebels of our own. Rebels, therefore, are with us not in such high favor as they were" ("A National Change of Heart," in *Lee at Appomattox*, 270).

80. [GS], "British Imperialism," *Nation*, September 12, 1901, 200–201; CFA, *"Imperialism,"* 19; Mark Twain, "To the Person Sitting in Darkness," *NAR*, February 1901, 161–77. On American atrocities committed in the Philippines, see Bain, *Sitting in Darkness*, 83–89; Schirmer, *Republic or Empire?*, 235–40. Led by, among others, Storey and CFA, the Anti-Imperialist League lobbied the U.S. Senate to hold hearings on the conduct of the war, which the Senate finally did in February 1902. On reading Twain's essay, an exultant ELG implored JB, "Do read Mark Twain in the *North American Review*. He is doing excellent work" (March 18, [1901], in ELG, *Gilded Age Letters*, 542).

81. [GS], "British Imperialism," *Nation*, September 12, 1901, 200–201. CWE sounded this regression theme when writing JB about concentration camps: "Isn't it a remarkable thing that three Christian nations [Spain, the United States, and Great Britain] at the end of the Nineteenth Century and the beginning of the Twentieth should have adopted a war measure which is really crueler than anything mankind has yet exhibited in a state of war." The "wholesale destruction of farms and villages" was troubling enough, but the concentration camp, he wrote, "seems to be a method of race extermination by killing off the children" (March 14, 1902, JB Papers).

82. CEN to ELG, July 21, 1901, ELG Papers; James Turner, *Liberal Education*; Armstrong, *ELG: A Biography*; Mary Higginson, *TWH*, 361.

83. CEN to FH, January 15, 1900, FH Papers, British Library of Political and Economic Science, London School of Economics, London, England; CWE to JB, August 18, 1903, JB to CWE, September 4, 1903, both in JB Papers; FH, "The Nineteenth Century: An Address Given to the Nineteenth Century Club of New York," in *George Washington and Other American Addresses*, 247; FH, "Impressions of America," *Nineteenth Century*, June 1901, 913–30; JB to GS, April 12, 1901, in Koss, *Pro-Boers*, 193; ELG to William James, February 21, 1902, in ELG, *Gilded Age Letters*, 547. See also LS, "The Good Old Cause," *Nineteenth Century*, January 1902, 11–23, which ascribes the supposed abandonment of ideals to an ambiguity in the meaning of liberalism. CEN also urged Morley to visit Cambridge after the wave of imperialism had subsided (January 30, 1904, CEN Papers).

84. ELG to Marion Bryce, November 18, 1899, in ELG, *Gilded Age Letters*, 526; CEN to FH, October 31, 1901, FH Papers; JB quoted in Wallace, *GS*, 201.

85. TWH, "How Should a Colored Man Vote in 1900?," reprinted in TWH and Meyer, *Magnificent Activist*, 402–4. TWH was outraged that Bryan criticized, in the *Commoner*, President Roosevelt for inviting Booker T. Washington to dine at the White House. "It is in my opinion an essential part of Democracy," TWH coldly informed the Great Commoner, "that social distinctions should be merely individual, not racial. Character is character; and education is education. What social gradations exist should be based on these, and these

alone; and even these should be effaced as rapidly as possible. What are you or what am I that we should undertake to advocate any social law that shall place us above men like Frederick Douglass or Booker Washington?" (November 27, 1901, TWH Papers).

86. TWH to JB, January 30, 1899, JB Papers. JB's Romanes Lectures were devoted to an analysis of the "advanced and backward races." For more on race as a theme in JB's writing, see Tulloch, *JB's "American Commonwealth."*

87. GS, *Commonwealth or Empire*, 45, 53; TWH, "American Home Rule," *Nineteenth Century*, May 1886, 801; [ELG], "Lynching," *Nation*, December 14, 1899, 440.

88. TWH, "Where Liberty Is Not, There Is My Country," *Harper's Bazaar*, August 12, 1899; TWH, "Higginson Answers Captain Mahan" (1902), reprinted in TWH and Meyer, *Magnificent Activist*, 404-10; CEN to S. G. Ward, October 7, 1901, CEN to Nariaki Kozaki, February 10, 1904, both in CEN, *Letters*, 2:311, 337. Such relativist thinking about civilization set TWH and CEN apart from many of their contemporaries. On the predominance of hierarchical thinking about civilization, see, for example, Bederman, *Manliness and Civilization*; Jacobson, *Barbarian Virtues*. For an imaginative treatment of Japanese-American cultural interchange, see Guth, *Longfellow's Tattoos*.

89. CEN to Nariaki Kozaki, February 10, 1904, CEN to S. G. Ward, September 13, 1905, both in CEN, *Letters*, 2:313, 357. A skeptical CFA dissented even from this achievement, grumbling in a letter to JB that Roosevelt (making "a somewhat dramatic first appearance as an international peace-maker") had merely shored up Russian autocracy (September 22, 1905, JB Papers).

90. CEN to GS, January 31, 1905, CEN Papers.

91. CEN to GS, August 30, 1905, CEN Papers.

92. JB to CEN, September 16, 1907, CEN Papers.

Epilogue

1. Virginia Woolf quoted in Stansky, *On or about December 1910*, 3.

2. See George Santayana, "The Genteel Tradition in American Philosophy," in Hollinger and Capper, *American Intellectual Tradition*, 2:102-13; Strachey, *Eminent Victorians*.

3. William James to Katharine Godkin, May 21, 1902, ELG Papers; William James to Henry James, August 20, 1891, February 1, 1889, April 19, 1888, November 30, 1907, Henry James to William James, October 1, 1887, September 1, 1891, William James to Alice Howe Gibbens James, July 31, 1890, all in William James, *Correspondence*, 2:185, 2:104, 2:85-86, 3:354-55, 2:72, 2:187-88, 7:77-78; Henry James to Alice James, February 17, [1875], in Henry James, *Henry James Letters*, 2:156-57.

4. See Charles Taylor, "Our Victorian Contemporaries," in *Sources of the Self*, 393-418. For studies that rely heavily on the modernist view of the Victorians, see, for example, Henry May, *End of American Innocence*; Singal, *War Within*.

5. ELG to CEN, December 29, 1895, in ELG, *Gilded Age Letters*, 475. In Henry James's estimation, this insecure cosmopolitanism prevented JRL from becoming, even with his "ambassadorial accretions, & the experience & fame that have come to him of late years,"

a true "'man of the world'" (Henry James to William James, October 1, 1887, in William James, *Correspondence*, 2: 72).

6. See TWH, "More Mingled Races?," in *Book and Heart*, 154–59; Johnson, "Autobiography," 483. With devastating economy, Johnson also revealed the limitations of the old colonel's antiracism when, after his minidisquisition on racial relativism, he admits that he would not consent to his daughter's marrying a black man. On TWH's lingering if limited antiracism, see McPherson, *Abolitionist Legacy*.

7. TWH, *Black Rebellion*. In addition to McPherson, editors of *Army Life* have included Howard Mumford Jones, E. Franklin Frazier, Howard N. Meyer, and John Hope Franklin.

8. For a discussion of some of the scholarship on the discourse model of politics, see, for example, Benhabib, "Liberal Dialogue"; Benhabib, "Toward a Deliberative Model"; Habermas, *Between Facts and Norms*; Gutman and Thompson, *Democracy and Disagreement*. On frames, see Matt Bai's discussion of the Berkeley linguist George Lakoff's analysis of political language in "The Framing Wars," *New York Times Sunday Magazine*, July 17, 2005.

9. On the Book-of-the-Month Club, see Rubin, *Making of Middlebrow Culture*; Radway, *Feeling for Books*; on the more self-consciously serious effort behind the Modern Library, see Satterfield, *World's Best Books*. On Oprah Winfrey's book club, see Farr, *Reading Oprah*. See also Rorty on "The Inspirational Value of Great Works of Literature," in *Achieving Our Country*, 125–40.

10. Hansen, *Lost Promise*, provides a helpful discussion of William James's role in providing a model for dissent.

Bibliography

Manuscript Collections

Boston, Mass.
  Massachusetts Historical Society
    John A. Andrew Papers
    Edward Atkinson Papers
    Henry W. Bellows Papers
    Caroline Dall Papers
    William E. Endicott Papers
    George F. Hoar Papers
    James Russell Lowell Papers
    Massachusetts Reform Club Papers
    Ellery Sedgwick Papers
    Moorfield Storey Papers
Burlington, Vt.
  University of Vermont Library
    George Perkins Marsh Papers
Cambridge, England
  University Library, Cambridge University
    Henry Acland Papers
    John Acton Papers
    American Lectureship, 1865–66, File
    Arthur Sedgwick Papers
    Robertson Smith Papers
    Stephen Family Papers
Cambridge, Mass.
  Harvard University Archives
    Charles W. Eliot Papers
  Houghton Library, Harvard University
    Francis J. Child Papers
    George William Curtis Papers
    E. L. Godkin Papers
    Thomas Wentworth Higginson Papers
    James Family Papers
    William James Papers
    Henry Wadsworth Longfellow Papers
    James Russell Lowell Papers

Nation Papers
North American Review
    Charles Eliot Norton Papers
Chicago, Ill.
  Newberry Library
    Henry Blake Fuller Papers
Dublin, Ireland
  National Library of Ireland
    John Elliot Cairnes Papers
London, England
  British Library
    John Bright Papers
    W. E. Gladstone Papers
  British Library of Political and
      Economic Science, London
      School of Economics
    Frederic Harrison Papers
Madison, Wis.
  Wisconsin Historical Society Library
    Rare Book Collection
New York, N.Y.
  New York Public Library
    Richard Watson Gilder Papers
    E. L. Godkin Papers
Oxford, England
  Bodleian Library, Oxford University
    James Bryce Papers
    A. H. Clough Papers
    Sir William Harcourt Papers, 1901–2
    Max-Muller Papers
    Miscellaneous Autograph Letters
      etc., 1882–1902
    Gilbert Murray Papers
    Rossetti Papers
    Toynbee Correspondence

San Marino, Calif.
  Huntington Library
    Century Manuscripts
    Huntington Manuscripts
Washington, D.C.
  Library of Congress, Manuscripts
    Division
    William A. Croffut Papers

Frederick Law Olmsted Papers
Carl Schurz Papers
Moorfield Storey Papers
Worcester, Mass.
  American Antiquarian Society
  Oscar Fay Adams Papers
  D. C. Heath Papers
  T. W. Higginson Papers

Periodicals

Atlantic Monthly
Century Magazine
Contemporary Review
Cornhill Magazine
The Crayon
Fortnightly Review
The Forum
Harper's Bazaar
Harper's New Monthly Magazine
Harper's Weekly
Macmillan's Magazine

The Nation
New England Loyal Publication
  Society Broadsides
New Princeton Review
The Nineteenth Century
North American Review
The Pioneer
Putnam's Magazine
Scribner's Magazine
Woman's Journal

Primary Printed Material

Adams, Charles Francis. *An Address Delivered at Cambridge, before the Society of the Phi Beta Kappa, 26 June, 1873.* Cambridge, Mass.: Wilson, 1873.

———. *"Imperialism" and "The Tracks of Our Forefathers": A Paper Read by Charles Francis Adams before the Lexington, Massachusetts, Historical Society, Tuesday, December 20, 1898.* Boston: Estes, 1899.

———. *Lee at Appomattox.* Boston: Houghton, Mifflin, 1902.

———. *Trans-Atlantic Historical Solidarity: Lectures Delivered before the University of Oxford in Easter and Trinity Terms.* Oxford: Clarendon, 1913.

Adams, Charles Francis, and Henry Adams. *Chapters of Erie, and Other Essays.* Boston: Osgood, 1871.

Adams, Henry. *Democracy: An American Novel.* New York: Holt, 1880.

———. *The Education of Henry Adams.* Washington, D.C.: Adams, 1907.

———. *The Great Secession Winter of 1860–61, and Other Essays.* Edited by George Hochfield. New York: Sagamore, 1958.

———. *The Letters of Henry Adams.* Edited by J. C. Levenson. 6 vols. Cambridge: Belknap Press of Harvard University Press, 1982–88.

———. *A Letter to American Teachers of History.* Washington, D.C.: Furst, 1910.

Amberley, John Russell. *The Amberley Papers: The Letters and Diaries of Bertrand Russell's Parents.* New York: Norton, 1937.

Arnold, Matthew. *Civilisation in America*. Philadelphia: Scott, 1888.

———. *Culture and Anarchy and Other Writings*. Edited by Stefan Collini. Cambridge: Cambridge University Press, 1993.

———. *Discourses in America*. London: Macmillan, 1885.

———. *Essays in Criticism*. Boston: Ticknor and Fields, 1865.

———. *The Letters of Matthew Arnold*. Edited by Cecil Y. Lang. 6 vols. Charlottesville: University Press of Virginia, 1996–2002.

Bradley, John Lewis, and Ian Ousby, eds. *The Correspondence of John Ruskin and Charles Eliot Norton*. New York: Cambridge University Press, 1987.

Bridgman, Raymond L. *The Independents of Massachusetts in 1884*. Boston: Cupples, Upham, 1885.

Bryce, James. *The American Commonwealth*. 3 vols. London: Macmillan, 1888.

———. *Briton and Boer: Both Sides of the South African Question*. New York: Harper, 1900.

———. *Handbook of Home Rule: Being Articles on the Irish Question*. London: Kegan Paul, Trench, 1888.

———. *Studies in Contemporary Biography*. Freeport, N.Y.: Books for Libraries, 1971.

———. *The Study of American History*. Cambridge: Cambridge University Press, 1921.

———. *University and Historical Addresses: Delivered during a Residence in the United States as Ambassador of Great Britain*. New York: Macmillan, 1913.

Burke, Edmund, and Edwin Lawrence Godkin. *Orations and Essays, the World's Great Books*. New York: Appleton, 1900.

Cairnes, John Elliott. *The Slave Power: Its Character, Career, and Probable Designs: Being an Attempt to Explain the Real Issues Involved in the American Contest*. New York: Carleton, 1862.

Carlyle, Thomas. *On the Choice of Books: The Inaugural Address of Thomas Carlyle, Lord Rector of the University of Edinburgh*. London: Hotten, 1866.

———. *Shooting Niagara: And After?* London: Chapman and Hall, 1867.

Channing, William Ellery. *Self-Culture: An Address Introductory to the Franklin Lectures, Delivered at Boston, September, 1838*. Boston: Dutton and Wentworth, 1838.

Clough, Arthur Hugh. *Correspondence of Arthur Hugh Clough*. Edited by Frederick L. Mulhauser. 2 vols. New York: Oxford University Press, 1957.

Conkling, Alfred. *The Life and Letters of Roscoe Conkling*. New York: Webster, 1889.

Curtis, George William. *Ars Recte Vivendi: Being Essays Contributed to the "Easy Chair."* New York: Harper, 1898.

———. *Early Letters of George Wm. Curtis to John S. Dwight: Brook Farm and Concord*. Edited by George Willis Cooke. New York: Harper, 1898.

———. *Equal Rights for Women. A Speech . . . in the Constitutional Convention of New York, at Albany, July 19, 1867*. Equal Rights Tract 7. New York: American Equal Rights Association, 1867.

———. *Homes of American Authors: Comprising Anecdotal, Personal, and Descriptive Sketches*. New York: Putnam, 1853.

———. *Literary and Social Essays*. New York: Harper, 1904.

———. *Machine Politics and the Remedy*. New York: Independent Republican Association, 1880.

————. *Nile Notes of a Howadji*. New York: Harper, 1851.

————. *Orations and Addresses of George William Curtis*. Edited by Charles Eliot Norton. New York: Harper, 1894.

————. *Party and Patronage: An Address Prepared for the Annual Meeting of the National Civil-Service Reform League*. New York: Peck, 1892.

————. *The Potiphar Papers*. New York: Putnam, 1853.

————. *Prue and I*. New York: Putnam, 1856.

————, ed. *The Correspondence of John Lothrop Motley*. London: Murray, 1889.

Dicey, A. V. *Lectures on the Relation between Law and Public Opinion in England during the Nineteenth Century*. London: Macmillan, 1905.

Dickens, Charles. *American Notes: A Journey*. 1842; reprint, New York: Fromm, 1985.

Du Bois, W. E. B. "The Souls of Black Folk." In *Three Negro Classics*. New York: Avon, 1965.

Eaton, Dorman, B. *The Civil Service in Great Britain: A History of Abuses and Reform and Their Bearing on American Politics*. New York: Harper, 1880.

Eliot, Charles W. *American Contributions to Civilization*. New York: Century, 1898.

Emerson, Ralph Waldo. *Ralph Waldo Emerson: Essays and Lectures*. New York: Library of America, 1983.

Essays on Reform. London: Macmillan, 1867.

Ford, Worthington Chauncey, Charles Francis Adams, and Henry Adams. *A Cycle of Adams Letters, 1861–1865*. Boston: Houghton Mifflin, 1920.

Gaskell, Elizabeth Cleghorn. *Letters of Mrs. Gaskell and Charles Eliot Norton, 1855–1865*. Edited and introduction by Jane Whitehill. London: Oxford University Press, 1932.

Gasparin, Count Agenor de. *Reconstruction: A Letter to President Johnson*. New York: Loyal Publication Society, 1865.

Gilder, Richard Watson. *Civic Patriotism: An Address at the Dinner of the New York Board of Trade and Transportation, February Third, 1894*. New York: privately printed, 1894.

————. *Grover Cleveland: A Record of Friendship*. New York: Century, 1910.

————. *The University Settlement and Good Citizenship: An Address at the Annual Meeting of the University Settlement Society of New York*. New York: n.p., 1897.

Gilder, Rosamond, ed. *Letters of Richard Watson Gilder*. Boston: Houghton Mifflin, 1916.

Gladstone, W. E., and James Bryce. *Handbook of Home Rule: Being Articles on the Irish Question*. London: Trench, 1887.

Godkin, Edwin Lawrence. *The Gilded Age Letters of E. L. Godkin*. Edited by William M. Armstrong. Albany: State University of New York Press, 1974.

————. *The History of Hungary and the Magyars: From the Earliest Period to the Close of the Late War*. London: Kent, 1856.

————. *Life and Letters of Edwin Lawrence Godkin*. Edited by Rollo Ogden. New York: Macmillan, 1907.

————. *Problems of Modern Democracy: Political and Economic Essays*. New York: Scribner's, 1896.

————. *Problems of Modern Democracy: Political and Economic Essays*. Edited by Morton Keller. Cambridge: Belknap Press of Harvard University Press, 1966.

————. *Reflections and Comments, 1865–1895*. New York: Scribner's, 1895.

————. *The Triumph of Reform: A History of the Great Political Revolution, November Sixth, Eighteen Hundred and Ninety-Four.* New York: Souvenir Publishing, 1895.

Godwin, Parke. "George William Curtis." In *Commemorative Addresses.* New York: Harper, 1895.

Guttsman, W. L., ed. *A Plea for Democracy: An Edited Selection from the 1867 Essays on Reform and Questions for a Reformed Parliament.* London: MacGibbon and Kee, 1967.

Harrison, Frederic. *Among My Books: Centenaries, Reviews, Memoirs.* London: Macmillan, 1912.

————. *The Choice of Books.* Chicago: Scott, 1891.

————. *George Washington and Other American Addresses.* London: Macmillan, 1901.

————. *National and Social Problems.* New York: Macmillan, 1908.

————. *Studies in Early Victorian Literature.* London: Arnold, 1895.

————. *Tennyson, Ruskin, Mill, and Other Literary Estimates.* London: Macmillan, 1899.

Haultain, Arnold. *Goldwin Smith: His Life and Opinions.* London: Laurie, 1913.

Higginson, Thomas Wentworth. *Army Life in a Black Regiment.* Boston: Fields Osgood, 1870.

————. *Atlantic Essays.* Boston: Osgood, 1871.

————. *Black Rebellion: Five Slave Revolts.* Introduction by James M. McPherson. New York: Da Capo, 1998.

————. *Book and Heart: Essays on Literature and Life.* New York: Harper, 1897.

————. "Charles Eliot Norton." In *Carlyle's Laugh, and Other Surprises.* Boston: Houghton Mifflin, 1909.

————. *Cheerful Yesterdays.* Boston: Houghton Mifflin, 1898.

————. *Common Sense about Women.* Boston: Lee and Shepard, 1882.

————. *Complete Civil War Journal and Selected Letters of Thomas Wentworth Higginson.* Edited by Christopher Looby. Chicago: University of Chicago Press, 2000.

————. *Contemporaries.* Boston: Houghton Mifflin, 1899.

————. *English Statesmen: Brief Biographies of European Public Men.* New York: Putnam's, 1875.

————. *Harvard Memorial Biographies.* Cambridge, Mass.: Sever and Francis, 1866.

————. *Henry Wadsworth Longfellow.* Boston: Houghton Mifflin, 1902.

————. *Hints on Writing and Speech-Making.* New York: Longmans Green, 1894.

————. *Letters and Journals of Thomas Wentworth Higginson, 1846–1906.* Edited by Mary Thacher Higginson. Boston: Houghton Mifflin, 1921.

————. *"Man Shall Not Live by Bread Alone": A Thanksgiving Sermon: Preached in Newburyport.* Newburyport, Mass.: Whipple, 1848.

————. *Margaret Fuller Ossoli.* Boston: Houghton Mifflin, 1884.

————. *Massachusetts in Mourning: A Sermon, Preached in Worcester, on Sunday, June 4, 1854.* Boston: Munroe, 1854.

————. *The Monarch of Dreams.* Boston: Lee and Shepard, 1887.

————. *Mr. Higginson's Address to the Voters of the Third Congressional District of Massachusetts.* Lowell, Mass.: Knapp, 1850.

————. *The New Revolution: A Speech before the American Anti-Slavery Society, at Their Annual Meeting in New York, May 12, 1857.* Boston: Wallcut, 1857.

————. *The New World and the New Book.* Boston: Lee and Shepard, 1892.

———. *Out-Door Papers*. Boston: Ticknor and Fields, 1863.

———. *Part of a Man's Life*. Boston: Houghton Mifflin, 1905.

———. *A Ride through Kansas*. New York: American Anti-Slavery Society, 1856.

———. "Ruskin and Norton: A Link between the Old and New Worlds." *Proceedings of the American Academy and National Institute of Arts and Letters* 1 (1910): 22–24.

———. "The School of Jingoes." In *Essays from the Chapbook*. Chicago: Stone, 1896.

———. *Studies in History and Letters*. Boston: Houghton Mifflin, 1900.

———. *Things Old and New: An Installation Sermon*. Worcester, Mass.: Earle and Drew, 1852.

———. *Travellers and Outlaws: Episodes in American History*. Boston: Lee and Shepard, 1889.

———. "Tribute to Professor Norton." *Proceedings of the Massachusetts Historical Society* 42 (1908): 33–35.

———. *The Unitarian Autumnal Convention: A Sermon*. Boston: Mussey, 1853.

———. *Unsolved Problems in Woman Suffrage*. New York: n.p., 1887.

———. "Visit to the John Brown Household." In James Redpath, *The Public Life of Capt. John Brown*. Boston: Thayer and Brown, 1860.

———. *Women and Men*. New York: Harper's, 1888.

———. *The Young Men's Party*. New York: Harper's, 1884.

Higginson, Thomas Wentworth, and Edward Channing. *English History for American Readers*. New York: Longmans Green, 1893.

Higginson, Thomas Wentworth, and Howard N. Meyer. *The Magnificent Activist: The Writings of Thomas Wentworth Higginson (1823–1911)*. Cambridge, Mass.: Da Capo, 2000.

Hirst, Francis W., Gilbert Murray, and J. L. Hammond. *Liberalism and the Empire*. London: Johnson, 1900.

Howells, W. D. *Literary Friends and Acquaintance: A Personal Retrospect of American Authorship*. New York: Harper, 1900.

Hughes, Thomas. *The Cause of Freedom*. London: Emancipation Society, 1863.

———. "Thomas Hughes and the American Civil War." *Journal of Negro History* 18:3 (July 1933): 322–29.

James, Henry. *The American Essays*. New York: Vintage, 1956.

———. *Hawthorne*. London: Macmillan, 1879.

———. *Henry James Letters*. Edited by Leon Edel. Vol. 2, 1875–83. Cambridge: Belknap Press of Harvard University Press, 1975.

James, William. *Correspondence of William James*. Edited by Ignas K. Skrupskelis and Elizabeth M. Berkeley. 12 vols. Charlottesville: University Press of Virginia, 1992–2004.

———. *Letters of William James*. Edited by Henry James Jr. 2 vols. Boston: Atlantic Monthly Press, 1920.

———. *Memories and Studies*. New York: Longmans, Green, 1911.

Johnson, James Weldon. "Autobiography of an Ex-Colored Man." In *Three Negro Classics*. New York: Avon, 1965.

King, Edward, and Thomas Wentworth Higginson. *French Political Leaders: Brief*

Biographies of European Public Men, by Thomas Wentworth Higginson. New York: Putnam's, 1876.

Lincoln, Abraham. *Lincoln: Selected Speeches and Writings*. Edited by Donald Fehrenbacher. New York: Library of America, 1992.

Lippmann, Walter. *The Phantom Public*. New York: Harcourt, Brace, 1925.

Lowell, James Russell. *Among My Books*. Boston: Osgood, 1876.

———. *The Anti-Slavery Papers of James Russell Lowell*. Edited by William Belmont Parker and Bruce Rogers. 2 vols. Boston: Houghton Mifflin, 1902.

———. *The Complete Poetical Works of James Russell Lowell*. Boston: Houghton Mifflin, 1896.

———. *Democracy, and Other Addresses*. Boston: Houghton Mifflin, 1887.

———. *Fireside Travels*. Boston: Ticknor and Fields, 1864.

———. *The Function of the Poet, and Other Essays*. Edited by Albert Mordell. Boston: Houghton Mifflin, 1920.

———. *Latest Literary Essays and Addresses of James Russell Lowell*. Boston: Houghton Mifflin, 1892.

———. *Letters of James Russell Lowell*. Edited By Charles Eliot Norton. 2 vols. New York: Harper, 1894.

———. *My Study Windows*. Boston: Osgood, 1871.

———. *The Old English Dramatists: Writings*. Cambridge, Mass.: Riverside, 1892.

———. *The Round Table*. Boston: Badger, 1913.

———. *The Writings of James Russell Lowell: In Ten Volumes*. Boston: Houghton, Mifflin, 1890.

Maitland, Frederic William. *The Life and Letters of Leslie Stephen*. London: Duckworth, 1906.

Melville, Herman. "Hawthorne and His Mosses." *Literary World*, August 17, 1850, 125–27; August 24, 1850, 145–47.

Mill, John Stuart. *The Collected Works of John Stuart Mill*. 33 vols. Toronto: University of Toronto Press, 1972–91.

———. "The Contest in America." In *Union Pamphlets of the Civil War, 1861–1865*, edited by Frank Freidel. 2 vols. Cambridge: Belknap Press of Harvard University Press, 1967.

———. *Suffrage for Women: Speech in the British Parliament on the Household Suffrage Bill, May 20th, 1867*. New York: American Equal Rights Association, 1867.

Morley, John. *Nineteenth Century Essays*. Edited by Peter Stansky. Chicago: University of Chicago Press, 1970.

———. *Recollections*. 2 vols. London: Macmillan, 1917.

Norton, Charles Eliot. "Charles Eliot Norton on Dime Novels." *Proceedings of the Massachusetts Historical Society* 50 (1917): 197–98.

———. *Considerations on Some Recent Social Theories*. Boston: Little, Brown, 1853.

———. "Harvard." In *Four American Universities: Harvard, Yale, Princeton, Columbia*. New York: Harper, 1895.

———. *Historical Studies of Church-Building in the Middle Ages: Venice, Siena, Florence*. New York: Harper, 1880.

————. *Letters of Charles Eliot Norton.* Edited by Sara Norton and M. A. De Wolfe Howe. Boston: Houghton Mifflin, 1913.

————. *The New Life of Dante: An Essay, with Translations.* Cambridge, Mass.: Riverside, 1859.

————. *Notes of Travel and Study in Italy.* Boston: Ticknor and Fields, 1860.

————. *The Soldier of the Good Cause.* Boston: American Unitarian Association, 1861.

Norton, Charles Eliot, James B. Thayer, and William Endicott Jr. *Report of the Executive Committee of the New England Loyal Publication Society.* Boston: New England Loyal Publication Society, 1865.

Redpath, James. *The Public Life of Capt. John Brown.* Boston: Thayer and Brown, 1860.

Rhodes, James Ford. *Historical Essays.* New York: Macmillan, 1909.

————. *History of the United States from the Compromise of 1850.* New York: Harper, 1893.

Roosevelt, Theodore. *An Autobiography.* New York: Scribner's, 1929.

Save the Republic. Boston: Anti-Imperialist League, 1899.

Smith, Goldwin. *The Civil War in America: An Address Read at the Last Meeting of the Manchester Union and Emancipation Society.* London: Simpkin Marshall, 1866.

————. *Commonwealth or Empire: A Bystander's View of the Question.* New York: Macmillan, 1902.

————. *The Conduct of England to Ireland: An Address Delivered at Brighton, Jan. 30, 1882.* London: Macmillan, 1882.

————. *Cowper.* New York: Harper, 1880.

————. *Does the Bible Sanction American Slavery?* Oxford, Eng.: Henry, 1863.

————. *The Empire: A Series of Letters, Published in the "Daily News," 1862, 1863.* Oxford, Eng.: Henry and Parker, 1863.

————. *Essays on Questions of the Day, Political and Social.* New York: Macmillan, 1893.

————. *In the Court of History: An Apology for Canadians Who Were Opposed to the South African War.* Toronto: Tyrrell, 1902.

————. *Irish History and Irish Character.* Oxford, Eng.: Parker, 1862.

————. *The Irish Question: Three Letters to the Editor of the "Daily News."* London: Ridgway, 1868.

————. *Lectures and Essays.* London: Macmillan, 1881.

————. *A Letter to a Whig Member of the Southern Independence Association.* London: Macmillan, 1864.

————. "Letters of Goldwin Smith to Charles Eliot Norton." *Proceedings of the Massachusetts Historical Society* 49 (October 1915–June 1916): 106–60.

————. *Life of Jane Austen.* London: Scott, 1890.

————. *Reminiscences.* Edited by Arnold Haultain, Herbert Parsons, and Mary Parsons. New York: Macmillan, 1911.

————. *A Selection from Goldwin Smith's Correspondence, Comprising Letters Chiefly to and from His English Friends, Written between the Years 1846 and 1910.* Edited by Arnold Haultain. London: Laurie, 1913.

————. *Shakespeare, the Man: An Attempt to Find Traces of the Dramatist's Character in His Dramas.* New York: Doubleday and McClure, 1900.

————. *The United States: An Outline of Political History, 1492–1871.* New York: Macmillan, 1893.

Stephen, Leslie. *An Agnostic's Apology, and Other Essays*. London: Smith, Elder, 1893.

———. *Essays on Freethinking and Plainspeaking*. London: Longmans, Green, 1873.

———. *History of English Thought in the Eighteenth Century*. 2 vols. London: Smith, Elder, 1876.

———. *Hours in a Library*. 3 vols. London: Smith, Elder, 1874–1904.

———. *Men, Book, and Mountains: Essays*. London: Hogarth, 1956.

———. *Social Rights and Duties: Addresses to Ethical Societies*. 2 vols. London: Sonnenschein, 1896.

———. *Selected Letters of Leslie Stephen*. Edited by John W. Bicknell and Mark A. Reger. Basingstoke, Eng.: Macmillan, 1996.

———. *Studies of a Biographer*. London: Duckworth, 1899.

———. *The "Times" on the American War: A Historical Study*. London: Ridgway, 1865.

Storey, Moorfield. *The Importance to America of Philippine Independence*. Boston: New England Anti-Imperialist League, 1904.

———. *Is It Right?* Chicago: American Anti-Imperialist League, 1900.

———. *Politics as a Duty and as a Career*. New York: Putnam, 1889.

Storey, Moorfield, and Marcial P. Lichauco. *The Conquest of the Philippines by the United States, 1898–1925*. New York: Putnam's, 1926.

Thompson, Henry Yates. *An Englishman in the American Civil War: The Diaries of Henry Yates Thompson, 1863*. Edited by Christopher Chancellor. London: Sidgwick and Jackson, 1971.

Tocqueville, Alexis de. *Democracy in America*. Edited by J. P. Mayer and translated by George Lawrence. New York: Harper and Row, 1969.

Trollope, Frances. *Domestic Manners of the Americans*. Edited by Richard Mullen. New York: Oxford University Press, 1984.

Twain, Mark. *A Connecticut Yankee in King Arthur's Court*. 1889; reprint, New York: Penguin, 1971.

Whitman, Walt. *Democratic Vistas and Other Papers*. 1871; reprint, Miami, Fla.: Fredonia, 2002.

Secondary Sources

Adams, Ephraim Douglass. *Great Britain and the American Civil War*. New York: Russell and Russell, 1958.

Adams, James Eli. *Dandies and Desert Saints: Styles of Victorian Manhood*. Ithaca: Cornell University Press, 1995.

Adelman, Paul. *Victorian Radicalism: The Middle-Class Experience, 1830–1914*. London: Longman, 1984.

Alexander, Edward. *Matthew Arnold and John Stuart Mill*. London: Routledge and Kegan Paul, 1965.

Allen, H. C. "Civil War, Reconstruction, and Great Britain." In *Heard Round the World: The Impact Abroad of the Civil War*, edited by Harold Hyman, 5–96. New York: Knopf, 1969.

―――. *Conflict and Concord: The Anglo-American Relationship since 1783.* New York: St. Martin's, 1959.

Altschuler, Glenn C., and Stuart M. Blumin. *Rude Republic: Americans and Their Politics in the Nineteenth Century.* Princeton: Princeton University Press, 2000.

Anderson, Stuart. *Race and Rapprochement: Anglo-Saxonism and Anglo-American Relations, 1895–1904.* Rutherford, N.J.: Fairleigh Dickinson University, 1981.

Annan, Noel. "The Intellectual Aristocracy." In *Studies in Social History,* edited by J. H. Plumb, 241–87. London: Longmans, 1955.

―――. *Leslie Stephen: The Godless Victorian.* Chicago: University of Chicago Press, 1984.

Armstrong, William M. *E. L. Godkin: A Biography.* Albany: State University of New York Press, 1977.

―――. *E. L. Godkin and American Foreign Policy, 1865–1900.* New York: Bookman, 1957.

―――. "The Freedmen's Movement and the Founding of the Nation." *Journal of American History* 53:4 (1967): 708–26.

Auld, John W. "The Liberal Pro-Boers." *Journal of British Studies* 14:2 (1975): 78–101.

Baetzhold, Howard G. *Mark Twain and John Bull: The British Connection.* Bloomington: Indiana University Press, 1970.

Bain, David Howard. *Sitting in Darkness: Americans in the Philippines.* Boston: Houghton Mifflin, 1984.

Baker, Paula. "The Domestication of Politics: Women and American Political Society, 1780–1920." *American Historical Review* 89:3 (1984): 620–47.

Barber, Benjamin R. *A Passion for Democracy: American Essays.* Princeton: Princeton University Press, 1998.

Bay, Mia. *The White Image in the Black Mind.* New York: Oxford University Press, 2000.

Beckert, Sven. "Democracy in the Age of Capital: Contesting Suffrage Rights in Gilded Age New York." In *The Democratic Experiment: New Directions in American Political History,* edited by Meg Jacobs, William J. Novak, and Julian E. Zelizer, 146–74. Princeton: Princeton University Press, 2003.

―――. *The Monied Metropolis: New York City and the Consolidation of the American Bourgeoisie, 1850–1896.* Cambridge: Cambridge University Press, 2001.

Bederman, Gail. *Manliness and Civilization: A Cultural History of Gender and Race in the United States, 1880–1917.* Chicago: University of Chicago Press, 1995.

Behm, Amanda. "Through Imperial Eyes: Race, Empire, and British Reactions to the American Civil War." Honors thesis, History Department, Dartmouth College, 2004.

Beisner, Robert L. *From the Old Diplomacy to the New, 1865–1900.* New York: Crowell, 1975.

―――. "Thirty Years before Manila: E. L. Godkin, Carl Schurz, and Anti-Imperialism in the Gilded Age." *Historian* 30:4 (1968): 561–77.

―――. *Twelve against Empire: The Anti-Imperialists, 1898–1900.* New York: McGraw-Hill, 1968.

Bell, Duncan S. A. *Building Greater Britain.* Princeton: Princeton University Press, forthcoming.

Bellows, Donald. "A Study of British Conservative Reaction to the American Civil War." *Journal of Southern History* 51:4 (1985): 505–26.

Beloff, Max. "Great Britain and the American Civil War." *History* 37 (February 1952): 40–48.

Bender, Thomas. *New York Intellect: A History of Intellectual Life in New York City, from 1750 to the Beginnings of Our Own Time*. New York: Knopf, 1987.

Benhabib, Seyla. "Liberal Dialogue versus a Critical Theory of Discursive Legitimation." In *Liberalism and the Moral Life*, edited by Nancy L. Rosenblum, 142–56. Cambridge: Harvard University Press, 1989.

———. "Toward a Deliberative Model of Democratic Legitimacy." In *Democracy and Difference: Contesting the Boundaries of the Political*, edited by Seyla Benhabib, 67–94. Princeton: Princeton University Press, 1996.

Bentley, Michael. *The Climax of Liberal Politics: British Liberalism in Theory and Practice, 1868–1918*. London: Arnold, 1987.

Berlin, Isaiah. *Four Essays on Liberty*. Oxford: Oxford University Press, 1969.

Bevington, Merle Mowbray. *The "Saturday Review," 1855–1868: Representative Educated Opinion in Victorian England*. New York: Columbia University Press, 1941.

Biagini, Eugenio F. "Exporting 'Western & Beneficent Institutions': Gladstone and Empire, 1880–1885." In *Gladstone Centenary Essays*, edited by David Bebbington and Roger Swift, 202–24. Liverpool: Liverpool University Press, 2000.

———. *Gladstone*. New York: St. Martin's, 2000.

———. "Liberalism and Direct Democracy: John Stuart Mill and the Model of Ancient Athens." In *Citizenship and Community: Liberals, Radicals, and Collective Identities in the British Isles, 1865–1931*, edited by Eugenio F. Biagini, 21–43. London: Cambridge University Press, 1996.

———. *Liberty, Retrenchment, and Reform: Popular Liberalism in the Age of Gladstone, 1860–1880*. Cambridge: Cambridge University Press, 1992.

Biel, Steven. *Independent Intellectuals in the United States, 1910–1945*. New York: New York University Press, 1992.

Blackett, R. J. M. *Divided Hearts: Britain and the American Civil War*. Baton Rouge: Louisiana State University Press, 2001.

Blake, Casey Nelson. *Beloved Community: The Cultural Criticism of Randolph Bourne, Van Wyck Brooks, Waldo Frank, and Lewis Mumford*. Chapel Hill: University of North Carolina Press, 1990.

Blanchard, Mary Warner. *Oscar Wilde's America: Counterculture in the Gilded Age*. New Haven: Yale University Press, 1998.

Bledstein, Burton. *The Culture of Professionalism: The Middle Class and the Development of Higher Education in America*. New York: Norton, 1976.

Blight, David W. *Race and Reunion: The Civil War in American Memory*. Cambridge: Belknap Press of Harvard University Press, 2001.

Blodgett, Geoffrey. *The Gentle Reformers: Massachusetts Democrats in the Cleveland Era*. Cambridge: Harvard University Press, 1966.

———. "The Mugwump Reputation, 1870 to the Present." *Journal of American History* 66:4 (1980): 867–87.

Bolt, Christine. *The Anti-Slavery Movement and Reconstruction: A Study in Anglo-American Cooperation, 1833–1877*. London: Oxford University Press, 1969.

————. *Victorian Attitudes to Race*. London: Routledge and Kegan Paul, 1971.

Bond, J. Arthur. "'Applying the Standards of Intrinsic Excellence': Nationalism and Arnoldian Cultural Valuation in the *Century Magazine*." *American Periodicals* 9 (1999): 55–73.

Bonner, Robert. *Mastering America: Proslavery Nationalists and the Crisis of the Union*. New York: Cambridge University Press, forthcoming.

Boyle, T. "The Venezuela Crisis and the Liberal Opposition, 1895–1896." *Journal of Modern History* 50:3 (1979): D1185–D1212.

Bradford, James C. *Crucible of Empire*. Annapolis, Md.: Naval Institute Press, 1993.

Bradley, Sculley. Introduction to *"The Pioneer": A Literary Magazine*, v–xxix. New York: Scholars' Facsimiles and Reprints, 1947.

Broaddus, Dorothy C. *Genteel Rhetoric: Writing High Culture in Nineteenth-Century Boston*. Columbia: University of South Carolina Press, 1999.

Brodhead, Richard H. *Cultures of Letters: Scenes of Reading and Writing in Nineteenth-Century America*. Chicago: University of Chicago Press, 1993.

————. "Literature and Culture." In *The Columbia Literary History of the Unites States*, edited by Emory Elliott, 467–81. New York: Columbia University Press, 1988.

————. *The School of Hawthorne*. New York: Oxford University Press, 1986.

Brooks, Van Wyck. *New England: Indian Summer, 1865–1915*. New York: Dutton, 1940.

Broughton, Trev Lynn. "Impotence, Biography, and the Froude-Carlyle Controversy: Revelations on Ticklish Topics." *Journal of the History of Sexuality* 7:4 (1997): 502–36.

————. *Men of Letters, Writing Lives: Masculinity and Literary Auto/Biography in the Late-Victorian Period*. London: Routledge, 1999.

Brown, R. Craig. "Goldwin Smith and Anti-Imperialism." *Canadian Historical Review* 43:2 (1962): 93–105.

Brown, Richard D. *The Strength of a People: The Idea of an Informed Citizenry in America, 1650–1870*. Chapel Hill: University of North Carolina Press, 1996.

Brownell, W. C. *American Prose Masters*. New York: Scribner's, 1909.

Budd, Louis J. *Mark Twain: Social Philosopher*. Bloomington: Indiana University Press, 1962.

Buell, Lawrence. *Emerson*. Cambridge: Harvard University Press, 2003.

————. *Literary Transcendentalism*. Ithaca: Cornell University Press, 1973.

————. *New England Literary Culture: From Revolution through Renaissance*. New York: Cambridge University Press, 1986.

Bundy, Carol. *The Nature of Sacrifice: A Biography of Charles Russell Lowell, 1835–1864*. New York: Farrar, Straus, and Giroux, 2005.

Burke, Martin J. *The Conundrum of Class: Public Discourse on the Social Order in America*. Chicago: University of Chicago Press, 1995.

Burrow, J. W. *The Crisis of Reason: European Thought, 1848–1914*. New Haven: Yale University Press, 2000.

————. *A Liberal Descent: Victorian Historians and the English Past*. Cambridge: Cambridge University Press, 1981.

————. *Whigs and Liberals: Continuity and Change in English Political Thought*. New York: Oxford University Press, 1988.

Butler, Leslie. "Investigating the 'Great American Mystery': Theory and Style in Henry

Adams's Political Reform Moment." In *Henry Adams and the Need to Know*, edited by William Merrill Decker and Earl S. Harbert, 80–103. Charlottesville: University Press of Virginia, 2005.

———. "Liberal Victorians and Foreign Policy in the Age of Empire." In *The Problem of Evil*, edited by Steve Mintz and John Stauffer. Amherst: University of Massachusetts Press, 2007.

———. "The Mugwump Dilemma: Democracy and Cultural Authority in Gilded Age America." Ph.D. diss., Yale University, 1997.

———. "Reconstructions in Intellectual and Cultural Life." In *Reconstructions: New Perspectives on Postbellum America*, edited by Thomas J. Brown. New York: Oxford University Press, 2006.

Cain, Peter. "Radicalism, Gladstone, and the Liberal Critique of Disraelian 'Imperialism.'" In *Victorian Visions*, edited by Duncan Bell. Cambridge: Cambridge University Press, forthcoming.

Campbell, Alexander E. *Great Britain and the United States, 1895–1903*. London: Longmans, Green, 1960.

Campbell, Charles Soutter. *Anglo-American Understanding, 1898–1903*. Baltimore: Johns Hopkins Press, 1957.

———. *From Revolution to Rapprochement: The United States and Great Britain, 1783–1900*. New York: Wiley, 1974.

———. *The Transformation of American Foreign Relations, 1865–1900*. New York: Harper and Row, 1976.

Campbell, Duncan Andrew. *English Public Opinion and the American Civil War*. Woodbridge, Eng.: Royal Historical Society, 2003.

Cannadine, David. *Ornamentalism: How the British Saw Their Empire*. Oxford: Oxford University Press, 2001.

Capaldi, Nicholas. *John Stuart Mill: A Biography*. New York: Cambridge University Press, 2004.

Carnes, Mark C., and Clyde Griffen, eds. *Meanings for Manhood: Constructions of Masculinity in Victorian America*. Chicago: University of Chicago Press, 1990.

Carwardine, Richard. *Transatlantic Revivalism: Popular Evangelicalism in Britain and America, 1790–1865*. Westport, Conn.: Greenwood, 1978.

Cary, Edward. *George William Curtis*. Boston: Houghton Mifflin, 1894.

Cashdollar, Charles D. *The Transformation of Theology, 1830–1890: Positivism and Protestant Thought in Britain and America*. Princeton: Princeton University Press, 1989.

Celozzi-Baldelli, Pia G. *Power Politics, Diplomacy, and the Avoidance of Hostilities between England and the United States in the Wake of the Civil War*. Translated by Elena Bertozzi and Cynthia DeNardi Ipsen. Lewiston, N.Y.: Mellen, 1998.

Charvat, William. *Literary Publishing in America*. Philadelphia: University of Pennsylvania Press, 1959.

Clark, J. Kitson. "'Statesmen in Disguise': Reflexions on the History of Neutrality in the Civil Service." In *The Victorian Revolution: Government and Society in Victoria's Britain*, edited by Peter Stansky, 61–88. New York: New Viewpoints, 1973.

Clarke, P. F. *Liberals and Social Democrats*. New York: Cambridge University Press, 1978.

Cmiel, Kenneth. *Democratic Eloquence: The Fight over Popular Speech in Nineteenth-Century America*. New York: Morrow, 1990.

Cohen, Nancy. *The Reconstruction of American Liberalism, 1865–1914*. Chapel Hill: University of North Carolina Press, 2002.

Collini, Stefan. *Arnold*. New York: Oxford University Press, 1988.

———. *English Pasts: Essays in History and Culture*. Oxford: Oxford University Press, 1999.

———. *Liberalism and Sociology: L. T. Hobhouse and Political Argument in England, 1880–1914*. Cambridge: Cambridge University Press, 1979.

———. "'Manly Fellows': Fawcett, Stephen, and the Liberal Temper." In *The Blind Victorian: Henry Fawcett and British Liberalism*, edited by Lawrence Goldman, 41–59. Cambridge: Cambridge University Press, 1989.

———. *Public Moralists: Political Thought and Intellectual Life in Britain, 1850–1930*. Oxford: Oxford University Press, 1991.

Collini, Stefan, Richard Whatmore, and Brian Young. *Economy, Polity, and Society: British Intellectual History, 1750–1950*. Cambridge: Cambridge University Press, 2000.

———. *History, Religion, and Culture: Essays in British Intellectual History, 1750–1950*. New York: Cambridge University Press, 2000.

Collini, Stefan, Donald Winch, and J. W. Burrow. *That Noble Science of Politics: A Study in Nineteenth-Century Intellectual History*. New York: Cambridge University Press, 1984.

Collison, Gary. *Shadrach Minkins: From Fugitive Slave to Citizen*. Cambridge: Harvard University Press, 1997.

Cook, Adrian. *The Alabama Claims: American Politics and Anglo-American Relations, 1865–1872*. Ithaca: Cornell University Press, 1975.

Cornford, James. "The Transformation of Conservatism in the Late Nineteenth Century." In *The Victorian Revolution: Government and Society in Victoria's Britain*, edited by Peter Stansky, 287–318. New York: New Viewpoints, 1973.

Cotkin, George. *William James, Public Philosopher*. Baltimore: Johns Hopkins University Press, 1990.

Coulling, Sidney. *Matthew Arnold and His Critics: A Study of Arnold's Controversies*. Athens: Ohio University Press, 1974.

Cowley, Malcolm. *After the Genteel Tradition: American Writers since 1910*. Gloucester, Mass.: Smith, 1959.

Crain, Caleb. *American Sympathy: Men, Friendship, and Literature in the New Nation*. New Haven: Yale University Press, 2001.

Crawford, Martin. "British Travelers and the Anglo-American Relationship in the 1850s." *Journal of American Studies* 12:2 (1978): 203–19.

Crook, David Paul. *American Democracy in English Politics, 1815–1850*. Oxford: Clarendon, 1965.

———. *The North, the South, and the Powers, 1861–1865*. New York: Wiley, 1974.

Cunningham, Hugh. "Jingoism in 1877–78." *Victorian Studies* 14:4 (1971): 429–53.

Dagger, Richard. *Civic Virtues: Rights, Citizenship, and Republican Liberalism*. New York: Oxford University Press, 1997.

Daunton, M. J., and Bernhard Rieger. *Meanings of Modernity: Britain in the Age of Imperialism and World Wars*. New York: Berg, 2001.

Davey, Arthur. *The British Pro-Boers, 1877–1902.* Cape Town, S.A.: Tafelberg, 1978.

Davis, David Brion. *Ante-Bellum Reform.* New York: Harper and Row, 1967.

———. *The Problem of Slavery in the Age of Revolution, 1770–1823.* New York: Oxford University Press, 1999.

———. *Slavery and Human Progress.* New York: Oxford University Press, 1984.

———. "Some Recent Directions in Cultural History." *American Historical Review* 73:3 (1968): 696–707.

Dawidoff, Robert. *The Genteel Tradition and the Sacred Rage: High Culture vs. Democracy in Adams, James, and Santayana.* Chapel Hill: University of North Carolina Press, 1992.

DeLaura, David. *Hebrew and Hellene: Newman, Arnold, and Pater.* Austin: University of Texas Press, 1969.

———. "Matthew Arnold and the American 'Literary Class': Unpublished Correspondence and Some Further Reasons." *Bulletin of the New York Public Library* 70:4 (1966): 229–50.

DiMaggio, Paul. "Cultural Entrepreneurship in Nineteenth-Century Boston: The Creation of an Organizational Base for High Culture in America." *Media, Culture, and Society* 4:1 (1982): 33–50.

———. "Cultural Entrepreneurship in Nineteenth-Century Boston, Part II: The Classification and Framing of American Art." *Media, Culture, and Society* 4:4 (1982): 303–22.

Dobson, John M. *Politics in the Gilded Age: A New Perspective on Reform.* New York: Praeger, 1972.

Donald, David Herbert. *Charles Sumner.* New York: Da Capo, 1996.

Douglas, Ann. *The Feminization of American Culture.* New York: Knopf, 1977.

Drescher, Seymour. "The Ending of the Slave Trade and the Evolution of European Scientific Racism." *Social Science History* 14:3 (1990): 415–50.

———. *The Mighty Experiment: Free Labor versus Slavery in British Emancipation.* New York: Oxford University Press, 2002.

———. "Public Opinion and the Destruction of British Colonial Slavery." In *From Slavery to Freedom: Comparative Studies in the Rise and Fall of Atlantic Slavery*, 57–86. New York: New York University Press, 1999.

———. "Servile Insurrection and John Brown's Body in Europe." *Journal of American History* 80:2 (1993): 499–524.

Dubbert, Joe L. *A Man's Place: Masculinity in Transition.* Englewood Cliffs, N.J.: Prentice-Hall, 1979.

Duberman, Martin B. *James Russell Lowell.* Boston: Houghton Mifflin, 1966.

DuBois, Ellen Carol. *Feminism and Suffrage.* Ithaca: Cornell University Press, 1999.

Dubrulle, Hugh. "'We Are Threatened with . . . Anarchy and Ruin': Fear of Americanization and the Emergence of an Anglo-Saxon Confederacy in England during the American Civil War." *Albion* 33:4 (2002): 583–613.

Duffy, Timothy P. "The Gender of Letters: Charles Eliot Norton and the Decline of the Amateur Intellectual Tradition." *New England Quarterly* 69:1 (1996): 91–109.

Duke, Alex. *Importing Oxbridge: English Residential Colleges and American Universities.* New Haven: Yale University Press, 1996.

Durrans, P. J. "A Two-Edged Sword: The Liberal Attack on Disraelian Imperialism." *Journal of Imperial and Commonwealth History* 10:3 (1982): 262–84.

Edel, Leon. *Henry James: A Life*. New York: Harper and Row, 1985.

Edelstein, Tilden G. "Emily Dickinson and Her Mentor in Feminist Perspective." In *Nineteenth-Century Women Writers of the English-Speaking World*, edited by Rhoda B. Nathan, 37–43. New York: Greenwood, 1986.

———. *Strange Enthusiasm: A Life of Thomas Wentworth Higginson*. New Haven: Yale University, 1968.

Edwards, Rebecca. *Angels in the Machinery: Gender in American Party Politics from the Civil War to the Progressive Era*. New York: Oxford University Press, 1997.

Eisenach, Eldon J., ed. *Mill and the Moral Character of Liberalism*. University Park: Pennsylvania State University Press, 1998.

Eldridge, C. C. *England's Mission: The Imperial Idea in the Age of Gladstone and Disraeli, 1868–1880*. London: Macmillan, 1973.

Elkins, Stanley M. *Slavery: A Problem in American Institutional and Intellectual Life*. Chicago: University of Chicago Press, 1959.

Ellison, Julie K. *Cato's Tears and the Making of Anglo-American Emotion*. Chicago: University of Chicago Press, 1999.

Ellison, Mary. *Support for Secession: Lancashire and the American Civil War*. Chicago: University of Chicago Press, 1972.

Epstein, James. "'America' in the Victorian Cultural Imagination." In *Anglo-American Attitudes: From Revolution to Partnership*, edited by Fred M. Leventhal and Roland Quinault, 107–23. Burlington, Vt.: Ashgate, 2000.

Everett, Edwin Mallard. *The Party of Humanity: The "Fortnightly Review" and Its Contributors, 1865–1874*. Chapel Hill: University of North Carolina Press, 1939.

Farr, Cecelia Konchar. *Reading Oprah: How Oprah's Book Club Changed the Way America Reads*. Albany: State University of New York Press, 2005.

Faust, Drew Gilpin. *A Sacred Circle: The Dilemma of the Intellectual in the Old South*. Baltimore: Johns Hopkins University Press, 1977.

Feinstein, Howard M. *Becoming William James*. Ithaca: Cornell University Press, 1984.

Ferguson, John Henry. *American Diplomacy and the Boer War*. Philadelphia: University of Pennsylvania Press, 1939.

Feske, Victor. *From Belloc to Churchill: Private Scholars, Public Culture, and the Crisis of British Liberalism, 1900–1939*. Chapel Hill: University of North Carolina Press, 1996.

Feuchtwanger, E. J. *Democracy and Empire: Britain, 1865–1914*. London: Arnold, 1985.

Filene, Peter G. *Him/Her/Self: Gender Identities in Modern America*. 3rd ed. Baltimore: Johns Hopkins University Press, 1998.

Filler, Louis. "The Early Godkin: Toward an Evaluation of a Significant Victorian." *Historian* 17:1 (1955): 43–66.

Finn, Margot C. *After Chartism: Class and Nation in English Radical Politics, 1848–1874*. Cambridge: Cambridge University Press, 1993.

Fishkin, James S. *Democracy and Deliberation: New Directions for Democratic Reform*. New Haven: Yale University Press, 1991.

Foerster, Norman. *American Criticism: A Study in Literary Theory from Poe to the Present*. Boston: Houghton Mifflin, 1928.

Foner, Eric. *Nothing but Freedom: Emancipation and Its Legacy*. Baton Rouge: Louisiana State University Press, 1983.

———. *Reconstruction: America's Unfinished Revolution, 1863–1877*. New York: Harper and Row, 1988.

Foner, Philip S. *British Labor and the American Civil War*. New York: Holmes and Meier, 1981.

Foner, Philip S., and Richard C. Winchester. *The Anti-Imperialist Reader: A Documentary History of Anti-Imperialism in the United States*. 2 vols. New York: Holmes and Meier, 1984.

Foote, Lorien. *Seeking the One Great Remedy: Francis George Shaw and Nineteenth-Century Reform*. Athens: Ohio University Press, 2003.

Franklin, John Hope, ed. *Three Negro Classics*. New York: Avon, 1965.

Fredrickson, George M. *The Black Image in the White Mind: The Debate on Afro-American Character and Destiny, 1817–1914*. New York: Harper and Row, 1971.

———. *The Inner Civil War: Northern Intellectuals and the Crisis of the Union*. New York: Harper and Row, 1965.

Freeden, Michael. *The New Liberalism: An Ideology of Social Reform*. Oxford: Clarendon, 1978.

Furstenberg, François. "Beyond Freedom and Slavery: Autonomy, Virtue, and Resistance in Early American Political Discourse." *Journal of American History* 89:4 (2003): 1295–1339.

Gardner, Lloyd C. *Safe for Democracy: The Anglo-American Response to Revolution, 1913–1923*. New York: Oxford University Press, 1984.

Garrison, Dee. *Apostles of Culture: The Public Librarian and American Society, 1876–1920*. New York: Free Press, 1979.

Gay, Peter. *The Cultivation of Hatred*. Vol. 3 of *The Bourgeois Experience: Victoria to Freud*. New York: Norton, 1993.

Gelber, Lionel Morris. *The Rise of Anglo-American Friendship: A Study in World Politics, 1898–1906*. Hamden, Conn.: Archon, 1966.

Gerlach, Murney. *British Liberalism and the United States: Political and Social Thought in the Late Victorian Age*. New York: Palgrave, 2001.

Gerstle, Gary. "The Protean Character of American Liberalism." *American Historical Review* 99:4 (1994): 1043–73.

Gibson, William. "Mark Twain and Howells: Anti-Imperialists." *New England Quarterly* 20:4 (1947): 435–70.

Gohdes, Clarence. *American Literature in Nineteenth Century England*. New York: Columbia University Press, 1944.

Goldman, Lawrence. "Exceptionalism and Internationalism: The Origins of American Social Science Reconsidered." *Journal of Historical Sociology* 11:1 (1998): 1–36.

———. *Science, Reform, and Politics in Victorian Britain: The Social Science Association, 1857–1886*. Cambridge: Cambridge University Press, 2002.

———, ed. *The Blind Victorian: Henry Fawcett and British Liberalism*. New York: Cambridge University Press, 1989.

Gossett, Thomas F. *Race: The History of an Idea in America*. Dallas: Southern Methodist University Press, 1963.

Gougeon, Len. *Virtue's Hero: Emerson, Antislavery, and Reform*. Athens: University of Georgia Press, 1990.

Graff, Gerald. *Professing Literature: An Institutional History*. Chicago: University of Chicago Press, 1987.

Graff, Gerald, and Reginald Gibbons. *Criticism in the University*. Evanston, Ill.: Northwestern University Press, 1985.

Grant, Mary Hetherington. *Private Woman, Public Person: An Account of the Life of Julia Ward Howe from 1819–1868*. Brooklyn, N.Y.: Carlson, 1994.

Gray, John. *Liberalisms: Essays in Political Philosophy*. London: Routledge, Chapman, and Hall, 1989.

Gray, Walter D. *Interpreting American Democracy in France: The Career of Édouard Laboulaye, 1811–1883*. Newark: University of Delaware Press, 1994.

Grimes, Alan Pendleton. *The Political Liberalism of the New York "Nation," 1865–1932*. Chapel Hill: University of North Carolina Press, 1948.

Grodzins, Dean. *American Heretic: Theodore Parker and Transcendentalism*. Chapel Hill: University of North Carolina Press, 2002.

Gross, John J. *The Rise and Fall of the Man of Letters: Aspects of English Literary Life since 1800*. London: Penguin, 1991.

Gunn, Simon. *The Public Culture of the Victorian Middle Class: Ritual and Authority and the English Industrial City, 1840–1914*. Manchester, Eng.: Manchester University Press, 2000.

Guth, Christine M. E. *Longfellow's Tattoos: Tourism, Collecting, and Japan*. Seattle: University of Washington Press, 2004.

Gutmann, Amy, and Dennis Thompson. *Democracy and Disagreement*. Cambridge: Belknap Press of Harvard University Press, 1996.

Habermas, Jürgen. *Between Facts and Norms: Contributions to a Discourse Theory of Law and Democracy*. Translated by William Rehg. Cambridge: MIT Press, 1998.

———. *The Structural Transformation of the Public Sphere*. Cambridge: MIT Press, 1989.

Habich, Robert D. "Emerson's Reluctant Foe: Andrews Norton and the Transcendental Controversy." *New England Quarterly* 65:2 (1992): 208–37.

Hale, Edward Everett. *James Russell Lowell and His Friends*. Boston: Houghton Mifflin, 1899.

Hall, Catherine. *Civilising Subjects: Colony and Metropole in the English Imagination*. Chicago: University of Chicago Press, 2002.

———. "Competing Masculinities: Thomas Carlyle, John Stuart Mill, and the Case of Governor Eyre." In *White, Male, and Middle-Class: Explorations in Feminism and History*, 255–95. New York: Routledge, 1992.

———. "The Economy of Intellectual Prestige: Thomas Carlyle, John Stuart Mill, and the Case of Governor Eyre." *Cultural Critique* 12 (1989): 167–96.

Hall, Catherine, Keith McClelland, and Jane Rendall. *Defining the Victorian Nation: Class, Race, Gender, and the British Reform Act of 1867*. Cambridge: Cambridge University Press, 2000.

Hall, David D. *Cultures of Print: Essays in the History of the Book*. Amherst: University of Massachusetts Press, 1996.

————. "The 'Higher Journalism' and the Politics of Culture in Mid–Nineteenth Century America." Unpublished paper in author's possession.

————. "The Victorian Connection." In *Victorian America*, edited by Daniel Walker Howe, 81–94. Philadelphia: University of Pennsylvania Press, 1976.

————. "A World Turned Upside Down?" *Reviews in American History* 18:1 (1990): 10–14.

Hall, Peter Dobkin. *The Organization of American Culture, 1700–1900: Private Institutions, Elites, and the Origins of American Nationality*. New York: New York University Press, 1982.

Hamburger, Joseph. "Individuality and Moral Reform: The Rhetoric of Liberty and the Reality of Restraint in Mill's *On Liberty*." *Political Science Reviewer* 24 (1995): 7–70.

————. *John Stuart Mill on Liberty and Control*. Princeton: Princeton University Press, 1999.

Hamer, D. A. *John Morley: Liberal Intellectual in Politics*. Oxford: Clarendon, 1968.

Hampton, Mark. "Liberalism, the Press, and the Construction of the Public Sphere: Theories of the Press in Britain, 1830–1914." *Victorian Periodicals Review* 37:1 (2004): 72–92.

————. *Visions of the Press in Britain, 1850–1950*. Urbana: University of Illinois Press, 2004.

Hansen, Jonathan M. *The Lost Promise of Patriotism: Debating American Identity, 1890–1920*. Chicago: University of Chicago Press, 2003.

Harp, Gillis J. *Positivist Republic: August Comte and the Reconstruction of American Liberalism, 1865–1920*. University Park: Pennsylvania State University Press, 1995.

Harrington, Fred Harvey. "Literary Aspects of American Anti-Imperialism, 1898–1902." *New England Quarterly* 10:4 (1937): 650–67.

Harris, Neil. *The Artist in American Society: The Formative Years, 1790–1860*. New York: Braziller, 1966.

Harrison, Brian Howard. *The Transformation of British Politics, 1860–1995*. Oxford: Oxford University Press, 1996.

Hartz, Louis. *The Liberal Tradition in America: An Interpretation of American Political Thought since the Revolution*. New York: Harcourt, Brace, 1955.

Harvie, Christopher. "Ideology and Home Rule: James Bryce, A. V. Dicey, and Ireland, 1880–1887." *English Historical Review* 91:359 (1976): 298–314.

————. *The Lights of Liberalism: University Liberals and the Challenge of Democracy, 1860–1886*. London: Lane, 1976.

Haskell, Daniel C., comp. *"The Nation," Volumes 1–105, New York, 1865–1917, Indexes of Titles and Contributors*. Vol. 2, *Index of Contributors*. New York: New York Public Library, 1953.

Haskell, Thomas L. *The Emergence of Professional Social Science: The American Social Science Association and the Nineteenth-Century Crisis of Authority*. Urbana: University of Illinois Press, 1977.

————. "Taking Exception to Exceptionalism." *Reviews in American History* 28:1 (2000): 151–66.

Hawkins, Angus. *British Party Politics, 1852–1886*. New York: St. Martin's, 1998.

Hawkins, Hugh. *Between Harvard and America: The Educational Leadership of Charles W. Eliot*. New York: Oxford University Press, 1972.

Held, David. *Models of Democracy*. Stanford: Stanford University Press, 1987.

Hernon, Joseph M. "The Use of the American Civil War in the Debate over Irish Home Rule." *American Historical Review* 69:4 (1964): 1022–26.

Herrick, Francis H. "The Second Reform Movement in Britain, 1850–1865." *Journal of the History of Ideas* 9:2 (1948): 174–92.

Hess, Earl J. *Liberty, Virtue, and Progress: Northerners and Their War for the Union*. New York: New York University Press, 1988.

Heyck, T. W. *The Transformation of Intellectual Life in Victorian England*. New York: St. Martin's, 1982.

Higginson, Mary Potter Thacher. *Thomas Wentworth Higginson: The Story of His Life*. Boston: Houghton Mifflin, 1914.

Higham, John. *From Boundlessness to Consolidation: The Transformation of American Culture, 1848–1860*. Ann Arbor, Mich.: Clements Library, 1969.

———. "The Reorientation of American Culture in the 1890s." In *The Origins of Modern Consciousness: Essays by John Higham*, edited by John Weiss, 25–48. Detroit: Wayne State University Press, 1965.

Higham, John, and Carl Guarneri. *Hanging Together: Unity and Diversity in American Culture*. New Haven: Yale University Press, 2001.

Hilton, Boyd. "Manliness, Masculinity, and the Mid-Victorian Temperament." In *The Blind Victorian: Henry Fawcett and British Liberalism*, edited by Lawrence Goldman, 60–70. Cambridge: Cambridge University Press, 1989.

Himmelfarb, Gertrude. *Poverty and Compassion: The Moral Imagination of the Late Victorians*. New York: Knopf, 1991.

———. *Victorian Minds*. New York: Knopf, 1968.

Hirshson, Stanley P. *Farewell to the Bloody Shirt: Northern Republicans and the Southern Negro, 1877–1893*. Gloucester, Mass.: Smith, 1968.

Hitchens, Christopher. *Blood, Class, and Nostalgia: Anglo-American Ironies*. New York: Farrar, Straus, and Giroux, 1990.

Hixson, William B., Jr. *Moorfield Storey and the Abolitionist Tradition*. New York: Oxford University Press, 1972.

Hofstadter, Richard. *The Age of Reform: From Bryan to F.D.R.* New York: Knopf, 1955.

———. *Anti-Intellectualism in American Life*. New York: Knopf, 1966.

———. *The Idea of a Party System*. Berkeley: University of California Press, 1969.

Hoganson, Kristin L. *Fighting for American Manhood: How Gender Politics Provoked the Spanish-American and Philippine-American Wars*. New Haven: Yale University Press, 1998.

Hollinger, David A., and Charles Capper. *The American Intellectual Tradition*. 5th ed. New York: Oxford University Press, 2006.

Holloway, John. *The Victorian Sage: Studies in Argument*. London: Archon, 1953.

Holt, Thomas C. *The Problem of Freedom: Race, Labor, and Politics in Jamaica and Britain, 1832–1938*. Baltimore: Johns Hopkins University Press, 1992.

Hoogenboom, Ari Arthur. *Outlawing the Spoils: A History of the Civil Service Reform Movement, 1865–1883*. Urbana: University of Illinois Press, 1961.

Hoppen, K. Theodore. *The Mid-Victorian Generation, 1846–1886.* Oxford: Oxford University Press, 1998.

Horsman, Reginald. *Race and Manifest Destiny: The Origins of American Racial Anglo-Saxonism.* Cambridge: Harvard University Press, 1981.

Houghton, Walter Edwards. *The Victorian Frame of Mind, 1830–1870.* New Haven: Yale University Press for Wellesley College, 1957.

———. "Victorian Periodical Literature and the Articulate Classes." *Victorian Studies* 22:4 (1979): 389–412.

———, ed. *The Wellesley Index to Victorian Periodicals, 1824–1900.* 5 vols. Toronto: University of Toronto Press, 1966–1989.

Howard, Leon. *Victorian Knight-Errant: A Study of the Early Literary Career of James Russell Lowell.* Berkeley: University of California Press, 1952.

Howard, Michael. *War and the Liberal Conscience.* Oxford: Oxford University Press, 1981.

Howe, Daniel Walker. *American History in an Atlantic Context: An Inaugural Lecture Delivered before the University of Oxford on 3 June 1993.* Oxford: Clarendon Press, 1993.

———. *Making the American Self: From Jonathan Edwards to Abraham Lincoln.* Cambridge: Harvard University Press, 1997.

———. *The Political Culture of the American Whigs.* Chicago: University of Chicago Press, 1979.

———. *The Unitarian Conscience: Harvard Moral Philosophy, 1805–1861.* Cambridge: Harvard University Press, 1970.

———, ed. *Victorian America.* Philadelphia: University of Pennsylvania Press, 1976.

Howe, M. A. De Wolfe. *The "Atlantic Monthly" and Its Makers.* Boston: Atlantic Monthly Press, 1919.

———. *James Ford Rhodes: American Historian.* New York: Appleton, 1929.

———. *Later Years of the Saturday Club, 1870–1920.* Boston: Houghton Mifflin, 1927.

———. *Portrait of an Independent: Moorfield Storey, 1845–1929.* Boston: Houghton Mifflin, 1932.

Hubbell, Jay B. *Who Are the Major American Writers?: A Study of the Changing Literary Canon.* Durham, N.C.: Duke University Press, 1972.

Hyman, Harold M. "The Election of 1864." In *History of American Presidential Elections,* edited by Arthur M. Schlesinger Jr., 1155–1244. New York: Chelsea House, 1971.

Ingraham, Patricia W. *The Foundation of Merit: Public Service in American Democracy.* Baltimore: Johns Hopkins University Press, 1995.

Ions, Edmund S. *James Bryce and American Democracy, 1870–1922.* London: Macmillan, 1968.

Jackson, Leon. "The Reader Retailored: Thomas Carlyle, His American Audiences, and the Politics of Evidence." *Book History* 2 (1999): 146–72.

———. "The Social Construction of Thomas Carlyle's New England Reputation, 1834–1836." *Proceedings of the American Antiquarian Society* 106:1 (1996): 165–89.

Jacobson, Matthew Frye. *Barbarian Virtues: The United States Encounters Foreign Peoples at Home and Abroad, 1876–1917.* New York: Hill and Wang, 2000.

Jaher, Frederic Cople. *The Urban Establishment: Upper Strata in Boston, New York, Charleston, Chicago, and Los Angeles.* Urbana: University of Illinois Press, 1982.

Jenkins, Brian. *Britain and the War for the Union*. Montreal: McGill–Queen's University Press, 1974.

———. *Fenians and Anglo-American Relations during Reconstruction*. Ithaca: Cornell University Press, 1969.

Jenkins, T. A. *The Liberal Ascendancy, 1830–1886*. New York: St. Martin's, 1994.

———. *Parliament, Party, and Politics in Victorian Britain*. Manchester, Eng.: Manchester University Press, 1996.

John, Arthur. *The Best Years of the "Century": Richard Watson Gilder, "Scribner's Monthly," and the "Century Magazine," 1870–1909*. Urbana: University of Illinois Press, 1981.

Jones, Aled. *Powers of the Press: Newspapers, Power, and the Public in Nineteenth-Century England*. Aldershot, Eng.: Scolar, 1995.

Jones, Howard. "History and Mythology: The Crisis over British Intervention in the Civil War." In *The Union, the Confederacy, and the Atlantic Rim*, edited by Robert E. May, 29–67. West Lafayette, Ind.: Purdue University Press, 1995.

———. *Union in Peril: The Crisis over British Intervention in the Civil War*. Chapel Hill: University of North Carolina Press, 1992.

Jones, Howard Mumford. Introduction to *Army Life in a Black Regiment*, by Thomas Wentworth Higginson, iv–xvii. East Lansing: Michigan State University Press, 1960.

Jones, Iva G. "Trollope, Carlyle, and Mill on the Negro: An Episode in the History of Ideas." *Journal of Negro History* 52:3 (1967): 185–99.

Jordan, Donaldson, and Edwin J. Pratt. *Europe and the American Civil War*. Boston: Houghton Mifflin, 1931.

Jordy, William H. *Henry Adams: Scientific Historian*. New Haven: Yale University Press, 1952.

Josephson, Matthew. *The Politicos, 1865–1896*. New York: Harcourt Brace, 1938.

Judis, John B. *The Paradox of American Democracy: Elites, Special Interests, and the Betrayal of the Public Trust*. New York: Pantheon, 2000.

Kahan, Alan S. *Aristocratic Liberalism: The Social and Political Thought of Jacob Burckhardt, John Stuart Mill, and Alexis de Tocqueville*. New York: Oxford University Press, 1992.

———. *Liberalism in Nineteenth-Century Europe: The Political Culture of Limited Suffrage*. New York: Palgrave, 2003.

Kantrowitz, Stephen. *Ben Tillman and the Reconstruction of White Supremacy*. Chapel Hill: University of North Carolina Press, 2000.

Kaplan, Amy, and Donald E. Pease, eds. *Cultures of United States Imperialism*. Durham, N.C.: Duke University Press, 1993.

Kasson, John F. *Rudeness and Civility: Manners in Nineteenth-Century Urban America*. New York: Hill and Wang, 1990.

Kateb, George. "Democratic Individuality and the Meaning of Rights," In *Liberalism and the Moral Life*, edited by Nancy L. Rosenblum, 183–206. Cambridge: Harvard University Press, 1989.

Katz, Philip Mark. *From Appomattox to Montmartre: Americans and the Paris Commune*. Cambridge: Harvard University Press, 1998.

Keller, Morton. *Affairs of State: Public Life in Late Nineteenth Century America*. Cambridge: Harvard University Press, 1977.

Kelley, Robert. *The Transatlantic Persuasion: The Liberal-Democratic Mind in the Age of Gladstone*. New York: Knopf, 1969.

Kennedy, Robert C. "Crisis and Progress: The Rhetoric and Ideals of a Nineteenth-Century Reformer, George William Curtis." Ph.D. diss., University of Illinois, 1994.

Kenny, Anthony. *The History of the Rhodes Trust, 1902–1999*. New York: Oxford University Press, 2001.

Kent, Christopher. *Brains and Numbers: Elitism, Comtism, and Democracy in Mid-Victorian England*. Toronto: University of Toronto Press, 1977.

———. "Higher Journalism and the Mid-Victorian Clerisy." *Victorian Studies* 13:2 (1969): 181–98.

Keyssar, Alexander. *The Right to Vote: The Contested History of Democracy in the United States*. New York: Basic Books, 2000.

Kijinski, John L. "John Morley's 'English Men of Letters' Series and the Politics of Reading." *Victorian Studies* 34:2 (1991): 205–25.

Kinzer, Bruce L. *The Ballot Question in Nineteenth-Century English Politics*. New York: Garland, 1982.

———. "J. S. Mill and Irish Land: A Reassessment." *Historical Journal* 27:1 (1984): 111–27.

Kinzer, Bruce L., Ann P. Robson, and John M. Robson. *A Moralist in and out of Parliament: John Stuart Mill at Westminster, 1865–1868*. Toronto: University of Toronto Press, 1992.

Kirkland, Edward Chase. *Charles Francis Adams, Jr., 1835–1915: The Patrician at Bay*. Cambridge: Harvard University Press, 1965.

Kloppenberg, James T. "From Hartz to Tocqueville: Shifting the Focus from Liberalism to Democracy in America." In *The Democratic Experiment: New Directions in American Political History*, edited by Meg Jacobs, William J. Novak, and Julie E. Zelizer, 350–80. Princeton: Princeton University Press, 2003.

———. *Uncertain Victory: Social Democracy and Progressivism in European and American Thought, 1870–1920*. New York: Oxford University Press, 1986.

———. *The Virtues of Liberalism*. New York: Oxford University Press, 1998.

Knickerbocker, Frances Wentworth Cutler. *Free Minds: John Morley and His Friends*. Cambridge: Harvard University Press, 1943.

Knights, Ben. *The Idea of the Clerisy in the Nineteenth Century*. Cambridge: Cambridge University Press, 1978.

Knupfer, Peter. "A Crisis in Conservatism: Northern Unionism and the Harpers Ferry Raid." In *His Soul Goes Marching On: Responses to John Brown and the Harpers Ferry Raid*, edited by Paul Finkelman, 119–48. Charlottesville: University Press of Virginia, 1995.

Koss, Stephen E. *The Pro-Boers: The Anatomy of an Antiwar Movement*. Chicago: University of Chicago Press, 1973.

———. *The Rise and Fall of the Political Press in Britain*. Chapel Hill: University of North Carolina Press, 1981.

Kramer, Paul. "Empires, Exceptions, and Anglo-Saxons: Race and Rule between the

British and United States Empires, 1880–1910." *Journal of American History* 88:4 (2002): 1315–53.

LaFeber, Walter. *The New Empire: An Interpretation of American Expansion, 1860–1898.* Ithaca: Cornell University Press, 1963.

Landow, George P. *Elegant Jeremiahs: The Sage from Carlyle to Mailer.* Ithaca: Cornell University Press, 1986.

Lasch, Christopher. "The Anti-Imperialists, the Philippines, and the Inequality of Man." In *The World of Nations: Reflections on American History, Politics, and Culture,* 70–79. New York: Knopf, 1973.

———. *The Revolt of the Elites and the Betrayal of Democracy.* New York: Norton, 1995.

———. *The True and Only Heaven: Progress and Its Critics.* New York: Norton, 1991.

Lawrence, Jon. *Speaking for the People: Party, Language, and Popular Politics in England, 1867–1914.* Cambridge: Cambridge University Press, 1998.

Leach, William. *True Love and Perfect Union: The Feminist Reform of Sex and Society.* Middletown, Conn.: Wesleyan University Press, 1989.

Lears, T. J. Jackson. *No Place of Grace: Antimodernism and the Transformation of American Culture, 1880–1920.* New York: Pantheon, 1981.

Levenson, J. C. *The Mind and Art of Henry Adams.* Boston: Houghton Mifflin, 1957.

Leventhal, Fred M., and Roland Quinault, eds. *Anglo-American Attitudes: From Revolution to Partnership.* Burlington, Vt.: Ashgate, 2000.

Levine, Lawrence W. *Highbrow/Lowbrow: The Emergence of Cultural Hierarchy in America.* Cambridge: Harvard University Press, 1988.

Levy, David M. *How the Dismal Science Got Its Name: Classical Economics and the Ur-Text of Racial Politics.* Ann Arbor: University of Michigan Press, 2001.

Lewis, David Levering. *W. E. B. Du Bois: Biography of a Race, 1868–1919.* New York: Holt, 1993.

Liddle, Dallas. "Salesmen, Sportsmen, Mentors: Anonymity and Mid-Victorian Theories of Journalism." *Victorian Studies* 41:1 (1997): 31–68.

Lightman, Bernard. *The Origins of Agnosticism: Victorian Unbelief and the Limits of Knowledge.* Baltimore: Johns Hopkins University Press, 1987.

Linderman, Gerald F. *The Mirror of War: American Society and the Spanish-American War.* Ann Arbor: University of Michigan Press, 1974.

Lippincott, Benjamin E. *Victorian Critics of Democracy: Carlyle, Ruskin, Arnold, Stephen, Maine, Lecky.* Minneapolis: University of Minnesota Press, 1938.

Looby, Christopher. "'As Thoroughly Black as the Most Faithful Philanthropist Could Desire': Erotics of Race in Higginson's *Army Life in a Black Regiment.*" In *Race and the Subject of Masculinities,* edited by Harry Stecopoulos and Michael Uebel, 71–115. Durham, N.C.: Duke University Press, 1997.

———. "Flowers of Manhood: Race, Sex, and Floriculture from Thomas Wentworth Higginson to Robert Mapplethorpe." *Criticism* 37:1 (1995): 109–56.

Lorimer, Douglas A. *Colour, Class, and the Victorians: English Attitudes to the Negro in the Mid–Nineteenth Century.* Leicester, Eng.: Leicester University Press, 1978.

Love, Eric T. L. *Race over Empire: Racism and U.S. Imperialism.* Chapel Hill: University of North Carolina Pres, 2004.

Macedo, Stephen. *Liberal Virtues: Citizenship, Virtue, and Community in Liberal Constitutionalism*. New York: Oxford University Press, 1990.

Machin, Ian. *The Rise of Democracy in Britain, 1830–1918*. London: Macmillan, 2001.

Mack, Edward Clarence, and Walter Harry Green Armytage. *Thomas Hughes: The Life of the Author of "Tom Brown's Schooldays."* London: Benn, 1952.

MacPherson, C. B. *The Political Theory of Possessive Individualism: Hobbes to Locke*. Oxford: Clarendon, 1962.

Mandler, Peter. "'Race' and 'Nation' in Mid-Victorian Thought." In *British Intellectual History, 1750–1950: History, Religion, and Culture: Essays in British Intellectual History, 1750–1950*, edited by Stefan Collini, Richard Whatmore, and Brian Young, 224–44. Cambridge: Cambridge University Press, 2000.

Mangan, J. A., and James Walvin, eds. *Manliness and Morality: Middle-Class Masculinity in Britain and America, 1800–1940*. New York: St. Martin's, 1987.

Martellone, Anna Maria. "In the Name of Anglo-Saxondom, for Empire, and for Democracy: The Anglo-American Discourse, 1880–1920." In *Reflections on American Exceptionalism*, edited by David K. Adams and Cornelis A. van Minnen, 83–96. Staffordshire, Eng.: Keele University Press, 1994.

Martin, Ged. "The Cambridge Lectureship of 1866: A False Start in American Studies." *Journal of American Studies* 7:1 (1973): 17–29.

Matthew, H. C. G. *Gladstone, 1875–1898*. Oxford: Oxford University Press, 1995.

———. *The Liberal Imperialists: The Ideas and Politics of a Post-Gladstonian Élite*. Oxford: Oxford University Press, 1973.

———. "Rhetoric and Politics in Great Britain, 1860–1950." In *Politics and Social Change: Essays Presented to A. F. Thompson*, edited by P. J. Waller, 34–58. Oxford: Oxford University Press, 1987.

Mattson, Kevin. *Creating a Democratic Public: The Struggle for Urban Participatory Democracy during the Progressive Era*. University Park: Pennsylvania State University Press, 1998.

May, Ernest. *American Imperialism: A Speculative Essay*. New York: Atheneum, 1968,

May, Henry Farnham. *The End of American Innocence: A Study of the First Years of Our Own Time, 1912–1917*. New York: Knopf, 1959.

Mayor, Mara N. "Norton, Lowell, and Godkin: A Study of American Attitudes toward England, 1865–1885." Ph.D. diss., Yale University, 1969.

Mazurek, Raymond. "'I Have No Monarch in My Life': Feminism, Poetry, and Politics in Dickinson and Higginson." In *Patrons and Protégées: Gender, Friendship, and Writing in Nineteenth-Century America*, edited by Shirley Marchalonis, 122–40. New Brunswick, N.J.: Rutgers University Press, 1994.

McCarthy, Kathleen D. *Noblesse Oblige: Charity and Cultural Philanthropy in Chicago, 1849–1929*. Chicago: University of Chicago Press, 1982.

———. *Women's Culture: American Philanthropy and Art, 1830–1930*. Chicago: University of Chicago Press, 1991.

McClay, Wilfred M. *The Masterless: Self and Society in Modern America*. Chapel Hill: University of North Carolina Press, 1994.

McCormick, Edgar L. "Higginson, Emerson, and a National Literature." *ESQ: A Journal of the American Renaissance* 37 (1964): 71–74.

———. "Thomas Wentworth Higginson: Poetry Critic for the Nation, 1877–1903." *Serif* 2:3 (1965): 15–20.

McCormick, Richard L. "Antiparty Thought in the Gilded Age." In *The Party Period and Public Policy: American Politics from the Age of Jackson to the Progressive Era*, 228–59. New York: Oxford University Press, 1986.

McGerr, Michael E. *The Decline of Popular Politics: The American North, 1865–1928*. New York: Oxford University Press, 1986.

———. "Political Style and Women's Power, 1830–1930." *Journal of American History* 77:3 (1990): 864–85.

McGreevy, John. *Catholicism and American Freedom: A History*. New York: Norton, 2003.

McLachlan, James. "American Colleges and the Transmission of Culture: The Case of the Mugwumps." In *The Hofstadter Aegis: A Memorial*, edited by Stanley Elkins and Eric McKitrick, 184–206. New York: Knopf, 1974.

McPherson, James M. *The Abolitionist Legacy: From Reconstruction to the NAACP*. Princeton: Princeton University Press, 1975.

———. *Ordeal by Fire: The Civil War and Reconstruction*. New York: Knopf, 1982.

———. *The Struggle for Equality: Abolitionists and the Negro in the Civil War and Reconstruction*. Princeton: Princeton University Press, 1964.

———. "'The Whole Family of Man': Lincoln and the Last Best Hope Abroad." In *The Union, the Confederacy, and the Atlantic Rim*, edited by Robert E. May, 131–58. West Lafayette, Ind.: Purdue University Press, 1995.

McWilliam, Rohan. "Radicalism and Popular Culture: The Tichborne Case and the Politics of 'Fair Play,' 1867–1886." In *Currents of Radicalism: Popular Radicalism, Organised Labour, and Party Politics in Britain, 1850–1914*, edited by Eugenio F. Biagini and Alastair J. Reid, 44–64. New York: Cambridge University Press, 1991.

Mehta, Uday Singh. *Liberalism and Empire: A Study in Nineteenth-Century British Liberal Thought*. Chicago: University of Chicago Press, 1999.

Menand, Louis. *The Metaphysical Club*. New York: Farrar, Straus, and Giroux, 2001.

———. *Pragmatism: A Reader*: New York: Vintage, 1997.

Meyer, Howard N. *Colonel of the Black Regiment: The Life of Thomas Wentworth Higginson*. New York: Norton, 1967.

Milder, Robert. "'The American Scholar' as Cultural Event." *Prospects* 16 (1991): 119–47.

Miller, Dale E. "John Stuart Mill's Civic Liberalism." *History of Political Thought* 21:1 (2000): 88–113.

Milne, Gordon. *George William Curtis and the Genteel Tradition*. Bloomington: Indiana University Press, 1956.

Mintz, Steven, *Moralists and Modernizers: America's Pre–Civil War Reformers*. Baltimore: Johns Hopkins University Press, 1995.

Montgomery, David. *Beyond Equality: Labor and the Radical Republicans, 1862–1872*. New York: Knopf, 1967.

———. *Citizen Worker: The Experience of Workers in the United States with Democracy and the Free Market during the Nineteenth Century*. Cambridge: Cambridge University Press, 1993.

Moorhead, James H. *American Apocalypse: Yankee Protestants and the Civil War*. New Haven: Yale University Press, 1978.

Morgan, H. Wayne. *From Hayes to McKinley: National Party Politics, 1877–1896.* Syracuse, N.Y.: Syracuse University Press, 1969.

Mott, Frank Luther. *American Journalism: A History, 1690–1960.* 3rd ed. New York: Macmillan, 1962.

———. *A History of American Magazines.* Vol. 2, *1850–1865.* Cambridge: Harvard University Press, 1938.

———. *A History of American Magazines.* Vol. 4, *1885–1905.* Cambridge: Harvard University Press, 1957.

Mulanax, Richard B. *The Boer War in American Politics and Diplomacy.* Lanham, Md.: University Press of America, 1994.

Newfield, Christopher. *The Emerson Effect: Individualism and Submission in America.* Chicago: University of Chicago Press, 1996.

Newsome, David. *The Victorian World Picture: Perceptions and Introspections in an Age of Change.* London: Murray, 1997.

Nicholson, Peter. "The Reception and Early Reputation of Mill's Political Thought." In *The Cambridge Companion to Mill,* edited by John Skorupski, 464–96. Cambridge: Cambridge University Press, 1998.

Ninkovich, Frank. *The United States and Imperialism.* Oxford: Blackwell, 2001.

Noer, Thomas J. *Briton, Boer, and Yankee: The United States and South Africa, 1870–1914.* Kent, Ohio: Kent State University Press, 1978.

O'Brien, Michael. *Conjectures of Order: Intellectual Life and the American South, 1810–1860.* 2 vols. Chapel Hill: University of North Carolina Press, 2004.

O'Day, Alan. *Irish Home Rule, 1867–1921.* New York: St. Martin's 1998.

O'Grady, Joseph P. *Irish-Americans and Anglo-American Relations, 1880–1888.* New York: Arno, 1976.

Okin, Susan Moller. "Humanist Liberalism." In *Liberalism and the Moral Life,* edited by Nancy L. Rosenblum, 39–53. Cambridge: Harvard University Press, 1989.

Ostrander, Gilman M. *Republic of Letters: The American Intellectual Community, 1776–1865.* Madison, Wis.: Madison House, 1999.

Painter, Nell Irvin. *Standing at Armageddon: The United States, 1877–1919.* New York: Norton, 1987.

Paludan, Phillip S. *A Covenant with Death: The Constitution, Law, and Equality in the Civil War Era.* Urbana: University of Illinois Press, 1975.

———. *A People's Contest: The Union and the Civil War, 1861–1865.* 2nd ed. Lawrence: University Press of Kansas, 1996.

Park, Joseph H. "Thomas Hughes and Slavery." *Journal of Negro History* 12:4 (1927): 590–605.

Park, T. Peter. "John Stuart Mill, Thomas Carlyle, and the U.S. Civil War." *Historian* 54:1 (1991): 93–106.

Parrington, Vernon Louis. *Main Currents in American Thought: An Interpretation of American Literature from the Beginnings to 1920.* 3 vols. New York: Harcourt, Brace, 1927–30.

Parrish, Peter. "Gladstone and America." In *Gladstone,* edited by Peter J. Jagger, 85–103. London: Hambledon, 1998.

Parry, Jonathan. *The Rise and Fall of Liberal Government in Victorian Britain*. New Haven: Yale University Press, 1993.

Peatling, Gary. *British Opinion and Irish Self-Government, 1865–1925: From Unionism to Liberal Commonwealth*. Dublin, Ire.: Irish Academic Press, 2001.

Pelling, Henry. *America and the British Left, from Bright to Bevan*. London: Black, 1956.

Perkins, Bradford. *The Great Rapprochement: England and the United States, 1895–1914*. New York: Atheneum, 1968.

Persons, Stow. *The Decline of American Gentility*. New York: Columbia University Press, 1973.

———. *Free Religion: An American Faith*. New Haven: Yale University Press, 1947.

Phillips, Paul T. *The Controversialist: An Intellectual Life of Goldwin Smith*. Westport, Conn.: Praeger, 2002.

Pletcher, David M. *The Awkward Years: American Foreign Relations under Garfield and Arthur*. Columbia: University of Missouri Press, 1962.

Pocock, J. G. A. *Politics, Language, and Time: Essays on Political Thought and History*. New York: Atheneum, 1971.

Pombeni, Paolo. "Starting in Reason, Ending in Passion: Bryce, Lowell, Ostrogorski, and the Problem of Democracy." *Historical Journal* 37:2 (1994): 319–41.

Porter, Bernard. *Absent-Minded Imperialists: Empire, Society, and Culture in Britain*. New York: Oxford University Press, 2005.

———. *Critics of Empire: British Radical Attitudes to Colonialism in Africa, 1895–1914*. London: Macmillan, 1968.

Potter, David M. *The Impending Crisis, 1848–1861*. New York: Harper and Row, 1976.

Pugh, Martin. "The Limits of Liberalism: Liberals and Women's Suffrage, 1867–1914." In *Citizenship and Community: Liberals, Radicals, and Collective Identities in the British Isles, 1865–1931*, edited by Eugenio F. Biagini, 45–64. New York: Cambridge University Press, 1996.

———. *The Making of Modern British Politics, 1867–1939*. Oxford: Blackwell, 1993.

Putney, Clifford. *Muscular Christianity: Manhood and Sports in Protestant America, 1880–1920*. Cambridge: Harvard University Press, 2001.

Quigley, David. *Second Founding: New York City, Reconstruction, and the Making of American Democracy*. New York: Hill and Wang, 2004.

Quinault, Roland. "Anglo-American Attitudes to Democracy from Lincoln to Churchill." In *Anglo-American Attitudes: From Revolution to Partnership*, edited by Fred M. Leventhal and Roland Quinault, 124–41. Burlington, Vt.: Ashgate, 2000.

Radway, Janice A. *A Feeling for Books: The Book-of-the-Month Club, Literary Taste, and Middle-Class Desire*. Chapel Hill: University of North Carolina Press, 1997.

Raleigh, John Henry. *Matthew Arnold and American Culture*. Berkeley: University of California Press, 1957.

Read, Donald. *Cobden and Bright: A Victorian Political Partnership*. London: Arnold, 1967.

Renehan, Edward. *The Secret Six: The True Tale of the Men Who Conspired with John Brown*. New York: Crown, 1995.

Reuter, Bertha Ann. *Anglo-American Relations during the Spanish-American War*. New York: Macmillan, 1924.

Reynolds, David. *John Brown, Abolitionist*. New York: Knopf, 2005.

Reynolds, Katherine Chaddock. "A Canon of Democratic Intent: Reinterpreting the Roots of the Great Books Movement." *History of Higher Education Annual* 22 (2002): 5–32.

Richardson, Heather Cox. *The Death of Reconstruction*. Cambridge: Harvard University Press, 2001.

Roach, John. "Liberalism and the Victorian Intelligentsia." In *The Victorian Revolution: Government and Society in Victoria's Britain*, edited by Peter Stansky, 323–53. New York: New Viewpoints, 1973.

———. "Victorian Universities and the National Intelligentsia." *Victorian Studies* 3:2 (1959–60): 131–50.

Robbins, William. "Matthew Arnold and Ireland." *University of Toronto Quarterly* 17 (1947): 52–67.

Robertson, Andrew W. *The Language of Democracy: Political Rhetoric in the United States and Britain, 1790–1900*. Ithaca: Cornell University Press, 1995.

Robson, John. "Civilization and Culture as Moral Concepts." In *The Cambridge Companion to Mill*, edited by John Skorupski, 338–71. Cambridge: Cambridge University Press, 1998.

Rodgers, Daniel T. *Atlantic Crossings: Social Politics in a Progressive Era*. Cambridge: Harvard University Press, 1998.

———. *Contested Truths: Keywords in American Politics since Independence*. New York: Basic Books, 1987.

———. "Exceptionalism." In *Imagined Histories: American Historians Interpret the Past*, edited by Anthony Molho and Gordon S. Wood, 21–40. Princeton: Princeton University Press, 1998.

———. *The Work Ethic in Industrial America, 1850–1920*. Chicago: University of Chicago Press, 1974.

Rodier, Katharine. "'Astra Castra': Emily Dickinson, Thomas Wentworth Higginson, and Harriet Prescott Spofford." In *Separate Spheres No More: Gender Convergence in American Literature, 1830–1939*, edited by Monika M. Elbert, 50–72. Tuscaloosa: University of Alabama Press, 2000.

Roper, Jon. *Democracy and Its Critics: Anglo-American Democratic Thought in the Nineteenth Century*. Boston: Unwin Hyman, 1989.

Rorty, Richard. *Achieving Our Country: Leftist Thought in Twentieth-Century America*. Cambridge: Harvard University Press, 1997.

Rose, Anne C. *Transcendentalism as a Social Movement*. New Haven: Yale University Press, 1981.

———. *Victorian America and the Civil War*. New York: Cambridge University Press, 1992.

Rose, Jonathan. *The Intellectual Life of the British Working Class*. New Haven: Yale University Press, 2000.

Rosenberg, John D. *Carlyle and the Burden of History*. Cambridge: Harvard University Press, 1985.

Rosenblum, Nancy L. *Another Liberalism: Romanticism and the Reconstruction of Liberal Thought*. Cambridge: Harvard University Press, 1987.

————. "Pluralism and Self-Defense." In *Liberalism and the Moral Life*, edited by Nancy L. Rosenblum, 207–26. Cambridge: Harvard University Press, 1989.

————, ed. *Liberalism and the Moral Life*. Cambridge: Harvard University Press, 1989.

Ross, Dorothy. "Liberalism." In *Encyclopedia of American History*, edited by Jack P. Green, 2:750–63. New York: Scribner's, 1984.

————. "Liberalism and American Exceptionalism." *Intellectual History Newsletter* 24 (2002): 72–83.

————. *The Origins of American Social Science*. Cambridge: Cambridge University Press, 1991.

Ross, Earle Dudley. *The Liberal Republican Movement*. New York: Holt, 1919.

Rossbach, Jeffery S. *Ambivalent Conspirators: John Brown, the Secret Six, and a Theory of Black Political Violence*. Philadelphia: University of Pennsylvania Press, 1982.

Rotunda, Ronald D. *The Politics of Language: Liberalism as Word and Symbol*. Iowa City: University of Iowa Press, 1986.

Rotundo, E. Anthony. *American Manhood: Transformations in Masculinity from the Revolution to the Modern Era*. New York: Basic Books, 1993.

Rowe, John Carlos. *New Essays on the Education of Henry Adams*. New York: Cambridge University Press, 1996.

Rubin, Joan Shelley. *The Making of Middlebrow Culture*. Chapel Hill: University of North Carolina Press, 1992.

Ryan, Alan. *J. S. Mill*. London: Routledge and Kegan Paul, 1974.

————. "Mill in a Liberal Landscape." In *The Cambridge Companion to Mill*, edited by John Skorupski, 497–54. Cambridge: Cambridge University Press, 1998.

Sacks, Kenneth S. *Understanding Emerson: "The American Scholar" and His Struggle for Self-Reliance*. Princeton: Princeton University Press, 2003.

Samuels, Ernest. *Henry Adams: The Major Phase*. Cambridge: Belknap Press of Harvard University Press, 1964.

————. *Henry Adams: The Middle Years*. Cambridge: Belknap Press of Harvard University Press, 1958.

————. *The Young Henry Adams*. Cambridge: Belknap Press of Harvard University Press, 1948.

Satterfield, Jay. *The World's Best Books: Taste, Culture, and the Modern Library*. Amherst: University of Massachusetts Press, 2002.

Schaeper, Thomas J., and Kathleen Schaeper. *Cowboys into Gentlemen: Rhodes Scholars, Oxford, and the Creation of an American Elite*. New York: Berghahn, 1998.

Schirmer, Daniel. *Republic or Empire?: American Resistance to the Philippine War*. Cambridge, Mass.: Schenkman, 1972.

Schmeller, Mark G. "The Importance of Having Opinions: Philosophy, Popular Sciences of Mind, and the Victorian Self." Unpublished paper in author's possession.

Schmidt, Barbara Quinn. "In the Shadow of Thackeray: Leslie Stephen as the Editor of the *Cornhill Magazine*." In *Innovators and Preachers: The Role of the Editor in Victorian England*, edited by Joel H. Wiener, 77–96. Westport, Conn.: Greenwood, 1985.

Schmidt, Leigh Eric. *Restless Souls: The Making of American Spirituality*. San Francisco: Harper and Row, 2005.

Schudson, Michael. *Discovering the News: A Social History of American Newspapers*. New
    York: Basic Books, 1978.
———. *The Good Citizen: A History of American Civic Life*. New York: Free Press, 1998.
———. *The Power of News*. Cambridge: Harvard University Press, 1995.
Scott, Patrick Greig, and Pauline Fletcher, eds. *Culture and Education in Victorian
    England*. Lewisburg, Pa.: Bucknell University Press, 1990.
Sedgwick, Ellery. *The "Atlantic Monthly," 1857–1909: Yankee Humanism at High Tide and
    Ebb*. Amherst: University of Massachusetts Press, 1994.
Semmel, Bernard. *Imperialism and Social Reform: English Social-Imperial Thought, 1895–
    1914*. New York: Doubleday, 1968.
———. *Jamaican Blood and Victorian Conscience: The Governor Eyre Controversy*. Boston:
    Houghton Mifflin, 1963.
———. *John Stuart Mill and the Pursuit of Virtue*. New Haven: Yale University Press,
    1984.
Shain, Charles E. "The English Novelists and the American Civil War." *American
    Quarterly* 14:3 (1962): 399–421.
Shannon, Richard. *Gladstone and the Bulgarian Agitation 1876*. London: Nelson, 1963.
———. *Gladstone: Heroic Minister, 1865–1898*. London: Lane, 1999.
Sheehan, James J. "Some Reflections on Liberalism in Comparative Perspective." In
    Deutschland und der Westen, edited by Henning Köhler, 44–58. Berlin: Colloquium,
    1984.
Silbey, Joel H. *The American Political Nation, 1838–1893*. Stanford, Calif.: Stanford
    University Press, 1991.
Simpson, Brooks D. *The Political Education of Henry Adams*. Columbia: University of
    South Carolina Press, 1996.
Simpson, Lewis P. *The Man of Letters in New England and the South: Essays on the History
    of the Literary Vocation in America*. Baton Rouge: Louisiana State University Press,
    1973.
Singal, Daniel Joseph. "Towards a Definition of American Modernism." *American
    Quarterly* 39:1 (1987): 7–26.
———. *The War Within: From Victorian to Modernist Thought in the South, 1919–1945*.
    Chapel Hill: University of North Carolina Press, 1982.
Skinner, Quentin. "Meaning and Understanding in the History of Ideas." *History and
    Theory* 8:1 (1969): 3–53.
Sklansky, Jeffrey. *The Soul's Economy: Market Society and Selfhood in American Thought,
    1820–1920*. Chapel Hill: University of North Carolina Press, 2002.
Skowronek, Stephen. *Building a New American State: The Expansion of National
    Administrative Capacities, 1877–1920*. New York: Cambridge University Press, 1982.
Smeed, J. W. "Thomas Carlyle and Jean Paul Richter." *Comparative Literature* 16:3
    (1964): 226–53.
Smith, George Winston. "Broadsides for Freedom: Civil War Propaganda in New
    England." *New England Quarterly* 21:3 (1948): 291–312.
Smith, Henry Nash. "Emerson's Problem of Vocation." *New England Quarterly* 12:1
    (1939): 52–67.

Smith, Herbert F. *Richard Watson Gilder*. New York: Twayne, 1970.

Smith, James Patterson. "The Liberals, Race, and Political Reform in the British West Indies, 1866–1874." *Journal of Negro History* 79:2 (1994): 131–46.

Smith, K. J. M. *James Fitzjames Stephen: Portrait of a Victorian Rationalist*. Cambridge: Cambridge University Press, 1988.

Smith, Rogers. *Civic Ideals: Conflicting Visions of Citizenship in U.S. History*. New Haven: Yale University Press, 1997.

Solomon, Barbara Miller. *Ancestors and Immigrants, a Changing New England Tradition*. Cambridge: Harvard University Press, 1956.

Spann, Edward K. *Ideals and Politics: New York Intellectuals and Liberal Democracy, 1820–1880*. Albany: State University of New York Press, 1972.

Spencer, Benjamin. *The Quest for Nationality: An American Literary Campaign*. Syracuse, N.Y.: Syracuse University Press, 1957.

Spragens, Thomas A. *Civic Liberalism: Reflections on Our Democratic Ideals*. Lanham, Md.: Rowman and Littlefield, 1999.

Sproat, John G. *"The Best Men": Liberal Reformers in the Gilded Age*. Chicago: University of Chicago Press, 1969.

Stansky, Peter. *Gladstone: A Politics in Progress*. Boston: Little, Brown, 1979.

———. *On or about December 1910: Early Bloomsbury and Its Intimate World*. Cambridge: Harvard University Press, 1996.

Stauffer, John. *The Black Hearts of Men: Radical Abolitionists and the Transformation of Race*. Cambridge: Harvard University Press, 2002.

Steel, Ronald. *Walter Lippmann and the American Century*. Boston: Little, Brown, 1980.

Steele, E. D. "J. S. Mill and the Irish Question: Reform and the Integrity of the Empire." *Historical Journal* 13:3 (1970): 419–50.

Stein, Roger B. *John Ruskin and Aesthetic Thought in America, 1840–1900*. Cambridge: Harvard University Press, 1967.

Stenfors, Brian D. *Signs of the Times: Leslie Stephen's Letters to "The Nation," 1866–1873*. New York: Lang, 1996.

Stephanson, Anders. *Manifest Destiny: American Expansionism and the Empire of Right*. New York: Hill and Wang, 1995.

Sterne, Richard Clark. *Political, Social, and Literary Criticism in the "New York Nation," 1865–1881: A Study in Change of Mood*. New York: Garland, 1987.

Stevenson, Louise L. *Scholarly Means to Evangelical Ends: The New Haven Scholars and the Transformation of Higher Learning in America, 1830–1890*. Baltimore: Johns Hopkins University Press, 1986.

———. *The Victorian Homefront: American Thought and Culture, 1860–1880*. New York: Twayne, 1991.

Story, Ronald. *The Forging of an Aristocracy: Harvard and the Boston Upper Class, 1800–1870*. Middletown, Conn.: Wesleyan University Press, 1980.

Strachey, Lytton. *Eminent Victorians*. New York: Putnam's, 1918.

Strysick, Michael. "Emerson, Slavery, and the Evolution of the Principle of Self-Reliance." In *The Emerson "Dilemma": Essays on Emerson and Society Reform*, edited by T. Gregory Garvey, 139–69. Athens: University of Georgia Press, 2001.

Sullivan, Eileen P. "Liberalism and Imperialism: J. S. Mill's Defense of the British Empire." *Journal of the History of Ideas* 44:4 (1983): 599–617.

Summers, Mark W. *The Era of Good Stealings*. New York: Oxford University Press, 1993.

———. *The Gilded Age; or, The Hazard of New Functions*. Upper Saddle River, N.J.: Prentice Hall, 1997.

———. *Party Games: Getting, Keeping, and Using Power in Gilded Age Politics*. Chapel Hill: University of North Carolina Press, 2004.

———. *The Press Gang: Newspapers and Politics, 1865–1878*. Chapel Hill: University of North Carolina Press, 1994.

———. *Rum, Romanism, and Rebellion: The Making of a President, 1884*. Chapel Hill: University of North Carolina Press, 2000.

Sussman, Herbert L. *Victorian Masculinities: Manhood and Masculine Poetics in Early Victorian Literature and Art*. Cambridge: Cambridge University Press, 1995.

Sweet, Matthew. *Inventing the Victorians*. New York: St. Martin's, 2001.

Taylor, A. J. P. *The Trouble Makers: Dissent over Foreign Policy, 1792–1939*. London: Hamilton, 1957.

Taylor, Charles. *Sources of the Self: The Making of the Modern Identity*. Cambridge: Harvard University Press, 1989.

Teichgraeber, Richard E. "'Our National Glory': Emerson in American Culture, 1865–1882." In *Transient and Permanent: The Transcendentalist Movement and Its Context*, edited by Charles Capper and Conrad Edick Wright, 499–526. Boston: Massachusetts Historical Society, 1999.

———. *Sublime Thoughts/Penny Wisdom: Situating Emerson and Thoreau in the American Market*. Baltimore: Johns Hopkins University Press, 1995.

Testi, Arnaldo. "The Gender of Reform Politics: Theodore Roosevelt and the Culture of Masculinity." *Journal of American History* 81:4 (1995): 1509–33.

Thistlethwaite, Frank. *The Anglo-American Connection in the Early Nineteenth Century*. Philadelphia: University of Pennsylvania Press, 1959.

Thompson, Andrew S. *Imperial Britain: The Empire in British Politics*. London: Longman, 2000.

———. "The Language of Imperialism: Imperial Discourse and British Politics, 1895–1914." *Journal of British Studies* 36:2 (1997): 147–77.

Thompson, Dennis F. *John Stuart Mill and Representative Government*. Princeton: Princeton University Press, 1976.

Thornton, A. P. *The Imperial Idea and Its Enemies*. New York: St. Martin's, 1959.

Titlow, Richard E. *Americans Import Merit: Origins of the United States Civil Service and the Influence of the British Model*. Washington, D.C.: University Press of America, 1979.

Tompkins, E. Berkeley. *Anti-Imperialism in the United States: The Great Debate, 1890–1920*. Philadelphia: University of Pennsylvania Press, 1970.

Tomsich, John. *A Genteel Endeavor: American Culture and Politics in the Gilded Age*. Stanford, Calif.: Stanford University Press, 1971.

Townsend, Kim. *Manhood at Harvard: William James and Others*. New York: Norton, 1996.

Trachtenberg, Alan. *The Incorporation of America: Culture and Society in the Gilded Age*. New York: Hill and Wang, 1982.

Trela, D. J. "Carlyle's *Shooting Niagara*: The Writing and Revising of an Article and
    Pamphlet." *Victorian Periodicals Review* 25:1 (1992): 30–34.
Tucker, David M. *Mugwumps: Public Moralists of the Gilded Age*. Columbia: University of
    Missouri Press, 1998.
Tulloch, Hugh. "Changing British Attitudes towards the United States in the 1880s."
    Historical Journal 20:4 (1977): 825–40.
———. *James Bryce's "American Commonwealth": The Anglo-American Background*.
    Wolfeboro, N.H.: Boydell, 1988.
Turner, Frank M. *Contesting Cultural Authority: Essays in Victorian Intellectual Life*.
    Cambridge: Cambridge University Press, 1993.
———. *The Greek Heritage in Victorian Britain*. New Haven: Yale University Press, 1981.
Turner, James. *The Liberal Education of Charles Eliot Norton*. Baltimore: Johns Hopkins
    University Press, 1999.
———. *Without God, without Creed: The Origins of Unbelief in America*. Baltimore: Johns
    Hopkins University Press, 1984.
Tuttleton, James W. *Thomas Wentworth Higginson*. Boston: Twayne, 1978.
Tyler, Alice Felt. *Freedom's Ferment: Phases of American Social History from the Colonial
    Period to the Outbreak of the Civil War*. Minneapolis: University of Minnesota Press,
    1944.
Urbinati, Nadia. *Mill on Democracy: From the Athenian Polis to Representative Government*.
    Chicago: University of Chicago Press, 2002.
Vance, Norman. *The Sinews of the Spirit: The Ideal of Christian Manliness in Victorian
    Literature and Religious Thought*. Cambridge: Cambridge University Press, 1985.
Vanderbilt, Kermit. *Charles Eliot Norton: Apostle of Culture in a Democracy*. Cambridge:
    Belknap Press of Harvard University Press, 1959.
Varg, Paul. *New England and Foreign Relations, 1789–1850*. Hanover, N.H.: University
    Press of New England, 1983.
Veysey, Laurence. *The Emergence of the American University*. Chicago: University of
    Chicago Press, 1965.
Vincent, John Russell. *The Formation of the British Liberal Party*. New York: Scribner,
    1967.
Vogeler, Martha Salmon. *Frederic Harrison: The Vocations of a Positivist*. Oxford:
    Clarendon, 1984.
———. "Matthew Arnold and Frederic Harrison: The Prophet of Culture and the
    Prophet of Positivism." *Studies in English Literature, 1500–1900* 2:4 (1962): 441–62.
Von Arx, Jeffrey Paul. *Progress and Pessimism: Religion, Politics, and History in Late
    Nineteenth Century Britain*. Cambridge: Harvard University Press, 1985.
Von Frank, Albert J. *The Trials of Anthony Burns: Freedom and Slavery in Emerson's
    Boston*. Cambridge: Harvard University Press, 1998.
Vorenberg, Michael. *Final Freedom: The Civil War, the Abolition of Slavery, and the
    Thirteenth Amendment*. New York: Cambridge University Press, 2001.
Wallace, Elisabeth. *Goldwin Smith, Victorian Liberal*. Toronto: University of Toronto
    Press, 1957.
Wallas, Graham. *Human Nature in Politics*. Boston: Houghton Mifflin, 1916.
Walters, Ronald. *American Reformers, 1815–1860*. New York: Hill and Wang, 1978.

Walzer, Michael. *The Company of Critics*. New York: Basic Books, 1988.

Wang, Xi. *The Trial of Democracy: Black Suffrage and Northern Republicans, 1860–1910*. Athens: University of Georgia Press, 1997.

Warren, Sydney. *American Freethought, 1860–1914*. New York: Columbia University Press, 1943.

Waugh, Joan. *Unsentimental Reformer: The Life of Josephine Shaw Lowell*. Cambridge: Harvard University Press, 1997.

Weaver, Stewart. "The Pro-Boers: War, Empire, and the Uses of Nostalgia in Turn-of-the-Century England." In *Singular Continuities: Tradition, Nostalgia, and Identity in Modern British Culture*, edited by George K. Behlmer and Fred M. Leventhal, 43–57. Stanford, Calif.: Stanford University Press, 2000.

Weinberg, Adelaide. *John Elliot Cairnes and the American Civil War*. London: Kingswood, 1968.

Welch, Richard E. *George Frisbie Hoar and the Half-Breed Republicans*. Cambridge: Harvard University Press, 1971.

———. *Response to Imperialism: The United States and the Philippine-American War, 1899–1902*. Chapel Hill: University of North Carolina Press, 1979.

Wells, Anna Mary. *Dear Preceptor: The Life and Times of Thomas Wentworth Higginson*. Boston: Houghton Mifflin, 1963.

White, Ronald C., Jr. *Lincoln's Greatest Speech: The Second Inaugural*. New York: Simon and Schuster, 2002.

Widmer, Edward L. *Young America: The Flowering of Democracy in New York City*. New York: Oxford University Press, 1998.

Wiebe, Robert H. *The Search for Order, 1877–1920*. New York: Hill and Wang, 1967.

———. *Self-Rule: A Cultural History of American Democracy*. Chicago: University of Chicago Press, 1995.

Wiener, Joel H. *Innovators and Preachers: The Role of the Editor in Victorian England*. Westport, Conn.: Greenwood, 1985.

Wiener, Martin J. *Between Two Worlds: The Political Thought of Graham Wallas*. Oxford: Clarendon, 1971.

Wilentz, Sean. *The Rise of American Democracy: Jefferson to Lincoln*. New York: Norton, 2005.

Williams, Gary. *Hungry Heart: The Literary Emergence of Julia Ward Howe*. Amherst: University of Massachusetts Press, 1999.

Williams, Raymond. *Culture and Society, 1780–1950*. New York: Columbia University Press, 1958.

———. *Keywords: A Vocabulary of Culture and Society*. Rev. ed. New York: Oxford University Press, 1983.

Williams, William Appleman. *The Tragedy of American Diplomacy*. New York: Norton, 1959.

Williamson, Chilton. *American Suffrage: From Property to Democracy, 1760–1860*. Princeton: Princeton University Press, 1960.

Wilson, Christopher P. *The Labor of Words: Literary Professionalism in the Progressive Era*. Athens: University of Georgia Press, 1985.

Winch, Donald. *Adam Smith's Politics: An Essay in Historiographic Revision*. New York: Cambridge University Press, 1978.

Winn, William E. *"Tom Brown's Schooldays* and the Development of 'Muscular Christianity.'" *Church History* 29:1 (1960): 64–73.

Winterer, Caroline. *The Culture of Classicism: Ancient Greece and Rome in American Intellectual Life, 1780–1910*. Baltimore: Johns Hopkins University Press, 2002.

Wohl, A. S. "'Dizzi-Ben-Dizzi': Disraeli as Alien." *Journal of British Studies* 34:3 (1995): 375–411.

Wolff, Leon. *Little Brown Brother: America's Forgotten Bid for Empire Which Cost 250,000 Lives*. New York: Kraus, 1970.

Wood, Marcus. "The Anatomy of Bigotry: Carlyle, Ruskin, Slavery, and a New Language of Race." In *Slavery, Empathy, and Pornography*, 346–97. New York: Oxford University, 2002.

———, ed. *The Poetry of Slavery: An Anglo-American Anthology, 1764–1865*. New York: Oxford University Press, 2003.

Workman, Gillian. "Thomas Carlyle and the Governor Eyre Controversy: An Account with Some New Material." *Victorian Studies* 18:1 (1974): 77–102.

Worth, George J. *Thomas Hughes*. Boston: Twayne, 1984.

Yacovone, Donald. "Abolitionists and the 'Language of Fraternal Love.'" In *Meanings for Manhood: Constructions of Masculinity in Victorian America*, edited by Mark C. Carnes and Clyde Griffen, 85–99. Chicago: University of Chicago Press, 1990.

Zakaria, Fareed. *The Future of Freedom: Illiberal Democracy at Home and Abroad*. New York: Norton, 2003.

Zastoupil, Lynn. "Moral Government: J. S. Mill on Ireland." *Historical Journal* 26:3 (1983): 707–17.

Ziff, Larzer. *Literary Democracy: The Declaration of Cultural Independence in America*. New York: Viking, 1981.

Zimmerman, Kristin. "Liberal Speech, Palmerstonian Delay, and the Passage of the Second Reform Act." *English Historical Review* 118:479 (2003): 1176–1207.

Zwick, Jim. "The Anti-Imperialist Movement, 1898–1921." In *Whose America?: The War of 1898 and the Battles to Define the Nation*, edited by Virginia Marie Bouvier, 171–92. Westport, Conn.: Praeger, 2001.

———. *Anti-Imperialism in the United States, 1898–1935*, <http://www.boondocksnet .com/ai/>. May 5, 2006.

Index